# *THE SMUGGLERS' WORLD*

# The Smugglers' World

## Illicit Trade *and* Atlantic Communities *in* Eighteenth-Century Venezuela

- - - - -

*Jesse Cromwell*

*Published by the*
OMOHUNDRO INSTITUTE OF
EARLY AMERICAN HISTORY AND CULTURE,
Williamsburg, Virginia,
*and the*
UNIVERSITY OF NORTH CAROLINA PRESS,
Chapel Hill

The Omohundro Institute of Early American History and Culture is sponsored by the College of William and Mary. On November 15, 1996, the Institute adopted the present name in honor of a bequest from Malvern H. Omohundro, Jr.


*Manufactured in the United States of America*

Jacket illustration: "The coast of Caracas, Cumana, Parla and the mouths of Rio Orinoco . . ." courtesy of the David Rumsey Map Collection, www.davidrumsey.com; "Brigatins des Isles de l'Amerique, Servants pour le Commerce quelquefois armêz en Course" from the JCB Archive of Early American Images, courtesy of the John Carter Brown Library at Brown University

LIBRARY OF CONGRESS CATALOGING-IN-PUBLICATION DATA
Names: Cromwell, Jesse, author. | Omohundro Institute of Early American History & Culture, publisher.
Title: The smugglers' world : illicit trade and Atlantic communities in eighteenth-century Venezuela / Jesse Cromwell.
Description: Williamsburg, Virginia : Omohundro Institute of Early American History and Culture ; Chapel Hill : University of North Carolina Press, [2018] | Includes bibliographical references and index.
Identifiers: LCCN 2018019919 | ISBN 9781469636887 (cloth : alk. paper) | ISBN 9781469636917 (ebook)
Subjects: LCSH: Smuggling—Venezuela—Atlantic Coast—History—18th century. | Venezuela—Commerce—History—18th century. | Spain—Colonies—America—History—18th century. | Spain—Commercial policy—18th century. | Smuggling—Social aspects. | Smuggling—Political aspects.
Classification: LCC F2322 .C76 2018 | DDC 987/.03—dc23
LC record available at https://lccn.loc.gov/2018019919

The University of North Carolina Press has been a member of the Green Press Initiative since 2003.

# *acknowledgments*

A decade of work on this project has left me in debt, in one form or another, to just about everyone I have ever known. Here is my shabby attempt at repayment. I start by thanking the four people most responsible for this book's existence. Ann Twinam, my dissertation supervisor, has been the rock of my professional life since I enrolled in her research seminar in the spring of 2006. The red-inked remains of my first chapter drafts represented tough love, encouragement, and even levity. She has been unwavering in her support of my work and my career. *Mil gracias,* Ann, for teaching me with good humor how to be a professional historian. Nadine Zimmerli has shepherded this manuscript from dissertation to book as my fearless editor. Her solutions are elegant and insightful. Whatever she is getting paid, it is not enough. Kris Lane and Christian Koot served as devoted peer reviewers of this book. I thank them for stress testing its contentions and for offering superb suggestions that greatly improved the final product. Any wayward arguments in the book are solely my fault.

My project received crucial funding and intellectual support from numerous organizations over the course of its development. The Graduate School, College of Liberal Arts, and Department of History at the University of Texas at Austin provided me with research and writing fellowships to conduct archival work in Venezuela, Spain, Colombia, and the United Kingdom and to finish writing my dissertation. I also had the pleasure of being a fellow at the Institute for Historical Studies (University of Texas at Austin). Likewise, grants from the College of Liberal Arts and the Arch Dalrymple III Department of History at the University of Mississippi enabled me to do follow-up research in Spain and attend academic conferences. A semester-long Alexander O. Vietor Memorial Fellowship at the John Carter Brown Library allowed me to consult new sources, write and revise important chapters of this book, and enjoy the scholarly kinship of that special place. I received generous travel grants to undertake research and / or present at fruitful seminars from the Program for Cultural Cooperation between Spain's Ministry of Culture and United States' Universities, the Summer Academy of Atlantic History, the Huntington Library, the Newberry Library, the McNeil Center for Early American Studies, the Omohundro Institute of Early American History and Culture, and the Johns Hopkins University Department of History. I thank *The Americas* for allowing me to republish portions of my article "Illicit Ideologies: Moral Economies of Venezuelan Smuggling and Autonomy in the Rebellion of Juan Francisco de León, 1749–1751," in this book.

My years spent in the Department of History at the University of Texas at Austin were hugely influential to the creation of this book. Jorge Cañizares-Esguerra always pushed me to make broader connections with my research. He was and continues to be a fierce advocate for his students' work. Julie Hardwick infused my writing with questions of consumer demand and early modern markets. She and Bob Olwell were important intellectual sounding boards and role models for maintaining proper work-life balance. Wisdom from Susan Deans-Smith, Virginia Garrard, Seth Garfield, Jonathan Brown, and Lina Del Castillo also helped shape my book. I found academic inspiration and warm friendship through an incredible cohort of fellow graduate students in the department, including Renata Keller, Cameron Strang, Chris Heaney, Cheasty Anderson, Jeff Parker, Mikki Brock, Laurie Wood, Juandrea Bates, Claudia Rueda, Kristie Flannery, María José Afanador-Llach, Dan Wold, Brian Jones, Chris Albi, Jen Eckel, and Takara Brunson.

For their kind and patient assistance with my research inquiries, I thank the staffs of the Archivo General de la Nación (Venezuela), the Archivo General de Indias, the Archivo General de la Nación (Colombia), the Academia Nacional de la Historia (Venezuela), the John Carter Brown Library, the Huntington Library, the British National Archives, the British Library, and the Nettie Lee Benson Latin American Collection. On research trips, numerous archivists and fellow researchers aided my work. In Venezuela, I am indebted to Carol Pérez, Jorge Isaac Flores, and Sebastián Navarro. In Spain, Pablo Mauriño Chozas, Luis Emilio Calenda Roa, Esther González, and Igor Pérez Tostado made a stranger feel at home and helped me understand the ways of the AGI. In Colombia, I wish to thank the AGN's Mauricio Ballesteros Tovar and Fabio Castro González in particular for their help. Ken Ward and Kim Nusco at the JCB are excellent archivists who became my friends.

The Arch Dalrymple III Department of History at the University of Mississippi has been a fine academic home to write and revise this book. My colleagues have been a support network, a broad base of experiential knowledge, and a cheerleading section when necessary. When my daughter was in the hospital, we did not cook for six weeks and, yet, the fridge overflowed with all their generosity. In particular, I wish to thank Darren Grem, Annie

Twitty, Jarod Roll, Marc Lerner, Zachary Kagan Guthrie, Mikaëla Adams, Sheila Skemp, Paul Polgar, Deirdre Cooper Owens, Jessie Wilkerson, Doug Sullivan-González, Oliver Dinius, Vivian Ibrahim, April Holm, Susan Gaunt Sterns, Rebecca Marchiel, Peter Thilly, Nicolas Trépanier, Jonathan Gienapp, and Kelly Brown Houston for personal and professional kindnesses. Here is a department that happily lunches together. What a rare blessing! My excellent chairs (Joe Ward, Noell Wilson, and Jeff Watt) have facilitated my research (and smoothed my path to tenure) in every way possible.

A web of scholars even more numerous than some of the smuggling rings profiled in this book added to its scope and offered comradery. Fabricio Prado and Ernesto Bassi are research brothers from another mother. Phil Morgan, Carla Rahn Phillips, James Sweet, Michael Kwass, and Claudia Schnurmann all read parts of the manuscript and provided valuable feedback. For reasons great and small, I wish to thank David Wheat, Erin Stone, Jane Landers, Jane Mangan, Arne Bialuschewski, Pablo Gómez, Elena Schneider, Bradley Benton, Linda Rupert, Olga González-Silen, April Hatfield, Carla Pestana, Wim Klooster, Cristina Soriano, Mark Hanna, Molly Warsh, Christian Crouch, Kaja Cook, Christine DeLucia, Charles Foy, Ralph Bauer, Claire Gherini, Rob Taber, Spencer Tyce, Frances Ramos, Melissa Morris, Gabriel Rocha, Daniel Hershenzon, Chris Parsons, Lauric Henneton, Matt Childs, Julia Sarreal, Philip Stern, Ada Ferrer, Casey Schmitt, Lauren MacDonald, and Phil Baltuskonis. I am grateful to Kim Morse, Peter Henderson, and a small army of RMCLASistas who took a young scholar under their collective wing over years of conferences. I hope I can someday repay the early mentors that put me on the path to the profession. They are Sam Cox, Michael Francis, Robert Douglas Cope, Onésimo Almeida, Stephanie Merrim, and James Woodard.

At the Omohundro Institute and University of North Carolina Press, I wish to thank Kristina Poznan and the William and Mary research associates for the laborious alchemy of copyediting they performed on my manuscript. Karin Wulf, Paul Mapp, Joshua Piker, and Fredrika Teute have all been champions of my project. I hope the final product lives up to their expectations. It has been a pleasure to work with Kathryn Burdette and Dino Battista. Christine Riggio drew the book's cogent maps.

On a personal note, I want to thank the friends, family, and caretakers who have provided comfort to me over these many years. Neil and Charles Hoffman and Josh Martinez have been great friends as well as constant sources of merriment, good food, and bad jokes. The Dads' Night crew has livened up my Tuesday nights and dispensed sage wisdom on parenting. Toward the end of revisions on this book, when our daughter's intrauterine growth restriction put her life in jeopardy, Drs. Justin Brewer, Bryan Darling, Ginger Pole, and a staff of dedicated nurses brought her into this world and nursed her to health. Teachers and administrators at First Baptist Weekday Day Care have provided a loving environment for our girls to thrive (and valuable time for me to work). Janet Cromwell, Gary Oba, Bob Levis, and Evie Williams gave me a roof over my head and emotional support at times. Janet Martin, Bob Martin, and Rosemarie Martin have been supportive and caring in-laws. My mother and father instilled in me the value of hard work and a deep love of learning. I hope this book makes them proud. My wonderful children, Alice and Lucy, have been the logistical engine and brakes of this endeavor. They have never known a dad without a book project and I hope they will forgive me for the presence of this phantom third child in their early lives. And finally, Laura. You are the *sine qua non* of these pages. You are my peace of mind, my often-sacrificing copilot, and my spiritual *media naranja*. Thank you. Thank you. Thank you.

# *contents*

# *illustrations*

FIGURES

MAPS

With appreciation from
the Omohundro Institute
of Early American
History & Culture

# abbreviations

ARCHIVAL SOURCES

| | |
|---|---|
| AGI | Archivo General de Indias, Seville |
| Caracas | Gobierno: Audiencia de Caracas |
| Ctdra | Contaduria |
| Esc | Escribanía de Cámara |
| Filipinas | Gobierno: Audiencia de Filipinas |
| Indif | Gobierno: Indiferente General |
| SD | Gobierno: Audiencia de Santo Domingo |
| SF | Gobierno: Audiencia de Santa Fe |
| AGNC | Archivo General de la Nación de Colombia, Bogotá |
| Contrabandos | Colonia: Fondo Contrabandos |
| AGNV | Archivo General de la Nación de Venezuela, Caracas |
| Comp Gui | Colonia: Compañía Guipuzcoana |
| Comisos | Colonia: Comisos |
| Diversos | Colonia: Capitanía General Diversos |
| León | Colonia: Insurreción del Capitán Juan Francisco de León |
| RO | Colonia: Reales Ordenes |
| BL | British Library, London |
| Add. MSS | Additional Manuscripts |
| MHS | The Massachusetts Historical Society, Boston |
| FRH | Francis Russell Hart Collection |
| NA | National Archives, Kew, U.K. |
| CO | Colonial Office |
| PC | Privy Council |
| SP | State Papers |

SECONDARY SOURCES

| | |
|---|---|
| *AHR* | *American Historical Review* |
| *Americas* | *The Americas: A Quarterly Review of Latin American History* |
| *BA* | *Boletín Americanista* |
| *BANHV* | *Boletín de la Academia Nacional de la Historia de Venezuela* |
| *BLAR* | *Bulletin of Latin American Research* |
| *HAHR* | *Hispanic American Historical Review* |
| *HEI* | *History of European Ideas* |
| *Itinerario* | *Itinerario: International Journal on the History of European Expansion and Global Interaction* |
| *NWIG* | *Nieuwe West-Indische Gids / New West Indian Guide* |
| *WMQ* | *William and Mary Quarterly* |

# THE SMUGGLERS' WORLD

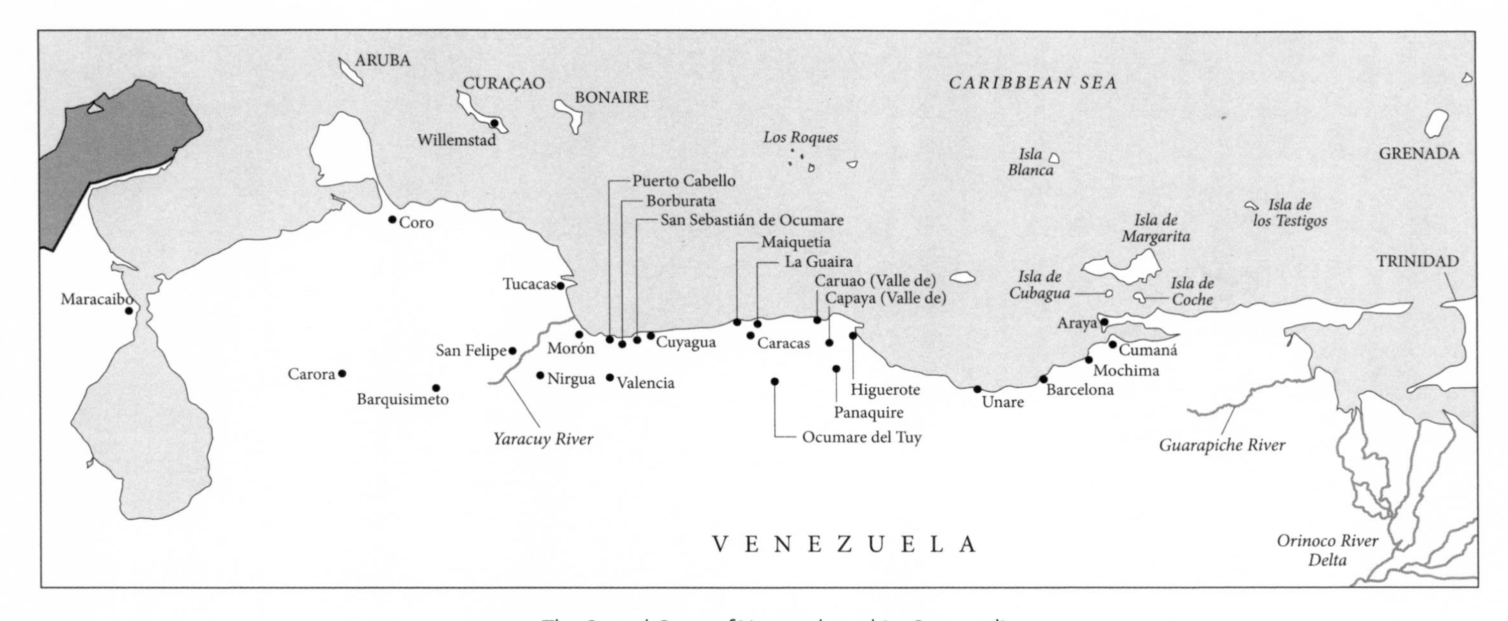


MAP 1. The Central Coast of Venezuela and Its Surroundings.
*Drawn by Christine Riggio*

# Prologue

Men in long coats and wigs stoop over pear-shaped pots and cauldrons. One froths the hot liquid inside with a mace-like wooden whisk called a *molinillo* that he spins by rubbing the handle between his palms. To the concoction, he might add sugar, cinnamon, cloves, vanilla, anise, achiote, almonds, orange flower water, nutmeg, corn, chile, *orejuela* flowers, dried roses, almonds, hazelnuts, allspice, and ambergris. Water, eggs, or milk might serve as a base. Another man kneels to pour contents from one of the pots into a delicate Chinese porcelain cup. Steam rises from the brew. The smell is heavenly. Chocolate.[1]

Panning outward from the improvised outdoor kitchen, the viewer takes in the tableau of a lively garden party. Waiters and cooks bring drinking chocolate to courtly gentlemen and ladies. Some guests sit formally around a table while others stand and mingle, dance, or flirt with one another. The scene is colorful and active, representing the eighteenth-century picture of civility, sophistication, and good feeling. The title of this painted ceramic panel, *La Xocolatada (The Chocolate Party)* (1710), gestures to the centrality of the beverage in the social rituals taking place around it.

In the early modern Atlantic, a mix of connoisseurship, religious strictures, new social spaces, and medicinal theories all stoked European enjoyment of chocolate. In the expanding world of early modern luxury commodities, a variety of implements for preparing and serving it demonstrated knowledge of and propriety over the finer things in life. Given chocolate's liquid properties yet nourishing contents, Catholics commonly drank it to dispel hunger during the ecclesiastical fast. Patrons regularly sipped chocolate in

1. For chocolate recipes and additives, see [Philippe Sylvestre Dufour], *The Manner of Making of Coffee, Tea, and Chocolate. . . . Newly Done out of French and Spanish,* trans. John Chamberlain (London, 1685), 72–73; Henry Stubbe, *The Indian Nectar; or, A Discourse concerning Chocalata. . . .* (London, 1662), preface, 13–14; Manuel Navas de Carrera, *Dissertacion historica phisico-chimica, y analysis del cacao, su uso, y dossis . . .* (Zaragoza, 1751), 38; Louis Evan Grivetti, "From Bean to Beverage: Historical Chocolate Recipes," in Grivetti and Howard-Yana Shapiro, eds., *Chocolate: History, Culture, and Heritage* (Hoboken, N.J., 2009), 99–114.

FIGURE 1. *La xocolatada* (The Chocolate Party), detail. Barcelona, 1710. *Legacy Joaquim de Càrcer, 1923, Museu del Disseny de Barcelona*

coffeehouses as part of new discourses of sociability and learning. The development of these venues and the merchant class that supplied and patronized them spread the beverage across Europe. Imbibers might even have believed that the drink regulated their humors, improved their moods, and augmented their sexual potency.[2]

2. Porcelain cups imported from China and biscuits or breads were also part of the service. The ingredients and additives were often rare and esoteric. See Lorinda B. R. Goodwin, *An Archaeology of Manners: The Polite World of the Merchant Elite of Colonial Massachusetts* (New York, 1999), 123; Wolfgang Schivelbusch, *Tastes of Paradise: A Social History of Spices, Stimulants, and Intoxicants,* trans. David Jacobson (New York, 1992), 62; Peter Brown, *In Praise of Hot Liquors: The Study of Chocolate, Coffee, and Tea-Drinking, 1600–1850* (York, 1995), 70–77; Susan Perkins, "Is It a Chocolate Pot? Chocolate and Its Accoutrements in France from Cookbook to Collectible," in Grivetti and Shapiro, eds., *Chocolate,* 158; Sophie D. Coe and Michael D. Coe, *The True History of Chocolate,* 3d ed. (London, 2013), 160; Navas de Carrera, *Dissertacion historica,* 49. On chocolate and Catholicism, see Manuel Aguilar-Moreno, "The Good and Evil of Chocolate in Colonial Mexico," in Cameron L. McNeil, ed., *Chocolate in Mesoamerica: A Cultural History of Cacao* (Gainesville, Fla., 2006), 283–287; Schivelbusch, *Tastes of Paradise,* trans. Jacobson, 87; Navas de Carrera, *Dissertacion historica,* 15–16, 56; [John Chamberlayne,] *The Natural History of Coffee, Thee, Chocolate, Tobacco . . . with Some Remarks upon that Liquor* (London, 1682), 14.

As Marcy Norton notes, chocolate might have created a market for coffee by introducing Europeans to dark, hot, stimulating beverages, rather than the other way around. Brian Cowan's research reveals that coffeehouses of the period might sell coffee, chocolate, tea, tobacco, and alcoholic beverages. Tea and coffee overtook chocolate in northern Europe as the eighteenth century wore on, but chocolate remained a reliable, if secondary, presence in coffeehouses throughout this period. See Norton, "Tasting Empire: Chocolate and the European Internalization of Mesoamerican Aesthetics," *AHR,* CXI (2006), 667; Cowan, *The Social Life of Coffee: The Emergence of the British Coffeehouse* (New Haven, Conn., 2005), 82. On the links between sociability, learning, and hot beverages, see James Delbourgo, "Slavery in the Cabinet of Curiosities: Hans Sloane's Atlantic World," British Museum, http://www.britishmuseum.org/pdf/delbourgo%20essay.pdf; Cowan, *Social Life of Coffee,* 2, 90–99;

FIGURE 2. *La xocolatada* (The Chocolate Party). Barcelona, 1710.
*Legacy Joaquim de Càrcer, 1923, Museu del Disseny de Barcelona*

Chocolate first came to Europe as a niche product and largely maintained this status for most of the sixteenth century. Spanish conquistadors were the first Europeans to taste the Mesoamerican ceremonial beverage. It likely crossed the Atlantic among the cargoes of elite merchants, sailors, and churchmen. Debate exists as to whether the beverage (until the eighteenth century, it was almost exclusively imbibed as a liquid) first came into widespread use as a drug or as a recreational pastime.[3]

Regardless of its intended purpose, chocolate took Spanish courts and noble houses by storm in the late sixteenth century. From Spain, chocolate passed to other European polities in the early seventeenth century. In 1685, one observer described how, at the Spanish court, "the great Ladies drink it in a morning before they rise out of their beds"; he also noted that chocolate was "lately much used in *England,* as Diet and Phisick with the Gentry." Back in Spain, the daily cup (or cups) of chocolate had long been something of an obsession among the well-to-do. "There are some [Spaniards] who are such aficionados that they would sooner go naked than give up drinking chocolate two or three times a day," wrote physician Manuel Navas de Carrera in 1751. In the eighteenth century, the beverage transcended class and began to attract a more diverse consumer base. During the reign of Charles III, consumption of chocolate in Madrid reached twelve million pounds per year. Eighteenth-century Europeans drank chocolate in these massive quantities because it was a mark of refinement, an entrée into social interaction, and a pleasurable experience. Chocolate's production and exchange lifted a faraway region up out of obscurity, shaped discussions of political economy and reform, and colored the social norms and legal interactions of those who trafficked in it.[4]

---

Brown, *In Praise of Hot Liquors,* 11–14, 17. On chocolate's perceived effect on humors, see Antonio Lavedan, *Tratado de los usos, abusos, propiedades y virtudes del tabaco, café, té y chocolate . . .* (Madrid, 1796), 212–213; [D. Quélus], *The Natural History of Chocolate: Being a Distinct and Particular Account of the Cocoa-Tree,* 2d ed. (London, 1730), 46–48; Stubbe, *Indian Nectar,* 141, 151–152; Navas de Carrera, *Dissertacion historica,* 33; [Dufour], *Manner of Making of Coffee, Tea, and Chocolate,* trans. Chamberlain, 94–95.

3. Sophie and Michael Coe assert that Europeans first drank chocolate to regulate humors and only later converted it into a recreational beverage. They equate it with other substances like tonic water, liqueurs, and absinthe that followed a similar pattern (Coe and Coe, *True History of Chocolate,* 126–130). Marcy Norton argues quite the opposite, pointing out that the time lag between when cacao had a negligible presence in Spain (1590) and when it became common in court (1610) shows that recreational use almost certainly preceded the substance's employment as medicine. See Norton, *Sacred Gifts, Profane Pleasures: A History of Tobacco and Chocolate in the Atlantic World* (Ithaca, N.Y., 2008), 141–146.

4. Coe and Coe, *True History of Chocolate,* 211. Chocolate allegedly came to France via

FIGURE 3. "Brigatins des Isles de l'Amerique, servants pour le commerce quelque fois armėz en course" (Traders Hail a Brigantine from the Shore), in Pierre Jacques Guéroult du Pas, *Les differens batimens de la mer oceanne, presentez a Monsieur deVanolles, grand audiencier de France et tresorier general de la marine* (Paris, 1709). *Courtesy of the John Carter Brown Library at Brown University*

The affairs of chocoholic Europeans matter to the history of eighteenth-century Spanish America because the best and most abundant source of raw chocolate (cacao) at this time of burgeoning appetites was the province of Venezuela. Connoisseurs of cacao and colonial officials alike coveted Venezuela's unusually flavorful cacao and helped augment Venezuela's reputation as the world's premier purveyor of the commodity. An anonymous English author observed that the English court accepted nothing less than Caracas cacao when preparing chocolate for the king. One bureaucrat tried to persuade the English to use Trinidad as a jumping-off point for invading Venezuela in 1797 by arguing that Venezuela "supplies not only all Europe with cocoa but also New Spain." François de Pons, a French traveler who visited Venezuela at the

---

Anna of Austria, who grew up drinking chocolate in the Spanish court and later married Louis XIII. The English, in turn, probably picked up a taste for the beverage from their ambassadors in Spain. See Schivelbusch, *Tastes of Paradise,* 91; Brown, *In Praise of Hot Liquors,* 9; [Dufour], *Manner of Making of Coffee, Tea, and Chocolate,* trans. Chamberlain, D4 [55]. "Aficionados": Navas de Carrera, *Dissertacion historica,* 57.

twilight of the Spanish Empire, said that Venezuelan cacao sold for almost twice the price of its counterpart from Guayaquil, Ecuador.[5]

The subject of my study is the untidy means by which early modern people sourced this delicacy for chocolate parties, as well as a host of other goods. An ocean away from the din of coffeehouse chatter and salon banter, foreign merchants and Spanish coastal subjects met covertly at the secluded beaches and principal ports of Venezuela to engage in extralegal trade. They did so in defiance of Spanish imperial law. African slaves planted and cultivated the stubby cacao trees that formed the principal reason for this commerce. They harvested the brilliantly hued yellow, orange, and magenta cacao pods and, in many cases, transported and sold the extracted beans in illicit coastal marketplaces themselves. Cacao, like many luxuries of the early modern global economy, was the fruit of black market transactions and oppressive labor systems. The products illegally obtained from covert sales sustained the communities that produced cacao. Grandees could sip chocolate because petty traders made hardscrabble transactions in the shadow economies of the interimperial Caribbean.

The experiences of a merchant named William Brundenburg exemplify the struggles and connections formed by illicit commerce. In 1731, the Flemish trader weighed anchor from Dutch Curaçao. Aboard his shallow-draft, single-masted sloop, the *Young William,* was a cargo of flour, liquor, and other sundries. His crew of German, Swiss, and Dutch mariners hopscotched among

5. For a late-seventeenth-century appraisal of Venezuelan cacao's high quality, see Stubbe, *Indian Nectar,* 41. Eighteenth-century Jesuit priest Antonio Julián said that Caracas cacao could only be matched by that of Soconusco in the Chiapas region of New Spain and that of the Magdalena River Delta of Colombia (Julián, *La perla de la America, provincia de Santa Marta, reconocida, observada, y expuesta en discursos historicos* [Madrid, 1787], 89). For a similar appraisal at the turn of the nineteenth century that also mentions the high-quality tobacco, see François Joseph de Pons, *A Voyage to the Eastern Part of Terra Firma, or the Spanish Main, in South-America, during the Years 1801, 1802, 1803, and 1804* (New York, 1806), I, v–vi. The king of Spain's special envoy to Venezuela in the 1720s, Pedro José de Olavarriaga, believed that Venezuelan hides were "much esteemed by foreigners" (Olavarriaga, *Instrucción general y particular del estado presente de la provincia de Venezuela en los años de 1720 y 1721* [1722; rpt. Caracas, 1981], 13); see also Eduardo Arcila Farias, *Economía colonial de Venezuela* (Mexico City, 1946), 77–89. On cacao in the English court, see [Chamberlayne], *Natural History of Coffee, Thee, Chocolate, Tobacco,* 16. "Supplies": Communication from Mr. Duff respecting the Island of Trinidad and Relations with the Mainland [Venezuela]; A Brief General Appraisal by the British Consul in Cadiz, 1797, FRH, box 1, folder 35, MHS. I wish to thank Elena Schneider for providing me with this reference. Price of Venezuelan cacao: de Pons, *Voyage to the Eastern Part of Terra Firma,* II, 294.

several Venezuelan ports, unloading this merchandise and picking up cacao from willing Venezuelan producers in defiance of Spanish mercantilist commercial statutes. Along with its cargo, Brundenburg's ship carried an array of cannons, mortars, and small arms because the smugglers had "heard news of corsairs cruising these coasts and felt obliged to defend themselves." Violence among traders and perpetuated by coast guard patrols was always a possibility in unregulated commerce such as this.[6]

The *Young William*'s capture near the small Venezuelan port of Patanemo by the maritime forces of the Caracas Company, a state-sanctioned royal trading company, reveal connections that crossed borders but were often intentionally shrouded. Spanish Americans and outsiders often knew each other, or at least the common conventions of interimperial exchange, to a degree that contradicted notions of discrete and mutually bellicose imperial polities. Spanish American prize court officials assessing the culpability of foreign-born mariners and their Spanish American accomplices sought to discover the partnerships that enabled smuggling. Brundenburg, like many captive contrabandists answering common questions from Spanish prize court officials, claimed not to know any of the Spanish subjects he dealt with on shore. Denying previous contact protected enduring smuggling networks.[7]

Brundenburg's story emphasizes the extent to which contraband commerce was a commonplace and necessary practice for both buyer and seller. He described trade between Dutch and Spanish subjects as a "daily" occurrence. Echoing the words of so many other illicit merchants, Brundenburg confessed that he recognized the illegality of his actions under Spanish law but entered into the trade anyway "to make a living." A similar, sustenance-based under-

6. For clarity with the nationalities of historical subjects, I have tried to transcribe Hispanicized names from the documents into their counterparts where appropriate. In this example, the smuggler Brundenburg showed up in the documents as "Guillermo Brundenbrug." Charles Nunn has noted how beguiling it can be to translate early modern Spanish renderings of non-Spanish names. Scribes often replaced foreign names with more traditionally Spanish ones ("Martin" into "Martínez"), literally translated a foreign word into a Spanish one ("John Waters" would become "Juan Aguas"), or phonetically spelled names as best they could ("Brundenbrug"). Adding to this confusion, foreigners living or visiting Spanish dominions often changed their names to mirror Spanish equivalents. In cases I have encountered, scribes have sometimes changed the spelling of names within the same case or even within the same document. See Charles F. Nunn, *Foreign Immigrants in Early Bourbon Mexico, 1700–1760* (Cambridge, 1979), 2. "Corsairs": Declaración de Guillermo Brundenbrug, Capitán de la balandra "Guillermo Joven," Puerto de Patanemo, abordo el navio San Ygnacio, July 9, 1731, AGI, SD, 781.

7. Declaración de Guillermo Brundenbrug, AGI, SD, 81.

standing of contraband trade was evident in the purchases of several unlucky *zambos* (men of mixed African and Indian ancestry) whom Spanish coast guard officials captured for trading with Brundenburg's men. Too poor to afford fine European apparel, which a petty trader like Brundenburg would not carry anyhow, the zambos had bought simple hats to shade themselves from the fierce tropical sun.[8]

Brundenburg and other captured smugglers in Venezuela and the Spanish Atlantic experienced severe punishments that did not fit the commonplace nature of their crimes. Individuals regularly engaged in on-the-ground relations with subjects of different empires, but their punishments contradicted the routine reality of illicit trade because they got caught. Spanish officials auctioned off the *Young William* and its contents. They sentenced its crew to work without pay for an unspecified period of time on Caracas Company ships and transported them across the Atlantic. In doing so, authorities ironically put contrabandists to work for the primary operatives of anticontraband policing. Sentences for similar offenses over the course of the eighteenth century suggest that it was common for smugglers to be turned over to massive Spanish convict labor programs on both sides of the Atlantic. Some convicted contrabandists built and manned forts in defensive outposts of the New World, whereas others worked in coast guard services, Spanish peninsular arsenals, or North African presidios. The whip, exposure, shackles on legs, stomach ailments, poor or inadequate food, infections, tuberculosis and other diseases of overcrowding, and vitamin deficiencies commonly weakened foreign and domestic contrabandists condemned to labor details. In all of these occupations, life expectancies were bleak.[9]

The meetings between foreigners like Brundenburg and Venezuelans shaped trade, politics, and social practice on the coast. Smuggling represented more than material transactions, crimes against commercial statutes, or acts of opportunistic self-interest. The mechanics of illegal exchange, along with efforts to obscure, explain, or prosecute it, can reveal the internal dynamics

8. Ibid.

9. On the sentencing of the *Young William*'s crew, see Auto de Sebastian Garcia de la Torre, Governor of Venezuela, Caracas, Dec. 17, 1731, AGI, SD, 781. Sentences for similar offenses: Expediente sobre prisión de holandeses y penas que se debían imponer a los extrangeros por ilícito comercio, Visto en el Consejo de Indias, 1736–1739, AGI, Indif, 1829. Punishments and short life expectancies for contrabandists: Ruth Pike, *Penal Servitude in Early Modern Spain* (Madison, Wis., 1983), 138–145; Pike, "Penal Servitude in the Spanish Empire: Presidio Labor in the Eighteenth Century," *HAHR*, LVIII (1978), 29; Manuel Martínez, *Los forzados de marina en la España del siglo XVIII (1700–1775)* (Almería, 2011), 57–64.

of communities immersed in clandestine economies in ways that commercial balance sheets cannot. This book, then, is a story of the ingenuity in subverting trade restrictions for sustenance and profit but also of the values that this process imparted.

Chocolate production and exchange brought the province of Venezuela out of obscurity, shaped discussions of political economy and reform, and colored the social norms and legal interactions of those who trafficked in it. The procurement of cacao for a *xocolatada* might contribute to criminal actions, suppressive countermeasures from imperial law enforcement agents, and violent revolt over these conditions. Encased in the trappings of civility that luxuries like chocolate bestowed was an unstable agreement between empire and colonial subject over how trade should work and whom it should serve.

# INTRODUCTION

## *Community from Criminality*

On the afternoon of April 20, 1749, a force of four to six hundred armed men gathered on Caracas's central plaza. Entering the city under blue and white flags emblazoned with red crosses and to the sounds of beating drums, the deployment comprised a cross section of Venezuela's races, social classes, and occupations. They followed Juan Francisco de León, a cacao planter and small-town sheriff *(teniente)*, and shouldered their weapons as a popular protest "in the name of the city [of Caracas], the nobility, and the masses." Disregarding the potentially ominous specter of so many armed insurgents, Caraqueños overwhelmingly welcomed León's troops with open arms. As one observer remarked, everyone in the city from shopkeepers "to the nuns give thanks to León, wishing him success and commending him to God."[1]

Royal Spanish officials and Caracas Company employees living in the city, however, felt none of these cordial sentiments. For the rebels, with León as their mouthpiece, declared the central aims of their uprising to be the extermination of the joint stock company and the expulsion of its hated Basque employees from the province. Approximately four hundred Basques fled the city, and the rebels put the governor of Venezuela under de facto house arrest while they presented their demands. Several days after the rebels entered Caracas, the hapless governor, Luis Francisco Castellanos, acceded to their terms, suspending the Company and formally expelling the outsiders. On April 23, a slave named Florenzio—the property of Simón Bolívar's father, Juan Vicente Bolí-

1. Certificación de Faustino Areste y Reina, vecino y escribano publico de Caracas, Caracas, May 23, 1749, AGI, Caracas, 937. "In the name of the city": Extracto de los Testimonios, y papeles que ha remitido el Govr., y de los que sobre ellos dice en quatro Cartas, una de 10 de Mayo, dos de 19 de Junio, y otra de 20 del mismo mes; con la Lysta de los 97 Capitulares y Nobles, que concurrieron a la Junta de 22 de abril que se refiere, Caracas, 1749, AGI, Caracas, 419.

var—read the news to a large crowd in the central plaza. When he rhetorically asked three times who had demanded the expulsion of the Caracas Company, the crowd enthusiastically cheered, "The whole province!" By August 1749, rumors circulated that León's forces numbered between four and seven thousand men throughout the province.[2] It would be the largest and arguably most important revolt witnessed in Venezuela before the independence wars.[3]

How did the Venezuelan colonial relationship reach this fever pitch of near insurrection? What passions and convictions brought Venezuelans from throughout the province into the streets of Caracas to upend the Caracas Company, the region's dominant commercial, economic, and political entity in the mid-eighteenth century? What threat did the Company pose to Venezuelan colonial society?

The León Rebellion presents an extreme example of the daily struggles over commercial control, subjecthood, and communal identity that illicit trade intensified in eighteenth-century Venezuela. Here, tensions over the Caracas Company's recent rejection of a centuries-observed *de facto* right to trade with little constraint (or to break the law with impunity, depending on one's point of view) came to a head. A long history of marginality and colonial neglect in the region had propelled Venezuelans into interimperial illegal trade for basic provisioning and profit. As legal Spanish transatlantic shipping routinely bypassed their shores for more profitable regions, Venezuelans had expanded

2. For the aims of the rebels, see Extracto de los Testimonios, y papeles que ha remitido el Govr., Caracas, 1749, AGI, Caracas, 419. "The whole province!": Diligencia del Escribano Gregorio del Portillo, Caracas, Apr. 23, 1749, AGNV, León, I, fols. 33–39, in Augusto Mijares, ed., *Documentos relativos a la insurrección de Juan Francisco de León* (Caracas, 1949), 55. On estimates of León's forces, see Auto de Gregorio del Portillo, Escribano Público, Caracas, Aug. 1, 1749, Auto del Teniente General Domingo de Aguirre y Castillo, Caracas, Aug. 2, 1749, in Juan Francisco de León, *Diario de una insurgencia, 1749* (Caracas, 1971), 115–116.

3. Other insurgencies of note in the province were the Coro Rebellion (1795) and the Gual y España Conspiracy (1795–1797). The former was much smaller than the León uprising and was, at its core, a series of slave revolts. The Gual y España Conspiracy advocated an end to Spanish rule and the formation of an independent republic, but it barely got off the ground before it was crushed. Although both movements were ideologically charged, neither uprising had the numbers, duration, or cross-class appeal of the León Rebellion. See Krisna Ruette-Orihuela and Cristina Soriano, "Remembering the Slave Rebellion of Coro: Historical Memory and Politics in Venezuela," *Ethnohistory*, LXIII (2016), 327–350; Michael P. McKinley, *Pre-Revolutionary Caracas: Politics, Economy, and Society, 1777–1811* (Cambridge, 1985), 125–138; H. Michael Tarver and Julia C. Frederick, *The History of Venezuela* (Westport, Conn., 2005), 46; Guillermo Morón, *A History of Venezuela*, trans. John Street (New York, 1963), 86; Linda M. Rupert, *Creolization and Contraband: Curaçao in the Early Modern Atlantic World* (Athens, Ga., 2012), 205–206.

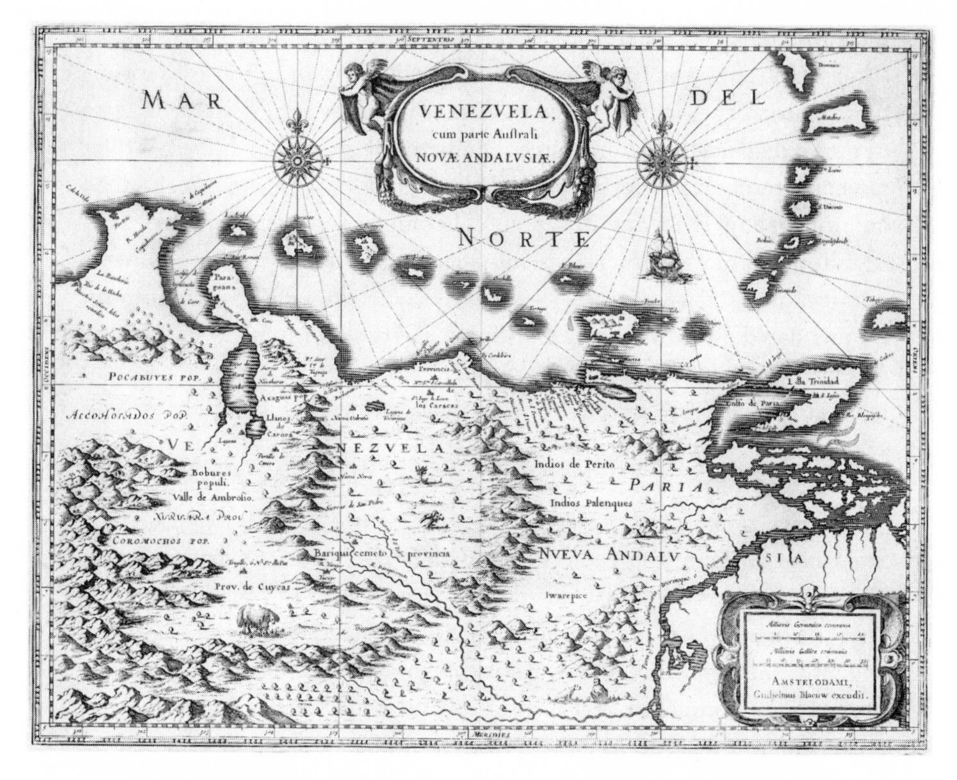


FIGURE 4. *Venezuela, cum parte Australi Novae Andalusiae* (Venezuela in the Mid-Seventeenth Century). By Willem Janszoon Blaeu. 1629–1662. *Courtesy of the John Carter Brown Library at Brown University*

their commercial gaze outward to non-Spanish markets and merchants. An arc of Dutch, English, and French Caribbean islands stretching from as far away as Jamaica to as close as Curaçao (only forty miles from the Venezuelan coast) made extralegal trading convenient and enticing. Coastal Venezuelan subjects and their non-Spanish partners developed a sense of statelessness from their commercial interactions and the relative weakness of the Spanish imperial presence in their lives. The material benefits, entrepreneurial enterprise, and local and interimperial community that blossomed from this necessary but legally prohibited commerce, in turn, helped stave off explosive colonial unrest like León's uprising.

As the Caracas Company (founded in 1728) and, by extension, the Bourbon state would come to find out, contraband commerce embodied something more expansive than simply a legal transgression or an economic transaction. Many Venezuelan coastal inhabitants and foreign visitors bought and sold smuggled goods, invented subterfuges to hide their smuggling, and sometimes endured the Spanish imperial state's strict punishments for their crimes. Unlicensed trade colored everyday social interactions and relationships. Participants in the illicit economy sent their slaves and employees out to smuggle for them. They protected associates who smuggled, formed partnerships and factions around smuggling, and bribed officials to enable their smuggling. These networks were not confined to a select few specialized merchants. They encompassed everyone: laborers, housewives, imperial administrators, sailors, clergymen, local elites, and the enslaved. The Company, with its stated mission to suppress contraband trade and revive the Venezuelan legal economy, ran into more than a stubborn commercial problem. It ran into a societal ethos.

Venezuela was but one node of coastal Caribbean smuggling circuits that sustained the economies of Spanish colonies in the Americas. Smuggling constituted more a normative state of commerce than an exotic indulgence for early modern inhabitants of Spanish America and the larger circum-Caribbean. While the metropole turned its attention to several large commercial and governmental hubs in the Caribbean basin, a profusion of littoral hamlets and towns languished in imperial neglect and mercantile isolation. These areas found connection and community through illicit exchange. The practice brought subjects of rival early modern empires into daily contact with one another. Their interaction contravened and contorted official statutes promoting imperial separation.[4]

4. A few notes on terminology and geography are useful here. The World-Systems implications of illicit trade impress Francisco Bethencourt, who believes, "It can be argued that the organisation of the Iberian Atlantic was due to two crucial economic developments: the slave trade and the contraband of silver" (Bethencourt, "The Iberian Atlantic: Ties, Networks, and Boundaries," in Harald E. Braun and Lisa Vollendorf, eds., *Theorising the Ibero-American Atlantic* [Leiden, 2013], 25). I employ the terms "Caribbean," "circum-Caribbean," "greater Caribbean," and "Caribbean basin" interchangeably to denote not only the islands of the Caribbean but also the coasts bordering the sea that bears that same name. Thus, northern South America, the Caribbean coast of Central America and Mexico, and the Gulf Coast shores of the present-day United States fall under these geographic terms. When speaking specifically of islands in the Caribbean Sea, I will use the term "Antilles."

Being on "the margins" of empire in Spanish America was probably a more normative experience than being at its center. Michiel Baud concludes that Spanish imperialism was essentially an urban ideology. However, "the paradox of Spanish colonialism was that, in spite of this centralist ideology, a great deal of marginal 'frontier'-activity took place. One could even say that colonial reality was determined more by individual colonists pushing forward the agricultural and colonial frontier than by imperial centralism. The Spanish crown could not prevent a great deal of uncontrolled economic activity within its borders.

The province of Venezuela's flourishing eighteenth-century black market, the subject of this book, illuminates the consequences of this widespread illegal trade for commerce, communication, legal understandings, imperial loyalties, and collective moral economies in the Spanish Atlantic world. Enabled by benign neglect since the colony's founding in 1522, illegal interimperial trade on the central coast was a hallmark of Venezuelan commerce and connectivity by the eighteenth century. Over that century, up to half of the province's trade came illegally from sources outside of the Spanish Empire.[5] By the late seventeenth and early eighteenth centuries, however, thriving cacao production had brought Venezuela's potential wealth to the attention of Spanish imperial

---

Even in smaller territories, such as the Caribbean islands, this paradox was clearly visible" (Baud, "A Colonial Counter Economy: Tobacco Production on Española, 1500–1870," *NWIG*, LXV [1991], 27).

I use the term "central coast" to indicate the area in Venezuela running from Coro in the west to Cumaná in the east. My study focuses on this middle stretch of present-day Venezuela's Caribbean coast, although I do draw some examples from areas farther to the west (Maracaibo), to the east (Trinidad, Tobago, and the Orinoco River delta), and out into the sea (the islands of Margarita and Los Roques).

5. Getting accurate estimates of the amount of contraband trade in Venezuela is difficult. Wim Klooster says that the Dutch owned at least a 30 percent share in Venezuelan cacao from the 1730s to the 1750s, even before unregistered cacao was counted. In the first half of the eighteenth century, Venezuelan hides made up 72 percent of the more than one million pounds annually of hides that Curaçao shipped to the Netherlands. Ramón Aizpurua believes that the value of total trade (licit plus illicit) per year in Venezuela was around 1,000,000 pesos, or double previous estimates of the value of licit trade alone. Celestino Araúz Monfante contends that by 1720, only one-third of Venezuelan cacao made its way legally to Spain. José de Abalos, the first intendant of Caracas, estimated that between 1766 and 1775, 500,000 pesos' worth of cacao was sold by Venezuelans to Mexico. However, during that time, 450,000 pesos from those sales ended up in foreign hands. Using Spanish imperial statistics, Stanley J. Stein and Barbara H. Stein have demonstrated that the province of New Granada, which encompassed Venezuela, smuggled at a much higher rate than New Spain or Peru. Between 1747 and 1761, smuggling claimed 3 million of the viceroyalty of New Granada's 5.5 million pesos of annual exports. Suffice it to say that the volume of contraband trade in the colony of Venezuela was large. See Klooster, *Illicit Riches: Dutch Trade in the Caribbean, 1648–1795* (Leiden, 1998), 185, 196; Klooster, "Curaçao and the Transit Trade," in Johannes Postma and Victor Enthoven, eds., *Riches from Atlantic Commerce: Dutch Transatlantic Trade and Shipping, 1585–1817* (Leiden, 2003), 216; Aizpurua, *Curazao y la costa de Caracas: Introducción al estudio del contrabando de la Provincia de Venezuela en tiempos de la Compañía Guipuzcoana, 1730–1780* (Caracas, 1993), 124; Araúz Monfante, *El contrabando holandés en el Caribe durante la primera mitad del siglo XVIII*, I (Caracas, 1984), 217; Eduardo Arcila Farías, *Economía colonial de Venezuela* (Mexico City, 1946), 260–261; Stein and Stein, *Apogee of Empire: Spain and New Spain in the Age of Charles III, 1759–1789* (Baltimore, 2003), 72.

policymakers. With an export commodity of value finally identified, fierce efforts to stanch interimperial exchange and reintegrate the province (comprising Caracas and most of the western and central coasts of the present-day country) into the Spanish imperial fold began. In 1728, an agreement between the Spanish monarchy and a group of Basque investors resulted in the formation of the Real Compañía Guipuzcoana de Caracas (colloquially known as the Caracas Company). In return for granting it a near monopoly over the Venezuelan cacao trade with Spain, the crown expected the Company to supply the province with European goods, to provide coast guard patrols that would deter foreign interlopers to Venezuelan trade, and to ship a fixed amount of cacao on Venezuelan planters' private accounts (usually around one-third of a Company ship's cargo). Despite the transformative economic and commercial potential of the Caracas Company for the colony, its imposition aroused bitter tensions with Venezuelans of all classes. Although the Company used its private fleet of coast guard ships to suppress smuggling, it failed to comply with its other mission to increase the flow of European goods into the province. Records of this period offer an unusually rich set of cases to examine a society enmeshed in and influenced by contraband commerce. Although distinctive in the extent of its imperial neglect and in the suddenness with which its economic and political conditions changed, the province's experience with extralegal trade generally mirrored that of the vast majority of imperial circum-Caribbean outposts.[6]

My book makes three broad arguments. First, communities on the coastal peripheries of the Spanish Empire formed moral economies from the ground up that included contraband trade as a basic tenet within them. E. P. Thompson's term for the schema by which eighteenth-century English bread rioters intertwined their marketplace interactions and their sense of justice functions here as a way to analyze traders' tacit beliefs about their actions. Despite differing levels of exposure to the black market, Venezuelan subjects generally came

6. For the initial royal order establishing the Caracas Company and its privileges, see Real Compañía Guipuzcoana de Caracas, *Real Cedula de la Fundacion de la Real Compañia Guipuzcoana de Caracas, y Reglas Economicas de buen govierno, con que la estableció la M.N. y M.L. Provincia de Guipuzcoa, en Junta General del año de 1728*... (Madrid, 1765). See also Montserrat Gárate Ojanguren, *La Real Compañía Guipuzcoana de Caracas* (San Sebastián, 1990), 41–43; Margarita Eva Rodríguez García, *Compañías privilegiadas de comercio con América y cambio político (1706–1765)* (Madrid, 2005), 30, 47; Aizpurua, *Curazao y la costa de Caracas,* 150. For additional concessions given to the Company, see Raquel Rico Linage, *Las reales Compañías de comercio con América: Los órganos de gobierno* (Seville, 1983), 7, 24; Gerardo Vivas Pineda, *La aventura naval de la Compañía Guipuzcoana de Caracas* (Caracas, 1998), 39; and Arcila Farías, *Economía colonial de Venezuela,* 209.

to accept unlicensed transimperial enterprise as a path to greater commercial choice and communal sustainability. Material want and consumer preference drove smuggling in the first place. Smuggling then cultivated local and interimperial power bases. Venezuelans defended these commercial connections through deception, further commercial disobedience, and popular protest against state and private attempts at mercantile enforcement. They did so reluctantly because they still felt a sense of loyalty to the Spanish Empire and because they hesitated to publicly support what they knew to be a criminalized practice. Yet in their own minds and intermittently in their public statements, participants in contraband commerce expressed the relativistic belief that their trade was no different in substance than licensed exchange—and sometimes a good deal fairer for colonial inhabitants.[7]

Second, subjects and officials living in areas of endemic illicit trade agreed upon acceptable levels of criminality and corruption. Coastal dwellers created these unspoken compromises to prevent monopolization of the market. In the relative absence of formal governmental regulation of illicit transactions, these agreements functioned as an alternate conceptualization of commercial law.[8]

7. Criticism of Thompson's moral economy argues that it concentrates exclusively on local markets and the idea that the informal agreements of economic fairness were antithetical to modern open markets. My formulation of the term expands its reach into wide-open interimperial exchange and argues that colonial subjects manifested conceptualizations of economic justice based on *freer* trade. This runs counter to Thompson's context, in which authorities sought to introduce open market forces to areas where rebellious peasants appealed to customary practice. Additionally, my work contends that the moral economy can exist in illegal contexts. See E. P. Thompson, "The Moral Economy of the English Crowd in the Eighteenth Century," *Past and Present,* L (1971), 78–79, 86, 98, 112. For representative critiques of Thompson's model, see Norbert Götz, "'Moral Economy': Its Conceptual History and Analytical Prospects," *Journal of Global Ethics,* XI (2015), 147–148, 154, 158; Adrian Randall and Andrew Charlesworth, "The Moral Economy: Riot, Markets, and Social Conflict," in Randall and Charlesworth, eds., *Moral Economy and Popular Protest: Crowds, Conflicts, and Authority* (New York, 2000), 12–13.

8. Acceptable criminality and lawbreaking without the violation of moral codes are ideas that transcend time periods and contexts. In her work on twentieth-century informal economies in Martinique, anthropologist Katherine E. Browne focuses on *débrouillardism,* a concept going back to Caribbean slavery that describes someone who makes economic profit through his or her own cleverness. In avoiding taxes, working off the books, and seeking economic autonomy, these figures "are seen to push the limits of French law, but not to violate the culturally prescribed limits of what is morally defensible." By contrast, Kristen Block's work uses the microhistories of several seventeenth-century historical actors to examine these individuals' reactions to violations of the moral compact. According to Block, "Ordinary people made pirates, sailors, pawns, and slaves by desperate circumstances, exploited and persecuted for any resistance to their constant debasement—responded to the

This book's third argument contends that conflict over illicit trade in the Spanish Atlantic is, in fact, a story of empire building. The process was a shared endeavor between coastal inhabitants and metropolitan imperial reformers. A Spanish imperial government that wished to maintain legitimacy in the eyes of littoral subjects had to accommodate a certain amount of smuggling. Likewise, locals had to cope with substantive changes to their commercial status quo directed by early Bourbon Reforms meant to streamline and increase colonial revenue sources. A tension between transimperial autonomy and imperial enforcement ran throughout circum-Caribbean Venezuelan trade. At issue was the state's right to control human movement even when it criminalized most viable options for commerce. In the absence of adequate or equitable legal trade, Venezuelan subjects who availed themselves of clandestine exchange saw it as an innocuous offense. Smuggled goods were ubiquitous, even in regions where the human consequences of trading them could be severe. This paradox reveals that the state and local actors both shaped colonial compacts of commerce and government.

Taken together, these arguments reveal how smuggling and its suppression exacerbated a mutual incomprehension between Spanish imperial reformers and Venezuelan subjects over the nature of trade. As the Spanish state had finite resources to devote to its vast empire, it exerted weak control over Venezuela for two centuries. When Iberian bureaucrats finally sought to whip Venezuela into shape in the early eighteenth century, their sudden and heavy-handed solutions made governing difficult. Bourbon political economists in Spain saw trade as economic and political insofar as it furthered organizational order and increased badly needed revenue for the empire. They perceived commercial crime as economic disorder at best and colonial disloyalty at worst. Venezuelan subjects, by contrast, viewed commerce as an unbounded social and communal right. In their eyes, the king and the Council of the Indies had legislated commercial exclusivism but then had abdicated their responsibility to adequately direct provisions to their provincial subjects. Venezuelans had quickly accepted this and made alternate trading arrangements with non-Spaniards. But they could countenance neither the constricting of non-Spanish sources of trade nor the simultaneous exploitation and outsourcing of their resources to a third party (the Caracas Company). As a result, im-

---

chaos with a reciprocal hostility that threatened the breakdown of any agreements about moral economy." See Browne, *Creole Economics: Caribbean Cunning under the French Flag* (Austin, Tex., 2004), 11; Block, *Ordinary Lives in the Early Caribbean: Religion, Colonial Competition, and the Politics of Profit* (Athens, Ga., 2012), 205.

perial politics in Venezuela became volatile from the late 1720s onward but held together mainly because smuggling acted as a safety valve.

## DEFINING LEGALITY AND ILLEGALITY IN EARLY MODERN COMMERCE

Understanding Venezuelan "contraband trade" and "smuggling" first requires defining these murky words. In the eighteenth-century Iberian world, the Real Academia's *Diccionario de la lengua castellana* of 1729 defined *contraband* as acts contrary to the law (literally, *contra bando)* and then discussed the word's most common meaning as merchandise, clothing, goods, and "all that is prohibited from entering these kingdoms as it comes from enemy nations barred from our trade." The entry finished by quoting the *Recopilación de las Leyes de los Reynos de Indias*'s interpretation of contraband as that which had not been examined and approved by port and customs officials. Perhaps the clearest historical understanding of smuggling would define it as "the illegal movement of goods across national boundaries to evade payment of taxes."[9]

Legal pluralism in the early modern world made for different meanings of this socially constructed term. What constituted smuggling to one empire was simply trade to another. This study focuses on the interimperial portion of what the commercial codes of the Spanish Empire identified as contraband trade: the movement of any goods between Spanish subjects and foreign traders without the explicit blessing of the Spanish House of Trade (Casa de Contratación).[10]

The most common confusion among casual observers of early modern history is that "smuggling" was just another sobriquet for "piracy." Illicit trade, privateering, and piracy were legally separate practices, but imperial authorities muddled the distinctions between state and private actions (and violence) when it benefited them to do so. Both smuggling and piracy were commercial crimes that redirected wealth from imperially exclusive systems of trade. Maritime subjects could be both pirates and smugglers in the same life course (or

9. "Contra bando": "Mercadería, ropa, ò géneros de *contrabando:* Se llama assi todo lo prohibido de introducir en estos Reinos por ser de Países enemigos, con los quales está cerrado el comércio," *Diccionario de la lengua castellana,* II (Madrid, 1729), 559. "Illegal movement of goods": Wim Klooster, "Inter-Imperial Smuggling in the Americas, 1600–1800," in Bernard Bailyn and Patricia L. Denault, eds., *Soundings in Atlantic History: Latent Structures and Intellectual Currents, 1500–1830* (Cambridge, Mass., 2009), 141.

10. On legal pluralism in the early modern world, see Lauren Benton, *Law and Colonial Cultures: Legal Regimes in World History, 1400–1900* (Cambridge, 2002), 3–6, 24.

even the same voyage). Both professions drew from the lower ranks of Caribbean society. However, key distinctions separated these illegal phenomena. Smugglers and their accomplices could be from all social classes and occupations, whereas piracy mostly recruited the poor and economically dispossessed. Moreover, from the evidence available, it appears that piracy's violent tendencies drew on or produced a higher quotient of antisocial, violent, and even sadistic practitioners.[11]

Even though they frequently shared common social origins, contrabandists and pirates conducted business differently. As piracy was, not consensual exchange, but maritime theft, it almost always involved force or the threat of force. Smuggling was mutually beneficial, if illegal, commerce that still involved the possibility of violence. Although pirates used coercive violence to obtain goods and to advertise their ruthlessness (making further resistance less likely), stealth and collusion were the principal qualities of a successful smuggler.[12]

Smuggling's reputation as a near-victimless crime contrasted with the painful legacy of destroyed ports and tortured subjects conjured by piracy. Although piracy occasionally took the form of "forced trade" *(comercio forzado),* a feigned coercion that masked simple smuggling, real contraband trade offered much more substantive benefits for Spanish American settlements. Smuggling's potential to provision and enrich outposts over and above legal trade meant that illicit commerce enjoyed official complicity and community

11. The association between piracy and smuggling is so pronounced that Alan L. Karras titled the second chapter of his thematic monograph on smuggling "It's Not Pirates!" His observations on the differences in social class, business practices, punishments for practitioners, and consequences for trade policy have informed some of the distinctions I provide here between the two crimes. See Karras, *Smuggling: Contraband and Corruption in World History* (Lanham, Md., 2010), 20–42. On the muddling of illicit trade, privateering, and piracy, see Alejandro Colás and Bryan Mabee, "The Flow and Ebb of Private Seaborne Violence in Global Politics: Lessons from the Atlantic World, 1689–1815," in Colás and Mabee, eds., *Mercenaries, Pirates, Bandits, and Empires: Private Violence in Historical Context* (New York, 2010), 85. On the common social background of pirates and smugglers, see Marcus Rediker, *Between the Devil and the Deep Blue Sea: Merchant Seamen, Pirates, and the Anglo-American Maritime World, 1700–1750* (Cambridge, 1987), 60–76. On distinctions between them, see Kris E. Lane, *Pillaging the Empire: Piracy in the Americas, 1500–1750* (Armonk, N.Y., 1998), 26; Mark G. Hanna, *Pirate Nests and the Rise of the British Empire, 1570–1740* (Williamsburg, Va., and Chapel Hill, N.C., 2015), 158–162.

12. Peter T. Leeson argues that pirates sought to cultivate "a piratical 'brand name'" that "improved their efficiency on the account, reaping greater rewards from their plunder (Leeson, *The Invisible Hook: The Hidden Economics of Pirates* [Princeton, N.J., 2009], 107–133, esp. 108).

consent. This reality, in turn, enabled foreign smugglers to maintain their anonymity and domestic ones to blend into their communities. By contrast, pirates became a notorious and commonly hunted menace at most Caribbean ports by the early eighteenth century. Although Spanish royal authorities fought and punished both pirates and smugglers as noxious threats to the empire, they showed more tolerance and leniency for the latter.[13]

Finally, the diplomatic and economic consequences of the two crimes differed dramatically. Smuggling and piracy disrupted the peace between Spain and its rivals. Yet smuggling gradually precipitated the opening of Spanish commercial systems to foreign influence. Piracy only reinforced a siege mentality among Spanish bureaucrats. There is an irony in piracy's infamy and smuggling's relative obscurity in the historiography of the early modern Atlantic. Whereas piracy inflicted sensational but sporadic damage on the Spanish imperial political economy over a concentrated period, smuggling quietly bled much greater revenue from Spain's economy over centuries.

These somewhat stiff definitions of illicit trade belied a reality where smuggling was apparently everywhere. Smuggling had arrived with foreign traders, swelled with the commercial fancies of Spanish American colonists, and breached the seawall of officialdom that was supposed to keep it out. In their 1749 watershed exposé of Spanish South America, *Discourse and Political Reflections on the Kingdoms of Peru,* Jorge Juan and Antonio de Ulloa described coastal cities where "not only do [officials] fail to stop the entrance of illicit goods but they also fawn over and court smugglers in order to get preference for their port over others and insure continuance of income from bribes."[14]

It is worth comparing this acknowledgment that seemingly everyone in Spanish America was caught up in interimperial contraband trade to documents that warned of its corrosive effects. One anonymous pamphleteer argued that decrees liberalizing trade *(comercio libre)* in Venezuela in 1789

13. For both private and state animosity against pirates, see Robert C. Ritchie, *Captain Kidd and the War against the Pirates* (1986; rpt. New York, 1998), esp. 232–238; Hanna, *Pirate Nests,* 330–415. For a concise separation between the illegal and illicit activities of pirates and the illegal but socially licit transactions of smugglers, see Alexandra Harnett and Shannon Lee Dawdy, "The Archaeology of Illegal and Illicit Economies," *Annual Review of Anthropology,* XLII (2013), 39–42.

14. Jorge Juan and Antonio de Ulloa, *Discourse and Political Reflections on the Kingdoms of Peru: Their Government, Special Regimen of Their Inhabitants, and Abuses Which Have Been Introduced into One Another, with Special Information on Why They Grew up and Some Means to Avoid Them* (1749), ed. John J. TePaske, trans. TePaske and Besse A. Clement (Norman, Okla., 1978), 51.

would restore to agriculture and to the arts the many vassals that are now occupied in [contraband trade] or its prevention. It would prevent the ruin of families, the depopulation of provinces, the perversion or relaxation of customs important to morality, and the extinction of patriotic spirit. Individual interests in obtaining desired goods that are absent from the kingdom or in acquiring them at a better price unite and conjoin our subjects with foreigners toward their own ends and intentions. This notorious threat alienates and distracts their spirits from the state.[15]

The conundrum of analyzing a consequential black market economy is how to reconcile grave portrayals of smuggling with its ubiquity. Illicit trade was an economic way of life and the most significant commercial activity in many Spanish American colonies. It was a normalized and humdrum feature of port life. Between the market forces that pushed subjects into smuggling and the administrative complicity that tolerated it, the operative question might be, Why call this trade contraband at all? By using words such as "smuggling," are we simply reifying terms of the state that no one much believed in anyway? Could we call this "free trade" or just plain "trade" and move on?

Despite their paradoxical demonization of a practice that was widespread and even necessary, the pronouncements of royal officials and commercial observers were not just window dressing to hide their own participation in illicit trade or doomsday material to justify their aspirational solutions. Many of these historical actors genuinely believed in the inherent criminality and perversity of unlicensed trade and wished to suppress it. By ignoring illicit trade in the historical record entirely or observing no distinction between it and legal trade, we lose something in terms of how early modern people thought about, followed, and circumvented the law.[16]

15. "Informe sobre el Real Decreto de Comercio Libre del 28 de febrero de 1789," in Antonio Arellano Moreno, ed., *Documentos para la historia económica en la Epoca colonial: Viajes y Informes* (Caracas, 1970), 496.

16. Harnett and Dawdy observe that the failure by scholars to take illegal economic activity into account "results in the nonsensical circular logic in which the definition of a state is a polity that successfully controls a market economy and that the definition of a market economy is one centralized and regulated by a state. It makes far more sense, judging from historical examples dating from antiquity to present time, to presume that a large percentage of a society's economic transactions, if not the majority, lie outside the successful regulation of the state. In fact, the more a state restricts economic activities, the greater the incentives are to evade regulation. That said, it is a common mistake to imagine the relation

Here, James C. Scott's well-worn concept of legibility is instructive. Preoccupations with smuggling were related to mobility and interimperial contact. For a host of itinerant groups, "efforts to permanently settle these mobile peoples (sedentarization) seemed to be a perennial state project." They represented "a state's attempt to make a society legible, to arrange the population in ways that simplified the classic state function of taxation, conscription, and prevention of rebellion." In this case, the Spanish state's attempt at legibility translated into ascribing moral connotations to the practice of smuggling. This stood in marked contrast to what most Spanish American subjects believed about smuggling, as demonstrated by their actions.[17]

Given the contradictions inherent in the discourse of commercial exclusion, perhaps the best way to interpret "contraband trade," "smugglers," and "smuggling" is, first, to reclaim these terms from the weighted moral connotations of the state. Approaching smuggling as an occupational and procedural category reveals much about the practices and hazards of commercial life in early modern coastal economies. Discussing it as part of a moral economy of Spanish American colonial communities offers a fuller picture of the everyday politics surrounding consumption and exchange. Instead of resorting to the anachronism of "free trader" or the vagueness of "trader," this book refers to interimperial merchants as "contrabandists" and "smugglers" to denote what the majority of colonial society knew them to be: purveyors of goods and bridges between empires in an era when commercial law and bureaucratic rhetoric militated against them.

Just as defining "smuggling" and "smugglers" is a conceptually slippery exercise, illicit trade resists periodization because of its uneven documentary footprint over a span of time. All the same, some broad trends and turning points in the history of Venezuelan contraband trade are helpful for understanding its intricate impact on the relationships of littoral dwellers. By the eighteenth century, smuggling had surpassed piracy as the most profitable means for foreign empires to penetrate the Spanish closed system of trade. Fully developed Caribbean colonies and merchant marines enabled non-Spanish merchants to conduct contraband trade on a much larger scale than ever before. Interimperial warfare was perhaps the most important noncommercial determinant influencing the intensity of smuggling. Formally declared

between economy and government to fall into black and white markets. The vast majority of day-to-day transactions take place in a gray zone" ("Archaeology of Illegal and Illicit Economies," *Annual Review of Anthropology*, XLII [2013], 46–47).

17. James C. Scott, *Seeing Like a State: How Certain Schemes to Improve the Human Condition Have Failed* (New Haven, Conn., 1998), 1–2.

conflicts between European powers in the eighteenth century brought legal Spanish trade in the Caribbean to a standstill and stimulated illicit commerce. Over the course of the century, Spanish trade suffered during the War of Spanish Succession (1701–1714), the War of Jenkins' Ear (1739–1748), the Seven Years' War (1754–1763), the American Revolutionary War (1776–1783), and the French Revolutionary Wars (1789–1802). Wartime shortages also prompted Spanish colonial officials to allow temporary trading with neutral empires.[18]

Domestic conflicts shaped the smuggler's business interests in Venezuela as well. In periods when the Caracas Company maintained firm political control over the colony, contrabandists saw their ventures curtailed. The 1730s and 1740s were decades when peak Company enforcement of trade laws produced many arrests and violent encounters. On the other hand, after the crown reduced Company privileges in Venezuela in the 1750s following León's Rebellion, smugglers had a considerably easier time plying their trade. The creation of free ports in the non-Spanish Caribbean in the 1750s and 1760s, which encouraged all nations to trade in these harbors, also lessened barriers to trans-imperial exchange.[19]

My study's time frame concludes with two dramatic developments that altered the landscape of smuggling in Venezuela and in the larger Spanish Atlantic. These historic shifts overturned or reconfigured many common patterns of illicit commerce in the colony. First, imperial administrators finally extended limited comercio libre between Spanish and Spanish American ports to Venezuela in 1789. Legalized and largely unrestricted commerce with other regions of the Spanish Empire, as well as a handful of specific concessions to trade with foreign colonies, provided Spanish American merchants with more options for conducting licit trade. In some cases, they used legal free trade as a jumping-off point for unregulated international exchange. Comercio libre also fulfilled various commercial niches and navigational circuits that would have been illegal under earlier Spanish trade law.[20]

18. In Klooster's estimation, the early eighteenth century was the period in which smuggling made a "qualitative leap" in the Atlantic. He especially highlights smuggling in the Caribbean due to the close geographic proximity of rival empires' colonies ("Inter-Imperial Smuggling," in Bailyn and Denault, eds., *Soundings in Atlantic History*, 162–163. Wars also stimulated and stifled attempts at imperial reform; see Allan J. Kuethe and Kenneth J. Andrien, *The Spanish Atlantic World in the Eighteenth Century: War and the Bourbon Reforms, 1713–1796* (New York, 2014), 346.

19. Rupert, *Creolization and Contraband*, 173–174; Klooster, *Illicit Riches*, 146–161.

20. Venezuela and New Spain (Mexico) were the last Spanish American colonies to receive this permission. Comercio libre decrees were extended to individual colonies and ports beginning in 1765. For merchants' options in licit trade, see John Fisher, *Commercial*

Second, chaotic patterns of late-eighteenth-century warfare crippled transatlantic Spanish commerce and diminished the criminality Spanish imperial authorities associated with smuggling. As a result of Spanish naval weakness, Spain's foes imposed blockades and embargoes at will upon the colonies from the Seven Years' War onward. Administrators of trade-starved provinces throughout the empire began to permit trade with neutral nations on an unprecedented scale. Along with this reform, Spanish American authorities became reluctant to prosecute those who brought much-needed goods to their colonies by quasi-legal or illegal means. The de facto and de jure decriminalization of aspects of contraband trade in Spanish America during the last quarter of the eighteenth century meant that smuggling displayed a markedly different character than earlier illegal exchange.[21]

## SOURCES, HISTORIOGRAPHICAL CURRENTS, AND METHODOLOGIES

The social foundations of early modern illicit economies like Venezuela's remain elusive. A reasonable consensus exists among historians of Spanish America that smuggling invigorated colonial economies, even as it ate away at the revenue streams of the Spanish treasury and empowered Spain's Atlantic rivals. However, many surveys of the Spanish commercial system have avoided substantial coverage of contraband trade. The basis for this omission is the difficulty in discerning the volume of an illegal practice that was, by its nature, secretive and usually undetected. Several valuable quantitative works have made projections based on records of captured goods or the bullion tallies from non-Spanish colonies to discuss smuggling's impact on the political economy of empires. This scholarship is inevitably incomplete, as it

---

*Relations between Spain and Spanish America in the Era of Free Trade, 1778–1796* (Liverpool, 1985), 89.

21. Adrian J. Pearce, "*Rescates* and Anglo-Spanish Trade in the Caribbean during the French Revolutionary Wars, ca. 1797–1804," *Journal of Latin American Studies,* XXXVIII (2006), 607, 621; Pearce, "British Trade with the Spanish Colonies, 1788–1795," *BLAR,* XX (2001), 233–234; Douglas Hamilton, "Rivalry, War, and Imperial Reform in the 18th-Century Caribbean," in Stephan Palmié and Francisco A. Scarano, eds., *The Caribbean: A History of the Region and Its Peoples* (Chicago, 2011), 270–271; John R. Fisher, *The Economic Aspects of Spanish Imperialism in America, 1492–1810* (Liverpool, 1997), 202–205. My survey of prize court cases from eighteenth-century Venezuela shows a significant drop in cases by the late 1770s and early 1780s. From this period onward, judges were more likely to fine convicted contrabandists than to dole out harsh labor, imprisonment, or exile sentences.

makes its estimates from the small number of smugglers caught in the act. In addition, studies of how smuggling altered individual colonial societies are few. This book grew out of the historiographical misinterpretation or outright exclusion of this lifeblood of the Spanish American economy. I read records of contraband trade, not to determine how much of it passed back and forth between empires, but instead to uncover the social history of subjects involved in it. Their struggles with imperial trade laws expose, at the granular level, the gap between how imperial planners envisioned colonial trade and how provincial subjects experienced and modified it.[22]

The archival sources documenting illicit commerce, when properly utilized, allow for a multiperspective analysis uncommon in colonial history. Contraband trade is a thematic topic that cannot be treated as a singular historical event or as a discrete colonial or national history. Nevertheless, it appears everywhere in the early modern collections of national and imperial archives. Smuggling figures as both a central category in eighteenth-century bureaucratic paperwork classifications and as a passing concern on memorandums highlighting other pressing matters of the day. Understanding these scattered writings on a mysterious business that was local and interimperial,

22. A few major works of Spanish American commercial historiography that agree with this contention are Geoffrey J. Walker, *Spanish Politics and Imperial Trade, 1700–1789* (Bloomington, Ind., 1979), ix, 14; Henry Kamen, *Empire: How Spain Became a World Power, 1492–1763* (New York, 2002), 436; Murdo J. MacLeod, *Spanish Central America: A Socioeconomic History, 1520–1720* (1973; rpt. Austin, Tex., 2008), xiii, 348–374; John Lynch, *The Hispanic World in Crisis and Change, 1598–1700* (Oxford, 1992), 242–264; Kenneth J. Andrien, *Crisis and Decline: The Viceroyalty of Peru in the Seventeenth Century* (Albuquerque, N.M., 1985), 11–49; Fisher, *Economic Aspects of Spanish Imperialism in America,* 72–91; Stanley J. Stein and Barbara H. Stein, *Silver, Trade, and War: Spain and America in the Making of Early Modern Europe* (Baltimore, 2000), 3–40; Kuethe and Andrien, *Spanish Atlantic World,* 70–73. For quantitative works, see, for example, Lance Grahn, *The Political Economy of Smuggling: Regional Informal Economies in Early Bourbon New Granada* (Boulder, Colo., 1997); Nuala Zahedieh, "The Merchants of Port Royal, Jamaica, and the Spanish Contraband Trade, 1655–1692," *WMQ,* 3d Ser., XLIII (1986), 570–593; Araúz Monfante, *El contrabando holandés;* Sergio Villalobos R[ivera], *Comercio y contrabando en el Río de la Plata y Chile, 1700–1811* (Buenos Aires, 1977). For works that address individual colonial development through smuggling, see Rupert, *Creolization and Contraband;* Christian J. Koot, *Empire at the Periphery: British Colonists, Anglo-Dutch Trade, and the Development of the British Atlantic, 1621–1713* (New York, 2011); Fabrício Prado, *Edge of Empire: Atlantic Networks and Revolution in Bourbon Río de la Plata* (Oakland, Calif., 2015); Thomas M. Truxes, *Defying Empire: Trading with the Enemy in Colonial New York* (New Haven, Conn., 2008); Zacarías Moutoukias, *Contrabando y control colonial en el siglo XVII: Buenos Aires, el Atlántico y el espacio peruano* (Buenos Aires, 1988); Klooster, *Illicit Riches;* Aizpurua, *Curazao y la costa de Caracas.*

an embarrassment to the empire and an obsession of political reformers, has proved difficult.[23] It involved striking an analytical balance between the imperial archive, with its metropolitan focus on political stability, revenues, and administration, and the colonial archive, which kept records of even the pettiest cases of commercial crime as a matter of judicial procedure. In this manner, I was able to explore the social impact of contraband trade from the level of the lowly village coast guard official all the way up to that of the king and the Council of the Indies in Spain. The study produced from these records examines prize court records of seized shipping, interrogations of contrabandists, governmental correspondence, and print material gathered from archives in Venezuela, Spain, Colombia, England, and the United States.[24]

These records are extraordinarily rich not only in their organization and diversity but also in the elucidative content they provide about enigmatic his-

23. The source material for illicit trade presents problems of brevity, omission, and credibility. Smugglers were guarded and developed deceptive scripts calculated to their circumstances. Still, the testimonies of captive merchants represent an entry point for reconstructing webs of commerce. The empire that judged these people saw them as common criminals to be processed through the legal system, not as subjects worthy of detailed and recurrent study. The vast majority of individual illicit peddlers appear just once in the historical record. Moreover, unlike legitimate businessmen, contrabandists kept few, if any, bills of sale or written correspondence, as these documents would be damning evidence in the event of their capture. Smugglers were also reticent to reveal their contacts. Divulging this information engendered the perception that the accused were habitual smugglers and could increase the severity of their punishments. Furthermore, offering details of the trade could endanger a smuggler's acquaintances or future contrabandists plying the same routes.

24. An extensive group of Venezuelan indexes written by Hermano Nectario María draw together the nation's prenational past. A rarity for the study of the colonial period, these indexes catalog in great detail documents related to Venezuelan colonial history in the Archivo General de Indias in Spain. The indexes enabled me to sift between local documents held in Venezuela and Colombia and imperial records in Spain. Venezuela's principal colonial archive, the Archivo General de la Nación, also has comprehensive unpublished indexes of its collections. Both of these sets of indexes were invaluable to my process of finding and sorting colonial records on illicit trade. In terms of document collections, I focused on the Comisos, Diversos, and Compañía Guipuzcoana collections in the Archivo General de la Nación. At the Archivo General de Indias, I drew most heavily on *legajos* from the Audiencia de Caracas, Audiencia de Santo Domingo, and Escribanía collections. In Caracas, I looked at prize court records in the Archivo General de la Nación and the Academia Nacional de la Historia. In Seville, I investigated more prize court records and imperial correspondence at the Archivo General de Indias. I also looked at documents pertaining to English smugglers in the National Archives in Kew and British Library in London. Regarding Venezuela's western border, I examined files in the Archivo General de la Nación in Bogotá. Finally, I surveyed print sources concerning cacao and the Caracas Company at the John Carter Brown Library in Providence, Rhode Island.

torical populations. Volumes upon volumes of documents catalogue smugglers' itineraries, contacts, opinions, and loyalties. These records speak of violent encounters, rebellion, bribery, and corruption, but also of cooperation, subaltern agency, geographic itinerancy, and sustained contact across vast distances and empires. Moreover, as with inquisition documents, the prosecution records against smugglers articulate the palpable voices of common people usually overlooked in the historical record. Colonial records that sought to document the prosecution unintentionally revealed the history of the prosecuted.[25]

Venezuela's eighteenth-century black market presents a cognitive conflict throughout this book. On one hand, illicit trade demonstrated the porousness of boundaries separating subjects of different empires in the Caribbean basin. Multinational, multiracial crews moved goods between way stations, negotiated local practices, and brought merchandise, information, and ideas across borders. On the other hand, the unlucky smuggler's experience with coast guards, prize courts, and criminal justice systems in a foreign land also underscored the extent to which "empire matters."[26]

The methodology of this study explores that tension between fluidity and rigidity. Smugglers and their allies fashioned for themselves and their communities a remarkably open existence that eschewed imperially demarcated borders. Contraband trade brought people together around a common littoral identity. Partakers in illicit commerce truly saw the world differently than the political economists of early modern imperialism who sought to partition

25. Here I draw on Karen B. Graubart's scholarship on indigenous women in Peru, which skillfully articulates how colonial systems' attempts to exclude various groups from positions of power and legitimacy in fact allowed these groups to remain a real force of contention in the documentary record. In a similar vein, Ann Laura Stoler argues for understanding subaltern subjects within, rather than against, the context of the arenas of oppositional authority that permitted their voices to be heard in the first place. She proposes that scholars treat archives "not as repositories of state power but as unquiet movements in a field of force, as restless realignments and readjustments of people and the beliefs to which they were tethered." See Graubart, *With Our Labor and Sweat: Indigenous Women and the Formation of Colonial Society in Peru, 1550–1700* (Stanford, Calif., 2007), 3; Stoler, *Along the Archival Grain: Epistemic Anxieties and Colonial Common Sense* (Princeton, N.J., 2009), 32–33.

26. As Elaine Carey and Andrae M. Marak have noted, borders imposed by modern states usually have the effect of creating networks meant to bridge or evade these barriers. See Carey and Marak, "Introduction," in Carey and Marak, eds., *Smugglers, Brothels, and Twine: Historical Perspectives on Contraband and Vice in North America's Borderlands* (Tucson, Ariz., 2011), 2–4. For further meditation on a paradox like this, see Trevor Burnard, "Empire Matters? The Historiography of Imperialism in Early America, 1492–1830," *HEI*, XXXIII (2007), 87–107.

English from French from Spanish from Dutch in a zero-sum game. The commercial lawbreaker's power derived from the accumulation of goods from many thousands of illicit transactions and from the unstated assumption that commercial transactions rarely followed all the legal stipulations imposed on them. Contrabandists' influence created a commercial "deviancy" that made a mockery of the law through its mundaneness. However, the imperialist's power sprang from more conventional sources such as armies, coast guards, treaties, and courts that could make war, police the populace, change the rules of the game, and punish transgressors. By regulating what was legal and illegal commerce, imperial representatives sought to define who could participate in a key activity of subjecthood.[27]

In many ways, the dispute between these groups was one of center versus periphery and mother country versus overseas subject. Yet many actors in this conflict existed at various points along the spectrum between these poles. Where, for example, would one place the loyalties of a local official, a privateer, or a runaway slave who communed with smugglers? How does one reconcile the fact that, even as they were harried by imperial officials, contrabandists

27. Here I borrow from Michael N. Pearson's concept of the "littoral society." Pearson makes a convincing theoretical case that "there is such a thing as littoral society, that is, that we can go around the shores of an ocean, or a sea, or indeed the whole world, and identify societies that have more in common with other littoral societies than they do with their inland neighbors." At a macro level, John R. Gillis agrees with Pearson that preindustrial coastlines were "zones of transfer and transmission, . . . seams rather than separations." Philip D. Morgan reiterates Pearson's perspective from the vantage point of individual colonies by discussing Jamestown and Roanoke, Virginia, as "islands" that shared a maritime perspective on settlement with the Caribbean Antilles. Scholars such as Ernesto Bassi, Juan Giusti-Cordero, and Linda Rupert have taken another approach to understanding littoral identity. They each acknowledge that inhabitants conceptualized geography quite differently than cartographers and imperial administrators. Thus two islands separated by a strait or an island straddling the mainland might be thought of as a common district by locals, even as maps viewed these configurations as separate geographic and imperial spaces. See Pearson, "Littoral Society: The Concept and the Problems," *Journal of World History,* XVII (2006), 353; Gillis, *The Human Shore: Seacoasts in History* (Chicago, 2012), 107; Morgan, "Virginia's Other Prototype: The Caribbean," in Peter C. Mancall, ed., *The Atlantic World and Virginia, 1550–1624* (Williamsburg, Va., and Chapel Hill, N.C., 2007), 345; Bassi, *An Aqueous Territory: Sailor Geographies and New Granada's Transimperial Greater Caribbean World* (Durham, N.C., 2017), 3–11, 55–84, 204–212; Giusti-Cordero, "Beyond Sugar Revolutions: Rethinking the Spanish Caribbean in the Seventeenth and Eighteenth Centuries," in George Baca, Stephan Palmié, and Aisha Khan, eds., *Empirical Futures: Anthropologists and Historians Engage the Work of Sidney W. Mintz* (Chapel Hill, N.C., 2009), 70–74; Rupert, "Contraband Trade and the Shaping of Colonial Societies in Curaçao and Tierra Firme," *Itinerario,* XXX (2006), 35.

depended on the illicit markets created by state prohibitions for their livelihoods and profits? In truth, mercantile enforcers, commercial transgressors, and ordinary subjects never resolved the conflict between competing visions of separation and connectivity in colonial commercial development.[28]

Paying attention to the mechanics of how separate societies traded and overlapped with one another uncovers more than just site-specific concerns. As contrabandists shaped local colonial processes, they also altered global commerce. The "social history of economic practice" embodied in their work reveals darker aspects to more rational and open trading arrangements emerging in the eighteenth century. Increased criminalization, state violence, and political turmoil surrounded efforts to quell extralegal exchange and public sympathy for it. Studying clandestine commerce demonstrates that the formation of free trade was a messy, bottom-up process that owed as much to the actions of illicit traders in the colonies as to the ideas of metropolitan reformers in Europe. Venezuelan contrabandists had a hand in shaping these broader developments.[29]

28. Shannon Lee Dawdy's and Michael J. Jarvis's monographs both perceive peripheral locations (New Orleans and Bermuda) as independent entities that, while maintaining contact, conflict, and loose loyalties with their imperial parents, evolved their own understandings of trade, colonial development, and interimperial interaction. See Dawdy, *Building the Devil's Empire: French Colonial New Orleans* (Chicago, 2009); Jarvis, *In the Eye of All Trade: Bermuda, Bermudians, and the Maritime Atlantic World, 1680–1783* (Williamsburg, Va., and Chapel Hill, N.C., 2010). On the implications of the state's rules in making the smuggler, see Peter Andreas, *Smuggler Nation: How Illicit Trade Made America* (New York, 2013), 1–10, 269, 336; Andreas, "Smuggling Wars: Law Enforcement and Law Evasion in a Changing World," in Tom Farer, ed., *Transnational Crime in the Americas: An Inter-American Dialogue Book* (New York, 1999), 85–98.

29. The "social history of economic practice" comes from Jane E. Mangan, *Trading Roles: Gender, Ethnicity, and the Urban Economy in Colonial Potosí* (Durham, N.C., 2005), 3. For a work that problematizes the early modern consumer revolution by revealing its more sinister elements in much the same way that my study discusses Atlantic commerce, see Michael Kwass, *Contraband: Louis Mandrin and the Making of a Global Underground* (Cambridge, Mass., 2014), 2–13. Elite society viewed reformers and physiocrats as men of authority and intelligence, whereas it judged most maritime criminals as unruly rabble. Yet, as Stuart B. Schwartz has observed in the context of religious tolerance and the budding Enlightenment, the behaviors of the poor and illiterate were often as responsible for the rise of intellectual paradigm shifts as the writings of the learned. In the more specific context of early modern global trade, Edward P. Pompeian reflects, "We also need to know about the less-privileged people—broadly defined—who kept the networks of global trade in motion without royal charters and other official rights or political aids. . . . The links between the wealthiest merchants and the rest are probably more important than we might otherwise suppose." See Schwartz, *All Can Be Saved: Religious Tolerance and Salvation in the Iberian Atlantic World*

Venezuela provides an ideal laboratory to study the colonial negotiation of trade law and notions of its legitimacy in peripheral communities. Contraband trade was endemic to many, if not most, kingdoms of Spanish America. Nevertheless, what makes the Venezuelan case informative is that Spanish subjects there developed deep roots in the illicit marketplace and then encountered intense state and private efforts to dislodge these entrenched interests. Spanish imperial officials allowed the province to grow up outside of legal Spanish trade circuits in the sixteenth and seventeenth centuries. The crown then reversed course in the second quarter of the eighteenth century, imposing rigid commercial control and refashioning Venezuela as a virtual company colony. The sudden imperial and business interest in Venezuelan trade generated concern for the enforcement of early modern trade law and the prosecution of its transgressors. A long history of smuggling, the peculiar administrative history of the province, the geographic proximity of foreign colonial trading partners, and favorable demographics combined to create a distinct species of commercial crime. Thus Venezuelan smuggling was related to that of other colonies but intensified due to these factors, making it a rich case study for examining the inner workings and social consequences of illicit trade.

My work probes the unsettled and obscured character of this smuggling society through eight chapters. As a backdrop to this study, Chapter 1 profiles Spanish Atlantic commercial structures and Venezuela's long history of imperial neglect and interimperial foraging within them. It argues that the colony's experience in the sixteenth, seventeenth, and early eighteenth centuries bred homegrown commercial and political solutions that resisted weakly imposed Spanish Atlantic systems of mercantilism. Chapter 2 analyzes the cultural value of smuggled cargoes in Spanish America as a means to understand eighteenth-century Venezuelans' acculturation to illicit activity. Colonists creatively employed smuggling to deal with a dearth of basic European goods and developed justifications and ruses for their quotidian illicit actions. Chapter 3 assesses the Spanish state's solution to Venezuelan commercial dysfunction through the establishment and tenure of the Caracas Company. Struggles between Company representatives, foreign and domestic smugglers, the Caraqueño elite, and the crown itself demonstrated that early Spanish Bourbon

(New Haven, Conn., 2008), 241; Pompeian, "Mind the Global U-Turn: Reorienting Early American History in a Global and Commercial Context," *Journal of the Early Republic*, XXXVI (2016), 735.

reformers underestimated how deeply contraband trade was stitched into the fabric of Venezuelan life.

The second half of this book reconstructs the social world of illicit traders and the human consequences of their commerce. Chapter 4 profiles Dutch, English, and French Caribbean contrabandists trading on the Venezuelan coast. They were, on the whole, multilingual and multiracial crews of petty traders who adapted to local conditions in order to maintain close economic and cultural connections with Venezuelan contacts ashore. Chapter 5 considers the other half of illicit commercial partnerships: Venezuelan merchants. I demonstrate how varying degrees of connection to bureaucratic, ecclesiastical, kinship, and criminal groups helped determine the success of Venezuelan illegal trading ventures. Chapter 6 details the role of Spanish colonial officials as facilitators of contraband trade. This chapter emphasizes that officials and colonial subjects reached a social compact regarding tolerable levels and types of smuggling and corruption. Illicit commerce's impact on the slave trade and Afro-Caribbean labor forms the subject matter of Chapter 7. As illicit cargo, free sailors, or enslaved laborers aboard smuggling ships and on the Venezuelan coast, Afro-Caribbeans balanced the prospects of wage earning and greater autonomy in labor with the risks of captivity and enslavement as they crossed imperial jurisdictions. Finally, Chapter 8 dissects the rebellion of Juan Francisco de León, the trade uprising against the Caracas Company that began this introduction. In their desires to return to a colonial status quo of measured commercial neglect and undeclared free trade, the León rebels illustrate the many ways in which contraband trade was an integral political force in Venezuela and Spanish America at large.

As a vocation and a state of market consciousness, smuggling created a mobility and mutability across the Atlantic that imperial bureaucrats found subversive. In the minds of Spanish functionaries, foreign interlopers broke up the cultural homogeneity and economic rationality these officials had worked so hard to cultivate. Moreover, transience and transnationalism undermined imperial defense systems and confounded plans for greater productivity in the colonies. By trading with other littoral societies, smugglers diverted American commodities into alternate distribution chains outside of state control. Ultimately, contrabandists in peripheral regions deeply influenced the development of these territories' commercial independence from colonial mercantile systems. In doing so, smugglers also forced colonial subjects to challenge the morality of early modern trade law and ask a fundamental question: Why was this vital and natural trade classified as "contraband" in the first place? The implications of whether the laws mattered and what sociocultural associations people produced in flouting them are at the heart of this study, just as they were at the heart of early modern imperial trade.

These wider truths applied to the eighteenth-century Venezuelan colonial relationship and Spanish imperial politics. Tolerating criminality and corruption in the commercial realm did not make Venezuelan merchants, producers, and consumers disloyal subjects. In fact, though they formed substantial relationships with foreigners, they almost never entertained thoughts of anticolonial rebellion. These subjects bristled, however, at Spain's attempts to monopolize the province's wealth. Stronger Bourbon attempts at commercial enforcement interrupted carefully calibrated community rhythms that revolved around buying, selling, possessing, and consuming contraband goods. Interimperial commerce substituted for an economy that the state could not meaningfully provide. Ironically, the outlawed practice of smuggling in Venezuela and the Spanish Empire at large was a fulcrum that brought stability to late colonial society.

# I

# *Old Habits*

## Commercial Neglect and Peripheral Innovation in Early Venezuela

In the Archivo General de Indias, in Seville, Spain, a large folder exists entitled "The Reestablishment of Indies Commerce" *(Restablecimiento del Comercio de Indias)*. It contains proceedings of the Council of Commerce *(Real y General Junta de Comercio)* in Madrid from 1705 to 1776. The contents point to a strange incongruity: that the Spanish Empire would need to "reestablish" commerce with territories that still belonged to it. Yet, as these minutes demonstrate, the turn of the eighteenth century was a time of extraordinary weakness for Spain in the Americas. In the last years of Habsburg rule, indecisive leadership, Spanish metropolitan economic stagnation, and sparse transatlantic shipping debilitated the Spanish presence in the Indies. One member of the Council of Commerce described Spanish trade with the Indies as "a body so sickly and exhausted, that, unless a remedy is applied, it will collapse." Another member singled out problems of neglect by pointing to Venezuela. He deduced that "if one was to say that the Dutch do business throughout the whole coast of the Province of Venezuela or Caracas, the response would be that there are no silver mines there, nor gold, but that the fruit and commerce [of the province] is generally cacao that will be quickly consumed if transported to Holland." The council was expressing almost two centuries of logic governing imperial prioritization of resources. Devoid of attention-grabbing mineral wealth, marginal colonies like Venezuela had been left to their own devices. As a result, foreign commerce infiltrated their coasts. In the council's

FIGURE 5. Chronology of Important Events for Eighteenth-Century Venezuela

| | |
|---|---|
| 1701–1714 | War of the Spanish Succession (ended by Treaty of Utrecht) |
| 1728 | Real Compañía Guipuzcoana de Caracas (Caracas Company) established |
| 1731–1732 | Andresote Rebellion. Andresote forced to flee to Curaçao |
| 1739–1748 | War of Jenkins' Ear |
| 1741 | San Felipe Uprising |
| 1749–1751 | Juan Francisco de León Rebellion. León jailed in 1752 |
| 1751 | Compañía Guipuzcoana reestablished. (More price controls, selling goods cheaper in Ven., Venezuelans given right to trade with Veracruz) |
| 1754–1763 | Seven Years' War |
| 1765 | End of Cádiz's monopoly on Spanish American trade. Santander, Gijón, La Coruña, Málaga, Cartagena, Alicante, and Barcelona are able to trade with Cuba, Santo Domingo, Puerto Rico, Margarita, and Trinidad. Successive decrees widen free trade in 1774, 1776, 1777, 1778 |
| 1766 | British Free Port Act begins era of more open and liberalized trade in the Caribbean |
| 1776 | Charles III creates Intendencia del Ejército y Real Hacienda (Caracas Intendancy) |
| 1777 | Charles III creates Gran Capitanía General de las Provincias Unidas de Venezuela |
| 1778 | Decree of Free Trade (*Reglamento de Libre Comercio*) (Charles III). All Spanish America under free trade except Venezuela and Mexico |
| 1781 | A royal order voids the Company's monopoly privileges |
| 1784 | Caracas Company dissolved |
| 1786 | Audiencia de Caracas created |
| 1789 | Venezuela and Mexico allowed free trade |
| 1793 | Real Consulado de Caracas established |
| 1797 | Mañuel Gual and José María España escape to Trinidad after their plot to foment revolution fails |
| 1806 | Francisco de Miranda arrives in Venezuela. His troops are routed |
| 1808 | Napoleonic invasion of Iberian Peninsula forces abdication of Charles IV |
| 1810 | Junta conservador organized in Caracas |
| 1811 | General Congress of United Provinces of Venezuela declares independence |

opinion, such realms required serious commercial reorganization—or inevitable abandonment.[1]

The conditions for illicit commerce in Venezuela grew out of an imperial disregard for the province because its settlement did not pay immediate dividends. Without bullion (like Mexico and Peru) or a sanctioned port to accommodate the Spanish trade fleets (like Havana, Panama, Veracruz, and Cartagena), Venezuela did not merit investment or the dispatch of regular shipping from the mother country. Spain's inattention to the colony's commercial life led to fragmentation. Instead of solely relying on the Spanish-Atlantic circuit of trunk lines, Venezuelan commercial participants pursued diverse legal and illegal pathways to trade. Once coastal inhabitants cultivated something of value to sell and gained non-Spanish colonial partners to buy it, smuggling transitioned from an occasional venue of interimperial interaction into a normalized economic practice. In short, neglect and adaptation created tendencies among the colonial population to engage in transactions that the state deemed criminal and subversive. Ultimately, the long roots of smuggling in coastal Venezuela would embed themselves in the province's social life and prove resilient against efforts of the state and private interests to eradicate them.

## SPANISH COMMERCIAL EXCLUSIVISM IN THE AMERICAS

Early Spanish philosophy on commerce shaped the choices of policymakers and colonial subjects for centuries to come. Compared to other imperial powers of the Americas, Spain's trade law was among the most exclusionary in its stance toward outsiders. There was good reason for this position early on. As Spain entered into European overseas expansion, it lacked a precedent for the logistical and infrastructural challenges of a transatlantic empire. Because of their primacy, sixteenth-century Spanish imperial organizers almost immediately confronted competitors seeking to rob their ships and ports of the vast bullion produced in Spanish American territories. As a result of

1. The Council of Commerce came into existence near the end of Habsburg rule and later proved responsible for many of the Bourbon plans to foment new industry and trade. See William J. Callahan, "A Note on the Real y General Junta de Comercio, 1679–1814," *Economic History Review,* N.S., XXI (1968), 519–528. "A body so sickly": Voto de D. Juan de Sotomayor y Garcia Martin, Jan. 13, 1706, AGI, Indif, 2046A. "If one was to say": Papeles de Don Manuel Garcia de Bustamante y uno de Don Ambrosio Doubenton tocante de la idea de la Compania Universal para Indias, sus reparos y de las otras navegantes propuesta, 1705–1706, AGI, Indif, 2046A. The specific document that refers to Venezuela is Cuenta de Comercio, Jan. 14, 1706.

these complications, as well as the influence of prevailing economic wisdom of the era, which envisioned the world's wealth as a zero-sum game built on a finite amount of specie, bullionism became the driving blueprint for running a resource-rich empire. Other empires later positioned themselves as the antithesis to this Spanish transatlantic trading system. Rather than invest in their own costly models of transatlantic shipping and commercial governance, Spain's rivals initially nibbled off the edges of Spanish wealth and later adopted more open and less codified maritime trading ventures. Smuggling in the Spanish colonies was, in part, a by-product of the lessons other empires believed they had learned from Spanish mistakes in empire building.[2]

Spanish transatlantic trade thus operated, in theory, as a closed system in which the ports, ships, and men involved in commerce were all Spanish and Catholic. Commercial law forbade trade with foreigners except under specific circumstances. From the founding of the House of Trade in 1503 onward, the sailors, passengers, and cargoes of outgoing or incoming Spanish ships had to be licensed, inspected, and registered in Seville. They could only travel to certain prescribed Spanish American ports (most notably Portobelo, Veracruz, Cartagena, and Havana). Moreover, the vast majority of shipping occurred in yearly convoyed fleets to protect bullion. Any trade taking place with foreigners, without licenses, or outside of these convoys, routes, and ports was considered contraband.

A detailed dissection of several hundred years of legal trade is beyond the scope of this investigation, but understanding the basic rhythms of the Spanish system helps to elucidate its purpose and problems. Imperial advisory councils first employed the fleet system *(Carrera de Indias)* in 1522 but did not make it a permanent fixture until 1561. The centrality of New Spain and Peru divided the carrera into one fleet that served Mexico and Central America (the *flota)* and another that supplied South America (the *galeones,* or galleons). Ideally, the flota left Spain in the beginning of April and headed for Veracruz, Mexico. The galeones left Spain for Portobelo (and Nombre de Dios until the seventeenth century) in Panama in August. After trading in these ports and spending the winter in the Indies, both fleets met up in Havana by March to sail home across the Atlantic. Ideally, during their time in the Indies, detachments of the fleets also would visit the principal ports of the Greater Antilles (Santo Domingo,

2. For an elegant discussion of the promise and problems of Spain's transatlantic primacy, see J. H. Elliott, *Empires of the Atlantic World: Britain and Spain in America, 1492–1830* (New Haven, Conn., 2007), 405–411. On this idea of Spain as the antithesis of a prosperous empire, see John Robertson, ed., *Andrew Fletcher: Political Works* (Cambridge, 1997), 86–90.

San Juan), northern South America (Cartagena, Santa Marta, Rio de la Hacha, La Guaira), and Central America (various ports in Honduras, Guatemala, and southern Mexico). Beyond the fleet system, the House of Trade occasionally licensed individual ships to sail to central and peripheral destinations in the New World as "register ships." This basic flow of trade continued with some slight alterations from the sixteenth century until the end of the galeones in 1740 and the flotas in 1789.[3]

Transatlantic commerce in the Americas reflected the motivations and limitations of imperial Spain. At trade fairs in Portobelo and Veracruz, Spanish merchants brought European manufactures, textiles, and food to trade with their Spanish American counterparts for American silver, gold, gemstones, and tropical agricultural products like sugar, tobacco, chocolate, cotton, and medicinal plants. The Iberian Peninsula could claim almost no domestic manufacturing sector, so Spanish merchants first purchased goods bound for the Americas from a range of European suppliers and then compensated them when the fleets returned flush with silver. As it had no colonial possessions or direct trading access to slaves on the west coast of Africa, the Spanish Empire also depended on other European powers to supply it with African slaves through a contract known as the *asiento.* The asiento operated from the early sixteenth until the mid-eighteenth century and served as the principal means of entry for the vast majority of legally trafficked Spanish American enslaved people, as well as a back door for illicit trade.[4]

Most regulations and transactions within the legal trading system existed to benefit small but extremely powerful merchant groups in Andalusia and, to a lesser extent, Mexico and Peru. Sevillian merchants successfully solicited the legal designation of a merchant guild *(consulado)* for their transatlantic businesses in 1543. This corporate entity of powerful merchant houses came to dominate the finances, logistics, and regulatory structure of Spanish overseas commerce for more than two centuries. Consulado members, as a result, had the ears of the Casa de Contratación and the Spanish court. The outsized im-

3. Clarence Henry Haring, *Trade and Navigation between Spain and the Indies in the Time of the Hapsburgs* (Cambridge, Mass., 1918), 201–213; John R. Fisher, *The Economic Aspects of Spanish Imperialism in America, 1492–1810* (Liverpool, 1997), 43–62.

4. On the history of the asiento, see Gregory E. O'Malley, *Final Passages: The Intercolonial Slave Trade of British America, 1619–1807* (Williamsburg, Va., and Chapel Hill, N.C., 2014), 219–263; Johannes Menne Postma, *The Dutch in the Atlantic Slave Trade, 1600–1815* (Cambridge, 1990), 26–51; Colin Palmer, *Human Cargoes: The British Slave Trade to Spanish America, 1700–1739* (Urbana, Ill., 1981), 1–79, 97–159; George H. Nelson, "Contraband Trade under the Asiento, 1730–1739," *AHR,* LI (1945), 55–67.

portance of Seville (and later Cádiz) as the embarkation and arrival point of all Indies shipping and seat of the Casa de Contratación centralized legal transatlantic commerce and its enforcement within Andalusia. Barriers specifying high minimums on tonnage of goods kept all but the wealthiest traders out of transatlantic shipping. From their commanding position, Andalusian merchants created intentional scarcities of European imports to drive up prices and profits in the Americas. The crown did not intervene in these manipulations because it believed that a steady supply of silver to pay debts and fund European wars trumped the material needs of colonists. The royal treasury also received frequent loans from Andalusian merchants. The result of transatlantic bullionism was a system that was extractive, exclusive, dependent on foreign suppliers of manufactured goods, and disadvantageous to Spanish American consumers.[5]

The commercial exclusivism represented in the Carrera de Indias system was not without merit. First and foremost, it protected the silver that funded Spain's ambitions and Europe's emerging market economies from maritime predation. Dutch privateer Piet Heyn's capture of the 1628 fleet at Matanzas Bay, Cuba, marked the only time foreign raiders seized an entire silver fleet. The system also centralized and regulated the overseas trade of an empire fractured by regional divides. Much of the state's revenue came from taxes levied on goods, ships, and licenses, as well as the royal fifth duty *(quinto)* on all silver imports. Checkpoints and inspections at specified ports provided at least some promise that officials would harvest this revenue and prevent its seepage into foreign coffers.

Moreover, the carrera system offered fringe benefits to a transatlantic empire. In terms of communication, the fleets were the de facto mail service of the Spanish Atlantic. They provided cultural continuity between the Old World

5. On the consulados, see C. H. Haring, *The Spanish Empire in America* (1947; rpt. New York, 1963), 300; J. H. Parry, *The Spanish Seaborne Empire* (1966; rpt. Berkeley, Calif., 1990), 125. On Andalusian merchants, see Stanley J. Stein and Barbara H. Stein, *Silver, Trade, and War: Spain and America in the Making of Early Modern Europe* (Baltimore, 2000), 3–18; Fisher, *Economic Aspects of Spanish Imperialism,* 54; Parry, *Spanish Seaborne Empire,* 125. Jeremy Baskes disputes the idea that a cabal of Gaditano merchants could have colluded so successfully in the Spanish transatlantic market, given their large numbers and the rivalries between them. He also argues that regulating the supplies that reached the Americas was essential to preventing oversaturated markets, decreasing risk, and maintaining the profitability of overseas trade. Although I do not disagree with these findings, they were imperatives that concerned and benefited major peninsular merchants at the expense of colonial consumers (Baskes, *Staying Afloat: Risk and Uncertainty in Spanish Atlantic World Trade, 1760–1820* [Stanford, Calif., 2013], 44–58).

and the New by sailing at regular intervals with news, passengers, and comforts from home. By determining who could legally enter the Americas on these Spanish ships, the House of Trade regulated the homogeneity of nationality, religion, and ethnicity in the colonies. The two-hundred-year longevity of this system attested to its stability.

Yet smuggling flourished precisely because of all the commercial activity that the Spanish closed system hindered or failed to control. Its strict configurations of trade and shipping routes allowed very little flexibility to adapt to changing market conditions. The logistical challenges of assembling yearly fleets and coordinating their cohesive voyages led to interminable delays. Slowdowns in the fleet's progress could be intentional as well. Seville and Cádiz merchants sometimes purposely delayed the departure of vessels bound for the Indies. This tactic drove up prices for goods and helped to extract more bullion from colonial consumers.[6]

Along with interruptions, numerous duties on goods as they crossed the Atlantic raised the cost of merchandise in the Americas. Spanish merchants and, by extension, traders and consumers in Venezuela paid a long list of possible duties. They all paid the *almojarifazgo,* a heavy tax required for the privilege of conducting business between multiple Spanish kingdoms. A 3 percent tax on merchandise called the *corso* (previously the *armada y armadilla)* financed the coast guard forces, and a 1 percent fee (the *avería)* on general trade to the colony funded the Venezuelan consulado after its late formation in 1793. Additional levies included an entry and exit port tax *(alcabala del mar),* another sales tax paid on land *(alcabala),* and a tax to fund the fleet *(almirantazgo).* Late in the eighteenth century, the crown also charged merchants the *subvención de guerra,* a fee to pay for the extraordinarily long period of war with the British. As a result, subjects trading legally received European manufactures infrequently and at great cost, even in colonial centers. Colonists beyond the fleets' major ports of call faced not only these inconveniences but also a noticeable drop in the quality of merchandise, as merchants offered them wares already picked over or reexported by imperial capitals.[7]

6. Geoffrey J. Walker, *Spanish Politics and Imperial Trade, 1700–1789* (Bloomington, Ind., 1979), 13.

7. On duties, see Manuel Lucena Salmoral, *Vísperas de la independencia americana: Caracas* (Madrid, 1986), 313–324; Roland Dennis Hussey, *The Caracas Company, 1728–1784: A Study in the History of Spanish Monopolistic Trade* (1934; rpt. New York, 1977), 57; Ramón Aizpurua, *Curazao y la costa de Caracas: Introducción al estudio del contrabando de la Provincia de Venezuela en tiempos de la Compañía Guipuzcoana, 1730–1780* (Caracas, 1993), 211; Haring, *Trade and Navigation,* 51, 62. For a thorough discussion of the inefficiencies and fraud char-

The deleterious effects of Spanish exclusivism extended beyond trade with the Americas into Spain's means of production. Because silver extraction became the paramount concern of the imperial commercial scheme, homegrown manufacturing and business enterprises languished. With the exception of limited textile production *(obrajes),* attempts to start manufacturing in the Americas faced either the indifference of imperial administrators, who wished to keep the colonies dependent on the mother country, or a dearth of necessary materials from Europe. Small merchants on both sides of the Atlantic were equally frustrated by the dominant presence of a group of traders in wealthy Andalusian and American consulados controlling direct transatlantic business.[8]

Ironically, the greatest casualty of Spanish commercial policy designed to exclude foreigners might have been the empire's sovereignty. Despite prohibitions on non-Spanish merchants in legal trade, most European goods aboard the official fleet came from Holland, Flanders, France, and England. Foreign traders either sold their goods outright to Andalusian firms or used Spanish stand-ins (called *prestanombres)* to legitimize what was actually foreign trade. Spanish merchants developed substantial debts to these outsiders. Likewise, the crown hemorrhaged silver to non-Spanish financiers who bankrolled its costly wars on the European continent. Spanish officials, under the informal insistence of the king and Spanish merchant interests, had to ignore persistent foreign penetration into transatlantic commerce or risk Spain's losing its credit abroad. The Spanish state was not oblivious to the threats of foreign commercial intrusion and moribund legal commerce. The writings of royal ministers and independent reformers acknowledged that the status quo presented serious impediments to functional legal trade and Spain's economic sovereignty, even as perversions of the system offered economic opportunities and material goods for Spanish American colonists. But overall, the Spanish state was too compromised by its dependence on silver and its obligations to foreign debtors and Andalusian merchants to meaningfully address these issues until the rise of the Bourbon dynasty in the first decades of the eighteenth century. Even after this shift, the economists tasked with overhauling Spanish American commerce proceeded with gradational responses designed to mitigate the worst aspects of a flawed system while keeping its basic structure intact.[9]

---

acteristic of mid-eighteenth-century shipping between Spain and New Spain, see Stanley J. Stein and Barbara H. Stein, *Apogee of Empire: Spain and New Spain in the Age of Charles III, 1759–1789* (Baltimore, 2003), 119–127.

8. Haring, *Trade and Navigation,* 125–136.

9. John Lynch, *Bourbon Spain, 1700–1808* (Oxford, 1989), 10; Stein and Stein, *Silver, Trade, and War,* 16, 47–66, 88, 156–159, 232; Stein and Stein, *Apogee of Empire,* ix, 22, 355.

For subjects in Spain and Spanish America, navigating an unreliable and overly regulated trading apparatus meant seeking out gray areas and weak points in the law. Unlicensed shipping from both foreign and domestic suppliers was a significant source of imports to the colonies even in major trading hubs. In peripheral locales, centuries of neglect had made illegal foreign trade the de facto marketplace for items that could not be produced in the Americas. Misreporting of cargo and payoffs to law enforcement officials became the norm among major merchants seeking to avoid onerous taxes in the transatlantic trade. Smaller buyers and sellers resorted to covert commerce with foreigners in order to supply trade-starved Spanish American outposts. They traded with non-Spanish smugglers of the greater Caribbean who saw illicit exchange as their only way to enter into Spanish markets. Some Spanish subjects no doubt felt conflicted between their loyalty to empire and the potential for profit and material comfort from smuggling. But over time, the ubiquity of illicit foreign trade quelled any sense of mutual exclusivity in all but the most die-hard advocates of Spanish bullionism.

By the turn of the eighteenth century, the starting point of this study, some mindsets and protocols of Spanish transatlantic trade had begun to change. The system's stability and traditions faltered. The Casa de Contratación moved from Seville to Cádiz in 1717, lessening the former's power in Atlantic commerce. By the last quarter of the eighteenth century, the volume of trade and silver imports had diminished greatly. Naval warfare during the War of the Spanish Succession (1701–1714) as well as the War of Jenkins' Ear (1739–1748) added to the stagnancy of maritime commerce. In fact, from 1680 until the end of the War of the Spanish Succession, the flotas and galeones completely ceased operations. With war disrupting fleets for years at a time and contraband-glutted markets cooling consumer interest in legal Spanish goods, the eighteenth century witnessed more unaccompanied register ships. In the best of times, the Carrera de Indias experienced temporary stoppages and delays. By midcentury, it was practically defunct.[10] The first decree of comercio libre in 1765 (and a more expansive decree in 1778) uncoupled Spanish trade from many of the strict regulations that had governed it. These reforms replaced a range of duties on transatlantic shipping with a straightforward 7 percent ad valorem tax. More important, comercio libre greatly increased the number of ports officially open

10. On changes in Spanish trade, see Josep M. Fradera, "The Caribbean between Empires: Colonists, Pirates, and Slaves," in Stephan Palmié and Francisco A. Scarano, eds., *The Caribbean: A History of the Region and Its Peoples* (Chicago, Ill., 2011), 174; Stein and Stein, *Silver, Trade, and War,* 191. On tax reform, see Haring, *Spanish Empire in America,* 319; Parry, *Spanish Seaborne Empire,* 316.

to direct trade from the Spanish peninsula, disbanded what was left of the coordinated trade fleets, and allowed for point-to-point travel between any licensed port in Spain or the Americas, ending the need to circulate all transatlantic trade through Cádiz, Veracruz, Portobelo, Cartagena, and Havana. The decrees also added a number of ports in Spain and the colonies to what had been a limited list of destinations under the fleet system.[11]

The legacies of Spanish exclusivism, however, remained, despite the breakdown of age-old trading arrangements in the eighteenth century. Trade with foreigners without special permission continued to be illegal. Imperial reformers replaced bullionism with mercantilism, gleaned from British and French examples. Monopolistic trading companies, including the Caracas Company in Venezuela, served as evidence of this shift. Most important for the status of illicit trade, imperial efforts to economically develop the periphery focused more on revenue extraction than improving the material conditions of inhabitants. Colonial officials presented subjects with few incentives to deter contraband trade and instead ramped up enforcement of the law. Suddenly, colonists came to grips with the end of long-term Habsburg conditions of imperial benign neglect regarding smuggling. International markets for Spanish American products grew at the same time that Bourbon reformers shunted resources to plugging commercial leaks. Just when often-ignored Spanish American colonies stood to make their greatest profits from smuggling, Spanish imperial administrators targeted the practice.[12]

## COMMERCIAL FRAGMENTATION AND PERIPHERAL ADAPTATION IN COLONIAL VENEZUELA

Like many Spanish circum-Caribbean colonies, Venezuela epitomized the incompatibility of narrow imperial models of commercial circulation with more diverse patterns of colonial development and interaction. The inability to derive quick profits from mineral resources discouraged regular Spanish metropolitan commerce to greater Venezuela. Though the fleet system proved to be a generally efficient and incredibly secure means to extract bullion from Mexico and Peru, it was inadequate for supplying Venezuela with European merchandise. Long before the eighteenth-century Bourbon Reforms, both im-

11. The decrees added thirty-five Spanish American ports and fourteen in Spain to those that could trade within the empire without first needing approval from Cádiz. See Jeremy Adelman, *Sovereignty and Revolution in the Iberian Atlantic* (Princeton, N.J., 2006), 29–34.

12. Haring, *Trade and Navigation,* 138.

perial policymakers and Venezuelan subjects failed in their attempts to harness the province's commercial potential within Spanish mercantile parameters.

From the province's founding in 1522, setbacks in development reinforced characterizations of Venezuela as an unproductive backwater with few discernible resources to exploit. One early colonization scheme involved the Welser Company, a private German enterprise given permission to explore Venezuela by Charles V in 1528. The sovereign allowed early company control of the area mainly to placate German and Flemish banking interests who were creditors to the crown. The Welsers searched for El Dorado but eventually focused their energies on indigenous slave trading rather than finding gold or founding towns. Philip II canceled their contract and reincorporated the colony under crown control in 1556. The region's only answer in the sixteenth century to the precious metal exports that made Spain the envy of Europe were the lucrative but quickly exhausted pearl-diving grounds of Margarita, Cumaná, and Cubagua.[13]

After failed attempts at quick, extractive ventures, settlers to the colony in the second half of the sixteenth century sought to create a steady indigenous tribute agriculture economy *(encomienda)* based around wheat production. It was the dominant export product of central Venezuela until the seventeenth century. Although trade with Spain was virtually nonexistent, merchants in La Guaira sent wheat flour to the circum-Caribbean destinations of Cartagena, Puerto Rico, Cuba, Santo Domingo, and even as far as the Canary Islands. This production, however, did little to attract imperial attention or drive serious population growth in Caracas, which existed as a city of only 40 tribute-receiving landowners *(encomenderos)* and around 320 total white inhabitants at the turn of the seventeenth century.[14]

The 1600s witnessed the transformation of the Venezuelan economy, if

13. John V. Lombardi, *Venezuela: The Search for Order, the Dream of Progress* (New York, 1982), 60–66; Guillermo Morón, *A History of Venezuela,* trans. John Street (New York, 1963), 38; Haring, *Trade and Navigation,* 99–101; Stein and Stein, *Silver, Trade, and War,* 33. For more information on pearl diving and trade, see Molly A. Warsh, *American Baroque: Pearls and the Nature of Empire, 1492–1700* (Williamsburg, Va., and Chapel Hill, N.C., 2018). Venezuela's pearl fishing past carried enough of a commercial cache that the eighteenth-century English merchant John Campbell's only remark on Venezuela's extractive prospects spoke almost exclusively about pearl fisheries ([Campbell], *The Spanish Empire in America: Containing, a Succinct Relation of the Discovery and Settlement of Its Several Colonies . . .* [1741; rpt. London, 1747], 200–203).

14. [Eduardo Arcila Farías], *Hacienda y comercio de Venezuela en el siglo XVII: 1601–1650* (Caracas, 1986), 48, 57; Robert J. Ferry, "Encomienda, African Slavery, and Agriculture in Seventeenth-Century Caracas," *HAHR,* XL (1981), 609.

not its relationship to the metropole, through the growth of American agricultural exports. The first of these products was tobacco. The leaf's value on world markets far surpassed foodstuffs like wheat. Tobacco, hides, and cotton were the principal exports of the colony for the first two decades of the seventeenth century. The international attention attracted by the former forced the Spanish crown to act to prevent outside intrusion into the tobacco-growing zones of Venezuela, Guyana, and Trinidad. English merchants illegally traded in the commodity to such an extent that Philip III imposed a ten-year ban on its cultivation in 1606. Later, Portuguese merchants dominated the tobacco trade. The Habsburg state's response to the cultivation and illicit trade of tobacco was indicative of policies emphasizing reactive and widely unenforceable prohibitions rather than active attempts to develop Venezuelan agricultural exports for Spanish imperial benefit.[15]

Despite the early promise of tobacco, it was cacao that truly unlocked Venezuela's economic potential. The commodity did not even appear on shipping manifests from Venezuela to Spain until 1607 and to New Spain until 1622. Yet over the following fifty years, it quickly eclipsed all other exports from the colony. By 1627, merchants regularly sent cacao shipments to New Spain as Venezuelan stock replaced that of Central America in the Mexican market. Its share of Venezuelan export production ticked steadily upward in the 1630s and 1640s. By 1650, cacao comprised 78.5 percent of all registered goods leaving the colony. Increased production also boosted the importation of slaves to tend trees and harvest beans. Although a cacao blight and competition in the Mexican market from Guayaquil, Ecuador, slowed this initial boom in the 1650s

15. On exports, see Eduardo Arcila Farías, *Economía colonial de Venezuela* (Mexico City, 1946), 77, 80–81; Ferry, "Encomienda, African Slavery, and Agriculture," *HAHR*, XL (1981), 609. Owing to increasing levels of tobacco smuggling with Spain's rivals in the Caribbean, the crown issued a royal *cédula* in 1606 prohibiting tobacco cultivation in the provinces of Venezuela, Margarita, and Cumaná. The prohibition was supposed to last for ten years, but public outcry made for its repeal in 1612. See Marcy Norton, *Sacred Gifts, Profane Pleasures: A History of Chocolate and Tobacco in the Atlantic World* (Ithaca, N.Y., 2008), 153; Kenneth R. Andrews, *The Spanish Caribbean: Trade and Plunder, 1530–1630* (New Haven, Conn., 1978), 214; Arcila Farías, *Economía colonial de Venezuela,* 82. For the early tobacco trade in the region, see Norton and Daviken Studnicki-Gizbert, "The Multinational Commodification of Tobacco, 1492–1650: An Iberian Perspective," in Peter C. Mancall, ed., *The Atlantic World and Virginia, 1550–1624* (Williamsburg, Va., and Chapel Hill, N.C., 2007), 251–273; Joyce Lorimer, "The English Contraband Tobacco Trade in Trinidad and Guiana, 1590–1617," in K. R. Andrews, N. P. Canny, and P. E. H. Hair, eds., *The Westward Enterprise: English Activities in Ireland, the Atlantic, and America, 1480–1650* (Detroit, Mich., 1979), 124–150. On prohibitions, see Engel Sluiter, "Dutch-Spanish Rivalry in the Caribbean Area, 1594–1609," *HAHR*, XXVIII (1948), 193–194; Haring, *Trade and Navigation,* 129.

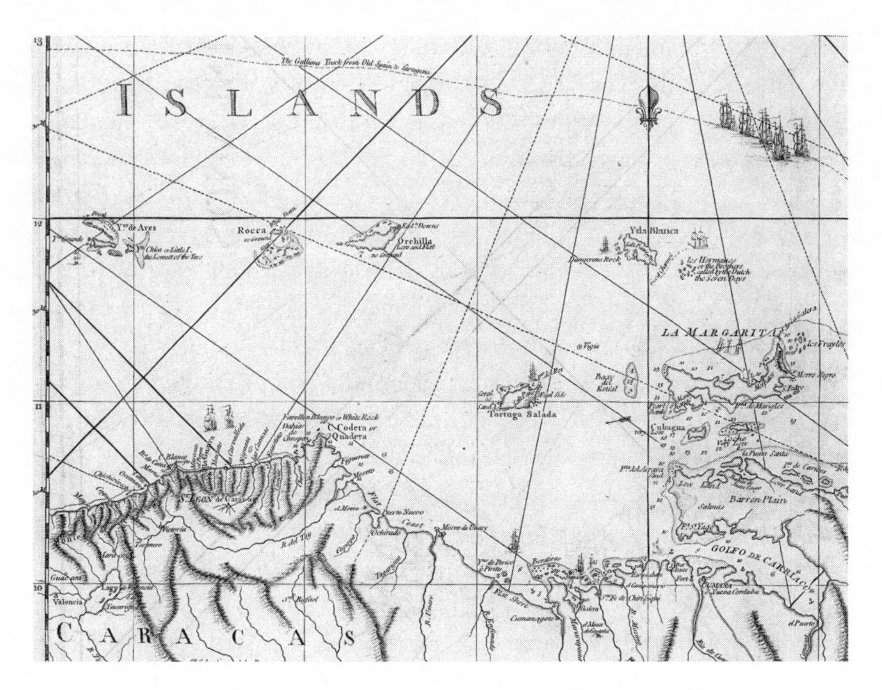


FIGURE 6. The Fleet Bypassing Venezuela. Detail of *The Coast of Caracas, Cumana, Parla, and the Mouths of Rio Orinoco, with the Islands of Trinidad, Margarita, Tobago, Granada, St. Vincent Etca.* By Thomas Jefferys. 1775. In the top right corner, the galleons can be seen passing from Spain to Cartagena. *The David Rumsey Map Collection, www.davidrumsey.com*

and 1660s, production and trade recovered by the 1670s. In 1677, a survey by the governor of Venezuela estimated that the colony contained 200,000 cacao trees and 6,000 slaves. The crown granted Venezuela a monopoly on the sale of cacao to Mexico by 1674. The colony would not relinquish it until the second half of the eighteenth century. By the end of the seventeenth century, cacao had gone from being one of many agricultural products in Venezuela to being the colony's main cash crop.[16]

Although the province of Venezuela experienced modest economic development in the first century and a half of its history, contact and commerce with Spain was minimal. The issue was demand; early Spanish merchants did not

16. On cacao shipping, see Lutgardo García Fuentes, *El comercio español con América, 1650–1700* (Seville, 1980), 351–352; [Arcila Farías], *Hacienda y comercio de Venezuela,* 6, 16, 66. On estimates in 1677, see Alex Borucki, "Trans-Imperial History in the Making of the Slave Trade to Venezuela, 1526–1811," *Itinerario,* XXXVI (2012), 33–35; Ferry, "Encomienda, African Slavery, and Agriculture," *HAHR,* XL (1981), 613, 627. On cacao's rise to Venezuela's only cash crop, see Arcila Farías, *Economía colonial de Venezuela,* 92.

yet prize the commodities that would later fuel the colony's rise from imperial economic obscurity. Venezuela's long-standing exports of cacao, tobacco, and hides inspired neither large-scale conquest expeditions to acquire them nor fleets to transport them. The utility of leather was obvious, but it could not make one rich. Tobacco and cacao remained exotic goods with few markets for much of the Spanish Empire's early history. The former, at least, became a moderately valuable commodity. Chocolate achieved popularity in Spain at the end of the sixteenth century, though it only became fashionable in the rest of Europe in the latter half of the seventeenth century.[17]

Estrangement from the metropole continued from Venezuela's founding until the first decades of the eighteenth century. The colony received almost no direct Spanish shipping in the sixteenth century. In theory, the crown allowed Venezuela to receive one unconvoyed register ship *(registro)* per year from Spain and to send two ships per year back to the metropole, as well as to load goods onto ships that broke off from the trade fleets *(naves sueltas).* In practice, however, these ships rarely materialized or failed to properly provision the colony. The South American galleons regularly bypassed Venezuela's harbors on their way to Cartagena and Panama. Licensed individual ships from Colombia, Panama, and New Spain brought Caracas merchants second-run goods that would not sell in more prosperous ports.[18]

Even after the rise of cacao cultivation, lapses in metropolitan contact were frequent. In the latter half of the seventeenth century, merchants sent fewer than five ships from Spain directly to Venezuela. No more than six vessels embarked for Venezuela from Spain between 1700 and 1728, and no ship made the return course directly between 1700 and 1721. Even the general galleon fleet to all of South America dropped off noticeably. From 1721 to 1737, only four galleon fleets went from Spain to Panama and Cartagena. After that period, only register ships made the journey. The complete breakdown of the Portobelo fair in Panama was yet another important signifier of the scarcity of legal trade in peripheral locales like Venezuela. Ideally, this annual trade fair of European products from the Spanish fleet system was supposed to supply Peru and all of northern South America. But between 1696 and 1720, the Portobelo fair gathered only once. The rise of serious and sustained foreign intrusions into Spanish America exacerbated difficulties in Spanish shipping.[19] During

17. Arcila Farías, *Economía colonial de Venezuela,* 88.

18. Federico Brito Figueroa, *La estructura económica de Venezuela colonial* (Caracas, 1963), 229; Morón, *History of Venezuela,* 74; Arcila Farías, *Hacienda y comercio de Venezuela,* 121–122.

19. On lapses in metropolitan contact, see Hussey, *Caracas Company,* 53–58; [Jean François Dauxion-]Lavaysse, *A Statistical, Commercial, and Political Description of Vene-*

the first half of the eighteenth century, warfare and the oversaturation of New World ports with contraband goods prompted frequent suspensions of the annual fleet. Even Spanish traders outside of the carrera shied away from Venezuela in this period. Some officials claimed that in the 1700s and 1710s, Canary Islands merchants gave up their right to trade with Venezuela for lack of profit. As these absences show, serious structural issues had emerged throughout the Spanish commercial system by the 1650s. Even if Spain had been inclined to focus its commercial attention on Venezuela, which it was not, the province would most likely have remained isolated from legal domestic trade.[20]

Infrequent contact meant continual scarcities of European products and general material insecurity for Venezuelans. One governor of the province noted in 1612, "I found the affairs of this province in such a bad condition that I cannot stop begging your majesty to feel sympathy for it, because [the province] is so poor, so exhausted, and its residents are so few." Lack of trade from the metropole was not the sole reason for shortages. As Venezuelan landowners ramped up cultivation of tobacco and cacao for external markets, whether to New Spain, the Caribbean, or Spain, local production of foodstuffs suffered. Throughout the seventeenth century, a continual shortfall of grain and occasional absences of meat, salt, cooking oil, and fish affected provincial life. Without European items to supplement domestic products, Venezuelans had no cushion in lean years. These deficiencies continued to plague the colony into the eighteenth century. At the start of the War of the Spanish Succession in 1701, the solicitor general *(procurador general)* of Caracas presented the governor with a dispatch detailing the complete lack of simple goods in Venezuela,

---

*zuela, Trinidad, Margarita, and Tobago* . . . (London, 1820), 17–18; Andrés Bello, *Resumen de la historia de Venezuela* (1810; rpt. Caracas, 1978), 44; José de Iturriaga, *Manifiesto, que con incontestables hechos prueba los grandes beneficios, que ha producido el establecimiento de la Real Compañía Guipuzcoana de Caracas* . . . ([Madrid?], 1749), 2v; Haring, *Spanish Empire,* 318. On galleon fleets and register ships, see Rafael Antunez y Acevedo, *Memorias históricas sobre la legislacion, y gobierno del comercio de los Españoles con sus colonias en las Indias occidentales* (Madrid, 1797), xxx–xxxiii. On the Portobelo fair, see Walker, *Spanish Politics and Imperial Trade,* 137. On foreign intrusions, see Ángel Alloza Aparicio, *Europa en el mercado español: Mercaderes, represalias y contrabando en el siglo XVII* (Salamanca, 2006), 201.

20. The tremendous costs of operating the fleets eventually led in 1739 to the creation of licenses for individual, unaccompanied register ships from Spain. These vessels replaced the galeones trade to South America in 1740 and intermixed with the Mexican flota until 1789, when the latter was finally abolished. See Stein and Stein, *Silver, Trade, and War,* 180–199. In 1734, a royal dispatch declared that the Portobelo fair would have to be closed again for the following year owing to a complete glut of foreign products in the Americas; see Real Despacho, San Ildefonso, Aug. 20, 1734, AGI, Caracas, 23. On Canary Island traders, see Iturriaga, *Manifiesto.*

such as wine and cooking oil. The severing of Spanish commerce combined with poor agricultural yields in the province that year pushed Venezuela into famine. The solicitor general's description was not exceptional. Gregorio de Robles, an inveterate traveler of Spanish America who visited nearly all of the major ports of the realm between 1688–1702, cited the west central Venezuelan coastal city of Coro in his appeal for increased Spanish trade to the Indies. In 1704, he wrote that the "inhabitants complain that Spanish ships neither arrive nor leave from [Coro] to relieve them with goods necessary for human life. Nor do they gather up these inhabitants' produce, hides, or brazilwood that exist in abundancy." He judged that "these vassals deserve help."[21]

The dearth of exchange with Spain also contributed to labor shortages in the colony just as it was attempting to develop its agricultural exports. Population growth in Venezuela through the first two centuries of colonization was sluggish. In 1696, only about 6,000 people lived in Caracas, the largest city in the province. That number had only grown by about 4,000 people since 1589. In contrast, in less than a century after the 1696 count, the capital city's population would quadruple to more than 24,000 inhabitants in 1772. Among these subjects, enslaved Africans were the most important laboring body for cacao production. Planters consistently exhorted officials and the crown to send more slaves for purchase from the late sixteenth through the early eighteenth century. Like European wares and foodstuffs, human cargo could not arrive fast enough to suit the needs of Venezuelan inhabitants.[22]

Given Spain's minimal presence in the province and the scarcities this caused, Venezuelans turned to several additional options for legal trade. Until the rise of the Caracas Company in the 1730s, the cacao trade to New Spain was the most important economic enterprise in Venezuela. Almost from the

21. "So poor, so exhausted": Federico Brito Figueroa, *La estructura social y demográfica de Venezuela colonial* (Caracas, 1961), 25. On shortages, see Stephanie Blank, "Patrons, Clients, and Kin in Seventeenth-Century Caracas: A Methodological Essay in Colonial Spanish American Social History," *HAHR,* LIV (1974), 264. For a document outlining supply failures over the course of the eighteenth century and making an argument for comercio libre late in that century, see "Informe sobre el Real Decreto de Comercio Libre del 28 de febrero de 1789," in Antonio Arellano Moreno, ed., *Documentos para la historia económica en la Epoca colonial: Viajes e informes* (Caracas, 1970), 489–510. On famine, see Arcila Farías, *Economía colonial de Venezuela,* 157–159. "Spanish ships neither arrive nor leave": Gregorio de Robles, *América a fines del siglo XVII: Noticia de los lugares de contrabando* (Valladolid, 1980), 90.

22. On labor shortages, see Brito Figueroa, *La estructura social,* 23, 25, 46–47. On shortages of slaves, see Borucki, "Trans-Imperial History," *Itinerario,* XXXVI (2012), 33, 36; Lombardi, *Venezuela,* 77.

beginning of cacao production in the colony in the 1620s, Venezuela had relied on licensed trade with New Spain to compensate for sparse commerce with Spain. Mexico was a crucial market for Venezuelan cacao and an important source of currency (Mexican silver) in return. Moreover, unlike the expensive transatlantic voyage to Spain, the Mexican route had lower transportation costs, allowing a larger and more diverse group of merchants to trade. From 1674 until the second half of the eighteenth century, Venezuelan cacao was the only raw chocolate that could be legally imported into New Spain. Shipments to Mexico comprised a large share of the early-eighteenth-century cacao trade. Over the first decade of the eighteenth century, for example, the 199,290 *fanegas* of cacao (a fanega equaling about 110 pounds) New Spain received from Venezuela dwarfed the 9,436 fanegas that Spain imported. In 1728, out of 50,000 fanegas of legally traded cacao, 20,000 remained in the New World for Mexican or Venezuelan consumption. Mexico's preeminence in the Venezuelan export market would continue until the Caracas Company shifted the cacao trade's alignment by the 1740s.[23]

In addition to Mexico, Venezuelan merchants and producers made use of smaller, but still legal, trading outlets in the Canary Islands and in the circum-Caribbean. The amount of business authorized between these colonies by the House of Trade varied from year to year, but figures point to sustained commerce. New Spain imported the lion's share of Venezuelan cacao from 1700 to 1710, but the Canaries purchased 3,208 fanegas, and Santo Domingo, Puerto Rico, Cartagena, and other Spanish colonies also received shipments of the cash crop.[24]

An extraordinary degree of administrative self-sufficiency in Venezuela also grew from Spanish commercial inattention. The province of Venezuela represented one of the most autonomous spaces in the Spanish Indies. Much of this autonomy owed to bureaucratic indecision as to whether the region fell under Andean or Caribbean jurisdictional authority. In practice, Venezuela did not exist as a coherent province in any functional way during the sixteenth and most of the seventeenth centuries. Western areas looked toward Cartagena on the coast and Andean Colombia in the interior. The central coast had the most

23. The first recorded shipments of cacao from Venezuela to New Spain occurred in 1622. See Eduardo Arcila Farías, *Comercio entre Venezuela y México en los siglos XVII y XVIII* (Mexico City, 1950), 18–20, 52. On cacao imports to Mexico, see Arcila Farías, *Economía colonial de Venezuela*, 92–96, 211; Joseph Pérez, *Los movimientos precursores de la emancipación en Hispanoamérica* (Madrid, 1977), 35; Brito Figueroa, *La estructura económica*, 240.

24. Brito Figueroa, *La estructura económica*, 229, 240.

contact with the Antilles, New Spain, the Canaries, and Seville. The eastern stretch of the province oriented itself toward Santo Domingo.[25]

The eighteenth-century shift to Bourbon governance shuffled control over the province between numerous administrative units. Under the new monarchy, imperial policymakers broke up massive jurisdictions into smaller, and theoretically more accountable, governmental districts. Reorganization occurred in fits and starts. Until 1717, Venezuela belonged to the viceroyalty of Peru, the principal political jurisdiction for all of South America. That year, the Council of the Indies moved Venezuela to the smaller viceroyalty of New Granada (centered in Bogotá). Venezuela returned to Peru in 1723, when the council briefly abolished New Granada due to concerns of rampant corruption among the viceroyalty's top officials. In 1742, the council reversed its decision, reconstituting New Granada and returning Venezuela to that viceroyalty for the remainder of the colonial period. The arrival of the intendancy system in the 1770s produced still larger changes to the structure of authority in the region.[26] The Intendancy of Venezuela (for commerce and finance) and the Captaincy General (for administrative, political, and military matters) largely superseded the authority of the viceroyalty in 1776 and 1777, respectively. Meanwhile, judicial authority for the province shifted back and forth between the *audiencias* (royal appeals courts) of Santa Fé de Bogotá and Santo Domingo. Venezuela was under the Caribbean Audiencia of Santo Domingo from 1526 to 1717, 1723 to 1739, and 1742 to 1786. It spent a brief period under the Andean Audiencia of Santa Fé from 1739 to 1742. Eventually, the province's judicial jurisdiction came to reside in its capital as the Audiencia of Caracas, from 1786 until the outbreak of independence struggles in 1810. For most of the colonial period, neither Santo Domingo nor Santa Fé shared economic interests with Venezuelans, nor did they interfere much in its affairs. The creation of the Audiencia of Caracas finally incorporated the provinces of Maracaibo, Cumaná, Margarita, Trinidad, Guyana, and Caracas under one court. It also

25. Ibid., 228–229. In general, jurisdictional ambiguity characterized coastal settlements of the Caribbean basin because their produce did little to enrich the empire in its first two hundred years of existence. Although the Venezuelan example is extreme, other Caribbean rim settlements had lax administrative oversight. See Andrews, *Spanish Caribbean,* 41–44.

26. The intendancy system centralized the chain of command beneath the viceroy by creating powerful intendants who received meaningful salaries to dissuade self-interested participation in local informal economies. These peninsular Spaniards acted independently of other officials and greatly increased the efficiency of tax collection in their provincial cities. See James Lockhart and Stuart B. Schwartz, *Early Latin America: A History of Colonial Spanish America and Brazil* (Cambridge, 1983), 352–356.

strengthened the city of Caracas's judicial, economic, and political dominance over greater Venezuela.[27]

The legacy of this complicated jurisdictional history was strong local control over the central coast. For most of the province's existence, viceregal courts and audiencias lacked the geographic proximity and administrative continuity to dominate Venezuela. Weak imperial order produced strange centers of power in the region. Caracas's *cabildo* (town council) and the province's governor were the most potent political forces in Venezuela. The cabildo maintained, between 1560 and 1733, the right to govern the province independently of any audiencia during interim periods between governors. This privilege was highly unusual in Spanish America and zealously guarded by the Caraqueño elite. Since governors rarely served more than five to ten years and often took considerable time to arrive from Spain, the cabildo took the reins of direct provincial control with regularity. It frequently undermined the governor's authority as the only visible imperial representative in the area and acted against new impositions from Spain. The cabildo projected power not only in the city but also throughout the province, as Caracas was the region's one true city of scale. Its influence in the region was on par with, and at times superior to, that of the viceregal government and the clergy.[28]

Social prestige in coastal Venezuela followed the same self-determined path as government. A powerful colonial elite dominated cabildo membership in Caracas. These *mantuanos,* as the first families of Caracas were known, formed a small and tight-knit group in the capital by the seventeenth century. To consolidate the central coast's modest resources, they married advantageously among themselves and strictly limited their number of heirs. By the eighteenth century, the mantuanos' designs had produced an intense concen-

27. The jurisdictional history of changes in viceroyalties and audiencias is compiled from David P. Henige, *Colonial Governors from the Fifteenth Century to the Present: A Comprehensive List* (Madison, Wis., 1970), 344; P. Michael McKinley, *Pre-Revolutionary Caracas: Politics, Economy, and Society, 1777–1811* (Cambridge, 1985), 4–5; Lombardi, *Venezuela,* 270; Morón, *History of Venezuela,* 64–65.

28. The cabildo often bypassed the governor and made petitions directly to the crown. Later in the colonial period, it advocated for the formation of the Audiencia of Caracas so that it could then play the governor against the audiencia, weakening both sides. See Ann Twinam, *Purchasing Whiteness: Pardos, Mulattos, and the Quest for Social Mobility in the Spanish Indies* (Stanford, Calif., 2015), 212–214; Alí Enrique López Bohórquez, *Los ministros de la Audiencia de Caracas, 1786–1810: Caracterización de una elite burocrática del poder* (Caracas, 1984), 64, 78–80. Despite its being the only sizeable city, Caracas's population did not reach 20,000 inhabitants until 1800. See Arcila Farías, *Economía colonial de Venezuela,* 33. On the cabildo's influence, see Morón, *History of Venezuela,* 68.

tration of land and wealth and had dedicated more acreage to the cultivation of agricultural exports than in previous centuries. While their familial partnerships found strength in exclusivity, the mantuanos' commercial relationships, like those of most coastal Venezuelans, looked to the broad and unbounded circum-Caribbean.[29]

## THE LONG HISTORY OF SMUGGLING

Spanish American intercolonial exchange was just one of many peripheral adaptations to mitigate neglect from the metropole by increasing autonomy and ignoring boundaries. In this sense, the province of Venezuela was no different from many other Spanish territories in the Caribbean Basin that the king and the Council of the Indies disregarded in order to protect more valuable assets. Spanish American settlements desired imperial protection from foreign raiding but loathed policing of trade policy violations that seemed inevitable given Spain's frequent commercial absenteeism in the region. Venezuela, in particular, developed self-sufficiency from its isolation in the sixteenth century and came to mediate its own contact with outsiders in the century thereafter. Imperial oversight of this exchange was nominal. Different municipalities upheld different standards of what constituted illegal interaction in practice. As Gregorio de Robles noted at the end of the seventeenth century, the governor of Maracaibo, who enforced anticontraband prohibitions, found himself in conflict with neighboring Spanish officials in Coro to the east, who did not. When it came to commercial and governmental standardization, Robles considered the large and decentralized province of Venezuela a place where "almost everyone lives by the laws of their choosing."[30]

Indeed, by far the most entrenched peripheral adaptation of Venezuelan subjects was interimperial smuggling. Commercially neglected and politi-

29. Blank, "Patrons, Clients, and Kin," *HAHR,* LIV (1974), 266; Brito Figueroa, *La estructura económica,* 176.

30. Scarano outlines a range of Caribbean colonial adaptations in his scholarship. See "Imperial Decline, Colonial Adaptation: The Spanish Islands during the Long 17th Century," in Palmié and Scarano, eds., *The Caribbean,* 179. For a comparable Dutch Atlantic case of peripheral adaptation to meet basic needs in the face of imperial neglect, see Bram Hoonhout, "Smuggling for Survival: Self-Organized, Cross-Imperial Colony Building in Essequibo and Demerara, 1746–1796," in Cátia Antunes and Amélia Polónia, eds., *Beyond Empires: Global, Self-Organizing, Cross-Imperial Networks, 1500–1800* (Leiden, 2016). On disregarded Spanish territories, see Andrews, *Spanish Caribbean,* 51. On Venezuela's self-sufficiency and outside contacts, see Aizpurua, *Curazao y la costa de Caracas,* 29–30. "Laws of their choosing": Robles, *América a fines del siglo XVII,* 89, 91.

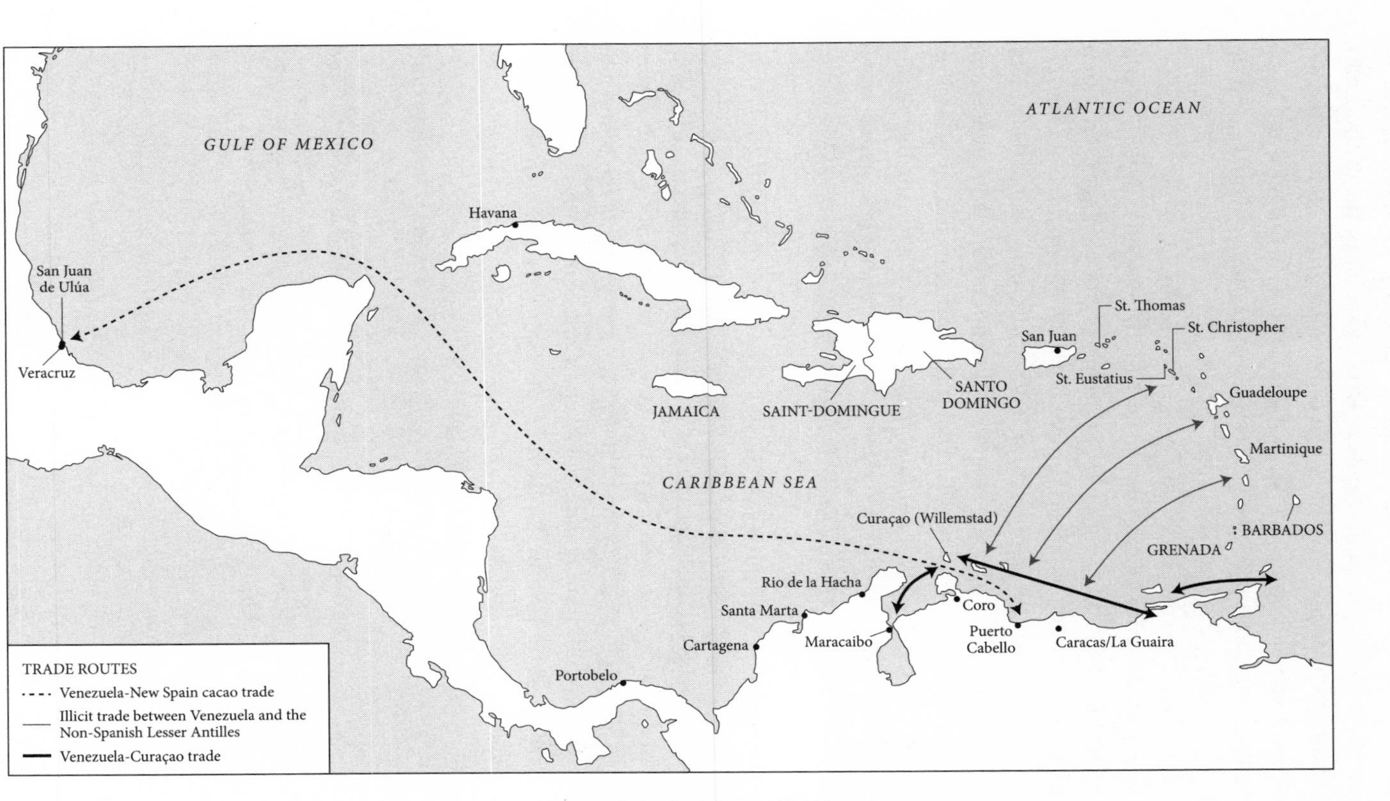


MAP 2. Venezuela in the Circum-Caribbean.
*Drawn by Christine Riggio*

cally autonomous, traders in the province developed relationships with foreign merchants early on. Distant royal authority and jurisdictional ambiguity contributed to the development of a transimperial space along the central coast. Hints of foreign penetration in the region came as early as the trading and privateering voyages of the Englishman Sir John Hawkins in the 1560s and 1570s. Many other adventurers combined commerce, extraction, and plunder on the coast. By the 1590s, the Dutch had moved into the pearl beds of Margarita and Cumaná (both to the east of the province of Venezuela in the province of Nueva Andalucía) as pearl gatherers and traders. They also illegally worked the salt flats of Nueva Andalucía's Araya Peninsula to extract salt for their fishing industries. Between 1601 and 1605, the governor of Nueva Andalucía calculated that as many as 120 Dutch ships stopped at Margarita, Cumaná, or Araya each year for these purposes. The crown noted a foreign presence in the circum-Caribbean, as well. In 1606 and 1614, Philip III issued royal cédulas reminding his subjects of blanket prohibitions on unauthorized trade and interaction with non-Spaniards in the Spanish American kingdoms. Many Dutch crews raided Spanish ships when they could not barter for or extract products themselves. Piracy and privateering were an unfortunate accompaniment to non-Spanish contact. Foreign intruders raided Caracas, Coro, Borburata, Puerto Cabello, Barcelona, and Cumaná in the seventeenth century.[31]

Foreign smuggling increased with the rise of permanent non-Spanish colonies in the Caribbean in the mid-seventeenth century. The Dutch seizure of nearby Curaçao in 1634 and their subsequent conversion of the island into arguably the premier trading entrepôt in the Caribbean regularized foreign influence in the region. From this island, Dutch commerce shifted west from Nueva Andalucía to the central coast of Venezuela. Between the 1650s and 1714, the Dutch were the leading legal and illegal slave traders to the region.[32] Under the auspices of the Dutch West India Company, Curaçaoan traders intermit-

31. For Hawkins's trading in Venezuela, see Harry Kelsey, *Sir John Hawkins: Queen Elizabeth's Slave Trader* (New Haven, Conn., 2003), 81. The governor's calculations come from Sluiter, "Dutch-Spanish Rivalry," *HAHR*, XXVIII (1948), 173–174, 178–179. See also Wim Klooster, *Illicit Riches: Dutch Trade in the Caribbean, 1648–1795* (Leiden, 1998), 24; Parry, *Spanish Seaborne Empire*, 258–259. On royal cédulas, see José Félix Blanco and Ramón Aizpurúa, eds., *Documentos para la historia de la vida pública del Libertador*, I (Caracas, 1977), 42; Arcila Farías, *Economía colonial de Venezuela*, 139. On foreign raiders, see Lombardi, *Venezuela*, 72–73; Klooster, *Illicit Riches*, 28.

32. The calculation of one-fourth of legal slave exports corresponds to 20,003 of 80,132 slaves shipped from Curaçao during the period. See Borucki, "Trans-Imperial History," *Itinerario*, XXXVI (2012), 36–38; see also Stein and Stein, *Silver, Trade, and War*, 34.

tently held the asiento to supply Spanish America with slaves. Regardless of whether or not they had permission to be in Venezuela, Dutch slavers traded African captives for cacao, tobacco, salt, and, occasionally, silver. Venezuelan merchants developed substantial credit entanglements with their Curaçaoan counterparts by the turn of the eighteenth century.[33]

The growth of Venezuelan cacao cultivation provided illicit traders with the most bankable export in the region's colonial history. Venezuela's central coast produced and still produces some of the finest cacao in the world. Rising European demand catalyzed an extraordinary cacao boom in the first half of the eighteenth century. Haciendas sprang up in previously uninhabited areas. In 1720, two million cacao trees existed in the province. By 1750, that number had risen to more than five million trees. Export estimates soared, as well. In 1697, the province exported 14,248 fanegas per year. By 1730, the governor of Venezuela's commissioned census projected that the colony was capable of exporting between 45,000 and 46,000 fanegas per year, a goal that the province exceeded by more than 10,000 fanegas according to some estimates.[34]

The eighteenth-century demographics of the central coast provided an ample labor force to transport and trade cacao surfeits illegally. The population of the province of Venezuela was majority *pardo* (free people of mixed white and African ancestry). The coast also experienced a large influx of Canary Islander immigrants *(Isleños)* in the late seventeenth and early eighteenth centuries as part of state-sponsored settlement projects. Isleños settled in out-of-the-way but fertile cacao regions such as the Tuy River valley, where the León Rebellion would begin in the town of Panaquire. Pardos and Isleños alike worked as urban artisans, petty traders, and small agricultural producers. Enslaved Africans never rose to more than 10 percent of the population in the province. Indian populations of the central coast were also small compared to most Spanish American settlements. This meant that Venezuela had a high percentage of free and non-tribute-bearing inhabitants who were more disposed

33. For the Dutch invasion and early settlement of Curaçao and its implications for seventeenth-century commerce in northern South America, see Pieter C. Emmer and Wim Klooster, "The Dutch Atlantic, 1600–1800: Expansion without Empire," *Itinerario,* XXIII (1999), 59; Linda M. Rupert, *Creolization and Contraband: Curaçao in the Early Modern Atlantic World* (Athens, Ga., 2012), 35–42.

34. On rising European demand for cacao in general, see Sophie D. Coe and Michael D. Coe, *The True History of Chocolate* (London, 1996), 160–176, 204–228; Norton, *Sacred Gifts, Profane Pleasures,* 158–169. On cacao trees, see Ferry, "Encomienda, African Slavery, and Agriculture," *HAHR,* XL (1981), 631. On exports, see Brito Figueroa, *La estructura económica,* 204; Arcila Farías, *Economia colonial de Venezuela,* 196.

to informal economic activities such as smuggling. Pardos and Isleños were not made to toil in coercive, race-based labor systems like plantation slavery, the encomienda, or the *repartimiento* (a compulsory rotating labor draft of indigenous people) that dominated other colonial societies with more Indians or enslaved Africans. Contraband trade was a potential occupation as well as a crucial means of attaining European goods and selling cacao.[35] Therefore, the socioracial composition of Venezuelan subjects meant that the colony not only had product to sell but people to sell it.[36]

Trends in production and demographics aligned with Spanish commercial decline to create an eighteenth-century "qualitative leap" in smuggling. The War of the Spanish Succession was the nadir of Spanish commercial control and influence in the province and Spanish America as a whole. Spanish maritime weakness during the conflict defanged threats to smugglers by coast guard ships throughout the empire. Foreigners filled this power vacuum. Philip V, the first Bourbon monarch of Spain, issued twelve decrees to stanch smuggling between the viceroyalty of Peru and French merchants in the first fifteen years of his reign. In Venezuela, the war interrupted connections with the metropole but boosted illicit slave imports. During and after the war, Vene-

35. In practice, the term *pardo* came to characterize a wide variety of mixed-race people and could be more synonymous with the term *casta* in the Spanish American colonial context. On the Venezuelan pardo majority, see H. Micheal Tarver and Julia C. Frederick, *The History of Venezuela* (Westport, Conn., 2005), 44; Frederick P. Bowser, "Colonial Spanish America," in David W. Cohen and Jack P. Greene, eds., *Neither Slave nor Free: The Freedmen of African Descent in the Slave Societies of the New World* (Baltimore, 1972), 37; J. L. Salcedo-Bastardo, *Historia fundamental de Venezuela* (Caracas, 1977), 145. On the history of Canary Islanders in Venezuela, see John Lynch, "Spanish America's Poor Whites: Canarian Immigrants in Venezuela, 1700–1830," in Lynch, *Latin America between Colony and Nation: Selected Essays* (New York, 2001), 58–73; María del Pilar Rodríguez Mesa, "Los blancos pobres: Una aproximación a la comprensión de la sociedad venezolana y al reconocimiento de la importancia de los canarios en la formación de grupos sociales en Venezuela," *Boletín academia nacional de la historia de Venezuela,* LXXX (1997), 133–188; James J. Parsons, "The Migration of Canary Islanders to the Americas: An Unbroken Current since Columbus," *Americas,* XXXIX (1983), 464–466. On occupations of pardos and Isleños, see Angelina Pollak-Eltz, *La esclavitud en Venezuela: Un estudio histórico-cultural* (Caracas, 2000), 8. Historians have best analyzed the socioracial breakdown of Venezuela for the end of the eighteenth century. For these demographics, see Brito Figueroa, *La estructura social,* 38–39, 58.

36. Discussing race in the colonial period is admittedly complicated. I mostly will use the terms "socioracial" and "socioracial group" to denote what we would call "race" in the twenty-first century, but what was much more fluid and multivariate in eighteenth-century Spanish America. For the basis of these distinctions, see Joanne Rappaport, *The Disappearing Mestizo: Configuring Difference in the Colonial New Kingdom of Granada* (Durham, N.C., 2014), 3–7, 208–209; Twinam, *Purchasing Whiteness,* 42–48.

zuelan cacao became a bedrock commodity to the illicit shipping transactions of many non-Spanish Caribbean colonies.[37]

Venezuela's proximity to Dutch Curaçao made the Dutch especially close trading partners. One Spanish Caribbean inhabitant described the island as "a dry crag that is nothing more than a warehouse for trading with the coast of Tierra Firme." Dutch smugglers followed Venezuela's coastline as they bartered European goods with locals in exchange for their valuable cacao. Pedro José de Olavarriaga, a special envoy of the king to Venezuela and a major commercial reformer, observed that the Dutch "could justly be called the merchants of Europe. They have recognized for a long time that they can derive a handsome profit from the anemic trade conducted by the Spanish." Statistics confirm observers' characterizations of Venezuelan-Curaçaoan exchange. The first three decades of the eighteenth century saw an average of 1,427,530 pounds of cacao consigned annually from the island to the Netherlands. For the next quarter century, Curaçaoan shipping consigned 1,274,843 pounds on average annually, despite much more stringent measures in Venezuelan against non-Spanish shipping. In the first half of the eighteenth century, cacao, overwhelmingly of Venezuelan origin, constituted 37 percent of exports from Curaçao to the United Provinces. Moreover, Dutch domination of the import trade of Spanish American cacao into Spain itself further proved that Olavarriaga's description was not hyperbole.[38]

After the War of the Spanish Succession, British commerce to Venezuela

37. "Qualitative leap": Wim Klooster, "Inter-Imperial Smuggling in the Americas, 1600–1800," in Bernard Bailyn and Patricia L. Denault, eds., *Soundings in Atlantic History: Latent Structures and Intellectual Currents, 1500–1830* (Cambridge, Mass., 2009), 162. On turn-of-the-century Spanish commercial stagnation, see Alloza Aparicio, *Europa en el mercado español*, 220–224. On the War of the Spanish Succession and trade, see Allan J. Kuethe and Kenneth J. Andrien, *The Spanish Atlantic World in the Eighteenth Century: War and the Bourbon Reforms, 1713–1796* (New York, 2014), 347; Aizpurua, *Curazao y la costa de Caracas*, 52; Morón, *History of Venezuela*, 74. Philip V's decrees were issued between 1703 and 1715. See Ruth Hill, *Hierarchy, Commerce, and Fraud in Bourbon Spanish America: A Postal Inspector's Exposé* (Nashville, Tenn., 2005), 108. On illicit slave imports, see Borucki, "Trans-Imperial History," *Itinerario*, XXXVI (2012), 39; Brito Figueroa, *La estructura económica*, 239.

38. "Dry crag": Juan de Stranal to Governor of Havana Dionisio Martinez de la Vega, Havana, Apr. 14, 1727, AGI, Indif, 1596. "Merchants of Europe": Pedro José de Olavarriaga, *Instrucción general y particular del estado presente de la Provincia de Venezuela en los años de 1720 y 1721* (Caracas, 1981), 102. On Curaçaoan shipping, see Wim Klooster, "Curaçao and the Caribbean Transit Trade," in Johannes Postma and Victor Enthoven, eds., *Riches from Atlantic Commerce: Dutch Transatlantic Trade and Shipping, 1585–1817* (Leiden, 2003), 211; Klooster, "Inter-Imperial Smuggling," in Bailyn and Denault, eds., *Soundings in Atlantic History*, 167. On Dutch cacao imports, see Haring, *Trade and Navigation*, 119.

came to rival Dutch activity in the province. After the Peace of Utrecht, the British gained the asiento to Spanish American slave trading from 1713 until 1739. During this period, British slavers brought more than 5,000 enslaved Africans to La Guaira, 900 to Maracaibo in the west, and 800 to the ports of Trinidad, Cumaná, and Margarita in the east. British imports cut Dutch slaving to Venezuela in half, even though Curaçaoan merchants continued to purchase Venezuelan cacao at steady rates. The legal merchandise aboard British asiento slave ships made up the vast majority of licit goods imported into the province between the end of the War of the Spanish Succession and the rise of the Caracas Company in 1728. Nevertheless, slave trading to Venezuela and to Spanish America at large served for British traders as merely a cloak for illicit commerce or as a foot in the door for eventual legal commerce with Spain's overseas dominions. Although the British never received this much desired unfettered legal access to Spanish American riches, they had wholeheartedly joined Dutch and occasionally French traders in competitive Venezuelan black markets by the 1710s.[39]

By the time the Spanish monarchy became acutely interested in Venezuela for its cacao potential, the genie of smuggling was already out of the bottle. The province's coastlines teemed with non-Spanish merchants and Venezuelan producers ready and willing to trade with them. Well before the crown and its ministers recast their gaze on the region, interimperial trade had been normalized into a peripheral strategy for survival.

## CONCLUSION

Ultimately, the exclusivity of the Spanish trade system and its near absence produced arrangements of commercial autonomy in Venezuela. A circuit that disseminated wealth and information back and forth between Spain and the Americas broke down in peripheral regions like Venezuela. The Spanish Empire was far too large for metropolitan Spain to provision and meaningfully support all of its territories. Whether because of negligence or other priorities, Spanish officials consigned slow-to-develop colonies to intermittent isolation. Although Venezuela represented an extreme example, many, if not most, colonies remained in the shadows by necessity. Venezuela only gained Spanish imperial attention once it developed a desirable cash crop. Before this, imperial disregard fostered frequent colonial impoverishment but also creative adap-

39. Borucki, "Trans-Imperial History," *Itinerario,* XXXVI (2012), 38; Arcila Farías, *Economía colonial de Venezuela,* 166; O'Malley, *Final Passages,* 142, 222.

tations. Venezuelan producers and traders developed connections with other Spanish circum-Caribbean colonies to mitigate the dearth of metropolitan trade. They created spheres of political and legal self-sufficiency as well. Most important, they acquired a habit of casting about for trading opportunities beyond the bounds of Spanish imperial borders and legal structures.

By the 1720s, smuggling had grown into an endemic feature of Venezuelan commerce and society. Under Habsburg rule, general anticontraband enforcement had been so lax that Venezuelans perceived an informal dispensation to smuggle as one of their political liberties. Spanish commercial administrators tolerated or ignored black market trade in the region when its resources were of modest value on the Atlantic market. However, the capacity of these steadily appreciating commodities to enrich foreigners in the late seventeenth and early eighteenth centuries demanded action from a new regime of Bourbon bureaucrats who took control of the Spanish state in the early 1700s. They broke with the past, making bold attempts to confront interimperial trade and extract colonial revenue.[40]

Spanish imperial solutions to the problem of contraband trade discounted or misinterpreted colonial perceptions of it. The consumer culture of illicit goods in Venezuela helps explain this disconnection. As the next chapter of this book argues, smuggling was a procedural mechanism rather than a legal transgression in the minds of eighteenth-century Venezuelan consumers. Analyzing their choices, rationales, and obfuscations reveals how their decision making normalized quotidian acts of illegality. Ordinary coastal inhabitants engaged with the black market to acquire a mix of basic goods and discretionary items. Deliberate preferences dictated why they purchased what they did. When under investigation, consumers carefully considered their answers and subterfuges. Yet it appears that the steady erosion of metropolitan Spanish commercial legitimacy washed away Venezuelan buyers' feelings of guilt when they partook in extralegal commerce.

40. Peggy K. Liss, *Atlantic Empires: The Network of Trade and Revolution, 1713–1826* (Baltimore, 1983), 52–53; Silvia Espelt Bombín, "Trade Control, Law and Flexibility: Merchants and Crown Interests in Panama, 1700–1750," in Francisco A. Eissa-Barroso and Ainara Vázquez Varela, eds., *Early Bourbon Spanish America: Politics and Society in a Forgotten Era (1700–1759)* (Leiden, 2013), 127–128; Lynch, *Bourbon Spain,* 145. A more theoretical overview of the Bourbon state's role as enforcer can be found in Michael C. Scardaville, "(Hapsburg) Law and (Bourbon) Order: State Authority, Popular Unrest, and the Criminal Justice System in Bourbon Mexico City," *Americas,* L (1994), 501–555.

# 2

# *Socialized into Smuggling*

## The Consumer Culture of the Black Market

Virtually from the beginning of his appointment as governor of Venezuela in 1732, Martín de Lardizabal was frustrated. Efforts by royal officials to stem the tide of illicit commerce had proved inadequate to the scale of the problem. Foreigners were embedded in the province's commercial affairs. Venezuela's economy and agriculture continued to mature, but not in a way that imperial administrators thought they could control. Rather than merely chasing smugglers, Lardizabal pursued a new and creative strategy in the mid-1730s. He focused on capturing revenue from the covert commerce he knew existed. Lardizabal sought to settle a backlog of outstanding cases and, like other officials, he offered pardons *(indultos)* for sale to those who had participated in smuggling or consumed smuggled goods. Where Lardizabal's scheme departed from those of his colleagues was in its scale. Instead of pardoning individuals, the governor drew up potential sums that *whole cities* could pay in order to nullify commercial crimes committed by their residents. This unorthodox approach revealed an inconvenient truth for regulators of the Spanish commercial empire: smuggling was not merely a problem of supply, demand, and non-Spanish purveyors. It also arose from the self-image and desires of the Spanish American colonial populace. By the eighteenth century, seemingly everyone in coastal regions of Venezuela had some contact with smuggling or smuggled goods. People adapted their consumer routines to constant, low-intensity structures of illegality and enforcement. In Lardizabal's thinking, if the preponderance of littoral inhabitants were complicit in some branch of the illegal economy, it was only natural to tax entire municipalities.[1]

1. Piezas de Autos Generales y Comision de Yndultos, 1734–1738, AGI, Ctdra, 1627. In general, this legajo is full of information about pardons and other bureaucratic devices to

We may very well ask, as did Lardizabal, why common people, who were neither contrabandists by trade nor scofflaws by nature, incurred the many risks of the illicit economy so often and with so little regard for Spanish commercial law. Despite official fulminations against illegal commerce, ordinary people rarely saw smuggling as a morally repugnant or particularly severe crime. They frequently aided in the diffusion of smuggled goods and stimulated underground markets through their buying choices. Notwithstanding dangers and disapprobation, they used illicit trade as a routine means of acquiring material goods.

One way to think about why people seek and send goods as they do would be to conceive of societal regulation and market competition as the twin forces determining the parameters of exchange. Put simply, contraband trade will spring up wherever there exists a market for it, as well as insufficient societal pressure to force people to comply with the law. In the early modern world, the prominence of specific goods in illicit trade had more to do with consumer desire than product output. This chapter examines demand as the impetus for contraband trade in eighteenth-century Venezuela; it profiles the material goods exchanged illicitly and identifies their everyday meanings for Venezuelan consumers.[2]

---

recover lost revenue from smuggling. Sums requested were great. The city of San Felipe, for example, was charged 10,000 pesos. There is no record that the cities listed in the legajo ever paid the sums requested of them. A few municipalities pledged to pay a measly percentage of the sums Lardizabal believed they owed.

2. Arjun Appadurai has theorized more elegantly that "the flow of commodities in any given situation is a shifting compromise between socially regulated paths and competitively inspired diversions" ("Introduction: Commodities and the Politics of Value," in Appadurai, ed., *The Social Life of Things: Commodities in Cultural Perspective* [Cambridge, 1986], 17). Scholars of consumption have stressed the pattern of consumer desire over product output. Breaking with earlier economic histories, Sidney W. Mintz first pioneered the approach of studying social and cultural demand rather than production in the rise of commodities (*Sweetness and Power: The Place of Sugar in Modern History* [New York, 1985]). John Brewer, Roy Porter, and a host of other contributors reified this approach in their important edited volume (Brewer and Porter, eds., *Consumption and the World of Goods* [London, 1993]). In my study, "material culture" follows historian Karen Harvey's definition as "not just the physical attributes of an object, but the myriad and shifting contexts through which it acquires meaning. Material culture is not simply objects that people make, use and throw away; it is an integral part of—and indeed shapes—human experience" ("Introduction: Practical Matters," in Harvey, ed., *History and Material Culture: A Student's Guide to Approaching Alternative Sources* [New York, 2009], 3). See also Jules David Prown, "Mind in Matter: An Introduction to Material Culture Theory and Method," *Winterthur Portfolio,* XVII (1982), 1–2. Slaves as a commodity will be analyzed somewhat in Chapter 7, but a deeper cultural inquiry into why people participated in slaving is beyond the scope of this project.

The study of smuggled goods reveals the nonmonetary reasons buyers and sellers traded and highlights the commercial localism of many early modern participants in the Atlantic economy. For Spanish colonial consumers, procuring the products they felt they needed was neither easy nor straightforward. They broke laws and risked punishment or harm to obtain a range of goods. They chose to enter the illicit economy because illegal imports possessed a cultural importance beyond their practical value.

The active pursuit of unlicensed products had a transformative social impact on the periphery. Smuggling involved navigating conflicts with authorities, creating systems of subterfuge, and reevaluating community standards of what constituted acceptable criminal behavior. By demonstrating the messy and extralegal means by which Spanish American subjects obtained their wares and what the process meant to them, this chapter challenges the teleological argument that ever-more-orderly and -streamlined commerce characterized the transition from the early modern to the modern world.[3]

Illicitly traded goods determined material conditions, shaped value systems, and socialized otherwise law-abiding subjects into circumstances of questionable legality. A range of sources—from official Spanish correspondence, ship manifests, Caracas city council resolutions, confiscation records of bodegas, and foreign traveler and merchant accounts—speak to how unremarkable both goods and the covert exchange of them were to Spanish American consumers. They made smuggling commonplace because their sense of self required access to the European goods that could distinguish them from Indians and Africans. Items that were ordinary in Europe were extraordinary in Venezuela, and Spanish American cravings for them made contraband commerce a regular affair.[4]

3. For examples of historiography observing the budding of an orderly transnational world, see David Hancock, *Oceans of Wine: Madeira and the Emergence of American Trade and Taste* (New Haven, Conn., 2009); and Pierre Gervais, "Neither Imperial, nor Atlantic: A Merchant Perspective on International Trade in the Eighteenth Century," *HEI,* XXXIV (2008).

4. James Deetz has described how ordinary consumer goods that were ideologically important sometimes get lost in the historical record as "small things forgotten" (Deetz, *In Small Things Forgotten: The Archaeology of Early American Life* [1977; rpt. New York, 1996). In the Venezuelan case, I am referring mostly to basic clothes and foodstuffs of European extraction. Ann Smart Martin and Sidney Mintz have pointed out that clothes and food, respectively, are often overlooked by those studying material culture and consumption due to their great ephemerality and therefore their unlikeliness to survive in the archival or archaeological record. See Martin, "Material Things and Cultural Meanings: Notes on the Study of Early American Material Culture," *WMQ,* 3d Ser., LIII (1996), 9; Mintz, "The

### THE INTERNAL LOGIC OF ILLICIT CONSUMPTION AND DEFENDANT TESTIMONIES

Both petty smugglers and those who pursued them reflected on the ethics, criminality, and justifications of commonplace extralegal trade. When caught, traders and consumers on the wrong side of the law justified their crimes against the Spanish treasury to themselves and judicial officials. The latter sometimes viewed smuggling as a character deficiency. By contrast, suspected contrabandists mostly explained their transgressions through a host of practical and logistical excuses meant to prove their innocence, or at least the innocence of their intentions. In the rarer instances when accused illegal traders confronted the moral implications of their crimes, they questioned the integrity of commercial law itself by pointing out the inescapability of market transactions in illicit wares for the vast majority of the Venezuelan population.

Smugglers and consumers of smuggled goods spoke of clandestine commerce in a matter-of-fact manner to lessen their legal culpability. Testimonies of the accused gave specific justifications for smuggling designed to mitigate stiff sentences. They were provided by desperate individuals looking to evade jail time and forced labor details. Although it is difficult to discern the extent of local knowledge about criminal proceedings for smugglers, suspects' responses to interrogations displayed patterns suggesting a practical awareness of which arguments might sway prize court judges. Defendants might have learned from their acquitted predecessors which details to omit, which tropes to stress, and when to tell a lie.

The accused believed that in the minds of royal officials, certain rationales could separate particularly flagrant and damaging smuggling from occasional and innocuous commercial indiscretions. Suspects emphasized the hardships that drove them to smuggle, downplayed their connections to habitual contrabandists, and underscored the extenuating circumstances of their cases that might point to their innocence in or ignorance of the crime.

Feigning unfamiliarity with the law and its specific provisions was the most common defense. Foreign and domestic contrabandists alike often responded that they did not realize their trading was illicit by Spanish commercial codes. One Dutch captain professed that "he did not know nor had he heard it said that there was a prohibition on trading on the coasts of this province." Other defendants claimed ignorance as to what goods constituted contraband or de-

---

Changing Roles of Food in the Study of Consumption," in Brewer and Porter, eds., *Consumption and the World of Goods*, 262–263.

nied knowing that certain items were in their possession at all. Some of the accused expressed their beliefs that various technicalities, such as deviations from their course owing to poor weather or mechanical malfunction, made their transactions acceptable.[5]

When this defense was exhausted, the accused often shifted to accentuating their inexperience in the trade and, by association, their harmlessness to legal commerce. This tactic, like others mentioned here, might have reflected the truth for some subjects. Nonetheless, novice and professional smugglers alike tried to pass as first timers. They claimed not to understand the dynamics of contraband transactions and highlighted, if possible, the small quantities of contraband goods they possessed. Suspects also vehemently denied personally knowing their trading partners, as long-standing associations could indicate the presence of larger smuggling networks.[6]

Finally, when presented with inescapable culpability, subjects might resort to justifications based on their material circumstances or request leniency on the grounds of their legal and social status. Captured traders claimed poverty and want as the reasons they entered into black market exchanges. One suspect got into smuggling "because he was poor and found no other way to make a living." Others said they participated to provide for their dependents. As prize courts rarely doled out harsh sentences to women, female buyers emphasized proscribed feminine gender roles as mothers and household managers in their testimonies. Defendants of indigenous or African descent told prize court judges stories stressing white Spaniards' stereotypical understandings of

5. "Prohibition on trading": Declaración de Juan Piñero, capitán de "La Perfecta," La Guaira, Aug. 19, 1778, AGNV, Comp Gui, XXXVIII, fol. 219–220. For examples of defenses, see Carta de Padres al Sr. Comandante General, Caracas, Feb. 6, 1737, AGNV, Diversos, XX, fol. 331; Ynforme de la Contaduria sobre Comiso de una Piragua con 2½ Barricas 1 Barril de Aguardientes, Tafia y 3 Votijas de miel, Cumaná; Apr. 6, 1756, AGI, Ctdra, 1662; Documentos relativos contra D. Francisco Morales y Simón Pérez, Caracas, Aug. 25, 1770, AGNV, Comp Gui, XXII, fols. 102–142; Testimonio de Andrés Joseph Miranda, marinero, Puerto de San Rafael, Aug. 2, 1779, AGNV, Comisos, XXXII, fols. 93–95; Cedula al Yntendente de Caracas, San Yldefonso, Aug. 14, 1803, AGI, Caracas, 836.

6. Confezion de Joseph Joachin, San Phelipe, Mar. 28, 1732, AGI, SD, 782; Declaración de Juan Piñero, Capitán de "La Perfecta," La Guaira, Aug. 19, 1778, AGNV, Comp Gui, XXXVIII, fols. 219–220. For examples of the rationalization of denying trading partners, see Testimonio de Domingo Viera, Valle de Moron, May 24, 1718, AGNV, Comisos, VI, fols. 171–173; Declaración de Maria Francisca de Espinoza, Caracas, May 23, 1721, AGI, SD, 763; Confesión de Andres, esclavo de Pascual Nuñez de Aguilar, Caracas, Jan. 3, 1752, AGNV, Comisos, XXV, fols. 246–248; Auto del Capt. Luis Lagarene, La Guaira, Nov. 29, 1764, AGNV, Comp Gui, VIII, fols. 284–285; Declaracion de D. Miguel Ruiz, La Guayra, Dec. 11, 1799, AGI, Caracas, 840.

these groups as simple-minded, poor, and easily deceived peons. Juan Cipriano Pérez, an Indian laborer from the inland plains who had transported contraband goods for a Venezuelan landowner, benefited from these preconceptions. Although captured with illicit items, he said he did not know they were contraband, "as he had worked the land all his life as a peon." An investigator agreed with Cipriano Pérez's professed ignorance of the situation, noting that he was simply a "miserable Indian," and dismissed the charges against him.[7]

The diverse legal strategies chosen by defendants demonstrate not only a sophisticated understanding of the prosecution's mindset but also the realization that these approaches worked. Pleading ignorance, amateurism, or poverty could secure freedom or at least a more favorable sentence. It is crucial to keep these realities in mind when parsing the thoughts of illicit buyers and sellers regarding their crimes.

Despite their sometimes formulaic quality, suspects' testimonies reflected important truths about Venezuelan material society and should not be dismissed as entirely fallacious. Records of their interrogations indicated that suspects realized the judicial deck was stacked against them. They could not question the nature of the commercial system in court. They could only defend themselves against accusations of their offenses against it. Defendants' words also betrayed that, in Venezuela, illicit trade's participants were numerous and connected to many levels of society. How else would captured contrabandists and consumers have learned the well-worn and effective talking points necessary to placate authorities? Furthermore, inhabitants' continual rationalization of illegal trade as a means to allay poverty and want suggested their belief that even prize court judges could grasp the conditions of material scarcity that characterized eighteenth-century coastal Venezuela.[8]

7. "No other way to make a living": Confession de Joseph de los Reyes, Caracas, May 6, 1732, AGI, SD, 782. For cases when women caught smuggling emphasized their ignorance of the situation, see Petizion de Manuel Martín Montenegro, fiscal nombrado en la causa que de oficio se sigue contra Maria Francisca de Espinoza, Caracas, May 29, 1721, AGI, SD, 763; Auto de D. Francisco Xavier Moreno de Mendoza, Maracaybo, Aug. 13, 1762, AGNC, Contrabandos, XXVIII, fols. 365–366. "Life as a peon": Confesión de Juan Cipriano Perez, Caracas, Mar. 3, 1755, y Auto de D. Phelipe Ricardos, Gobernador y Capitan General, Caracas, Aug. 8, 1755, AGNV, Comisos, XXV, fols. 315–324.

8. Tamar Herzog has profiled how illiterate frontier dwellers in Iberia and in South America, who were not jurists, nonetheless had a vernacular sense of successful legal strategies to employ in representing themselves in border disputes and trespasses. The repetition of certain phrases, rationales, and justifications by arrested contraband participants no doubt speaks to a similar oral transmission of knowledge of the law (*Frontiers of Possession: Spain and Portugal in Europe and the Americas* [Cambridge, Mass., 2015], 263).

In the infrequent instances when illegal traders and their accomplices reached beyond stock rationales and vocalized the deeper ethical contexts of smuggling, they used their testimonies to portray black market commerce as a permissible act of the masses. Take the case of Joseph Morales Guachico, who stood accused of smuggling with Governor Francisco Xavier Moreno in Maracaibo in 1764. Morales Guachico responded to questions of whether he understood black market commerce to be a crime by stating, "Although in some manner this grave insult and offense could not be hidden . . . it occurred to everyone to buy from the ships that frequently and publicly traded on the coasts." Morales Guachico implicitly questioned the degeneracy and illegality of smuggling by highlighting its prevalence in colonial society.[9]

For officials removed from this casual business or earnestly attempting to quell it, smuggling seemed like a moral contagion. Often, bureaucrats lumped commercial crimes together with civil misdeeds, implying an ethical failure on the part of the contrabandist. Officials interrogating Governor Moreno from Maracaibo as part of a wave of prosecutions in that region in 1747 illustrate this point. The investigators asked Moreno, whom they suspected of trading with a group of Jesuits involved in a smuggling ring, whether his transgressions meant that he had no respect for religion. That line of questioning reflected standard interrogations of contrabandists. Officials routinely inquired whether the accused understood that smuggling was a grave crime "against commerce and the monarchy" and a mark of "disorder and debauchery." Such inquires framed contraband as not just the theft of tax revenues but also as a treasonous, sinful offense.[10]

9. Here my analysis builds on Ann Laura Stoler's meditations on archival patterns. Stoler emphasizes the importance of understanding the logic of archival voices, no matter how scripted these documents may seem. However, she also counsels the reader of these texts to look for rationales outside of the norm. She admits, "Coherence is seductive for narrative form but disparities are, from an ethnographic perspective, more compelling. It is the latter that opens onto competing conventions of credibility about what and whose evidence could be trusted and those moments in which it could not" (Stoler, *Along the Archival Grain: Epistemic Anxieties and Colonial Common Sense* [Princeton, N.J., 2009], 185). "Publicly traded on the coasts": Confesión de Joseph Morales Guachico, 1764, AGNC, Contrabandos, XVI, fol. 627. Guachico's testimony could be applied to many early modern situations of material deprivation. Heather Shore has shown that in urban eighteenth-century London, neighbors of poorer districts saw certain crimes such as prostitution, workplace theft, and pilfering as part of the "canvas of the plebeian life-cycle." Venezuelan popular toleration of smuggling followed a similar logic. See Shore, "Crime, Criminal Networks, and the Survival Strategies of the Poor in Early Eighteenth-Century London," in Stephen King and Alannah Tomkins, eds., *The Poor in England, 1700–1850: An Economy of Makeshifts* (Manchester, U.K., 2003), 156.

10. On smuggling as moral failure, see Pedro José de Olavarriaga, *Instrucción general y par-*

Imperial administrators sought to correct what they believed to be relativism among the Spanish American populace. In 1776, José de Gálvez, the secretary of the Indies, requested on behalf of the king that clergy in the Americas condemn smuggling in moral terms. Gálvez opined that one of the reasons contraband trade persisted was that Spanish American subjects did not know it to be a sin. He implored clergy to remind their parishioners "in the pulpits and confessionals . . . that in the practice of this execrable vice, they not only break the laws of man and are unfaithful to our lord the king, but also to divine precepts. They make themselves criminals in front of God, our august sovereign, and mankind." The bishop of Venezuela enthusiastically agreed to spread the word among his priests and parishioners. In this effort, Gálvez followed the same path as many administrative protectors of borders both before and after him: he sought to create a moral panic that would shake up how administrators and subjects alike viewed a revenue-draining crime. This conjoining of smuggling and sin seemingly failed to gain traction among the populace of Venezuela. A French traveler to the province, François de Pons, echoed the popular belief that smuggling hurt nothing and no one except for royal revenues. Remarking on the clergy's attempts to convey this message in 1806, de Pons wrote, "There is no time worse employed than that which the priest spends in making this publication; for there is no act in the whole ecclesiastic liturgy which makes less impression on the Spaniard." Parishioners' intransigence on the matter also might have been strengthened by the hypocrisy of clergymen who engaged in covert commerce themselves.[11]

---

*ticular del estado presente de la Provincia de Venezuela en los años de 1720 y 1721* (1722) (Caracas, 1981), 96. On the investigation of Moreno, see Cargo al Don Francisco Xavier Moreno, Confesión, n.d., AGNC, Contrabandos, XVI, fols. 610–611. "Against commerce and the monarchy": Decreto del Virrey de Santa Fe Don Jorge de Villalonga, Santa Fe, Jan. 23, 1722, AGI, SD, 759. Other examples of this style of interrogation include Confesión de Juan Miguel de la Rosa, Caracas, Nov. 2, 1752, AGNV, Comisos, XXV, fols. 154–155, and Testimonio de Graham de Langhe, La Guaira, Apr. 30, 1731, AGI, SD, 781. "Disorder and debauchery": Comiso de una Valandra Española, Caracas, May 24, 1756, AGI, Ctdra, 1634.

11. "Practice of this execrable vice": "Despacho del Obispo de Venezuela, Mariano Martí, donde se condena al contrabando," in Felícitas López Portillo Tostado, ed., *Historia Documental de Venezuela,* I (Mexico City, 2003), 76–78. On various states' uses of moral panics regarding smuggling and open borders, see Josiah McC. Heyman and Howard Campbell, "Afterword: Crime on and across Borders," in Elaine Carey and Andrae M. Marak, eds., *Smugglers, Brothels, and Twine: Historical Perspectives on Contraband and Vice in North America's Borderlands* (Tucson, Ariz., 2011), 188; Peter Andreas, *Smuggler Nation: How Illicit Trade Made America* (New York, 2013), 191–207. "No time worse employed": F[rançois Joseph] de Pons, *A Voyage to the Eastern Part of Terra Firma, or the Spanish Main, in South America, during the Years 1801, 1802, 1803, and 1804 . . . ,* II (New York, 1806), 329. As Thomas M.

The large cohort of coastal inhabitants involved with smuggling or smuggled goods came to interpret the practice as a quotidian, victimless, and even desirable indiscretion. In the words of one judge, "This city [Caracas] and province is in such disorder, that foreign goods are introduced and stocked in [subjects'] homes and sold publicly at all hours on the streets." Bureaucrats upholding the Spanish mercantile system tried to tar contrabandists with the same brush they used for murders and thieves, but the characterization never stuck. Trying to change consumer perceptions of smuggling or deny the practice's influence in daily life proved to be a losing battle. If, however, they could not make popular perceptions of smuggling more negative, officials could try to make the practice of smuggling more difficult.[12]

## THE UNFORESEEN CONSEQUENCES OF SMUGGLING AND SMUGGLED GOODS

Smuggling and smuggled goods dominated commercial circumstances in the colonial Americas and also intervened in less overt community dynamics. In Venezuela, surveillance and policing of the population increased in the eighteenth century to keep pace with foreign commerce. Royal investigations could turn neighbor against neighbor. In other instances, people protected and sheltered contrabandists, who were more a part of their world than legal traders or officials. Women, who rarely smuggled on the water, figured prominently in accounts of raids of homes and shops inland. As irregular war raged between smugglers and law enforcement, sporadic violence plagued maritime occupations and disrupted relationships between Venezuelan subjects and inhabitants of the greater Caribbean that had developed over long periods of imperial neglect. Turbulence engulfed the "social life of things" in the province when minor merchants and producers found themselves enmeshed in the illicit trafficking of goods as likely to provoke conflict as to satisfy consumer demand.[13]

---

Truxes's elaborate study of colonial New York's illicit trade with the enemy French during the Seven Years' War demonstrates, the impulse to view unlicensed trade as a benign offense despite adverse geopolitical circumstances was not unique to Venezuela (*Defying Empire: Trading with the Enemy in Colonial New York* [New Haven, Conn., 2008], 2–7, 202–203). Priestly smuggling will be discussed in greater detail in Chapter 5.

12. Sentencia contra D. Marcos de Castro y Vetancurt, Apr. 20, 1731, AGI, Esc, 1194.

13. Appadurai proposes "that we treat demand, hence consumption, as an aspect of the overall political economy of societies. Demand, that is, emerges as a function of a variety of social practices and classifications, rather than a mysterious emanation of human needs, a mechanical response to social manipulation (as in one model of the effects of advertising in our own society), or the narrowing down of a universal and voracious desire for objects

The transition from Habsburg to Bourbon rule ushered in more stringent policing and surveillance of Venezuelan coastal inhabitants and their commercial practices. Beginning shortly after the War of the Spanish Succession, the crown and Venezuelan royal officials expanded sea patrols. Colonial governors throughout Spanish America also increased the use of spies and inspectors to keep track of colonists' purchasing habits and guard against the diffusion of illicit goods. Pedro José de Olavarriaga, a special envoy of the king to Venezuela, proposed the addition of "both public and secret guards and spies in the places and paths where [the contrabandists] turn up." He also defended the right of officials to search any house or store in the province.[14]

In addition, royal authorities encouraged priests to be vigilant against smuggling among their flocks in a more active manner than just preaching against it. Officials in Cumaná, a province to the east of Venezuela, asked churchmen for information about suspected contrabandists in the area in 1730. In particular, they hoped to learn whether the clergy knew anything about allegations of illicit trading against Juan de la Tornera Sota, the governor of the province. Although the priests pledged their support, their answers to an eleven-point questionnaire demonstrated either a lack of cooperation or complete ignorance regarding criminal activities in their jurisdiction. Friction between secular and ecclesiastical authorities concerning enforcement of commercial crimes was common because royal officials were essentially asking churchmen to betray the confidence of their parishioners.[15]

---

to whatever happens to be available." In other words, demand for material things cannot be removed from the culture and context that produces this desire. The illicit context of many consumer goods in eighteenth-century Venezuela led to rampant disregard for commercial law and inherently unstable social and commercial conditions on the coast. These circumstances, in turn, could produce collusion or violence. See Appadurai, "Introduction: Commodities and the Politics of Value," in Appadurai, ed., *Social Life of Things*, 29. For more on the social construction of demand, see Kenneth Pomerantz and Steven Topik, *The World That Trade Created: Society, Culture, and the World Economy, 1400-the Present* (Armonk, N.Y., 1999), xiv–xv.

14. On Spanish policing, see G. Earl Sanders, "Counter-Contraband in Spanish America: Handicaps of the Governors in the Indies," *Americas*, XXXIV (1977), 77; Vincente de Amézaga Aresti, *Vincente Antonio de Icuza: Comandante de corsarios* (Caracas, 1966), 16–18; Lance Grahn, "Guarding the New Granadan Coasts: Dilemmas of the Spanish Coast Guard in the Early Bourbon Period," *American Neptune*, LVI (1996), 19–28; Ramón Aizpurua, *Curazao y la costa de Caracas: Introducción al estudio del contrabando de la provincia de Venezuela en tiempos de la Compañía Guipuzcoana, 1730–1780* (Caracas, 1993), 148–158. "Secret guards and spies": Petición de Jose de Olavarriaga, director de la Real Compañía Guipuzcoana, Caracas, Sept. 2, 1732, AGI, Caracas, 925.

15. Auto de Dn. Juan Chrisos, Comisarios del Santo Oficio de la Ynquisicion Vicario

More stringent patrols meant inconveniences and hassles for interregional trade. By the 1780s, one foreigner lamented the plight of Venezuelans in the inland plains *(llanos)* who had to make a one-hundred-league circuit around the Orinoco and Guarapiche Rivers to purchase clothes and avoid patrols, which "entirely cut off all former communication and rendered the wretched Inhabitant still more miserable." Though descriptions such as these were often exaggerated to promote foreign sorties into valuable yet neglected Spanish territories, the extent to which many of them spotlighted Venezuela indicated a kernel of truth to the logistical obstacles Venezuelans faced.[16]

Imperial surveillance of consumption led to a clampdown on access to some provincial paths and waterways. Just as the *llaneros* found their trading routes cut off in the backcountry, coastal consumers also dealt with limited mobility. For many years, colonial officials had considered routes that ran inland from the sea to be suspicious. Dispatches spoke of cacao and illicit goods trafficked on secret paths carved out of the wilderness by contrabandists. Official accounts also portrayed trails and rivers as sites of potential ambush by foreign interlopers.[17]

To prevent such attacks and lessen covert commerce in the countryside, the colonial government tried to regulate Venezuelan transportation. Officials mandated that newly founded towns and older settlements wishing to retain their charters curtail access to the sea and tributary waterways. There was even talk among the audiencia of Santo Domingo in 1737 of closing the port of Coro to all seagoing traffic to avoid rampant smuggling there. As Coro was one of the largest ports in Venezuela at the time, this rejected proposal would have been a drastic measure. Notwithstanding strict prohibitions on freedom of movement throughout the province and region, smugglers and travelers alike continued to construct unregulated pathways for commerce and convenience. Joseph Luis de Cisneros wrote in 1764 that San Felipe, a town inland from Puerto Cabello and the site of a trade riot in 1741, was "a refuge of contraban-

---

Superintendente en Cumaná, Cumaná, May 10, 1730, AGI, SD, 635; Declaracion del R.P. Fray Domingo Rubio, Cumaná, May 12, 1730, AGI, SD, 635.

16. Observations on the Carraccas and Province of Cumaná by Louis Flislale to Major General John Dalling, Governor of Jamaica, Nov. 16, 1782, BL, Add. MSS, 36806, fol. 176.

17. Luis Enrique González F., *La Guayra, conquista y colonia* (Caracas, 1982), 119; El Cabildo Secular to the King, Caracas, June 24, 1712, AGI, SD, 751. In 1723, Agustín Reinaldo, a coast guard officer, described how he and his men found harvested cacao on one of these footpaths near the Tuy River. As they were confiscating the illicit wares, a much superior Dutch force surprised Reinaldo and his patrol and forced them to flee the site (Testimonio de Agustín Reinaldo, Caracas, Feb. 17, 1727, AGNV, Comisos, VII, fols. 561–562).

dists" because "its center is three short leagues from the Yaracuy River which can be navigated easily to the sea . . . while many paths penetrate its rugged mountains." Colonial regulation of roads and rivers limited the communication, transportation, and trade of many Venezuelans. Their resistance to this intrusion demonstrated the limits of state control.[18]

The eighteenth-century surge in commercial surveillance brought battles over smuggling directly to the doorsteps of more urban colonists. Even for Venezuelans who rarely trekked around the backlands as professional smugglers, contact with contraband in the home and store was routine. So were raids on these sites of consumption.

Authorities questioned many Venezuelan subjects suspected of involvement in smuggling who were not large-scale coastal participants with foreign merchants but rather were consumers and petty traders. These subjects' responses underscored the normalization of illicit foreign goods and anticontraband enforcement in daily life. Take the case of María Francisca de Espinoza, a Caracas widow arrested for possessing foreign cloth. Acting on the tip of an anonymous informant *(denunciador)*, authorities searched her home but failed to find anything; later, they discovered more than one hundred yards of cloth in the home of a neighbor. When questioned about how she came to own the cloth, Espinoza said that a man she had never met came to her home late one night asking her to temporarily store a bag containing the textiles. Her neighbor, in turn, volunteered to look after the goods. Both Espinoza and her neighbor claimed to be unaware that the rolls of cloth were contraband.[19]

Although the veracity of Espinoza's tale seems doubtful, her case and testimony confirmed how intricately smuggled goods fit within patterns of commonplace neighborly interaction. Small-time contraband busts often featured an informant. Denunciadores might receive anywhere from 10 percent to one-

18. Curiepe, a newly founded town of free blacks, was established on the condition that local officials limit access to sea routes. See Lucas Guillermo Castillo Lara, *La aventura fundacional de los Isleños: Panaquire y Juan Francisco de León* (Caracas, 1983), 166. Local governors closed a road to the sea in the town of Petaquire to avoid illicit commerce in 1740. See Cierre del camino de Petaquiere al mar para evitar comercio ilícito, 1740, AGNV, Diversos, XXII, fols. 92–93. On Coro, see Consejo de Indias a D. Simon Mozo de la Torre, Madrid, Oct. 14, 1737, AGI, SD, 784. "A refuge of contrabandists": Joseph Luis de Cisneros, *Descripción exacta de la Provincia de Venezuela* (1764) (Caracas, 1981), 152–153.

19. Testimonio de Auttos fhos contra Maria Francisca de Espanosa sobre haverse Rezeptado en su Cassa Generos de Extrajeria de los quales se hallaron algunos en la Casa ynmediata de su Vezina Paula de los Rios, El Sargento Don Pedro Martin Beato por Comission del exmo, Sr. Virrey de Este Distrito, Caracas, May 21, 1721, AGI, SD, 763.

third of the revenues from the sale of impounded illegal wares. Though the identities of these individuals almost always remained anonymous in court records, it is a reasonable assumption that a combination of fiscal gain and previous grievances toward the accused motivated them. That an informant would turn in María Francisca de Espinoza, even though her cloth was worth relatively little, indicated that she probably had made her share of local enemies.[20]

Conversely, the passing of goods in Espinoza's case demonstrated how neighbors formed networks of obfuscation concerning illicit items. If we buy even parts of Espinoza's story, she was willing to hide the cloth for the man who came to her door, just as her neighbor agreed to harbor it for her. This tantalizing glimpse into covert distribution chains raises more questions than it answers. Nonetheless, the Espinoza case implies that the number of buyers and sellers involved in the processes of smuggling was much larger than what authorities netted in raids.

Subjects who handled contraband goods became savvy about the law and how to negotiate a favorable place within it. Espinoza, like many other minor contraband buyers, was almost certainly aware of the legal repercussions of possessing illicit products despite her feigned obliviousness. She probably knew the package to be smuggled goods and had formulated her defenses accordingly. Why else would she be so willing to accept the bag's contents yet so hesitant to let the goods continue to reside in her house? Denying knowledge of the items' illicit nature was presumably a strategy to lessen punishment. On the other hand, Espinoza's open admission that she had had substantial contact with the goods most likely signaled that she considered her crime trifling and did not expect a harsh reprimand from the law. Her calculations proved accurate. Given that she was an old widow with only small quantities of contraband goods, authorities released Espinoza and confined her punishment to a few already-served days in jail and the confiscation of the cloth.[21]

20. In one proclamation from 1786, informants are promised 10 percent. See Ynforme del Yntendente de Caracas en vista de los dos testimonios de Autos que remite causados en la aprehension de la lancha Santa Rita y solicita Real Aprobacion de la sentencia pronunciada en ellos, Caracas, Sept. 19, 1786, AGI, Caracas, 839. In a letter from the king in 1802, one-quarter of the money raised from the seized assets is alloted to the informant. See Despacho del Rey, Madrid, July 16, 1802, AGI, Indif, 1835. In his study of smuggling, Lance Grahn puts the number at one-third (*The Political Economy of Smuggling: Regional Informal Economies in Early Bourbon New Granada* [Boulder, Colo., 1997], 25).

21. This defensive script was common. Aline Helg outlines a similar case in Colombia from 1796, where a woman of color named María Gervasia Guillén was caught with a parcel of contraband goods. Gervasia Guillén argued that she was ignorant of whom the goods

Taking into account the extension of contraband policing from the coast into the home, it is not surprising that women like María Francisca de Espinoza sometimes ran afoul of the law over their consumer preferences and entrepreneurial decisions. Women in colonial society were keepers of their households and also key participants in the family economy of makeshifts and avid petty traders. They often viewed contraband goods as raw materials for professional use, surplus income, or financial assets.[22]

The presence of women as defendants in smuggling investigations showcases the extent to which smuggled goods penetrated domestic economic routines. For women in particular, contraband goods often represented the fundamental supplies of artisanal production. In 1721, authorities found a cache of foreign fabric rolls and swatches, yarn, and thread under the bed of María Candelaria Jaramillo. The great variety of small quantities of illicit textiles at her home indicated that she was probably a seamstress who had purchased the contraband items for her occupation.[23]

Just as unlicensed trade could augment a woman's income or means of production, it could also prove financially detrimental if detected in a household. Because authorities viewed illicit goods as part of an individual's personal wealth, they usually froze all of a suspected contrabandist's assets. One woman in the town of San Sebastián de Ocumare wrote to the governor of Venezuela in Caracas, complaining that her husband had been in jail as an alleged smuggler for a month. During this time, officials had embargoed all the family's as-

---

came from and did not know they were illegal (*Liberty and Equality in Caribbean Colombia, 1770–1835* [Chapel Hill, N.C., 2004], 107). Espinoza's release: Testimonio de Auttos fhos contra Maria Francisca de Espanosa, May 21, 1721, AGI, SD, 763.

22. Judith M. Bennett has revealed the crucial role of women in bringing in extra household income in early modern Europe. Despite the illegal elements of their trade, Venezuela's female petty traders were not unlike Bennett's brewsters in their willingness to use the market in order to keep family finances solvent (*Ale, Beer, and Brewsters in England: Women's Work in a Changing World, 1300–1600* [New York, 1996], esp. 7, 145–150). For Spanish American examples of female petty traders and their role within family structures, see Jane E. Mangan, *Trading Roles: Gender, Ethnicity, and the Urban Economy in Colonial Potosí* (Durham, N.C., 2005), 134–160. Although Linda M. Rupert and Michael Kwass have both noted women as contraband consumers in the eighteenth century, early modern historiography on petty trading and smuggling has neglected how female subjects incorporated unlicensed goods into their market interactions and occupations. See Rupert, *Creolization and Contraband: Curaçao in the Early Modern Atlantic World* (Athens, Ga., 2012), 164; Kwass, *Contraband: Louis Mandrin and the Making of a Global Underground* (Cambridge, Mass., 2014), 10.

23. Testimonio de Autos fulminados contra María Candelaria Jaramillo sobre haversele hallado unos xeneros de Yllicito Comerzio en su cassa, Caracas, June 6, 1721, AGI, SD, 763.

sets, including her slave and the goods that comprised her dowry. Whether or not the smuggler's wife was aware of her husband's misdeeds, she felt the hardships of commercial enforcement in her home.[24]

In most routine arrests of women, gendered understandings of criminality worked in a female suspect's favor. It is difficult to parse the thoughts of judges from their terse comments. However, their sentences for female suspects suggest that judges either considered women incapable of habitual participation in illicit activities or were unwilling to reprimand them harshly. Punishments for women, unlike their male counterparts, demonstrated swiftness and leniency. Authorities concluded proceedings within days and deemed the confiscation of extralegal items, a small fine, and a few days in jail sufficient.[25]

However, in the few specific instances where authorities suspected that women were associated with powerful smuggling interests, they investigated more seriously. María Joseph de Escurra of Maracaibo sold small amounts of her own cacao to a middleman trader in exchange for china and glassware. The middleman transported her cacao, along with a much bigger shipment belonging to Second Lieutenant *(alférez)* Luciano Luzardo, to Curaçao for sale to Dutch traders. When authorities uncovered the business arrangements, they subjected Escurra to a thorough interrogation. She claimed she had purchased the goods in order to resell them and care for her sick mother with the profits. She denied knowing that the goods were contraband or that her cacao was headed for Curaçao. Escurra successfully marshaled witnesses to testify to these points and to confirm the hardships she had endured in supporting her mother. More important, Luzardo possessed a larger fiscal share of the confiscated shipment than Escurra, and his behavior was suspicious. During the proceedings, he sought asylum in a convent. The governor of Maracaibo eventually pardoned Escurra, declaring her "free of wider involvement" *(libre de sindicación)* in criminal networks. The case indicates that, even though María Joseph de Escurra's contact with large-scale smuggling might have been incidental and subsistence oriented, it could have cost her dearly had officials been able to prove more substantial connections.[26]

24. Josepha Antonia Quintero to the Governor, October 21, 1752, AGNV, Comisos, XXV, fols. 153–154.

25. See, for example, the cases of Maria Ygnacia Suarez and Rosalia Guevara, two women caught with smuggled goods in their homes. Their cases can be found respectively in Cedula al gobernador intendente de Maracaybo, Madrid, Oct. 8, 1796, AGI, Caracas, 837, and Cedula al Yntendente de Caracas, San Yldefonso, Aug. 14, 1803, 837.

26. The full case is Luzardo Balues, Luciano, Causa que le siguió Francisco de la Rocha Ferrer, gobernador y capitán general de Maracaibo, por comercio ilícito de mercancías y

As the prosecution of smuggling at the household level confirmed, contrabandists might be friends, neighbors, or kin. Therefore, it is not surprising that sections of the Venezuelan populace protected smugglers. One Spanish bureaucrat wrote to José de Gálvez, the minister of the Indies, "The Spanish in Caracas punctually advise their Dutch friends in Curaçao of the numbers of the coast guard, the date of their embarkation, and the coarse they chart." José Diguja y Villagómez, an official from Cumaná, agreed that "the poor . . . permit the elaborate, peaceful, and open landing [of Dutch ships]. Additionally, there are those that guard their illicit commerce so that it is available to all *(por ser común de todos)*." Affinity for smugglers diverged from the hostility many minor Venezuelan producers and store owners felt toward legal traders. François de Pons noted that smuggling had a "blind protection which no Spaniard, rich or poor, refuses it. — A vessel driven by a storm on the Spanish coasts, is robbed and plundered by the country-people, if the cargo is covered by legal papers: they succour and protect it, if contraband."[27]

For coastal inhabitants, the consequences of aiding or associating with contrabandists proved unpredictably violent owing to sporadic warfare waged between smugglers and customs officials. Coast guard patrols and foreign ships engaged one another in skirmishes, ship seizures, and theft throughout the eighteenth century. Informal practices of ship confiscations ensured that coast guard sailors received a greater percentage of a prize if they had faced violent resistance in capturing it.[28] All factors encouraged the escalation of conflict in the Caribbean. "The clandestine trade is so prodigiously advantageous that [English merchants] will venture estate, body and soul," reasoned an English governor in Bermuda in 1724. The presence of these foreigners encouraged the Spanish American coast guard's cruelty toward them. Finally, the

---

cacao entre dicho puerto y Curazao, Maracaibo, 1718, AGNC, Contrabandos, XIV, fols. 815–950.

27. "Advise their Dutch friends": Informe de Agustín Moreno Enríquez, remitido al Ministerio de Indias, José de Gálvez, Amsterdam, Feb. 11, 1778 (document reproduced in Aizpurua, *Curazao y la costa de Caracas,* 387). "Guard their illicit commerce": Comercio ilícito en la Gobernación de Cumaná, José Diguja y Villagómez, Cumaná, Dec. 22, 1761, in Antonio Arellano Moreno, ed., *Documentos para la historia económica en la Epoca colonial: Viajes e informes* (Caracas, 1970), 321. "Succour and protect it": de Pons, *Voyage to the Eastern Part of Terra Firma,* II, 329.

28. Numerous scholars have discussed the role of legal prohibitions and increased enforcement of commercial statutes in the development of violence and ever more organized crime. See, for example, George T. Díaz, "Twilight of the Tequileros: Prohibition-Era Smuggling in the South Texas Borderlands, 1919–1933," in Carey and Marak, eds., *Smugglers, Brothels, and Twine,* 76; Andreas, *Smuggler Nation,* 241–243, 336.

governor concluded that Spanish atrocities inspired indiscriminate piracy and low-intensity warfare.[29]

Cycles of war worsened relations and entrapped Venezuelan consumers between marauding parties and retributive attacks. The squishy boundaries separating empires in the Caribbean made for an unpredictable mix of international cooperation and hostility. Relations between, say, the Spanish and the Dutch rarely reached entanglement as defined by a declared war over smuggling. Yet, by consuming goods that required foreign commerce, Venezuelan coastal inhabitants unintentionally positioned themselves in the crossfire between hostile factions.[30]

Interimperial skirmishes over commerce bred disorder and made the threat of conflict ever present, even between willing traders. French Jesuit Jean-Baptiste Labat was no stranger to illicit trade. He described a typical meeting between French and Spanish contrabandists as a polite but uneasy standoff where both sides calculated each other's fighting capabilities:

> The merchant and a few men, all well-armed, stand behind this counter, and are guarded by armed members of the crew on the poop. The captain and the rest of the crew, all armed to the teeth, remain on deck to welcome the visitors, give them drinks, and see them politely into their canoes as soon as they have made their purchases . . . above all it is necessary to be on your guard, and also to be always the stronger, for if the Spaniards see a chance of seizing the ship it is very seldom that they fail to do so.[31]

Covert trade could be an apprehensive affair, because if might trumped right, the aggrieved could not count on the law for protection. Encounters

29. "Estate, body and soul": Lieutenant Governor Hope to the Council of Trade and Plantations, Bermuda, Aug. 21, 1724, CO, 37 / 11. Officials inadvertently encouraged violent conduct as they promised greater paydays for sailors who encountered martial resistance from smugglers. In 1783, Intendant Francisco de Saavedra and coast guard commander Vincente Antonio de Icuza formally codified what had been established practice for most of the eighteenth century. See Aizpurua, *Curazao y la costa de Caracas,* 174–175.

30. Lauren Benton has theorized that "because effective imperial control was defined by sets of narrow corridors and clusters of enclaves, multiple imperial powers could operate in the same region without producing abutting or conflicting spheres of control. The reach of jurisdiction could follow a snaking pattern of travel and trade routes that might cross or parallel other passages without entanglement" (*A Search for Sovereignty: Law and Geography in European Empires, 1400–1900* [Cambridge, 2010], 37).

31. [Jean-Baptiste Labat], *The Memoirs of Père Labat: 1693–1705,* trans. John Eaden (1931; rpt. London, 1970), 172–173.

with extralegal commerce might be just as anxiety-ridden for small-time, individual traders. La Guaira patrols arrested one such novice, a family man named Miguel Ruíz. Ruíz had bought a measly three and a half pesos' worth of smuggled textiles "to clothe his family . . . and to take care of necessities in his house." The unfortunate amateur almost failed to complete the purchase, "as he suspected that he might be robbed by the contrabandists." Ruíz arrived armed to the transaction site, as it was "an unpopulated area far from any neighborhood." The unregulated and persecuted trade in daily goods could transform the act of provisioning the home into a cloak-and-dagger affair.[32]

Conflicts over material consumption also influenced less-commercial aspects of quotidian life like transportation and residency. Stricter enforcement of Spanish commercial law and jurisdictional boundaries affected not just inland subjects moving through the province but also colonists who used the Caribbean Sea as a waterway. As smuggling ships were plentiful and tended to follow the coast, Venezuelan residents knowingly or unknowingly used them for passage between points. Ubaldo de Arcia, a free pardo living in Mochima on Venezuela's eastern coast, employed such a strategy. Arcia and his wife sought transport from Mochima to the city of Cumaná to get treatment for an undisclosed illness they had contracted. According to the two, they were unaware that the ship they traveled in carried smuggled goods. They were the only occupants not to flee the vessel when coast guard officials seized it, suggesting their innocence.[33]

Passengers on other coastal journeys walked a finer line between the role of bystander and contrabandist. A Spanish coast guard patrol stopped Alejo Almario aboard a ship carrying Venezuelan cacao and hides between Isla de Aves and nearby Curaçao. Though Almario claimed to be simply a passenger, his presence aboard a vessel carrying strictly cargo for illicit interimperial commerce cast doubt on this contention. Likewise, authorities were loath to believe Pedro Mariño de Lovera, a native of Coro, who had embarked on a voyage to Santo Domingo to place his daughter in a convent. He claimed that he

32. Declaracion de Don Miguel Ruiz, natural de la villa de Santellana en las montañas de valladolid y vecino de La Guayra, La Guayra, Dec. 11, 1799, AGI, Caracas, 840.

33. This was not an uncommon strategy throughout the Atlantic world. Jean-Francois Reynier and Maria Barbara Knoll, two well-known Moravian religious seekers and Atlantic travelers of the eighteenth century, used a smuggling ship for passage between Surinam and St. Thomas. See Aaron Spencer Fogleman, *Two Troubled Souls: An Eighteenth-Century Couple's Spiritual Journey in the Atlantic World* (Chapel Hill, N.C., 2013), 149. Arcia: Ynforme de la Contaduria sobre comiso de una piragua con 2½ barricas 1 barril de aguardientes, tafia y 3 votijas de miel, Cumaná, Apr. 6, 1756, AGI, Ctdra, 1662.

became involved in contraband shipping only to secure his passage back home. Mariño de Lovera's circuitous course, which included stopovers at several foreign islands and an arrest in Cumaná on the far opposite coast from Coro in the west, belied his defense.[34]

The policing of consumption in the province influenced where subjects could live as well as how they traveled. Laws designed to keep suspicious people out of regions prone to smuggling could be rigid. A French surgeon and apothecary named Pedro Vigot petitioned the governor of Venezuela and the Spanish crown to allow him to stay in Caracas. Vigot had lived and worked in the city for fourteen years, married a Spanish woman, fathered two children, and donated medicines to the poor in the local hospital. Yet a law published in 1736 mandated the expulsion of all foreigners from the province within sixty days to reduce smuggling. Authorities in Spain eventually made an exception for Vigot, but not before his wife and children temporarily went into hiding to avoid expulsion themselves.[35]

The extenuating circumstances of enforcing commercial law on the Venezuelan coast produced a chaotic existence for colonial consumers. Caught between trade parameters that inhibited widespread participation in the world of goods and unrestricted commerce that presented danger in its very criminality, Venezuelan subjects adapted to their situation. They created ruses to cover up illicit activity and used particular circumstances in their cases to argue for leniency. They sought to avoid danger but also developed contingency plans in case it came looking for them. Finally, they exploited the chaos and illegality of smuggling to facilitate transportation and profit for themselves and their families. Smuggling was not an ideal gateway to material provisioning or peaceful daily life, but it nonetheless formed an essential part of the colonial economy of makeshifts.

34. Almario: Autos sobre el apreso de la goleta española de Manuel Rodríguez con cacao y cueros sin licencia de navegar en 27 Jul. 1770 entre Curazao y Isla de Aves, Decs. de Manuel Rodríguez y Alejo Almario, patrón y pasajero, Caracas, Nov. 24, 1770, AGNV, Comp Gui, XXII, fols. 143–178. Lovera: Declaraciones ante Justicia Mayor de la Guaira de Francisco Santoya, Ten de balandra corsaria "Nuestra Señora de Aránzazu," 35, Fran. Loreto, 46, José Vincente Amestoy, 22, marineros, y Pedro Mariño de Lovera, dueno de goleta apresada, 34, La Guaira, Aug. 1–2, 1760, AGNV, Comp Gui, X, fols. 153–161.

35. Memorial de Don Pedro Vigot, Caracas, July 6, 1737, AGI, Caracas, 365. Periodic calls to round up unnaturalized foreigners in the Indies were common throughout the colonial period. They usually came at times when the empire was at war or when its finances were particularly tight. See Charles F. Nunn, *Foreign Immigrants in Early Bourbon Mexico, 1700–1760* (Cambridge, 1979), 86; Carlos F. Duarte, *La vida cotidiana en Venezuela durante el período hispánico,* II (Caracas, 2001), 127.

For those expecting smuggling to possess a certain quality of outlaw chic, perhaps the most surprising aspect of Venezuelan coastal dwellers' engagement with illicit commerce was the mundaneness of their purchases. Eighteenth-century Venezuelans interacted with the interimperial black market as practical buyers. They generally bartered the increasingly valuable cacao, tobacco, and hides they had rather than the hard currency they lacked. Owing to the merchandise shortfalls caused by anemic legal trade, most items they purchased illegally were routine staples from Europe. Although enslaved Africans were the most valuable individual imports into Venezuela, with the price of a single slave reaching as high as several hundred pesos, the number of slaves transported to Venezuela was small, and slaves appeared only sporadically in most inventories of smuggled goods.[36]

One packet of documents (legajo) detailing forty-two contraband seizures conducted in small shops (bodegas), homes, streets, and forests in and around Caracas and the central coast of Venezuela in 1721 and two legajos detailing thirty-eight similar seizures throughout the whole province from 1773 to 1793 provide an intriguing glimpse of smuggled goods that trickled down into Venezuelan daily life. These cases serve as detailed snapshots of Venezuelan contraband imports during specific years of the eighteenth century rather than a representative sample of all eighteenth-century illicit trade. Yet the confiscations give a good sense of many products commonly smuggled into Venezuelan shops and homes throughout the period. Terrestrial, as opposed to shipboard, seizures zero in on sites of consumption and illustrate buyer preferences. This documentary record of the consumption patterns of Venezuelan subjects suggests that smuggling succored neglected communities with staple goods and, in some cases, supplanted legal trade entirely.[37]

36. At the auction for a confiscated cargo of enslaved Africans in La Guaira in 1757, healthy male laborers sold for an average of 270 pesos each while even sick Africans sold for 150 to 200 pesos each. See Autos en Testimonio de los formados sobre el apreso que hiso el Jabeque Nobrado San Francisco Xavier Guardacosta de la Rl. C. G. el dia 21 de Julio de 1757, en la Ysleta de Piritu de una balandra olandesa nombrada Fee, Esperanza y Amor con Carga de Cacao, Cueros, y algunos Negros Bozales, La Guaira, Jan. 21, 1758, AGI, Caracas, 892.

37. The 1721 inventory comes from Comisos de Géneros Extranjeros, Testimonio de autos sobre varios comisos de géneros extranjeros, Provincia de Caracas, Caracas, 1721, AGI, SD, 763. The 1773–1793 cases come from AGI, Caracas, 839 and 841. Case names in the 1773–1793 documents have been omitted to keep footnotes uncluttered and succinct. Whereas comisos involving ship seizures are plentiful in Venezuelan and Spanish archives, documentary evidence of seized goods from homes, stores, roadsides, and other inland venues are less

Confiscation lists noted fabric for garment production as the single most frequent black market import. Most of this cloth was coarse cotton or linen of questionable quality that was meant to cover the body rather than appeal to the latest eighteenth-century fashions. *Coleta,* a cheap cotton, and *ruan,* a lightweight and coarse linen from the Rouen region of Normandy, figured most prominently in the house, store, and street contraband seizures. Behind these fabrics were *listado* (striped linen), *cotonia* (a Flemish cotton), *bretaña* (linen from Brittany of slightly higher quality), and *olandilla* (pressed and dyed linen). As the latter two names indicate, most fabrics found among the confiscated goods came from northern Europe (France, Holland, England, and Flanders). Authorities uncovered yarn, thread, twine, and cheesecloth used in the production of clothing. Officials also identified many finished apparel items, including stockings, shirts, shoes, handkerchiefs, and hats, as being of northern European extraction.[38]

Venezuelans not only sought European textiles and manufactures; they also craved Old World foodstuffs. Regardless of the fertile soil and plentiful hunting grounds of the colony, cultural preferences dictated that Venezuelans import many food items from Europe. The inflated prices and paltry stock of legal Spanish goods assured that Venezuelans would obtain many of these edibles through clandestine means. Typical confiscations in 1721 included wheat flour, salted European meats and fish, as well as alcoholic beverages ranging from French wine to rotgut liquor. The 1773 to 1793 seizures contained a significant quantity of foreign tobacco from Virginia, probably as a means to

---

common. This accounts for the odd date ranges of the documents presented here. To give as accurate a sense as possible of land-based comisos, I have culled the 1773–1793 cases in Caracas 1839 and 1841 down from several hundred records to include just land-based comisos with specific goods listed. To do this, I removed cases with obvious references to bodies of water and ships, cases where goods were not specified (but rather referred to only generically as "generos extranjeros"), and cases where all goods seized were outgoing Venezuelan products suspected of being future illicit exports.

38. Other fabrics appearing in small quantities included *seda, angaripola, zarasa, pruciana,* chambray, and *choleta.* My descriptions of fabrics are based on Peter Boyd-Bowman, "Spanish and European Textiles in Sixteenth Century Mexico," *Americas,* XXIX (1973), 336–353; Elena Phipps, "The Iberian Globe: Textile Traditions and Trade in Latin America," in Amelia Peck, ed., *Interwoven Globe: The Worldwide Textile Trade, 1500–1800* (New Haven, Conn., 2013), 34; Robert S. DuPlessis, *The Material Atlantic: Clothing, Commerce, and Colonization in the Atlantic World, 1650–1800* (Cambridge, 2016), 62–69; Stanley J. Stein and Barbara H. Stein, *Silver, Trade, and War: Spain and America in the Making of Early Modern Europe* (Baltimore, 2000), 78; Aizpurua, *Curazao y la costa de Caracas,* 104–105; Wim Klooster, *Illicit Riches: Dutch Trade in the Caribbean, 1648–1795* (Leiden, 1998), 178; de Pons, *A Voyage to the Eastern Part of Terra Firma,* II, 330–333.

evade the Bourbon tobacco monopoly. The presence of imported comestibles demonstrates that colonists considered simple European foodstuffs essential for civilization no matter how difficult or potentially illegal they were to procure.[39]

In addition to fabrics and food, household, store, and street raids in 1721 and 1773–1793 reveal a proliferation of manufactured European tools. Country folk frequently traded for machetes and other agricultural implements. They also bought guns and gunpowder. Despite the heavy emphasis on cheap import staples, a few luxury products made their way into homes and stores according to the confiscation records. Silk and velvet, both fabrics of the wealthy, figured most prominently among big-ticket items. Chinese satin and paper (probably to make screens) came to the province by way of New Spain and the Manila galleon trade. The registers also document culinary treats such as raisins, cinnamon, and black pepper.[40]

The scarcity of these indulgences, however, only underscores the subsistence character of smuggling in Venezuela. As other documents of the period testify, many small-time Venezuelan buyers frequently chose to trade in the black market merely to meet personal needs. One such consumer, a free man of color named Joseph Joachim, from the central Venezuelan town of Morón, openly admitted to bartering with his cacao to obtain small amounts of cloth, thread, wax, and gunpowder in 1732. According to Joachim, the textiles were to clothe his children, and the wax and gunpowder would embellish his town's Corpus Christi celebration. Like many amateur contrabandists trying to extricate themselves from a bad situation, Joachim stressed that he had entered into the business only to satisfy unremarkable personal wants.[41]

José Diguja y Villagómez, a royal official in Cumaná, noted the combination of poverty and cultural perceptions that drove smuggling among the population. He admitted,

> Some tolerance [of smuggling] was indispensable because without it, the population of Spaniards would go naked in the short span of eight

39. Surprisingly, very few of the 1773–1793 seizures include much in the way of food. Wheat flour seems to have been the most common comestible in these seizures. By contrast, cloth dominated confiscating goods. It was present in 76 percent of the cases.

40. Joseph Luis de Cisneros remarked on the common use of iron tools by agricultural laborers in his description of the province (*Descripción exacta de la provincia de Venezuela,* 138–139). For luxury products, see Ross W. Jamieson, "Bolts of Cloth and Sherds of Pottery: Impressions of Caste in the Material Culture of the Seventeenth Century Audiencia of Quito," *Americas,* LX (2004), 444.

41. Confesión de Joseph Joachim, San Phelipe, Mar. 28, 1732, AGI, SD, 782.

> months, *as if they were Indians.* The common outfit of all the poor is the long shirt and britches worn by mariners and made of cheap, ordinary coleta. He who has two changes of clothes is considered well off; these clothes often being so mean that they fall apart. Moreover, [without smuggling] the fields would cease to be cultivated for lack of tools, which break quickly due to their poor quality.

Luxury was clearly absent from Diguja y Villagómez's reckoning of how the needs of home animated market behavior.[42]

Household and storefront confiscations paralleled inventories of ship seizures in some ways (both types were referred to as *comisos)* but also displayed important differences. As with maritime arrests, the land-based 1721 and 1773–1793 comisos featured cheap cloth most prominently, followed by agricultural implements and firearms. Maritime comisos contained greater quantities of goods, particularly food and alcohol, than their terrestrial counterparts. This was because one ship might supply many shops and homes and could use its mobility to protect cargo from confiscation. As seaborne smugglers rarely conducted just one transaction per voyage, foreign coastal vessels, unlike inland contraband depots, held a mix of both imports still left to be traded and exports like tobacco and cacao. Maritime comisos also contained a greater variety of goods. Slaves, an unheard-of commodity in bodegas, showed up in shipboard confiscations, along with luxury items like gin and castile soap. These specialized items imply that interimperial smugglers might have brought them with specific buyers in mind. By contrast, the humble bodega sold to a range of retail consumers, whom petty merchants could not count on to purchase niche items.[43]

As documentation of both shipboard and town arrests substantiate, the combination of unreliable and expensive licit wares and a crackdown on smuggling squeezed colonial consumers. Material scarcity drove subjects to treat their natural consumption patterns and very survival as bound up in the cir-

42. Comercio ilícito en la Gobernación de Cumaná, José Diguja y Villagómez, Cumaná, Dec. 22, 1761, in Arellano Moreno, ed., *Documentos para la historia económica,* 321 (emphasis added).

43. The following footnotes contain cases with examples of these broader trends found in a range of ship seizures. As mentioned above, case titles have been omitted to keep the footnotes uncluttered: AGNV, Comisos, XVI, 1735, fols. 96–307. For quantities of goods in maritime comisos, see AGNV, Comisos, XV, 1736, fols. 201–244; AGNV, Comp Gui, XIX, 1768, fols. 314–376. On mixed cargoes of imports and exports, see AGNV, Comisos, XVI, 1735, fols. 96–307. On slaves and luxury items, see AGNV, Comisos, XVIII, 1737, fols. 1–252; AGNV, Comp Gui, XXVIII, 1775, fols. 120–176; AGNV, Comisos, XXIV, 1750, fols. 261–367.

cumvention of commercial law. Colonists' difficulty in procuring goods encouraged violence and criminality but also the belief that they could best make ends meet through their own clandestine arrangements.[44]

Nonetheless, material scarcity of European goods alone could not account for the profusion of smuggled goods for petty retail sale and personal consumption. Given the inherent dangers of smuggling and its possible legal repercussions, colonists could have reduced risk by trading for stray legal merchandise or by making do with items produced in Venezuela or the broader Spanish American colonies. Why not just eat indigenous food and wear homespun cloth? Although European food and clothes provided no more nourishment or cover to colonists than New World items, creoles of European descent and newly arrived Spaniards linked their cultural superiority to these imports. This belief in the loftier quality of European products also made them valuable for Venezuelan retailers hoping to resell contraband goods. Such preferences also enabled colonial buyers to tolerate the criminal consequences of illicit trade.

Venezuelan consumers and smugglers esteemed European goods for more than merely their monetary value. The consumption of European foods and textiles was crucial for settlers attempting to assert their whiteness and place within the colonial hierarchy. Clothes were essential for reproducing Europeanness in the public sphere of Latin America. The accoutrements of white European society went into making a home *(casa* or *hogar)* as opposed to poor and uncivilized Indian dwellings *(bohio, choza, jacal,* or *ruca)*. Since racial and ethnic distinctions in these societies were, after all, socially constructed rather than biologically determined, material possessions were pivotal to establishing hierarchies.[45]

44. For an in-depth analysis of the commercial pressures facing Venezuelan subjects at the turn of the nineteenth century, see Manuel Lucena Samoral, *Vísperas de la independencia americana: Caracas* (Madrid, 1986).

45. Both Arnold J. Bauer and Rebecca Earle assert the importance of clothes, material goods more broadly, and even dwellings in differentiating between Spanish and Indian identities (Bauer, *Goods, Power, History: Latin America's Material Culture* [Cambridge, 2001], 74; Earle, "Luxury, Clothing and Race in Colonial Spanish America," in Maxine Berg and Elizabeth Eger, eds., *Luxury in the Eighteenth Century: Debates, Desires, and Delectable Goods* [New York, 2003], 221–225). Beverly Lamire seconds Bauer and Earle's arguments for the early modern Atlantic, noting, "From the early modern to the dawn of the modern times, textiles for home or personal apparel represented the most important investments for the majority of the population. These goods were also imbued with complex economic and cultural meanings. Interactions between societies, East and West, as well as the evolving colonial projects in the Americas, can be discerned through the trade, use and evolution

Food played a similar role. In addition to reminding Spanish immigrants of the tastes of home, Old World dietary products sated their physiology and self-esteem. White Spanish subjects and their descendants in the New World perceived food, next to climate, as the most important influence on their humors. Following humor theory, they believed that too much New World food could alter their constitutions, leaving them unprotected from the damp and treacherous environments of the Americas and making them more like Indians. Food aided the construction of bodily differences in the early modern mind. Colonial society linked procuring European food to whiteness and elevated status in the racial pecking order. This was borne out in Venezuela. White individuals ate wheat bread and drank wine and chocolate, whereas poorer and darker-skinned subjects ate corn cakes and black beans and drank *guarapo* (a liquor made from fermented sugar syrup).[46]

In purely monetary terms, Venezuelans' consumer choices placed them into unequal exchange with Dutch, English, and French contrabandists. In Spanish America in general, trade-starved consumers often esteemed basic clothing and food from Europe to be worth much more than non-Spanish traders did. European manufactures of questionable quality commanded far greater sums in the Americas than they would have in the Old World or even in the English, French, and Dutch colonies. Some goods sold to Spanish subjects

---

of materials, as well as through the needlework that constructed everyday items" (Lamire, "Draping the Body and Dressing the Home: The Material Culture of Textiles and Clothes in the Atlantic World, c. 1500–1800," in Harvey, ed., *History and Material Culture,* 85). In her analysis of clothing and racialization in colonial Louisiana, Sophie White agrees about clothing's power for identity construction but also finds that identity highly malleable and argues that cross-dressing between clothing of different ethnic and racial groups was common and acceptable to Europeans as long as it was temporary (White, *Wild Frenchmen and Frenchified Indians: Material Culture and Race in Colonial Louisiana* [Philadelphia, 2012], 1–6, 17–20). Adrienne D. Hood's study of the material culture of textiles in eighteenth-century rural Pennsylvania provides a comparative British Atlantic context. She finds that the resource and time investment in homespun clothing versus increased Atlantic access to European textiles meant that "the use of homespun was limited to the 'lower sorts,' especially servants and slaves, and to less visible household textiles like sheets" (Hood, "The Material World of Cloth: Production and Use in Eighteenth-Century Rural Pennsylvania," *WMQ,* 3d Ser., LIII [1996], 64). On the construction of racial and ethnic difference through consumption, see Karen B. Graubart, *With Our Labor and Sweat: Indigenous Women and the Formation of Colonial Society in Peru, 1550–1700* (Stanford, Calif., 2007), 8, 19–20; DuPlessis, *Material Atlantic,* 164, 188, 226–227.

46. On humoral theory in the colonies, see Rebecca Earle, "'If You Eat Their Food . . .': Diets and Bodies in Early Colonial Spanish America," *AHR,* CVX (2010), 690. On Venezuelan foodways, see Duarte, *La vida cotidiana en Venezuela,* II, 33, 41.

amounted to nothing more than refuse. The English merchant Lewes Roberts wrote that his compatriots looking to trade on the Caracas coast should bring "*English* Commodities, Serges, all kinds of *Norwich* Stuff; all sorts of Stockings," since "no Stuffs in *England* wearable but are here saleable." Sir James Modyford, brother to the governor of Jamaica, composed a similar list of inexpensive items that could be hawked at high markups along the coast of Colombia and Venezuela in 1667. The exploitation of Spanish American buyers even trickled down into the market for human beings. Foreign merchants sometimes sent "refuse slaves" who could not be sold in the Caribbean sugar colonies. Foreign plenty and Spanish dearth fostered unequal trade relationships in which non-Spanish merchants sold valuable Venezuelan commodities such as cacao and tobacco well below their European offering prices in return for European, but substandard, goods. Even so, Venezuelan traders who carried on commerce with foreigners received a more reliable supply of wares for their cacao than they did in dealing with Spanish suppliers.[47]

Despite this commercial vulnerability, it was vital, even in peripheral societies like Venezuela, to acquire coletas, bretañas, flour, olive oil, and wine no matter how coarse, bitter, shoddy, or expensive they were. In practical terms, reliably obtaining European products in most of Spanish America meant participating in contraband trade.

## CONCLUSION

Although it is tempting to view smuggling as an elaborate game of cat and mouse between black market merchants and law enforcement, both sides would lack a raison d'être without consumer demand. As Benjamin Franklin famously wrote, "There is no kind of dishonesty into which otherwise good people more easily and frequently fall, than that of defrauding government

47. "*English* Commodities": Lewes Roberts, *The Merchants Map of Commerce: Wherein the Universal Manner and Matter of Trade Is Compendiously Handled. . . .* (London, 1671), 63. Modyford's list of items: A. P. Thornton, "The Modyfords and Morgan: Letters from Sir James Modyford on the Affairs of Jamaica, 1667–1672, in the Muniments of Westminster Abbey," *Jamaican Historical Review,* II (1952), 47–48. "Refuse slaves": Colin Palmer, *Human Cargoes: The British Slave Trade to Spanish America, 1700–1739* (Urbana, Ill., 1981), 62; Gregory E. O'Malley, *Final Passages: The Intercolonial Slave Trade of British America, 1619–1807* (Williamsburg, Va., and Chapel Hill, N.C., 2014), 62. On unequal trade relationships and wares that could be acquired with cacao, see Aizpurua, *Curazao y la costa de Caracas,* 340; Francisco Morales Padrón, *Rebelión contra la Compañía de Caracas* (Seville, 1955), 22–23; Joseph Pérez, *Los movimientos precursores de la emancipación en Hispanoamérica* (Madrid, 1977), 35.

of its revenues, by smuggling when they have an opportunity, or encouraging smugglers by buying their goods." The desire for cacao in Europe and European textiles, food, and manufactures in Venezuela stimulated contraband trade along commodity chains that stretched across the Atlantic. In the colonial context, smuggling allowed for the provisioning of culturally favored products but also infused daily life with conflict and uncertainty.[48]

Records of illicit trade in Venezuela add much to the study of consumer behavior. The meanings human beings attach to objects form the crux of material culture and consumption research. As most Venezuelan imports and exports from the eighteenth century were comestibles or cheap consumer goods, they have long since disintegrated. Criminal cases documenting the exchange of illicit wares represent some of the only persistent markers of their existence.

The deeper contextualization of these goods within trading relationships and legal systems can help uncover how they affected the communities in which they were exchanged. Here, cases of clandestine commerce, which tend to offer detailed notations of the circumstances surrounding exchange and consumption, are particularly instructive. For the Venezuelan buyer, smuggling was a business capable of producing violence, risk, and hassle, but also monetary and material gain. In the colony, the eighteenth century marked not an orderly progression into a rational Atlantic trading system but a hard scramble for commercial autonomy and inclusivity through illegal channels possessing their own, idiosyncratic logic.[49]

Everyone, from unassuming storekeepers to cutthroat pirates-cum-contrabandists, was socialized into smuggling. Venezuelans who otherwise had no dealings with criminal elements freely ventured into the illicit commercial world in myriad ways. Buying a new shirt, cooking with olive oil, or trimming weeds with a fresh machete were all behaviors that could imply knowing or oblivious participation in the clandestine economy. Venezuelan consumers' willingness to alter patterns of daily life in the pursuit and consumption of material objects demonstrates, on one hand, conditions of need in Venezuela and, on the other, the tremendous material and cultural worth they ascribed to certain black market goods.

Bourbon reformers were less willing to tolerate colonial subjects' commercial and social familiarity with smuggling than their Habsburg predeces-

48. Benjamin Franklin, "On Smuggling, and Its Various Species," *London Chronicle,* Nov. 24, 1767, in *The Memoirs of Benjamin Franklin . . .* (Philadelphia, 1837), 460.

49. On the messy and bellicose process of eighteenth-century commercial globalization, see Kwass, *Contraband,* 359.

sors. The creation of the Caracas Company, the subject of Chapter 3, was an (unsuccessful) attempt to change this troubling culture. Analyzing the Spanish state's logic for enabling and supporting this entity over the majority of the eighteenth century offers insight into how the state sought to rehabilitate communities given to illicit commerce. In the public-private partnership of a trading company, the Caracas Company represented a novel solution that, nevertheless, would not upend the traditional structures of trade in the Spanish Atlantic. The establishment of the Company was also the crown's tacit acknowledgment that experimentation on the periphery could not make the situation worse than it already was. The monarchy came to this realization as it deduced that increases in the commercial viability of cacao had finally made Venezuela worth saving. The paradox in these positions would drive conflict between reformers, Company administrators, and colonial subjects throughout the venture's existence.

# 3

## New Cures

### The Caracas Company, the Crown, and Commercial Control

In 1720, backers of the future Caracas Company in the province of Guipuzcoa wrote a proposal to the king asking permission to trade in Venezuela as a royal company. Their petition emphasized the terrible state of trade in the province of Venezuela, arguing that cacao commerce "sadly has been taken away from Spaniards and put under the control of foreigners who possess it impudently as if it was their own." In the document, the investors lamented the high price that Dutch traders were making Spanish merchants pay in Europe to sell them cacao grown in Spanish territories. They went on to promise, among other things, the formation of a squadron of Company warships to dislodge the Dutch.[1]

Overtures like this played well to the mindsets of early-eighteenth-century political economists. Mercantilism and favorable balances of trade would gain new importance for English, French, and Spanish imperial policies in this period. Political theorists and governmental ministers wrote with great urgency about commerce as war by another name. A "jealousy of trade" animated thinkers of competing empires to envision commercial policy as formative to political prosperity. European acquisition of colonial possessions

1. Quote from La Provincia hizo la solicitud formal al rey para el comercio con Caracas, Archivo General de Gipuzkoa, sec. 2, neg. 22, leg. 72, cited in Montserrat Gárate Ojanguren, *La Real Compañía Guipuzcoana de Caracas* (San Sebastián, 1990), 20-21. See also Margarita Eva Rodríguez García, *Compañías privilegiadas de comercio con América y cambio político (1706-1765)* (Madrid, 2005), 27.

overseas only agitated this viewpoint. But what if crime and idleness blighted commercial virtue and, by extension, the state's vigor?[2]

To appreciate smuggling as a social practice and not simply as a set of economic transactions, it is necessary to understand the logic behind early modern commercial laws. After all, without the restrictions states placed on trade, illicit commerce, as well as the relationships of cooperation and suppression it produced, would not exist. Eighteenth-century empires did not uphold commercial stipulations simply out of hidebound deference to tradition, naïveté, or greed. Rather, their decisions to exclude groups from trading with their kingdoms and to hunt lawbreakers corresponded to the political and economic concerns of the time. In the case of coastal Venezuela, and the Spanish circum-Caribbean in general, the Spanish Empire attempted to capitalize on the export agricultural revitalization of its territories as early as the 1720s. This initiative took place in the midst of an immense reorganization of the troubled empire. Integrating peripheral colonies into the Spanish Empire would entail wrenching them free from foreign commercial domination typified by contraband trade. It is only by understanding the implementation of Spanish strategies for preventing illicit commerce that a clearer picture emerges of smuggling's hold over eighteenth-century Venezuela.[3]

The question of how to achieve commercial control over the empire in order to channel its resources productively and establish primacy among the world's powers confounded Spanish Bourbon imperial reformers. They hoped to assert this command, in part, by cracking down on contraband trade and providing government support to some private trading ventures. The Real Compañía Guipuzcoana de Caracas represented one of the first concrete steps of early Spanish Bourbon policymakers to arrest the decay and deceit that they perceived in Spanish imperial trade.[4]

2. Istvan Hont, *Jealousy of Trade: International Competition and the Nation-State in Historical Perspective* (Cambridge, Mass., 2005), 1-8; Ángel Alloza Aparicio, *Europa en el mercado español: Mercaderes, represalias y contrabando en el siglo XVII* (Salamanca, 2006), 10; Ernesto E. Bassi Arévalo, "Between Imperial Projects and National Dreams: Communication Networks, Geopolitical Imagination, and the Role of New Granada in the Configuration of a Greater Caribbean Space, 1780s-1810s" (Ph.D. diss., University of California, Irvine, 2012), 25.

3. Barbara H. Stein and Stanley J. Stein, *Edge of Crisis: War and Trade in the Spanish Atlantic, 1789-1808* (Baltimore, 2009), 4, 13; Richard M. Morse, "Trends and Patterns of Latin American Urbanization, 1750-1920," *Comparative Studies in Society and History*, XVI (1974), 423.

4. The historiography of Bourbon commercial reforms is complex and contested. The long stretch of time and rotating cast of monarchs, court favorites, and ministers blurs neat chronological divisions. With some disagreements, historians generally separate these re-

Owing to its early date of formation, the Caracas Company and its objective of Venezuelan commercial transformation adds much to our understanding of the efficacy and paradoxes of Bourbon commercial initiatives. The province was an initial focal point in the dual Bourbon projects of commercializing agricultural exports and stanching contraband trade in the empire. The establishment of the Caracas Company was an early expression of Bourbon reformers' plans to transform former backwaters like Venezuela into connected and productive revenue generators for the empire. Some of these thinkers believed the Company's creation was a half measure. The pre-Bourbon commercial status quo had allowed for the steady accretion of Andalusian merchant power over imperial politics in the previous two centuries. Most reformers saw developing the Caracas Company as the boldest action they could take within the structure of Spanish political economy. Forming a private trading company was a truly jarring approach in the context of fleet-based exclusivism. Across the ocean, events confirmed this supposition. Sudden Company control over the colony's economic engine and stricter enforcement of anti-smuggling laws made Venezuela a hotly contested zone of reform.

The Caracas Company's long tenure of economic and political control over the colony (from 1728 to 1784) demonstrates the evolution of Bourbon commercial thought. In essence, the Company was an early solution that outlived the trends in political economy that had created it. Its longevity reveals the shifting sands of Bourbon Reform projects and the autonomy of such ideas once imperial planners had brought them to life. Although many Venezuelan subjects resented the Company almost from its founding, even metropolitan reformers singled it out for abuse as a counterproductive relic later on. Yet, de-

---

forms into pre- and post-1759 epochs. The bulk of the historiography has focused on the more dramatic moves toward limited free trade after the coronation of Charles III in 1759 and the watershed Spanish surrender of Havana to the British in 1762. The earlier period (1714-1759) has received less attention and generally been treated as an era of big dreams but few actions. Scholars of Bourbon trade policies have wondered to what extent reforms represented a concerted plan versus piecemeal solutions; see, for example, John R. Fisher, *The Economic Aspects of Spanish Imperialism in America, 1492-1810* (Liverpool, 1997), 3-5. Others have described the restructuring of trade as the gentle mitigation of the worst of imperial dysfunction, but not a fundamental shift away from entrenched interests of the Habsburg period; see, for example, Stanley J. Stein and Barbara H. Stein, *Silver, Trade, and War: Spain and America in the Making of Early Modern Europe* (Baltimore, 2000), viii. Finally, recent work has documented how interimperial warfare and reform reinforced one another in Spanish imperial decision making, especially Allan J. Kuethe and Kenneth J. Andrien, *The Spanish Atlantic World in the Eighteenth Century: War and the Bourbon Reforms, 1713-1796* (Cambridge, 2014), 25, 346.

spite being a window into the *longue durée* of Bourbon commercial tinkering on the ground in Spanish America, the Caracas Company has been understudied by scholarship on the period.[5]

The Company's mandate to assimilate a peripheral space via the trafficking of its most valuable export (cacao) and to police its commerce was difficult to achieve and only partially successful. On the one hand, for much of its history, the organization earned steady profits for its shareholders and the crown and provided infrastructure to Venezuela as an ancillary benefit. The Company militarized commercial enforcement and ended a period of almost total permissiveness toward unlicensed foreign trade. On the other hand, it could neither stop the flow of contraband nor diminish illicit trade's importance in central coast communities. The Company's mission to include the colony's population in the larger circulation patterns of the Spanish Empire ironically excluded these inhabitants. The Guipuzcoana's near-monopoly control, enforcement of smuggling prohibitions, and poor prices paid to cacao producers deprived colonists of the fruits of their land's own economic revival. In the end, the indifference to Venezuelan needs that characterized the Compañía Guipuzcoana's rule bolstered illicit trade.

Metropolitan Spanish reformers were not so naïve as to think that the Company could eradicate contraband trade entirely. Ingrained local interests in Spain and Spanish America constricted absolutism and demanded fiscal and commercial compromises to combat the dry rot of empire. Nor were Spanish political economists in unanimous agreement as to how to confront the problem. A substantial faction of them, nevertheless, envisioned the Company as a pragmatic experiment in controlling peripheral Spanish American commerce. The Company's existence was an agreement between the monarchy and a regional sector of Spanish maritime capital. Reformers hoped this com-

5. In English, only Roland Dennis Hussey and Robert J. Ferry have devoted more than a chapter to the Caracas Company. See Hussey, *The Caracas Company, 1728-1784: A Study in the History of Spanish Monopolistic Trade* (1934; rpt. New York, 1977); Ferry, *The Colonial Elite of Early Caracas: Formation and Crisis, 1567-1767* (Berkeley, Calif., 1989). For Spanish-language works focusing on the Company, see Alejandro Cardozo Uzcátegui, *Los mantuanos en la Corte española: Una relación cisatlántica (1783-1825)* (Bilbao, 2013); Gerardo Vivas Pineda, *La aventura naval de la Compañía Guipuzcoana de Caracas* (Caracas, 1998); María Teresa Zubiri Marín, "Etapa final y caída de la Compañía Guipuzcoana de Caracas (1777-1785)," *Pedrables*, XI (1991), 155-164; Vincente Amézaga Aresti, *Hombres de la Compañía Guipuzcoana* (Caracas, 1963); Francisco Morales Padrón, *Rebelión contra la Compañía de Caracas* (Seville, 1955); José Estornés Lasa, *La Real Compañía Guipuzcoana de Navegación de Caracas* (Buenos Aires, 1948); Gárate Ojanguren, *La Real Compañía Guipuzcoana.*

pact would, in turn, patch gaping holes in the Spanish mercantile system and diminish the need to bargain with Venezuelan elites and contrabandists.[6]

From the second quarter of the eighteenth century onward, Spanish ministers and reformers thought practically and experimentally about how to confront unlicensed interimperial trade within the realities of the empire's existing structures of power. With the formation of the Caracas Company, they defined the parameters of interaction for illicit trade's principal agents and antagonists. This intrusion into previous, unspoken arrangements of semiautonomous commerce unleashed a half-century-long struggle over who controlled trade and access to the coast. Spanish imperial ministers could see smuggling only as an obstacle to incorporation, a drain on Spanish economic potential, and a criminal act. Unlike coastal inhabitants, they could not envision an organic web of multi-imperial buyers, sellers, officials, and everyday subjects—in short, a normative, parallel system to mercantile designs. Early reformers' attempts to control a broad maritime space also hampered their successors' strategies for how to develop a colony. That early Bourbon thinkers' understandings of economic productivity and colonial progress squared with neither smuggling-inured Venezuelans nor later metropolitan reformers exemplified the competing and nonconversant visions of trade's purpose in the region.

## GOALS OF THE EARLY REFORMERS

The death of Charles II in 1700 presented the opportunity to reimagine the Spanish Empire on many levels. The shift to Bourbon rule and the subsequent War of the Spanish Succession (1701–1714) was the first dynastic shift since Charles V took control of the monarchy in 1516. When the French-backed Philip V ascended to the Spanish throne, he inherited a commercially adrift Atlantic empire. His reign began during perhaps the weakest period of transatlantic shipping and trade enforcement in the history of the empire. In Venezuela, the lack of access to legal markets, shipping, information, and imperial oversight was particularly acute. In theory, a single unreliable register ship from Spain, another from the Canaries, and four or five vessels from New Spain represented the entirety of the province's allotted legitimate annual commerce.

6. This line of argument draws its understanding of the nonhegemonic and conflicted nature of imperial projects, specifically Spanish Atlantic ones, from Alejandra Irigoin and Regina Grafe, "Bargaining for Absolutism: A Spanish Path to Nation-State and Empire Building," *HAHR*, LXXXVIII (2008), 173-209; Ann Laura Stoler and Frederick Cooper, "Between Metropole and Colony: Rethinking a Research Agenda," in Cooper and Stoler, eds., *Tensions of Empire: Colonial Cultures in a Bourgeois World* (Berkeley, Calif., 1997), 21-22.

In practice, legal trade had been considerably lighter. Caracas Company authorities noted, for example, that no ship had left Caracas for Spain between 1706 and 1721. For Philip, successive Bourbon monarchs, and their ministers, this stagnancy and the smuggling that accompanied it were symptoms of a disease of indulgence that had developed over the Habsburg period. Standardizing and enforcing laws, revoking special dispensations, and rationalizing commerce piqued their interests.[7]

To attack the entwined problems of commercial inactivity and illicit trade, imperial ministers in the first half of the eighteenth century championed a set of mercantile principles that dated back to the previous century. Late-seventeenth-century Habsburg reformers called *arbitristas* had wished to confront these difficulties by increasing the efficiency of revenue extraction from existing sources. These men lionized the former greatness of the empire and believed a path back to it was possible through conventional means. Early-eighteenth-century Spanish thinkers known as *proyectistas,* by contrast, concentrated less on milking surviving revenue streams and more on creating new ones. Statesmen and economists like José Patiño, José del Campillo y Cossio, Gerónimo de Uztáriz y Hermiaga, and the marqués de la Ensenada all looked to France for a solution to Spanish problems.[8]

7. Allotted legitimate shipping tallies come from Pedro José de Olavarriaga, *Instrucción general y particular del estado presente de la provincia de Venezuela en los años de 1720 y 1721* (1722; rpt. Caracas, 1981), 96. Company portrayals of Venezuelan commerce come from José de Iturriaga, *Manifiesto, que con incontestables hechos prueba los grandes beneficios, que ha producido el establecimiento de la Real Compañía Guipuzcoana de Caracas . . .* ([Madrid?], 1749), 2v. Roland Hussey and Guillermo Morón agree with the Company's depiction (Hussey, *Caracas Company,* 51-53; Morón, *A History of Venezuela,* trans. John Street [New York, 1963], 71).

8. For Bourbon views on the problems with trade and reforms, see J. H. Elliott, *Empires of the Atlantic World: Britain and Spain in America, 1492-1830* (New Haven, Conn., 2006), 230; Henry Kamen, *Empire: How Spain Became a World Power, 1492-1763* (New York, 2003), 440-441. On arbitristas and proyectistas, see Gabriel B. Paquette, *Enlightenment, Governance, and Reform in Spain and Its Empire, 1759-1808* (New York, 2008), 95; Stanley J. Stein and Barbara H. Stein, *Apogee of Empire: Spain and New Spain in the Age of Charles III, 1759-1789* (Baltimore, 2003), 30; Stein and Stein, *Silver, Trade, and War,* 4-5, 104. Examples of their own writings include José del Campillo y Cosio, *Nuevo Sistema de gobierno económico para la América: Con los males y daños que le causa el que hoy tiene, de los que participa copiosamente España; y remedios universales para que la primera tenga considerables ventajas, y la segunda mayores intereses* (Madrid, 1789), 59-64; and Gerónimo de Uztáriz, *The Theory and Practice of Commerce and Maritime Affairs,* trans. John Kippax (London, 1751), 92-130. On the willingness of these reformers to emulate French examples, see Anthony McFarlane, "The Bourbon Century," in Francisco A. Eissa-Barroso and Ainara Vázquez Varela, eds., *Early Bourbon Spanish America: Politics and Society in a Forgotten Era (1700-1759)* (Leiden, 2013), 183.

In the seventeenth century, Louis XIV's minister of finance, Jean-Baptiste Colbert, had advocated for the forceful state subsidization of French imperial commerce in order to generate a self-sufficient French economy and military. Colbert perceived trade as another form of warfare. In his view, France would be stronger for the export agriculture, industry, professional navy, and merchant marine that trade would build. To enable such commercial gains, Colbert wished to topple impediments to internal trade, including certain onerous and outmoded taxes, while strongly prohibiting commerce with other nations.[9]

Spanish reformers found this model appealing and potentially adaptable to their own circumstances. In particular, they valued commercial exclusivism, not simply as a means to hoard bullion, but rather as a way to jump-start a range of industries and infrastructure. Increased trade would stimulate imperial shipping, agriculture, mining, homegrown industry, and the developments of ports and roads. All of this growth would, in turn, reinforce a positive balance of trade internationally. Moreover, structured commercial exclusivism would fit with broader Bourbon goals of simplifying power relations between the monarchy and its subjects by eliminating intermediaries (in this case, smugglers).[10]

In translating Colbertian theory into Spanish transatlantic commercial practice, reformers worked within the confines of the already-established Spanish closed system while at the same time trying to exploit new opportunities for wealth generation and to eliminate the worst of the system's abuses. Steps proposed toward this process included reinstituting a more efficacious version of the fleet system, promoting agricultural export crops in peripheral regions, and ending the Cádiz peninsular monopoly on transatlantic trade. Additionally, early reformers suggested stanching contraband trade and ex-

9. Xabier Lamikiz, *Trade and Trust in the Eighteenth-Century Atlantic World: Spanish Merchants and Their Overseas Networks* (Rochester, N.Y., 2010), 14; D. A. Brading, *Miners and Merchants in Bourbon Mexico, 1763-1810* (Cambridge, 1971), 25-26; Hont, *Jealousy of Trade,* 24; Stein and Stein, *Silver, Trade, and War,* 39, 156.

10. On the topic of these early reformers and their views, see Antonio García-Baquero González, *Cádiz y el Atlántico (1717-1778): El comercio colonial español bajo el monopolio gaditano,* I (Seville, 1976), 67-86; John Robert McNeill, *Atlantic Empires of France and Spain: Louisbourg and Havana, 1700-1763* (Chapel Hill, N.C., 1985), 51-53; Stein and Stein, *Silver, Trade, and War,* 5-8, 86, 156, 164; Fisher, *Economic Aspects of Spanish Imperialism,* 129. For a discussion of the ideology behind eliminating intermediaries between the monarchy and subjects, see Charles F. Walker, *Shaky Colonialism: The 1746 Earthquake-Tsunami in Lima, Peru and Its Long Aftermath* (Durham, N.C., 2008), 14; McFarlane, "The Bourbon Century," in Eissa-Barroso and Vázquez Varela, eds., *Early Bourbon Spanish America,* 184.

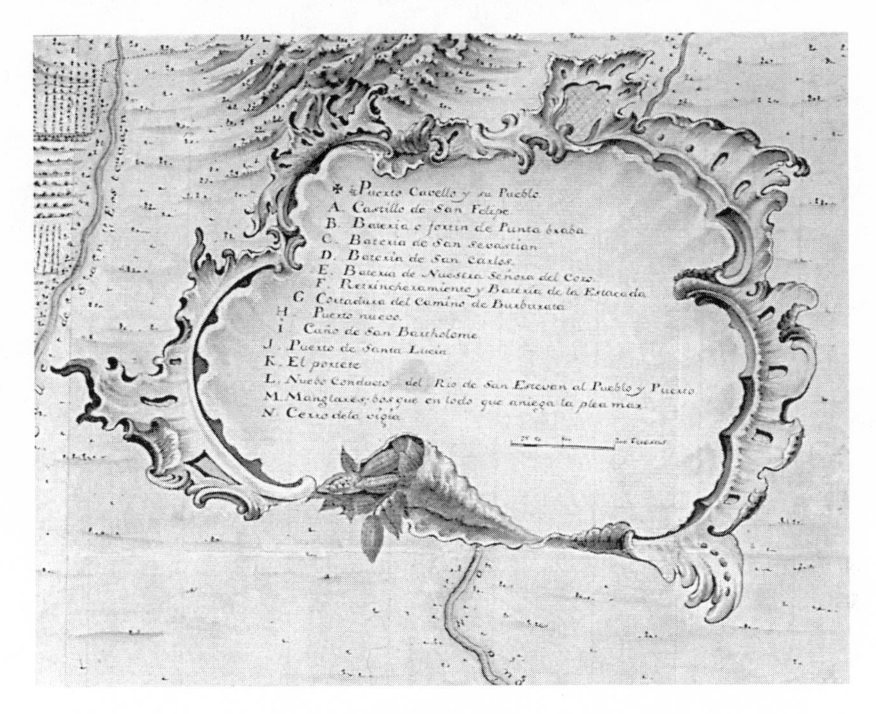


FIGURE 7. Cacao Cornucopia in a Cartouche. Detail from *Plano de Puerto Cabello, en Venezuela.* 1764. The cartouche of this map of Puerto Cabello demonstrates what made Venezuela noteworthy in the minds of imperial policymakers. Ministerio de Educación, Cultura y Deporte. Archivo General de Indias, Mapas y Planos, Venezuela, 149

panding limited private commercial undertakings alongside the fleets. Owing to the overwhelming influence of Andalusian merchants, who thwarted most efforts at change, the crown's ministers realized the last of these aims only during the first two decades of Bourbon rule. Even the creation of the Caracas Company in 1728 angered traders in Cádiz by damaging their absolute control over transatlantic trade. These merchants were not misguided in their assumptions that reformers sought to reduce their power over Spanish shipping. Royal companies, of which the Caracas Company was by far the most successful, controlled around 20 percent of Spanish Atlantic shipping between 1730 and 1778, whereas they had scarcely existed before this period.[11]

11. On early reforms, see Josep M. Fradera, "The Caribbean between Empires: Colonists, Pirates, and Slaves," in Stephan Palmié and Francisco A. Scarano, eds., *The Caribbean: A History of the Region and Its Peoples* (Chicago, 2011), 175; Fisher, *Economic Aspects of Spanish Imperialism,* 129; Stein and Stein, *Silver, Trade, and War,* viii. On royal companies' share of shipping, see García-Baquero González, *Cádiz y el Atlántico,* 136. On Cádiz merchants' opposition to early Bourbon Reforms, see Eduardo Arcila Farías, *Economía colonial de Vene-*

In its inception, the Company appeared to fulfill most of the criteria prized by reformers. Unlike the foreign asientos that had shipped slaves to Spanish America, the Caracas Company was an in-house solution to market inefficiencies. Its business sought to bring a developing Venezuelan cacao sector into the fold of legal Spanish imperial commerce and increase consumption of legal European goods in the province. Economic integration would lead, with any luck, to a deeper political connection with the metropole. To operate in the colony, the Guipuzcoana would need to invest in Venezuela's infrastructure as well. Back in Spain, the Company's founding would offer another port of departure, Pasajes, for the Americas than those of Andalusia and potentially integrate the Basque Country more fully into Madrid's sphere of influence. Perhaps most important for reformers considering granting concessions to the Caracas Company, the firm dramatically reduced the costs of commerce and trade enforcement by providing its own private fleet to transport goods and pursue contrabandists. Finally, the Company likely benefited from the metropolitan view of Venezuelan legal trade as so defunct that experimentation could only help it.[12]

## THE GENESIS OF A PRAGMATIC SOLUTION

The involvement of a monopoly company headed by Basque merchants in the province of Venezuela was not an obvious fit from the start. This development came about because the Company functioned at the pragmatic juncture between the interests of several Basque provinces and the commercial aims of the crown in the early eighteenth century. Its involvement in Venezuela lacked historical antecedents. Instead, the impetus for the venture was the convergence of upstart Basque maritime enterprises and Bourbon understandings of Venezuela as a trouble spot ripe for economic development. The potential profits to be derived from this marriage of convenience overcame questions regarding the Company's suitability for the territory it would inhabit.

Basque settlement in Venezuela predated the Company's arrival. Basque immigrants had been in the area as merchants and landowners since the sixteenth century. Simón Bolívar's eponymous forebear was among their numbers in the late sixteenth century. Nonetheless, immigration had been individual and sporadic before the eighteenth century. Basque inhabitants of

*zuela* (Mexico City, 1946), 84; Kuethe and Andrien, *Spanish Atlantic World,* 126; Stein and Stein, *Silver, Trade, and War,* 202.

12. Hussey, *Caracas Company,* 51.

MAP 3. Greater Iberian Connections to Venezuela.
*Drawn by Christine Riggio*

Venezuela comprised no more than several hundred individuals in this period. Pathways to the Company's establishment in Venezuela did not spring from deep ancestral receiving networks.[13]

Although Venezuela had no implicit significance in their plans, by the late seventeenth century Basque merchants around the ports of San Sebastián and Pasajes were expressing more interest in entering Indies commerce. Residents of northwestern Spain were generally maritime oriented, commercially minded. They had withstood Spain's seventeenth-century economic depres-

13. Vicente de Amézaga Aresti, *El elemento vasco en el siglo XVIII venezolano* (Caracas, 1966), 11; Arantzazu Amezaga Iribarren, "La Real Compañía Guipuzcoana de Caracas: Crónica sentimental con una visión historiográfica: Los años áuricos y las rebeliones (1728-1751)," *Sancho el Sabio,* XXIII (2005), 198.

sion better than the rest of the peninsula. Unfortunately for them, the Andalusian monopoly on imperial trade to the Americas impeded the aspirations of other peninsular regions. Undeterred after its founding in 1682, the consulado of San Sebastián advocated for Basque trade in the Indies. The merchant organization united with leaders of the province of Guipuzcoa in their support of overseas enterprises and an eventual trading company. At this time, the geographic destinations of Basque traders remained murky.[14]

Crown commercial needs and preferences gradually dictated where Basque merchants would land. Imperial ministers wanted to revitalize Spain's transatlantic merchant marine and trade more extensively in areas traditionally underserved by the trade fleets. Spanish reformers could experiment with new forms of administration and political economy most easily in the Spanish American periphery, where creole commercial and governmental power was less entrenched than in Mexico and Peru. Caracas and its hinterlands were among the most attractive testing grounds for new agricultural and commercial development. Crown officials also hoped to integrate heretofore marginal regions of the Iberian Peninsula into Spain's commercial affairs. This would serve the complementary purpose of destabilizing Andalusian traders, whose sway had prevented substantial reforms to a stagnant imperial trading system. Given the sorry state of the Spanish treasury, they also needed cost-effective measures to accomplish their goals. These factors, along with Basque enthusiasm for transatlantic commerce, coalesced into permission for a private trading company in Venezuela.[15]

The crown concession only materialized after a series of debates and frustrated efforts in the first quarter of the eighteenth century. Habsburg mon-

14. Gárate Ojanguren, *La Real Compañía Guipuzcoana,* 11, 20.

15. For Spanish economic experimentation on the periphery, see Paquette, *Enlightenment, Governance, and Reform,* 94. As José Miguel Delgado Barrado points out, privileged companies in Iberia were an inversion of those in the rest of Europe. In other European countries, companies were a response to a lack of governmental support and regulation of commercial activities and a way to centralize commerce for a commercial task. In Spain, the commercial system was already rigid and firmly in place. Companies were potentially a way of loosening a commercial system dominated by southern Spanish merchants and centuries-old concessions they had extracted from the crown (Delgado Barrado, "Reformismo borbónico y compañías privilegiadas para el comercio americano [1700-1756]," in Agustín Guimerá, ed., *El reformismo borbónico: Una visión interdisciplinar* [Madrid, 1996], 137). On undermining the dominance of Andalusian merchants through companies, see also Kenneth R. Maxwell, "Hegemonies Old and New: The Ibero-Atlantic in the Long Eighteenth Century," in Jeremy Adelman, ed., *Colonial Legacies: The Problem of Persistence in Latin American History* (New York, 1999), 80; Rodríguez García, *Compañías privilegiadas,* 21, 29-31; Stein and Stein, *Apogee of Empire,* 21.

archs had been unable to launch royal companies because they lacked leverage with Andalusian and creole merchant guilds, both of which hated the idea. The Bourbon era, beginning in 1701, reinvigorated old ideas for commercial reform, yet visions remained divided. As discussed in Chapter 1, several proposals and rebuttals between 1705 and 1706 from the Real y General Junta de Comercio (Council of Commerce) in Madrid typified these divisions in the early Bourbon court. A privileged trading company was only one of many options for reform on the table. Distracted by the War of the Spanish Succession, the Council of the Indies and the Junta de Comercio rejected or delayed nearly all suggestions and opted instead to maintain the creaky status quo.[16]

Due to these ongoing quarrels, reformers rebuffed several Guipuzcoan proposals to start a company in the first decade of the eighteenth century. Yet the crown was still interested in Venezuela. It permitted a proposed Honduras Company the opportunity to send four ships to Caracas in 1714 as part of a larger trading venture to Venezuela and Honduras. This company never raised sufficient funds, however, to get its enterprise off the ground.[17]

With the 1717 transfer of the House of Trade (Casa de Contratación) from Seville to Cádiz, reforms to the Spanish transatlantic commercial system began in earnest. Company advocates, sensing the moment, found two influential backers in Pedro José de Olavarriaga and José Patiño y Rosales. Olavarriaga connected general calls for reform and increased commerce to the specific locale of Venezuela. More than any other single figure, Olavarriaga expressed Venezuela's agricultural and commercial promise to a wider audience and championed the creation of a privileged company there. The crown appointed the Basque native as a special judge of commercial affairs *(juez de comisión)* to Venezuela in 1718. Along with co-judge Martín Beato, Olavarriaga traveled extensively through the province as part of his mission to root out

16. On Habsburg policy, see Arcila Farías, *Economía colonial de Venezuela,* 180. On the Madrid Council of Commerce, see William J. Callahan, "A Note on the Real y General Junta de Comercio, 1679-1814," *Economic History Review,* N.S., XXI (1968), 519-528. Other ideas for reform included replenishing naval infrastructure, combining sailings of traditional trade fleets with individual register ships, and pursuing more widespread and open trade between Spanish American ports in the model of the later comercio libre. Some proposals even allowed for a modicum of highly regulated commerce with foreigners. To energize licit trade and smother smuggling, several members of the junta proposed the creation of a general Spanish company of the Indies patterned after the French Compagnie des Indes occidentales (Papeles de Don Manuel Garcia de Bustamante y uno de Don Ambrosio Doubenton tocante de la idea de la Compania Universal para Indias, sus reparos y de las otras navegantes propuesta, 1705-1706, AGI, Indif, 2046a).

17. Gárate Ojanguren, *La Real Compañía Guipuzcoana,* 14-18.

contraband and commercial fraud. Carrying out his orders embroiled Olavarriaga in a series of legal battles against royal officials complicit in smuggling operations. Olavarriaga's experiences as an outsider confronting entrenched provincial factions in the contraband trade shaped his perception of Venezuela's commercial potential, problems, and solutions. His sojourns and conflicts led him to write his 1722 *Instrucción general y particular del estado presente de la provincia de Venezuela en los años de 1720 y 1721.*[18]

The *Instrucción* proved that Spanish officials were not blind to or unmoved by commercial stagnancy in the periphery. In it, Olavarriaga bemoaned what he saw as the Venezuelan paradox of potential bounty amid disorder and poverty. Olavarriaga remarked, "The Province of Venezuela could be one of the best and most fertile of all the Indies if it was cultivated, but the weakness of its residents is so pronounced that instead of abundance, they barely procure life's necessities." Although Olavarriaga had harsh words for Venezuelan subjects, he also chastised military and civilian royal officials who acquiesced to illicit trade in order to supplement their poor salaries. Even if these men had had the will to prosecute smuggling, the underwhelming condition of coastal fortifications, arms, and troop discipline hindered efforts to keep foreigners out. In a port-by-port tour, Olavarriaga profiled in exhaustive detail how mobile Dutch merchants plied their trade across the stopovers of the central coast. The region was, in Olavarriaga's opinion, a defensive and economic liability to the crown. The lack of legitimate trade to the colony impoverished it and failed to provide a counterweight to Dutch trade. To shame the meager Spanish commerce along the central coast and emphasize the Dutch threat, Olavarriaga praised the latter's efficiency and thrift. The Dutch could sell more cheaply, he felt, because they had better ships, fewer duties to pay, and less red tape.[19]

Overall, the *Instrucción* encouraged an increase in Spanish transatlantic contact and investment to unlock the province's cacao riches. The book promoted greater production and circulation of cacao through legal channels. Not only would this place a Spanish American product back under Spanish control, but it would assure a steady stream of tax revenue from its importation

18. On the transfer from Seville to Cádiz, see Clarence Henry Haring, *Trade and Navigation between Spain and the Indies in the Time of the Hapsburgs* (Cambridge, Mass., 1918), 138; Gárate Ojanguren, *La Real Compañía Guipuzcoana,* 16-18. Chapter 6 discusses Pedro José de Olavarriaga's legal battles in detail as part of its analysis of factionalism and smuggling in officialdom.

19. "Best and most fertile of all the Indies": Olavarriaga, *Instrucción general y particular,* 13. See also 19-21 (critiques), 30-69 (Dutch incursions), and 96-103 (colonial liabilities to Spain and Dutch advantages).

and sale. Paying more generous salaries to local officials (tenientes) would recover more revenue, as they would no longer need to provide for themselves by smuggling or accepting smugglers' bribes. Olavarriaga spoke of Venezuela as more than simply a place to be exploited for imperial gain; he proposed inducements to legal behavior as much as he chastised illegal activities. For a sustained transformation of the province, Olavarriaga believed Venezuelans would need a steady supply of European provisions to reduce their reliance on interimperial markets. He also recommended distribution of land to immigrants, particularly the Canary Islanders who had populated the colony since the late seventeenth century. Olavarriaga considered some of the territory they occupied "the worst terrain" in the province. Granting hardworking immigrants fertile parcels of land would encourage them to generate wealth through productive agriculture rather than illicit trade. It would even fix individuals in one place, cutting down on the suspect mobility of rootless people *(vagabundos),* who currently had "no other means than the cloak and dagger by which they steal from others and sleep where they can." In sum, greater attention needed to be paid to improving Venezuela's material conditions in order to re-Hispanicize its cash crop.[20]

The *Instrucción*'s diagnosis of Venezuela's commercial ailments had a profound impact on imperial designs for the region and the future of contraband trade there. It offered a pathological assessment of illicit commerce in the colony and more broadly in Spanish America. Olavarriaga enabled imperial reformers to differentiate Venezuela from other vague sites of potential economic revival. His treatise provided policymakers and Basques who would follow him with accurate information about the geography, agriculture, commerce, and politics of the province. All of this knowledge came from a trusted royal official who had dirtied his hands investigating the legal squabbles and factionalism involved in commercial graft. Olavarriaga's writing became the driving rationale for the creation of the Caracas Company and a new attitude toward trade in Venezuela, since he identified smuggling as a fatal flaw to be expunged.[21]

After the 1722 *Instrucción,* work proceeded rapidly on the necessary logistics and permissions to bring the Company to life. Olavarriaga met with im-

20. Ibid., 100 (production and tax revenue), 96 (enticements to legal trade), 15-16 ("the worst terrain" and land distribution).

21. Mario Briceño Perozo, *Magisterio y ejemplo de un vasco del siglo XVIII* (Caracas, 1965), 139, 155; Rosario Salazar Bravo, *El comercio diario en la Caracas del siglo XVIII: Una aproximación a la historia urbana* (Caracas, 2008), 44-45; Amézaga Aresti, *Hombres de la Compañía Guipuzcoana,* 17-18; Gárate Ojanguren, *La Real Compañía Guipuzcoana,* 19.

portant financial backers in the Basque Country in 1726. At the same time, the Basque province of Guipuzcoa appointed Felipe de Aguirre, the secretary of the Junta Foral committee on privileges, as its representative to meet with the king of Spain and discuss the terms of the Company's charter. Olavarriaga also attempted to raise a fleet of four ships to make the Company's first transatlantic voyage. On September 25, 1728, the crown approved the Real Compañía Guipuzcoana de Caracas's charter as it officially became a royal company. Olavarriaga would serve as the Caracas Company's first factor in Venezuela from 1728 to 1731. The three ships that made the first company voyage to Venezuela brought Olavarriaga as well as the next governor of Venezuela, a Basque named Sebastián García de la Torre, in 1730. Five hundred sixty-one Real Compañía Guipuzcoana employees and a range of commercial goods also filled the ships to establish control in the colony. On July 15, 1730, the Company began operations in Venezuela.[22]

During Olavarriaga's tenure as factor and even after his period of directorship, he served as a steady voice for connecting the province to the empire, encouraging its agricultural production and suppressing its contraband economy. A 1732 petition he wrote, for example, talked about reforming coast guard procedures so that patrol ships would not always need to bring back their captured prizes to a prize court judge or the governor if it was inconvenient to do so. The petition in general asserted Company rights to enforcement above the rights of colonial subjects. Later, Olavarriaga complained that poor roads between towns hindered the legal cacao trade. Before he could improve the colony's infrastructure, however, this vocal advocate of Basque transatlantic involvement in Venezuela died in 1735 in Caracas.[23]

Olavarriaga's overtures might have fallen on deaf ears had they not had the metropolitan support of José Patiño y Rosales. Patiño became minister of the

22. Basque financial backers: Amézaga Aresti, *Hombres de la Compañía Guipuzcoana,* 25. Negotiation of the Company's charter: Hussey, *Caracas Company,* 60. Raising a fleet: Ramón Aizpurua, *Curazao y la costa de Caracas: Introducción al estudio del contraband de la Provincia de Venezuela en tiempos de la Compañía Guipuzcoana, 1730-1780* (Caracas, 1993), 151. García de la Torre (1730-1732) would be the first of a string of three Basque governors, succeeded by Martín de Lardizabal (1732-1737) and José Gabriel de Zuloaga (1737-1747) (Amezaga Iribarren, "La Real Compañía Guipuzcoana de Caracas," *Sancho el Sabio,* XXIII [2005], 190). On the Company's arrival and establishment of control, see Luis Enrique González F., *La Guayra, conquista y colonia* (Caracas, 1982), 123; Eugenio Piñero, "The Cacao Economy of the Eighteenth-Century Province of Caracas and the Spanish Cacao Market," *HAHR,* LXVIII (1988), 77.

23. Petición de Jose de Olavarriaga, Director de la Real Compañía Guipuzcoana, Sept. 2, 1732, AGI, Caracas, 925.

navy in 1717, the first of several high-level posts he would hold, including minister of war, minister of finance, minister of the Indies, and secretary of state. He served in these appointments until his death in 1736. During the 1720s and early 1730s, Patiño largely ran the imperial government. The most pronounced part of his reform agenda was to increase legal trade by suppressing its foreign competition. To this end, Patiño promoted a stronger transatlantic navy, merchant marine, and coast guard. His *Proyecto de flotas y galeones* desired to strengthen maritime commerce and defense by reviving the yearly trade fleets. In the Americas, he chose to increase funding to coast guard units and furnish more privateering licenses. Despite his interest in revitalizing the fleets for the purposes of commercial circulation, Patiño had no particular affinity for the Andalusian monopoly over the Indies trade. As an adherent of a more systematic mercantilism according to a Colbertian model, he wished to centralize control in Madrid over the transatlantic economy, and his rise to the position of minister of the Indies in 1726 worried the Cádiz consulado.[24]

Patiño and Olavarriaga's interests overlapped in their support of privileged trading companies. Patiño saw company trading as a means of increasing money to the Spanish treasury and giving life to stagnant trading patterns by shaking up deeply rooted merchant interests. In court, he was the strongest promoter of the company model. As plans developed for the Caracas Company, he smoothed the path to royal approval of its charter. Patiño and Olavarriaga were friends, and the former's ascendance in court in the 1720s aided the Caracas Company's prospects. Patiño's enthusiasm for Olavarriaga's plan was such that he did not even consult with the Cádiz consulado before recommending that the Basque-backed Compañía Guipuzcoana receive royal protection. As an early reformer who would influence future Spanish imperial thinkers, including José del Campillo and the marqués de la Ensenada, Patiño's advocacy for the Company transferred to his protégés in Madrid after his death in 1736.[25]

Spanish political economists had mixed opinions about the fast-tracking

24. On Patiño, see John Lynch, *Bourbon Spain, 1700-1808* (Oxford, 1989), 95; McNeill, *Atlantic Empires*, 53. On his coastal policies, see Geoffrey J. Walker, *Spanish Politics and Imperial Trade, 1700-1789* (Bloomington, Ind., 1979), 98-106; Fradera, "The Caribbean between Empires," in Palmié and Scarano, eds., *The Caribbean*, 175; Kuethe and Andrien, *Spanish Atlantic World*, 349. On his trade views and later career, see Rodríguez García, *Compañías privilegiadas*, 27-31; Briceño Perozo, *Magisterio y ejemplo*, 155.

25. Gárate Ojanguren, *La Real Compañía Guipuzcoana*, 17; Briceño Perozo, *Magisterio y ejemplo*, 155; Rodríguez García, *Compañías privilegiadas*, 29; Kuethe and Andrien, *Spanish Atlantic World*, 126-128.

of the Caracas Company. Spanish economist Miguel de Zavala y Auñón, for one, supported it. He believed that the commerce generated by a company would stimulate manufacturing in regions of Spain where these companies were headquartered. Zavala subscribed to the argument that the Americas were the future economic engine of Spain, and therefore any organization that could plug wayward colonies back into the Spanish imperial matrix was worth supporting. For Zavala and like-minded others, privileged companies represented a transitional solution that would unite capital with merchants to provision the American market and thereby impede foreigners from doing so. It was hoped that these companies would help stimulate a virtually nonexistent Spanish peninsular manufacturing sector as well.[26]

The strongest dissenting voice among political economists was Gerónimo de Uztáriz y Hermiaga. Uztáriz, whose *Theórica y prática de comercio y de marina* (1724) was one of the most important treatises on the Spanish economy in the first half of the eighteenth century, saw trading companies as distractions from more substantive issues in the Spanish transatlantic economy. The most serious problem Spain faced was its appalling dependence on the manufactured goods of imperial rivals to provision its subjects, both legally and illegally. He did not believe that companies could be the catalyst for manufacturing and, by extension, a decline in smuggling. Instead, total mercantilism, wherein Spanish-produced goods would be shipped on Spanish vessels to Spanish American consumers, was necessary to end Spain's commercial woes. But men like Uztáriz were in the minority. Over Uztáriz and his followers' objections, the Caracas Company received royal status.[27]

The foundational arrangements of the business that would come to dominate Venezuelan shipping and commercial enforcement revealed a partnership between Basque and crown interests. Like most privileged companies, the Compañía Guipuzcoana needed shareholders and the royal concession of a commercial monopoly (or near monopoly) over a territory. One of the reasons the Company received royal protection in the first place was that it offered to pay off substantial debts that the Spanish royal treasury had incurred. In its initial years, shareholders in the Caracas Company were all Basques, specifically illustrious Guipuzcoans, with the exception of José Patiño and the king.[28] The

26. Rodríguez García, *Compañías privilegiadas,* 37-43, 75-76.

27. Gerónimo Uztáriz, *The Theory and Practice of Commerce and Maritime Affairs,* trans. John Kippax (London, 1751), 7-8, 181-186.

28. On the Company's establishment and early shareholders, see John V. Lombardi, *Venezuela: The Search for Order, the Dream of Progress* (New York, 1982), 102; Delgado Barrado,

Company would report to Madrid but run operations from the Basque Country. This was a major concession to Basque autonomy given Andalusia's usual dominance of transatlantic shipping. The Company's headquarters were in the city of San Sebastián, and its ships were built in, launched from, and returned to Pasajes. Compañía Guipuzcoana ships could travel directly from the Basque Country to Venezuela but needed to stop in Cádiz on the return voyage in order to have cargoes assessed and pay duties. The Company built its Venezuelan offices in La Guaira and Puerto Cabello, the two largest ports on the central coast. Company founders constructed an enterprise that was logically organized, autonomously administered, and favorable to the crown's bottom line.[29]

## EXPECTATIONS AND REALITIES OF THE CARACAS COMPANY IN VENEZUELA

The terms of the Caracas Company's founding gave it generous privileges, with the expectation of great benefits for the crown and the province. Basque investors and merchants received royal protection and almost exclusive rights to ship cacao between Venezuela and Spain. Although the Company did not have a complete monopoly over the cacao trade in its first decade of existence, its dominance allowed the Basques to corner the market. It enjoyed reductions in port duties *(derechos de toneladas)* and, as stated earlier, the freedom from disembarking its goods at the House of Trade in Cádiz before departing for the Americas. Although Company trading was supposed to focus on the central

---

"Reformismo borbónico y compañías privilegiadas," in Guimerá, ed., *El reformismo borbónico,* 125. Kenneth Pomeranz and Steven Topik argue that monopoly over a marketplace or region and the fixed military costs of preserving such a monopoly from outside interlopers are mutually reinforcing (Pomeranz and Topik, *The World That Trade Created: Society, Culture, and the World Economy, 1400–the Present* (Armonk, N.Y., 1999), 37, 165.

29. Large shares in the Company cost 500 pesos each, whereas small shares cost 100 pesos each. To be a voting shareholder, an individual had to own eight large shares. The king owned two hundred large shares in the Company when it was formed. The Company set out with the goal of raising 3 million pesos for its establishment. However, it was only able to secure 1.5 million pesos by 1730 (Monserrat Gárate Ojanguren, "La Real Compañía Guipuzcoana de Caracas: Una historia económica," in Ronald Escobedo Mansilla, Ana M. Rivera Medina, and Alvaro Chapa Imaz, eds., *Los vascos y América: Actas de las jornadas sobre el comercio vasco con América en el siglo XVIII y la Real Compañía Guipuzcoana de Caracas . . .* [Bilbao, 1989], 292; Federico Brito Figueroa, *La estructura económica de Venezuela colonial* [Caracas, 1963], 254; Gárate Ojanguren, *La Real Compañía Guipuzcoana,* 90, 169-170). On the Company's American offices, see Gárate Ojanguren, *La Real Compañía Guipuzcoana,* 170-172, 199.

coast, once it had supplied this region, it then could trade with Cumaná, Trinidad, Guyana, and Margarita.

Additional concessions followed in the 1740s. The Company received a formal monopoly over cacao trade from Venezuela and Maracaibo to Spain in 1742. That same year, the Company extended its geographic reach by securing limited rights to ship cacao to New Spain, Venezuela's other major legal trading partner. By 1744, the crown freed ships of the Guipuzcoana from their obligation to stop in Cádiz on their return trips to the Iberian Peninsula as well.

In return for these grants, the crown expected the Compañía Guipuzcoana to supply Venezuela with at least two register ships' worth of European goods per year. This obligation did not give them a monopoly over imports into the province, as this level of importation was beyond their means. It did, however, represent a sizable commitment for the organization. The Company would also provide coast guard patrols. Two-thirds of the auctioned profits of any goods confiscated by Company ships went to its treasury, while the captain and crew of the patrol ship divvied up the other one-third. Finally, the Company pledged to ship a fixed amount of cacao for the private profit of Venezuelan planters (called the *tercio* because it was usually around one-third of a ship's cargo). By gaining rights to exclusive trade and its own naval and coastal forces, the Compañía Guipuzcoana's status as a private business venture blurred with its role as an enforcer of Spanish commercial policy.[30]

In many ways, the Caracas Company owed its longevity to its capacity for visibly developing Venezuela's economy and infrastructure even as the monetary gains from these improvements rarely stayed in the province. The Company's carte blanche control over Venezuelan ports ushered in the province's

30. For the initial royal order establishing the Caracas Company and its privileges, see Real Compañía Guipuzcoana de Caracas, *Real Cedula de Fundacion de la Real Compañia Guipuzcoana de Caracas, y Reglas Economicas de buen govierno, con que la estableció la M.N. y M.L. Provincia de Guipuzcoa, en Junta General del año de 1728 . . . .* (Madrid, 1765). See also Gárate Ojanguren, *La Real Compañía Guipuzcoana,* 41-43; Rodríguez García, *Compañías privilegiadas,* 30, 47; Aizpurua, *Curazao y la costa de Caracas,* 150. For additional concessions given to the Company, see Raquel Rico Linage, *Las reales Compañías de comercio con America: Los organos de gobierno* (Seville, 1983), 7, 24; Vivas Pineda, *La aventura naval,* 39; Arcila Farías, *Economía colonial de Venezuela,* 209. For meditations on how state-sponsored trading companies muddled boundaries between public and private responsibilities, see Patricia Owens, "Distinctions, Distinctions: 'Public' and 'Private' Force?" in Alejandro Colás and Bryan Mabee, eds., *Mercenaries, Pirates, Bandits, and Empires: Private Violence in Historical Context* (New York, 2010), 27; P. W. Klein, "The Origins of Trading Companies," in Leonard Blussé and Femme Gaastra, eds., *Companies and Trade: Essays on Overseas Trading Companies during the Ancien Régime* (Leiden, 1981), 23.

first substantial legal trading system, dramatically increased royal revenues coming from the colony, and generally brought Venezuela positive economic attention from Madrid for the first time. Annual Venezuelan cacao exports to Spain between 1700 and 1730 had averaged approximately 21,000 fanegas (or about 2.3 million pounds in today's measurements). During the first eighteen years of the Caracas Company's existence (1730–1748), annual Venezuelan cacao exports to the mother country more than doubled to around 50,000 fanegas (5.5 million pounds). The Company built permanent and stable port structures on top of what had been ramshackle port complexes in La Guaira, Puerto Cabello, and San Felipe. In its first twenty years, it also improved the ports, defenses, and roads of major coastal cities and towns to facilitate smoother commerce. Such infrastructure connected Caracas to interior regions of the province. Company shipping increased communication and cacao trade between Venezuela and New Spain, Havana, and Puerto Rico.[31]

The Company also proved its mettle as a coastal policing power. Throughout the colonial period, tepid imperial financial support and contradictory crown policies, which emphasized hindering contraband while not provoking war with foreign powers, had doomed sustainable coast guard operations. The fleets and land-based units that had sprung up were locally financed, ineffectual, and sporadically operational.[32] In contrast, the Caracas Company prom-

31. On early developments to Venezuela's economy and imperial revenues, see F[rançois Joseph] de Pons, *A Voyage to the Eastern Part of Terra Firma, or the Spanish Main, in South America, during the Years 1801, 1802, 1803, and 1804: Containing a Description of the Territory under the Jurisdiction of the Captain-General of Caraccas . . .*, II (New York, 1806), 271-277; Morales Padrón, *Rebelión contra la Compañía de Caracas*, 89; Otto Pikaza, *Don Gabriel José de Zuloaga en la gobernación de Venezuela (1737-1747)* (Seville, 1963), 90-91; Amézaga Aresti, *Hombres de la Compañía Guipuzcoana*, 31. On the rise in cacao exports, see de Pons, *Voyage to the Eastern Part of Terra Firma*, II, 273; Vivas Pineda, *La aventura naval*, 43; Morales Padrón, *Rebelión contra la Compañía de Caracas*, 19. During the following fifteen years (1749-1764), annual Company cacao exports to Spain would reach the 50,000 fanega mark only twice, in 1763 and 1764 (*Real Compañía Guipuzcoana de Caracas: Noticias historiales practicas de los sucessos, y adelantamientos de esta Compañía, desde su fundacion año de 1728, hasta el de 1764 . . .* [(Madrid?), 1765], 158-159). On infrastructural improvements, see Iturriaga, *Manifiesto*, 9v-14f; Mercedes M. Alvarez F., *Comercio y comerciantes y sus proyecciones en la independencia venezolana* (Caracas, 1964), 25; Andrés Bello, *Resumen de la historia de Venezuela* (1810; rpt. Caracas, 1978), 43-45; Amézaga Aresti, *El elemento vasco*, 17; Piñero, "Cacao Economy of the Eighteenth-Century Province of Caracas," *HAHR*, LXVIII (1988), 97; Lombardi, *Venezuela: The Search for Order*, 97; Estornés Lasa, *La Real Compañía Guipuzcoana de Navegación de Caracas*, 66-75.

32. In 1723, the crown gave two Cádiz merchant financiers, Alonzo Ruiz Colorado and Juán Francisco Melero, permission to send two ships to the central coast of Venezuela as for-

ised a substantial and regular *armadilla* at little cost to the imperial treasury. Using its own vessels instead of relying on Spanish ships offered the Company strategic advantages, as well. Its private fleet insulated the Company somewhat from both the vagaries of shipping costs and more pronounced governmental oversight of its patrols.[33]

The Company's initial tenure in Venezuela witnessed the most stringent anticontraband measures in the colony's history. A paramilitary fleet of between ten and twenty ships and several hundred men a year patrolled coastal waters, harassing foreign and domestic shipping suspected of illicit trade. Slave trade numbers from Curaçao testify to the Company's initial success in policing contraband. The 1730s marked the lowest decade of slaves imported into Curaçao for resale between 1657 and 1778, indicating that the market for them in Venezuela had been thoroughly disrupted. One researcher found 263 entries of Company coast guard impoundments *(presas)* of foreign and Venezuelan ships between 1750 and 1780 in the admittedly incomplete records of the Archivo General de la Nación. In 1764, Company literature claimed that it had spent 4,800,000 pesos over the previous thirty years on coast guard expenses. Fighting against the prospects of trade liberalization, Company leaders argued that "only by the fire and vigilance of the coast guard" could the commerce of the province be defended against foreign powers.[34]

The Company's economic and military capacities quickly made it the primary governing force in the province. Like other trading companies of the era, the Caracas Company demonstrated its sovereignty as a sort of state unto

---

profit anticontraband forces. Their business was short-lived and of negligible importance in enforcing Spanish trade law in the region. See Contrabando en las Costas de Venezuela, y en Caracas, Real orden sobe destinación de guardacostas para celarlo, Cádiz, Apr. 12, 1723, AGNC, Contrabandos, VII, fols. 576-587; G. Earl Sanders, "Counter-Contraband in Spanish America: Handicaps of the Governors in the Indies," *Americas*, XXXIV (1977), 59-80.

33. Vivas Pineda, *La aventura naval*, 34, 44.

34. The records of the Archivo General de la Nación (Venezuela) list only some of the many ship confiscations carried out by Company coast guard patrols over the course of its tenure. Other presas are in the Archivo General de Indias and the Archivo General de la Nación (Colombia). Additionally, many ship confiscations were, no doubt, never recorded, owing to fraud. See Vicente de Amézaga Aresti, *Vicente Antonio de Icuza: Comandante de corsarios* (Caracas, 1966), 200. On the Company's coast guard, see *Real Compañía Guipuzcoana de Caracas: Noticias historiales*, 114; de Pons, *Voyage to the Eastern Part of Terra Firma*, II, 276; Pikaza, *Don Gabriel José de Zuloaga*, 64. On its effects on the slave trade, see Alex Borucki, "Trans-Imperial History in the Making of the Slave Trade to Venezuela, 1526-1811," *Itinerario*, XXXVI (2012), 39. "Only by the fire and vigilance of the coast guard": *Real Compañía Guipuzcoana de Caracas: Noticias historiales*, 104.

itself through the creation or management of legal and political institutions. Its maritime forces asserted the legitimacy of Company jurisdiction and distinguished licit merchants from interlopers. It handpicked the governor, usually from among Basque candidates. The governor then received a yearly payout of between two and four thousand pesos from the Company for his role as an arbiter *(juez conservador)* for the venture in Venezuela. His secretary received one thousand pesos annually to defend the legal suits and rights of the Company. At the lower administrative rungs, the Company helped appoint prize court judges to deliberate over ships seized by its maritime forces, uniting coast guard and maritime judiciary functions under Company prerogative. Caracas and Maracaibo municipal administrations became a revolving door for former Company employees, many of whom never returned to the Basque Country. These far-reaching manipulations quickly made the province's judicial and administrative systems intolerant of anything contrary to the Company's interests.[35]

The Company also brought a large and occupationally diverse population to Venezuela that altered the province's social fabric. Mariners, merchants, carpenters, office workers, and sailors all came to populate the colony. At its peak, the Company had nearly seven hundred armed Basques at its disposal. These outsiders were a tight-knit group that gradually infiltrated Venezuelan society.[36]

35. Philip J. Stern has argued that the British East India Company's ability to make laws, collect taxes, provide protection, punish interlopers, and regulate economic and civic life made it a state untethered from the British nation-state. He contends that scholars, in this case, could apply concepts of state formation to a corporation. Although the Caracas Company's control was neither as all-encompassing nor unregulated as that of the EIC, it certainly assumed some state functions in the realms of commerce, politics, and law (Stern, *The Company-State: Corporate Sovereignty and the Early Modern Foundations of the British Empire in India* [New York, 2011], 3-14, 29-31, 44-46). On Company presence in the province's government, see Lucas Guillermo Castillo Lara, *La aventura fundacional de los Isleños: Panaquire y Juan Francisco de León* (Caracas, 1983), 63, 185-188, 196-198; Luis Alberto Sucre, *Gobernadores y capitanes generales de Venezuela* (1928; rpt. Caracas, 1964), 257-268; Morales Padrón, *Rebelión contra la Compañía de Caracas,* 75; Enrique Bernardo Nuñez, *Miranda; o, El tema de la libertad / Juan Francisco de León; o, El levantamiento contra la Compañía Guipuzcoana* (1950; rpt. Caracas, 1979), 67; Belin Vázquez de Ferrer, "Maracaibo y su Puerto en la dinámica del poder local y regional, 1574-1821," in Johanna von Grafenstein Gareis, ed., *El Golfo-Caribe y sus puertos,* I, *1600-1850* (Mexico City, 2006), 167; Cardozo Uzcátegui, *Los mantuanos,* 164-165.

36. Amezaga Iribarren, "La Real Compañía Guipuzcoana de Caracas," *Sancho el Sabio,* XXIII (2005), 197-199; Amézaga Aresti, *El elemento vasco,* 18; Alvarez F., *Comercio y comerciantes,* 6-9.

The Caracas Company supported its dominance over Venezuelan affairs by channeling monetary aid to the crown and to royal projects. During the War of Jenkins' Ear (1739–1748), the Company gave 300,000 pesos to the monarchy to help pay for the fleet at El Ferrol in northwestern Spain and donated five ships to carry one thousand reinforcements to the Caribbean theater of that war. Company ships participated in the defense of Havana against the British in 1742 and of La Guaira and Puerto Cabello in 1743. It claimed to have lost eight ships to the British over the course of the conflict. Between 1747 and 1749 alone, the Company averred that it had paid nearly fifty million reales to the royal treasury in taxes and donations. It also boasted of spending 320,000 pesos to build or upgrade fortifications in La Guaira, Puerto Cabello, Cumaná, Margarita, and Trinidad.[37]

Despite the Caracas Company's promises of greater prosperity for Venezuela as a whole, locals rapidly came to resent the intrusion of these outsiders. At first, the possibilities of using Company resources to stimulate provincial development enticed Caracas's power brokers. According to one chronicler, "The principal subjects of the city, excessively supported the seductive persuasions of Olavarriaga and Beato . . . and embraced without reservation their proposals." Over time, however, elites saw the Company's meddling in government as a threat to their political control over the province through the cabildo.[38]

Moreover, both elite and petty merchants perceived the danger to their interests posed by the Company's ascendancy in the cacao trade. With its dominant share of the province's legal commerce, the Caracas Company depressed the prices it would pay producers for their cacao and controlled access to loans. From a pre-Company rate of around twenty-two pesos per fanega (equaling 110 pounds), the going price for cacao during the Company's first twenty years plummeted to an average of eight pesos per fanega and in some cases as low as four to five pesos per fanega. To curtail private cacao trading to New Spain, Company ship captains deployed a strategy known as the *alter-*

37. Kuethe and Andrien, *Spanish Atlantic World,* 142; Amezaga Iribarren, "La Real Compañía Guipuzcoana de Caracas," *Sancho el Sabio,* XXIII (2005), 188; *Real Compañía Guipuzcoana de Caracas: Noticias historiales,* 8; Amézaga Aresti, *Vicente Antonio de Icuza,* 13; Iturriaga, *Manifiesto,* 10f-10v.

38. Extracta de carta del Gobernador de Caracas, n.d., AGI, Caracas, 418; Francisco Morales Padrón, "La Real Compañía Guipuzcoana de Caracas y la sociedad venezolana," in Escobedo Mansilla, Rivera Medina, and Chapa Imaz, eds., *Los vascos y América,* 217; Morales Padrón, *Rebelión contra la Compañía de Caracas,* 33-34, 43. "Excessively supported the seductive persuasions of Olavarriaga and Beato": Blas José Terrero, *Teatro de Venezuela y Caracas* (Caracas, 1967), 58.

*nativa* system. Because the alternativa gave Company vessels the privilege of loading their cargoes at Venezuelan docks before any private traders could do so, Company mariners intentionally delayed filling their ships to capacity until they had boxed Venezuelan merchants out of the Mexican trade and into bad deals. Company buyers purchased only what the overseas market would buy at a high price and left excess cacao to rot in port. The Company also later retracted its promise to reserve one-third of its ships' capacity for Venezuelan planters' private cacao trading. The inability of Venezuelan producers to sell their crop legally at anything approaching a fair market price ruined their fortunes.[39]

Moreover, the Company wavered in its commitment to another pillar of its contract: provisioning the colony. On paper, the Compañía Guipuzcoana noticeably increased imports to the province. In addition to the intercolonial trade Venezuelan subjects already engaged in with Mexico and the Spanish Caribbean, they now received at least two ships per year loaded with products from the Caracas Company. Its official papers heralded the great bounty of items it brought into the province from all corners of Spain, including cotton, silk, wool, and taffeta fabric, ribbons and thread, and finished clothes and accessories such as handkerchiefs and hats. The Company also brought dry goods like tableware, firearms, nails, paper, and wood for furniture. Finally, it claimed to import foods such as olive oil, sardines, wine, and flour. According to midcentury Company literature, its shipments only supplemented an independent retinue of goods and consumables coming from New Spain, the Canary Islands, Mérida, Cumaná, Cartagena, Santo Domingo, the Orinoco River delta, and from illicit Dutch sources in the Caribbean. These facts, in the opinion of Compañía Guipuzcoana officials, struck down claims of a despotic Company monopoly or of material shortages. They argued that the surest way to a commercially "fatal epoch of ruin" would be a return to individual register

39. On cacao prices, see Junta, Caracas, Apr. 22, 1749, AGI, Caracas, 937; Don Julian de Arriaga y Rivera to Don Juan Manuel de Goyzueta and Don Mathiais Urroz, Caracas, Mar. 29, 1750, AGI, Caracas, 418; Ferry, *Colonial Elite,* 138; Nuñez, *Miranda / Juan Francisco de León,* 66; Brito Figueroa, *La estructura económica,* 256. On the alternativa and its effects, see Ynforme de la Provincia y Cavildo Esclesiastico de Santiago de Leon de Caracas sobre la pretension y estado del Cacao que sale de aquella Provincia segun el deznio que esta dentro, Caracas, Nov. 7, 1734, AGI, Caracas, 438; Interrogatorio (made by Juan Francisco de León), n.d., AGI, Caracas, 418; Gárate Ojanguren, *La Real Compañía Guipuzcoana,* 301. For information on the alternativa system, see Ferry, *Colonial Elite,* 165, 182; Kuethe and Andrien, *Spanish Atlantic World,* 162. The tercio system was not codified by a cédula but had been common practice since the Company's founding. See Arcila Farías, *Economía colonial de Venezuela,* 195.

ships or the movement to free trade. In the minds of Company directors, these misguided plans would minimize legal goods entering the province.[40]

But Company claims never squared with the realities of Venezuelan importation. Though lists of what the Company could obtain and transport from Spain were impressive, the Basque organization's ships rarely arrived so full. Even if they did, two Company ships probably would have been inadequate for the region's appetites. In 1744, Philip V wrote to Caracas Company directors regarding Caraqueño complaints of a dearth of wheat flour, liquor, and clothing. The monarch scolded Company officials for allowing conditions in the province to reach a point where "the necessities of eating and clothing themselves oblige residents to take from foreigners what this company should be offering them in abundance." Some of this scarcity was due to wartime predation by the British, which inhibited the ability of private ships to enter and exit Venezuela's ports. Nonetheless, even when cargoes did arrive, merchandise sold almost exclusively in Company stores at prices 20 percent higher on average than Dutch contraband. According to one British observer, Venezuelan consumers received in return "such Wares and Merchandize as probably have been lodged in their stores for 20 years a back." Despite the increase in legal goods entering the colony because of the Company's shipping capabilities, the province might have experienced a net decline in imports during the Company's heyday (1728–1749) owing to its zealous patrolling of coastal waters for contraband.[41]

Locals expressed their dismay at how the Company shirked its responsibilities to provision the colony. Complaints of inadequate, substandard, and prohibitively expensive goods and foodstuffs were common. On several occa-

40. *Real Compañía Guipuzcoana de Caracas: Noticias historiales,* 129, 140-142; Iturriaga, *Manifiesto,* 5v-6f.

41. Consider that, before the Caracas Company, Venezuela had only sporadic coast guard patrols with little central organization. It is not surprising, therefore, that the number of contraband seizures in the Comisos and Diversos sections of the AGNC and various Audiencia sections of the AGI spike with the arrival of the Caracas Company in 1728. "Oblige residents to take from foreigners": El Rey a los Señores Directores de la Real Compania Guipuzcoana de Caracas, Madrid, Sept. 30, 1744, AGI, Caracas, 928. "Such Wares and Merchandize": Observations on the Carraccas and Province of Cumaná by Louis Flislale to Major General John Dalling, Governor of Jamaica, Nov. 16, 1782, BL, Add. MSS, 36806, fol. 173. On British contributions to trade scarcities, see Celestino Andrés Arauz Monfante, *El contrabando holandes en el Caribe durante la primera mitad del siglo XVIII,* I (Caracas, 1984), 135; de Pons, *Voyage to the Eastern Part of Tierra Firme,* II, 310-319. On Company stores, see Morales Padrón, *Rebelión contra la Compañía de Caracas,* 74; Aizpurua, *Curazao y la costa de Caracas,* 105.

sions, lapses in Company shipping forced Venezuelan residents to petition to buy flour from neighboring colonies. Clothes became so scarce that in 1749, the rector of the university in Caracas issued an impassioned plea for additional supplies. The province's population of 140,000 needed roughly one million pieces of clothing "to cover their nudity." He opined that just as "the laws of god and man oblige one to solicit covering for beasts, so do they for the necessity of the human condition." The rector chastised the Company that "since its establishment has allowed for a continual dearth of the most common and usual goods, of foodstuffs and supplies . . . subjecting [the province's] inhabitants to an intolerable nudity and compelling them by necessity to look for a remedy wherever the possibility presents itself." When Company merchandise did reach Venezuela, price gouging frequently put it out of the populace's reach. One complaint noted that the Company bought barrels of flour at ten pesos each and then sold them to the general public at twenty-three pesos per barrel.[42]

At the same time that Venezuelans went without basic supplies, the Company hauled in tidy profits. Shareholders earned dividends between 20 and 30 percent in the 1730s and 1740s. A twenty-peso difference between the Company's buying and selling price on cacao per fanega easily covered overhead expenses.[43]

These developments fueled a shared anxiety among Venezuelan coastal inhabitants that the Company had come to monopolize the province's economic and political resources for its own extractive gain. The wealthiest cacao producers mitigated this dominance as best they could. They grudgingly formed

42. For complaints against the Company, see Declaración de Don Juan Camejo, vecino de Caracas, Caracas, Dec. 14, 1747, and Declaración de Francisco Domingo Bejaramo, Caracas, Dec. 15, 1747, AGI, Caracas, 891; Governor Luis Francisco de Castellanos to the King, La Guaira, Oct. 15, 1749, AGI, Caracas, 418; Gárate Ojanguren, *La Real Compañía Guipuzcoana,* 301; Morales Padrón, *Rebelión contra la Compañía de Caracas,* 22-23; Morón, *History of Venezuela,* 33. The problem of insufficient flour continued over the course of the eighteenth century, particularly in the outer reaches of Venezuela (El Gobernador y Oficiales Reales de Cumaná a D. Julián de Arriaga, Cumaná, Nov. 8, 1771, AGI, Caracas, 541). "To cover their nudity" and clothing shortages: Petición del Sr. Rector de la Real y Pontificia Universidad, Caracas, June 12, 1749, AGI, Caracas, 419. For price gouging, see Interrogatorio, n.d., AGI, Caracas, 418. Subjects of Havana, Cuba, experienced similar problems of inadequate provisioning and price gouging in dealing with another Basque monopoly company, the Real Compañía de Comercio de la Habana, from 1740 to 1790 (Sherry Johnson, *Climate and Catastrophe in Cuba and the Atlantic World in the Age of Revolution* [Chapel Hill, N.C., 2011], 11, 35).

43. Gárate Ojanguren, *La Real Compañía Guipuzcoana,* 46; Vivas Pineda, *La aventura naval,* 43; Morón, *History of Venezuela,* 70.

economic, if not political, alliances with the Basques decades after the Company's arrival. Many prominent families of Caracas became shareholders in the Company after membership was opened to creoles in 1751. By contrast, petty merchants and planters without influence felt cut out from their own province's wealth and commercial boom.[44]

Undergirding this concern was the Caracas Company's role in smuggling enforcement. Whether through neglect or commercial restrictions, Venezuelans were used to sparse legal trade opportunities. As one governor of Venezuela put it in the year before the Company's founding, his subjects benefited from "the disorder whereby foreigners take cacao and tobacco from this province and introduce clothing" into it.[45] But the initiation of Company patrols cut into the provincial refuge of smuggling. Venezuelan illicit trade dropped during the first twenty years of Company rule. Coast guard ships rounded up contrabandists in record numbers (their fifty-six years of prize court cases encompass forty-two volumes in Venezuela's Archivo General de la Nación). The regulations of corsairing allowed maritime patrols to collect between one-third and one-half of the value of impounded contraband. In 1750, the Company's board of directors proposed further crew member compensation for captured goods to make up for planned cuts in salaries. Coast guardsmen therefore had every incentive to seize goods, whether they were illicit or not. Prize money from contraband caused jurisdictional disputes between royal officials and Company men that made the former resent the organization's presence in Venezuela. Coastal traders coming into contact with these forces had more to fear than just property loss; Company coast guard patrols frequently assaulted both foreign and domestic smugglers, earning coast guardsmen a violent reputation.[46]

44. Joseph Luis de Cisneros, *Descripción exacta de la Provincia de Venezuela* (1764; rpt. Caracas, 1981), 121-122; Gárate Ojanguren, *La Real Compañía Guipuzcoana,* 87.

45. "Disorder whereby foreigners take cacao and tobacco": Auto de Diego Portales y Meneses, Governor of Venezuela, AGNV, Diversos, XII, fol. 180.

46. I agree with the evidentiary basis of scholarly estimates on the drop in illicit trade. Eugenio Piñero, for example, points to the increase in cacao prices in Amsterdam during this period as proof of decreased smuggling (Piñero, "Cacao Economy of the Eighteenth-Century Province of Caracas," *HAHR,* LXVIII [1988], 91). Also see Hussey, *Caracas Company,* 76; Aizpurua, *Curazao y la costa de Caracas,* 154-159; Wim Klooster, *Illicit Riches: Dutch Trade in the Caribbean, 1648-1795* (Leiden, 1998), 146-152. On financial incentives for enforcement, see Lance Grahn, *The Political Economy of Smuggling: Regional Informal Economies in Early Bourbon New Granada* (Boulder, Colo., 1997), 25; González F., *La Guayra,* 122; Gárate Ojanguren, *La Real Compañía Guipuzcoana,* 42; Klooster, *Illicit Riches,* 148; Aizpurua, *Curazao y la costa de Caracas,* 15. On problems between the coast guard and royal officials and

Tighter enforcement of illicit trade by the Company did nothing to quiet Venezuelans' persistent whispers that Company officials themselves were deeply involved in smuggling. Tax fraud resulting from Company ships' transporting undeclared cacao to Spain and untaxed luxury items to Venezuela was common. Mariners and ship captains frequently overloaded these vessels with undeclared items to such an extent that the ships became unseaworthy. In 1738, customs officials in Spain seized one Company ship that had failed to declare 40,000 pesos of Mexican silver. Company men in port proved no more scrupulous than their seafaring counterparts. Local exasperation with the Caracas Company and its hypocrisy began very soon after its arrival in Venezuela, but it took another generation for metropolitan admiration for the venture to dissipate.[47]

## NEW IDEAS OF REFORM AND THE DISMANTLING OF THE CARACAS COMPANY

In the latter half of the eighteenth century, the Bourbon relationship with the Caracas Company soured. In part, the unrest caused by the Company's low cacao prices, poor provisioning, and heavy-handed commercial enforcement frightened the king and his ministers in Madrid. The rebellion of Juan Francisco de León from 1749 to 1751 served as a wake-up call for imperial authorities to recognize the growing colonial frustration with the Company. This insurgency—which developed out of subjects' anxieties about low prices paid for cacao, Basque control over Venezuelan institutions, and crackdowns on smuggling—had as its stated goal the removal of the Compañía Guipuzcoana from Venezuela. It signaled Venezuelan merchants' frustration with the Company's brand of productive, but manipulative, legal commerce. Small cacao producers and traders spearheaded the rebellion in an attempt to defend understandings of economic fair play bound up in extralegal trade and lax imperial oversight of coastal communities. At the height of the uprising, a multiclass group of protestors destabilized colonial control by temporarily expelling both the governor of Venezuela and the Company from Caracas. The Company's first incarnation (between 1728 and 1749) came undone because its directors re-

---

Venezuelans, see ibid., 159, 204-205. This book will discuss coast guard violence more thoroughly in Chapters 4 and 5.

47. Expediente sobre aberiguar el fraude de 13 cajones que se tubo noticia traia de Caracas el navio de la Compania Santa Ana que arrivo a Cadiz, Caracas, 1738, AGI, Caracas, 926; Vivas Pineda, *La aventura naval,* 18, 64-66.

fused to acknowledge the constraints of the existing commercial situation and instead sought simultaneously to squeeze merchants and rip up smuggling by the roots. After León's rebellion, a worried Spanish monarchy reinstituted the Company in a chastened form by stripping it of much of its commercial autonomy and involving Venezuelan creoles in its decision making.[48]

Aside from local factors, the larger cause of the Company's fall from favor was that it was out of step with evolving philosophies of Bourbon political economy. A new crop of reformers, such as Pedro Rodríguez de Campomanes y Pérez, José de Gálvez, and Francisco Saavedra de Sangronis, emphasized trade liberalization as the means to Spanish commercial revival. Although unrestricted free trade with foreign empires was a bridge too far for these officials, they proposed greatly expanding the number of Spanish and Spanish American ports that could trade with one another. Comercio libre within the empire threatened Company privileges of exclusivity. Reformers saw old monopolies as antithetical to commercial circulation that would encourage the growth of agricultural exports in peripheries like Venezuela. New wealth generation relied on free exchange of these products rather than closed commerce in precious metals.[49]

Although the Company had promoted Venezuelan cacao for decades, reformers from the reign of Charles III onward criticized the deleterious effects of its monopoly. In the 1760s and 1770s, Campomanes, a political economist, and Gálvez, the minister of the Indies, both singled out the Caracas Company as a symbol of commercial backwardness in the empire. Campomanes blamed the Company for destabilizing Venezuela with its price fixing, its cacao cartel, and its unwillingness to supply the province with goods. Rather than further provincial integration into the Spanish Empire, the Compañía Guipuzcoana had increased Venezuelan smuggling by cutting subjects off from profitable markets. Campomanes even blamed the decline of the Basque whaling industry on the Company, which had convinced scores of seafarers to serve on its ships rather than whaling vessels. He recommended remedying the "vice

48. Pedro Rodríguez Campomanes, *Reflexiones sobre el comercio español a Indias* (1762) (Madrid, 1988), 76; Alí Enrique López Bohórquez, *Los ministros de la Audiencia de Caracas (1786-1810): Caracterización de una elite burocrática del poder español en Venezuela* (Caracas, 1984), 38; Miguel Izard, "Contrabandistas, comerciantes e ilustrados," *BA*, XXVIII (1978), 27; Aizpurua, *Curazao y la costa de Caracas*, 17. Chapter 8 deals with the specifics of crown reforms to the Company after the León Rebellion in more detail.

49. For the viewpoints of these later reformers, see Stein and Stein, *Apogee of Empire*, ix, 20-40, 295, 351; Stein and Stein, *Edge of Crisis*, 4; Cardozo Uzcátegui, *Los mantuanos*, 31, 49; Kuethe and Andrien, *Spanish Atlantic World*, 291.

of exclusivity" that had rendered the Company inefficient and decadent by revoking its monopoly over Venezuela and allowing it to trade freely in the Americas as recompense. José de Gálvez cited the commercial inefficiency of the Company as well as the projections of Spanish economists who claimed annual trade from the province might increase from 400,000 pesos per year to as much as 800,000 to 1,000,000 pesos if trade there were liberalized. Gálvez echoed Campomanes's concerns about the Company's trading potential; in addition, he lost confidence in its defensive capabilities when a group of Company ships he had dispatched to serve on a wartime transatlantic convoy fell into the hands of British admiral George Rodney in 1780, near the Basque port of Finisterre.[50]

Bureaucrats in charge of the province agreed with highly placed metropolitan reformers. From the time of his appointment in 1777, José de Ábalos, the first intendant of Venezuela after the institution was established in the colony in 1776, condemned the Compañía Guipuzcoana for neither living up to its promises to provision the colony nor fully exploiting its cacao riches. Company domination had presented Venezuelan "vassals with the pitiful setback that came from misallocating the considerable benefits found in their soil into a few privileged hands." Ábalos pointed to widespread smuggling throughout the ranks of Caracas Company employees as proof that even its vaunted antismuggling efforts had been disingenuous. He argued that demolishing the Company would allow the province "to finally breathe freely and to bring to light the riches that, sadly until now, have remained buried to the detriment of the state and the common good of two continents." In the last year of the Company's tenure, 1783, Francisco Saavedra, the second intendant and a disciple of Gálvez, described the Company as "ruinous" to cacao producers. Its monopoly enabled employees to shortchange these planters. Drawing an obvious contrast to the Company, he contended that "commerce subdivided into many hands would make this province flourish." Saavedra and Ábalos both

50. For Gálvez and Campomanes's critiques of the Company's monopoly, see Campomanes, *Reflexiones sobre el comercio español,* 76-77; Vivas Pineda, *La aventura naval,* 36; María Teresa Zubiri Marín, "Etapa final y caída de la Compañía Guipuzcoana de Caracas (1777-1785)," *Pedrables,* XI (1991), 158-161; Hussey, *Caracas Company,* 277. "Vice of exclusivity": Campomanes, *Reflexiones sobre el comercio español,* 68. Rodney's seizure seems to have played a significant role in the Caracas Company's losing its commercial monopoly over Venezuelan cacao trading with Spain in 1781. See Lourdes Díaz-Trechuelo, "De 'Compañía Guipuzcoana de Caracas' a 'Compañía de Filipinas,'" in Escobedo Mansilla, Rivera Medina, and Chapa Imaz, eds., *Los vascos y América,* 363-364; Vivas Pineda, *La aventura naval,* 347, 349.

believed that an influx of liberalized legal trade would deter smuggling more effectively than costly maritime patrols.[51]

In addition to these attitudes, changing commercial legislation meant that the Company's days were numbered. The comercio libre decrees guaranteed many Spanish American ports unfettered trade with each other and a host of peninsular ports in 1765. Many more harbors received these rights in 1774, 1776, 1777, and 1778. New Spain and Venezuela did not gain similar status until 1789.[52] This lag hurt the province when ports in Spanish South America gained the right to trade with New Spain in 1774. Soon, cacao shipped from the Ecuadorian coastal port of Guayaquil outpaced Venezuelan stock in Mexico. Whereas the Company could only legally send 20,000 fanegas of cacao to New Spain via Veracruz, there were no restrictions on the cacao Guayaquil's merchants could bring into New Spain through Acapulco.[53]

51. "Bring to light the riches": Joseph de Ábalos to Joseph de Gálvez, Caracas, Sept. 29, 1780, AGI, Caracas, 784. For further information on Ábalos's objections, see Manuel Lucena Giraldo, "Introducción," in Lucena Giraldo, ed., *Premoniciones de la independencia de Iberoamérica: Las reflexiones de Jose de Ábalos y el Conde de Aranda sobre la situación de la América española a finales del siglo XVIII* (Madrid, 2003), 26; María Teresa Zubiri Marín, "José de Ábalos, primer intendente de Venezuela (1777-1783)," *BA,* XXXVIII (1988), 297. Saavedra's opinions on the value of lower prices and more abundant legal trade versus the inefficacy of punishing smugglers were common to late-eighteenth-century reformers (Paquette, *Enlightenment, Governance, and Reform,* 104). "Commerce subdivided into many hands": Cardozo Uzcátegui, *Los mantuanos,* 100, 102. For Ábalos's preference for comercio libre over coast guard patrols, which royal officials in Veracruz, Mexico, supported, see "Representación del Intendente Electo de Venezuela al Secretario del Despacho Universal, D. José de Gálvez," *Revista de historia,* V (1960), 91-103; "Informe de los oficiales reales de Veracruz sobre la representación del Intendente de Caracas," ibid., VI (1961), 156, 174. For Campomanes's argument for a similar Caribbean-wide approach encouraging liberal commerce over enforcement, see Campomanes, *Reflexiones sobre el comercio español,* 75.

52. The dates in which various ports and colonies gained comercio libre rights to trade freely with other Spanish ports are as follows: Santo Domingo, Puerto Rico, Margarita, Trinidad, Cádiz, Seville, Alicante, Cartagena, Málaga, Barcelona, Santander, Coruña, and Gijón (1765), Louisiana and Campeche (1768), Yucatán (1770), New Granada, Peru (1774), Santa Marta (1776), Rio de la Hacha (1777), Buenos Aires and Chile (1778), New Spain and Venezuela (1789). See Arcila Farías, *Economía colonial de Venezuela,* 349-350.

53. Guillermina del Valle Pavón, "Cacao de Guayaquil y apertura comercial: La promoción del comercio de cacao y azúcar a través del Consulado de México," in Nikolaus Böttcher, Bernd Hausberger, and Antonio Ibarra, eds., *Redes y negocios globales en el mundo ibérico, siglos XVI-XVIII* (Orlando, Fla., 2011), 239-240, 262; "Representación del intendente electo de Venezuela," *Revista de historia,* V (1960), 91-94; "Informe de los oficiales reales de Veracruz," ibid., VI (1961), 152; Díaz-Trechuelo, "De 'Compañía Guipuzcoana de Caracas' a 'Compañía de Filipinas,'" in Escobedo Mansilla, Rivera Medina, and Chapa Imaz, eds., *Los vascos y América,* 363.

Even before the 1789 arrival of comercio libre to Venezuela, some Bourbon provisions benefited the province. Metropolitan authorities abolished old duties on certain commercial items, legalized the direct sale of Venezuelan mules to Spanish Caribbean islands, and permitted locals to purchase a pardon *(composición)* for illicit goods they had bought unknowingly. A subsequent round of 1777 reforms opened up trading with the French Antilles for food in wartime, as well as slaves and hard currency during peacetime. The only restriction was that Venezuelans merchants were not to sell cacao for these items.[54]

In the late 1770s and early 1780s, two developments assured the Company's demise by revoking its most treasured privileges. The 1776 creation of the Intendancy of Caracas hobbled the Company's profitability. With the arrival of this new administrative jurisdiction, the crown removed coast guard powers from the Company. From then on, the intendant, rather than any company official, became the ultimate judge over ship seizures. In 1781, a royal order voided the Company's monopoly concessions over Venezuelan cacao commerce to Spain. By forfeiting its monopoly and the right to patrol Venezuelan waters, the Caracas Company not only lost its dominance over legal trade; it gave up its unobstructed ability to smuggle.[55]

Despite earning the distaste of Bourbon reformers in the latter half of the eighteenth century, the Company was a survivor. Its presence and profitability (until the last decade of its life) made Venezuela one of the last two colonies in the empire to receive comercio libre privileges. In essence, an early Bourbon Reform retarded the attempts of a later one to take root.

## CONCLUSION

Bourbon Reform projects were multifaceted and, at times, contradictory. The under-studied Caracas Company is noteworthy in this context for several reasons. First, its long tenure allows for the mapping of changing commercial ideologies through the lens of one specific entity over nearly the whole course of the Bourbon Reform period. Second, in very few instances over the course of the eighteenth-century reformulation of the Spanish Empire did experimentation become so far-reaching or so dominant. The Company gained mastery

54. Aizpurua, *Curazao y la costa de Caracas,* 183; P. Michael McKinley, *Pre-Revolutionary Caracas: Politics, Economy, and Society, 1777-1811* (Cambridge, 1985), 39; Arcila Farías, *Economía colonial de Venezuela,* 351, 357.

55. Cardozo Uzcátegui, *Los mantuanos,* 157-159.

over the political, economic, and military apparatus of the province in the century before its independence. Assessing Venezuelan history over the lion's share of the eighteenth century without accounting for the Company is nearly impossible. Third, the Company was the most successful of Spain's transatlantic monopoly trading companies. As such, it represents an important yardstick for assessing the efficacy of this approach in the Iberian Atlantic.[56]

The Caracas Company came into existence at a crucial juncture for the Spanish Atlantic system. As a new dynasty arose and the trade fleet model of exclusive commerce disintegrated, novel port regulations and developments tried to contribute new revenue streams into imperial coffers. Reformers also sought to improve finances by eradicating the old colonial vice of illicit trade. Despite its imperfections, the Caracas Company exemplified a first initiative to reignite an atrophied scheme of imperial trade. In the eyes of reformers, the outsourced entity might serve as a corrective to the endemic extralegal behavior that enveloped a recently thriving province. But modifying the commercial culture of Venezuela proved to be a lengthy and contested process.

The Company's time in Venezuela reveals that economic development and colonial (or community) development were not the same thing. The Caracas Company's balance sheets appeared stout for most of its existence. It significantly raised Venezuela's profile within the Spanish imperial system. Although comercio libre and economic liberalism ultimately propelled Venezuela to an economic boom in the 1790s, the metropolitan connections and infrastructural improvements that the Company fostered from 1728 to 1784 were significant contributing factors. Nevertheless, Venezuelan subjects of various stripes continued to believe that the Caracas Company had cut them out of their colony's own economic rejuvenation. Furthermore, the Company had impeded the traditional coastal mainstay of smuggling. As an outside entity, it had become burdensome to Venezuelan trade. On this, for very different reasons, peripheral subjects and metropolitan political economists could agree.[57]

56. Ibid., 36. Seven monopoly trading companies were envisioned over the course of the eighteenth century, but only four actually came into existence. They were the Real Compañía Guipuzcoana de Caracas, the Real Compañía de la Habana, the Real Compañía de San Fernando de Sevilla, and the Real Compañía de Barcelona (Patrick O'Flanagan, *Port Cities of Atlantic Iberia, c. 1500-1900* [Burlington, Vt., 2008], 85). On the success of the Compañía Guipuzcoana compared to other companies, see Fisher, *Economic Aspects of Spanish Imperialism,* 129.

57. John Fisher, *Commercial Relations between Spain and Spanish America in the Era of Free Trade, 1778-1796* (Liverpool, 1985), 45, 76; Fisher, *Economic Aspects of Spanish Imperialism,* 156, 176.

The movement from enforcement strategies to transgressions requires a mental reorientation. The granular character of smuggling both interacted with and defied overarching attempts to regulate the Spanish Atlantic. The next three chapters shift from the perspective of the state to that of its antagonists and accomplices. What emerges is a different colonial history. In the internal dynamics of contraband commerce, imperial identity faded to the background, while concepts of trust and accepted criminality came to the fore. Smuggling was not an "honor among thieves" enterprise. Yet mutual understandings between non-Spanish contrabandists, Venezuelan merchants, and Spanish officials established an equilibrium of how much illicit trade could take place. In the daily interimperial interaction of smuggling, different groups learned evasion, balanced risk and reward, and facilitated a consistent marketplace. The deep integration of these systems of exchange into Venezuelan coastal life opened its participants' social horizons beyond the confines of empire-bound territorialism.

# 4

# *Networking Statelessness in a Bordered World*

## Foreign Smugglers

Despite the laws and intentions of imperial bureaucrats, coastal Spanish America was an international marketplace. Shoals, coves, and harbors teemed with foreign merchants buying the agricultural and mineral bounty of Spanish America in return for European finished products unavailable to many Spanish Americans through intraimperial trade. Whereas Spanish trade fleets provided for the centers of imperial power in the Americas (mainly Mexico and Peru), inhabitants of more far-flung crown possessions like Venezuela depended on the illegally imported wares provided by foreigners. Regional, multipoint contraband trade shaped the economies and social interactions of coastal Venezuelan towns and made their shores a crossroads for a motley composition of maritime businessmen. Smugglers tested the boundaries of mercantilism and internationalized commerce in an empire legally closed to outside business.

Consider the case of Manuel Michel, a French captain from Martinique accused of smuggling. Spanish coast guard forces captured Michel and his eight crewmen in eastern Venezuela in 1768. The French captain claimed that his ship, the *Saint Charles,* had anchored on the coast to make essential repairs before continuing on to Dutch Curaçao. He held licenses from the French monarchy to trade in the Indies, though not in Spanish territories. His vessel transported mostly liquor and a few slaves bound for Dutch Curaçao, but it had stopped off already in English Grenada to trade some of its cargo. The multi-imperial voyage, along with the fact that the *Saint Charles* had landed on Spanish shores, raised the suspicions of commercial officials that he had intended to trade illegally with Spanish subjects. Michel objected to these suppositions, claiming his goods never made landfall in the Spanish dominions. Despite his complaints, Spanish authorities confiscated his ship and its cargo.

The most fascinating part of Michel's testimony was that he conceived of the Caribbean and its surrounding territories as a collection of commercial routes independent of national designations. As a transimperial traveler and trader, he argued that Spanish commercial law applied only "to the offenses of those subjects bound to the [Spanish] king." The Spanish coast guard's liberal interpretation of what constituted incursion into Spanish territory impeded his basic ability as a businessman "to trade and transport cargo with ease." Michel stated that he had followed the rules of his sovereign (in France) and would be obedient to the laws of his destination (in Dutch Curaçao). He concluded that it was his compliance with these strictures, not those of the lands and seas he passed en route, that truly mattered. Within the framework of an imperially divided region, the French captain had asserted his right to navigate and trade freely. Michel's pluralistic legal views on eighteenth-century Caribbean commerce reflected the antagonisms inherent in interpreting wrongdoing among the overlapping colonial jurisdictions of the early modern world.[1]

We still know very little about individuals like Michel who, through their illicit voyages, blurred the cartographic lines demarcating empires. Historians have illustrated the social and economic dimensions of the Spanish-Atlantic fleet systems, large merchant firms, and transatlantic sailing. Yet those who plied the vibrant and multi-imperial coastal trading routes of the Americas are faint sketches by comparison. A host of seafaring petty traders, peddlers, and foreign merchants did business in the Spanish Empire.[2]

1. Autos contra Don Manuel Michel, Capitán de la balandra francesa "San Carlos" en 18 Marzo 1768 . . . , Caracas, July 28, 1768, AGNV, Comp Gui, XIX, fols. 314–376. For theory on convergent legal jurisdictions in the early modern world, see Lauren Benton, *Law and Colonial Cultures: Legal Regimes in World History, 1400–1900* (Cambridge, 2002), 264.

2. For existing historiography on Spanish-Atlantic trade, see Jeremy Baskes, *Staying Afloat: Risk and Uncertainty in Spanish Atlantic World Trade, 1760–1820* (Stanford, Calif., 2013); Pablo E. Pérez-Mallaína, *Spain's Men of the Sea: Daily Life on the Indies Fleets in the Sixteenth Century,* trans. Carla Rahn Phillips (Baltimore, 1998); Phillips, *Six Galleons for the King of Spain: Imperial Defense in the Early Seventeenth Century* (Baltimore, 1986); García-Baquero González, *La carrera de Indias: Suma de la contratación y océano de negocios* (Seville, 1992); Antonio García-Baquero González, *Cádiz y el Atlántico (1717–1778): El comercio colonial español bajo el monopolio gaditano,* 2 vols. (Seville, 1976); Enriqueta Vila Vilar, *Los Corzo y los Mañara: Tipos y arquetipos del mercader con Indias* (Seville, 1991); Pierre Chaunu and Huguette Chaunu, *Séville et l'Amérique au XVIe et XVIIe siècles* (Paris, 1977); Susan Midgen Socolow, *The Merchants of Buenos Aires 1778–1810: Family and Commerce* (Cambridge, 1978); J. H. Parry, *The Spanish Seaborne Empire* (New York, 1966); Clarence Henry Haring, *Trade*

This chapter uncovers the social history of foreign smugglers who served as the sinew and bone of coastal commerce in Venezuela and, by association, most of Spain's maritime peripheries. Their occupation sprang not only from Spanish American material want but also, for many, from their socioeconomic circumstances. Smuggling was one of several maritime professions open to men who were neither masters nor slaves and who thus struggled to find their place within the plantation complex that dominated the circum-Caribbean. Contraband trade provided economic opportunity and occupational stability against marginalization. From their livelihood crossing borders, illicit maritime laborers embraced views on imperial politics that emphasized statelessness and maritime transnationalism. Nevertheless, the prospect of being ensnared by the enforcement measures of the same Spanish colonies whose subjects coveted their business placed non-Spanish traders in an uneasy position.[3]

Commercial law enforcement and the evasion of it complicate any occupational portrayal of smugglers. Questions about the representativeness or truthfulness of documentation on contraband trade have caused historians to shy away from studying its practitioners. As most foreign traders appear in Spanish prize court records just once, recovering the stories of individual smugglers proves challenging. Examined as a group, however, their testi-

---

*and Navigation between Spain and the Indies in the Time of the Hapsburgs* (Cambridge, 1918). Likewise, Michael J. Jarvis points out that, for British maritime historiography, "we know much more about British and Anglo-American mariners involved in transatlantic trades than about the thousands of Anglo-American mariners and entrepreneurs who animated the equally important coastal trades" (Jarvis, *In the Eye of All Trade: Bermuda, Bermudians, and the Maritime Atlantic World, 1680–1783* [Chapel Hill, N.C., 2010], 122). In the recent literature of that field, Gregory E. O'Malley, Daniel Vickers, and W. Jeffrey Bolster have expressed serious interest in the topic (O'Malley, *Final Passages: The Intercolonial Slave Trade of British America, 1619–1807* [Chapel Hill, N.C., 2014]; Vickers with Vince Walsh, *Young Men and the Sea: Yankee Seafarers in the Age of Sail* [New Haven, Conn., 2005]; Bolster, *Black Jacks: African American Seamen in the Age of Sail* [Cambridge, Mass., 1997]). Ernesto Bassi has conducted the most thorough investigation of Spanish American coastal trading routes (Bassi, *An Aqueous Territory: Sailor Geographies and New Granada's Transimperial Greater Caribbean World* [Durham, N.C., 2016]).

3. Here my work is informed by Daviken Studnicki-Gizbert's explanation for Portuguese royal opposition to international networks of crypto-Jewish traders. He writes, "What propelled this opposition movement was the sense that the Portuguese mercantile nation represented, in act and in expression, the antithesis of the 'true' commonwealth, one based on fixity (rather than mobility), political and economic boundedness (rather than transnationalism), the subordination of commerce to royal prerogative (rather than economic naturalism), religious purity (rather than hybridity and heterodoxy), and undivided loyalty (rather than cosmopolitanism)" (Studnicki-Gizbert, *A Nation upon the Ocean Sea: Portugal's Atlantic Diaspora and the Crisis of the Spanish Empire, 1492–1640* [New York, 2007], 13).

monies reveal patterns in the motivations, itineraries, working conditions, and socioeconomic statuses of crucial imperial go-betweens.[4]

This chapter divides its investigation of foreign contrabandists into four sections. First, it dissects the practice of smuggling. Contrabandists' ruses, networks, and common procedures for working in a hostile environment reveal both their expertise and their understanding of Spanish commercial enforcement mechanisms. The second section contemplates what sort of person became a smuggler. Though clandestine foreign merchants had ambivalent relationships with the imperial goals of their home countries, they generally shared commonalities of religion, age, and class with one another. Smugglers' trials and tribulations with the Spanish American criminal justice system comprise a third unit of analysis. Arrest, trial, sentencing, and a range of punishments for contrabandists dramatized the fact that, despite its ubiquity, interimperial commerce still constituted a highly illegal economic practice with potentially severe consequences in the Spanish colonies. A final section examines how illicit trade precipitated sporadic but long-lasting violence in coastal waters, as smugglers and coast guardsmen sought to avenge each other's raiding.

More than a portrait of one occupational group in the early modern world, the social study of smugglers offers a different vantage point on colonial history. It is time to reevaluate what the multi-imperial, polyglot crews that frequented the Spanish American coasts meant for Spanish colonial development and identity formation.[5] Smugglers were savvy and adaptable to local market conditions, customs, languages, and coast guard operations. Insider knowledge of this sort demonstrates the extent to which sailors exchanged

4. Obviously, many clandestine traders moved through the Spanish Empire undetected and never appeared in colonial records. Even when captured, illicit traders often divulged as little as possible about themselves and their associates or cloaked their true circumstances and intentions in well-worn deceptions. The vast majority of foreign activities in Spanish territories were illegal, meaning that embattled illicit merchants and chagrined Spanish American officials alike might prefer to keep records of the former's presence to minimum. But, as Kristen Block discusses in her search for evidence of Northern Europeans in similar seventeenth-century Spanish Caribbean records, "Here and elsewhere, what was recorded only once turned out to be a key revelation of an open secret" (Block, *Ordinary Lives in the Early Caribbean: Religion, Colonial Competition, and the Politics of Profit* [Athens, Ga., 2012], 8).

5. Political scientists Itty Abraham and Willem van Schendel contend that highly mobile people like smugglers "often appear in social theory as obscure, fleeting figures, as peripheral social actors with a lowly status in the world order, and as faceless outsiders who fit imperfectly into neat representations of social reality" (Abraham and van Schendel, "Introduction: The Making of Illicitness," in van Schendel and Abraham, eds., *Illicit Flows and Criminal Things: States, Borders, and the Other Side of Globalization* [Bloomington, Ind., 2005], 11).

information in port and formed mutually beneficial bonds with habitual trading partners on shore. Moreover, non-Spanish familiarity with Spanish American territories and subjects illustrates a worldview where imperial subjecthood was of secondary importance to commerce. Beyond the reach of metropolitan policymakers, small-time but well-connected contrabandists provided material comfort for themselves and Spanish America's neglected provinces while they sewed together dominions that mercantilism sought to keep apart. From their actions, the common social and procedural foundations of free trade arose.[6]

## THE PRACTICE AND NETWORKS OF SMUGGLING

A skilled smuggler tracing the coastlines of Spanish America had innumerable methods to bend and break Spanish commercial law. The range of practices and routes employed by illicit traders was truly astounding. The word "smuggler" brings to mind ingenious criminals slipping like cat burglars past border guards and customs officials. Certainly, covert activity of this kind comprised a significant portion of unlicensed trade. But clandestine maneuvers marked only one of many strategies concocted between foreign sellers and Spanish American buyers to exchange goods in eighteenth-century Venezuela. In addition to stealth, the art of smuggling relied on veniality, deception, necessity, and apathy. Whether they trafficked their illegal merchandise furtively or with the discreet consent of law enforcement officers, foreign contrabandists in Venezuela depended on wide-ranging networks of foreign and Spanish commercial contacts in the province and throughout the Caribbean to stock their inventories, facilitate safe passage, and serve as willing trading partners.

No matter how many trusted associates they amassed, most contrabandists still sold their wares in quiet coves, on out-of-the-way beaches, and at shallow anchorages, often under the cover of night. The experiences of Captain Louis Lagarene and his crew followed this example. Lagarene, a French national, led a trading expedition to Venezuela on behalf of a prominent Curaçaoan merchant in 1763. The trader, a Dutch Jew named Abraham Henrique

6. As Ana Crespo Solana theorizes, it was contraband trade, more than any Spanish crown initiatives, that encouraged potentially prosperous Spanish American agricultural zones to look outward toward external commerce and to produce crops for export rather than subsistence. Non-Spanish smugglers merely responded to the structural realities of peripheral areas (Crespo Solana, *Mercaderes atlánticos: Redes del comercio flamenco y holandés entre Europa y el Caribe* [Córdoba, 2009], 263).

Morón, furnished Lagarene with a passport from the governor of Curaçao and a letter introducing him to a commercial contact in Venezuela named Miguel de Acosta Andrade. Henrique Morón might have placed trust in Acosta Andrade because evidence suggests that Acosta Andrade was a Sephardic Jewish trading agent himself. Captain Lagarene's instructions called for him to bring the ship and European consumer goods belonging to Henrique Morón to the Venezuelan coast. Lagarene would find Acosta Andrade, barter the goods for his mules, and then ship the mules to French Martinique. When they returned to Curaçao, the crew would divvy up profits from the sale of the mules with Henrique Morón.[7]

Unfortunately for the crew, events did not go as planned. Though they made the voyage safely from Curaçao to the Venezuelan coast, they could not find Acosta Andrade. They spent almost three months searching for their contact in vain. Nonetheless, they eventually managed to barter some of their cargo with two Venezuelan merchants for a handsome sum of cacao. They returned to Curaçao with the cacao, only to be told by Henrique Morón that he would not receive them until they had made the agreed-upon transactions with Acosta Andrade. Henrique Morón ordered them to pick up more consumer goods on the Dutch island of Bonaire and again go looking for the Venezuelan. Following the stopover in Bonaire, they claimed they ran short of fresh water and had to reprovision on shore in the small inlet of Unare in eastern

7. Several scholars identify Henrique Morón as a significant trading house in Curaçao and Jamaica in the eighteenth century, with significant ties to large European cities such as Amsterdam and London. Abraham was the son of Aron Henrique Morón (or "Henriquez Morao," in Curaçao) and the grandson of Isaac Henrique Morón. The family dated back to 1674 in Curaçao and was involved in trading, shipping, insurance, and plantation agriculture on the island. Miguel de Acosta Andrade's identity is less certain. He might have descended from the Acosta Andrade family of merchants who were active in Curaçao in the late seventeenth and early eighteenth centuries and had family connections to the Jewish communities of Martinique and Amsterdam. This genealogy reveals two things about the case in question: first, that these particular smugglers had the backing of important members in the Curaçaoan merchant community, and second, that the route taken by the venture might have involved calling on Sephardic trading agents in French Martinique and Spanish Venezuela. Assuming my supposition about Miguel de Acosta Andrade's identity is correct, the latter would have been a place where authorities strictly prohibited Acosta Andrade's presence, as he was both an unlicensed trader and a Jew. See Isaac S. Emmanuel, *Precious Stones of the Jews of Curaçao: Curaçaon Jewry, 1656–1957* (New York, 1957), 145–146, 200–202, 382–383; Stephen Alexander Fortune, *Merchants and Jews: The Struggle for British West Indian Commerce, 1650–1750* (Gainesville, Fla., 1984), 133; Ramón Aizpurua, *Curazao y la costa de Caracas: Introducción al estudio del contrabando de la provincia de Venezuela en tiempos de la Compañía Guipuzcoana, 1730–1780* (Caracas, 1993), 263.

Venezuela. After the crew had been there three days, the Spanish coast guard detected the Curaçaoan smugglers and took their ship by force.[8]

The Lagarene voyage emphasizes that covert operations were both vital to the fulfillment of daily trade in the Caribbean basin and fraught with potential legal conflict. The Dutchmen provided Venezuelan subjects with welcome goods and a market for their cacao. Their actions were also highly illegal. According to Spanish commercial statutes, they were guilty of trespassing into Spanish territory, associating and bartering with Spanish subjects, and exporting Spanish cacao. Though they held a Dutch passport, much of their trade took place outside the protection of Dutch mercantile law.

Effective smugglers worked discreetly to avoid these legal snafus and did so with a regularity that make their actions seem ordinary. Lagarene's crew might have continued their travels unimpeded had not the need for freshwater made them prey for coast guard boats. By the time of their arrest, after all, they had made two trips to Venezuela. During the better part of three months, they had explored the coast in search of Acosta Andrade and surreptitiously traded without detection. Avoiding capture required local knowledge and elusiveness that Lagarene and his crew clearly possessed. And yet the mundane way in which the captured Dutch sailors discussed an itinerary that would have required them to navigate Dutch, Spanish, and French commercial conventions suggests that they perceived nothing uncommon in this type of multi-imperial exchange. Even when their commercial contact failed to materialize, Lagarene confidently improvised. He arranged substitute trading partners to salvage some profit from the voyage.

Of course, backwater trading was just one implement in the smuggler's toolkit. In many instances, commercial interlopers entered more-traveled ports with the tacit endorsement of local authorities. Although officially assisted smuggling involved an infinite number of variations, the three most common practices were as follows: allowing a smuggler to make landfall under the guise of maritime exigencies, such as repairing the ship or taking on water, food, or firewood; ignoring a foreign merchant's entrance into port (usually for a bribe or kickback); or pretending to detain a contrabandist while arranging for the private sale of his merchandise.

The practice of superfluously seeking provisions and repairs was often the easiest of the three ruses to carry out, since it could be employed with or with-

8. Declaraciones de Louis Lagarene, Capitan de "La Catharina," 49, Abraham Pineda, Escribano, 45, marineros Juan Lorenzo Cristián y Jacobo de Varas, 22, La Guaira, November 29, 1763, AGNV, Comp Gui, VIII, fols. 284v–290.

out official cognizance and participation. Captain Philip Jongh was among seven sailors who left Dutch Curaçao in 1760 to trade in Grenada. According to their testimonies, a broken rudder and navigational mishaps forced the men toward Margarita Island, off the coast of Venezuela, in search of freshwater and a place to repair their ship. Had they not been pursued by the Caracas Company's coast guard ships, the men testified, they would have sought permission from the governor of Margarita to fix their ship and replenish water supplies. An inventory of the ship revealed it to be full of clothes, meat, bacon, butter, flour, and wine. Spanish officials were unconvinced by the Curaçaoan sailors' story. Numerous declarations of smugglers caught in the Spanish net include similarly questionable and convenient emergencies.[9]

Administratively assisted smuggling might even involve some mix of all three tactics. Père Labat, the French Jesuit chronicler who crisscrossed the Caribbean aboard numerous vessels in the seventeenth and early eighteenth centuries, explained as much in his memoirs. Labat instructed his readership,

> If you wish to enter one of their ports to trade, you say that you are short of water, fuel, or victuals, or that you have a split mast, or a leak which cannot be plugged without removing the cargo. An officer is sent to explain all these things to the Governor, and, by giving him a good present, makes him believe what you wish him to believe. His officers can be made blind in the same way if necessary, and then permission is granted to enter the port and unload the ship in order to repair her. All formalities are carefully observed. A seal is placed on the door of the warehouse by which the cargo is brought in, but equal care is taken that there is another door left unsealed by which it is taken out at night, and replaced by cases of indigo, cochenille, vanilla, cacao, tobacco, etc., etc., and silver in bars and specie. As soon as this has been done one finds the mast repaired, the leak plugged, and the ship ready to sail.

As long as illicit traders and Spanish American bureaucrats followed the minimum protocol to provide the latter with an air of plausible deniability, any number of creative deceptions could facilitate illegal trade.[10]

9. Declaraciones de Capitan Felipe de Jongh, 49, Mercader Juan Pierrote, 45, Contramaestre Antonio Marcos (negro libre), 35, Contestable Juan Pedro (negro libre), 29, 2 españoles Domingo Antonio Acuña y Juan José de la Cruz, 40 y 28, y Francisco Martínez, Marinero Contrabandista, 30, La Guaira, July 9 y 11, 1760, AGNV, Comp Gui, VII, fols. 339–345.

10. Père Labat, *The Memoirs of Père Labat: 1693–1705,* trans. John Eaden (1931; rpt. London, 1970), 170–171.

Smuggling did not always involve the support or tacit acknowledgment of officials. François de Pons, an early-nineteenth-century French traveler to Venezuela, marveled at the mix of hazard and ease in covert and unassisted smuggling. Breaking down the various modes of illicit exchange, de Pons described the clandestine trade practiced by men like Louis Lagarene as the most difficult and demanding. The practice required its participants "to unload the contraband on a part of the coast distant from frequented ports, and to carry the merchandises by land, to the place of their destination. This method, more decided and direct . . . is also the most dangerous. A risk is hazarded, not only of being taken by the guards, but of suffering damages more or less considerable." De Pons was "struck with the fidelity and good faith of the conductors" and came to view them "as prodigies." As the traveler's depictions made clear, some contrabandists either could not count on or chose not to accept the helping hand of pliable officials. Aware of the shifting fortunes of life in a coastal borderland, these men had good reason to aim for remote harbors.[11]

Even without bureaucratic support, willing Spanish subjects might help foreign smugglers to cloak illicit trade in the guise of legal commerce. As many contrabandists were well connected in the Spanish and Spanish American merchant communities, they often piggybacked their illicit items on top of legitimate shipments or activities. Foreigners bought a place for their goods aboard legal Spanish vessels. Permits for cargo space aboard individually licensed register ships typically were sold to the highest Spanish bidder in seventeenth-century Seville. Dutch traders would then pay off Spanish merchants to take on fictitious ownership of the Dutch businessmen's goods. The merchandise made its way successfully across the Atlantic under the names of royally permitted Spanish traders, but most of the profits cycled back to the original foreign purveyors. English and French interlopers successfully co-opted Spanish merchant activities aboard the great Spanish trade fleets, as well. In the early years of the Bourbon alliance, French privateers tasked with policing Spanish American waters against pirates even used their privateering licenses *(patentes de corso)* as cover to land on Spanish colonial shores and trade illegally.[12]

11. François Joseph de Pons, *A Voyage to the Eastern Part of Terra Firma, or the Spanish Main, in South-America, during the Years 1801, 1802, 1803, and 1804 . . .* (New York, 1806), II, 327–328. De Pons's nineteenth-century observations mainly square with eighteenth-century practice. There is every reason to believe that the main difference between what he described and precommercial liberalization smuggling of the first three-quarters of the eighteenth century was that smuggling without official participation was more common in this earlier period because laws were less permissive to permutations in trading patterns.

12. For Dutch examples, see Zacarias Moutoukias, "Power, Corruption, and Commerce:

In Venezuelan coastal waters, this ambiguity between licit and illicit commerce took the form of foreign smugglers employing Spanish subjects as middlemen. These *prácticos,* as they were called, were often experienced coastal traders whose business coast guard patrols might construe as legal. In the second half of the eighteenth century, Spanish free trade decrees, which allowed for limited licensed trade between Spanish colonies, provided additional cover for Spanish sailors and merchants to roam around the Caribbean basin. During this period, frequent shortages of basic provisions owing to war also forced Venezuelan officials to send merchants to nearby foreign islands in search of foodstuffs. Clandestine trade bloomed out of these missions of necessity, as traders bought products in addition to those comestibles enumerated in their licenses. In this way, war functioned as an unintended corrective to trade imbalances produced by imperially exclusive commerce.[13]

Spanish authorities suspected Salvador Rexat, a Catalan trader working out of Guyana, of being a práctico. Coast guard forces stopped Rexat's vessel off the coast of Guyana to perform a routine inspection. On board they found various unregistered goods in the hold, including several barrels of gunpowder, two pairs of new boots, and even a few barrels of liquor cleverly hidden in the ship's water stores. According to Rexat, he had left French Martinique with the intent of purchasing Venezuelan cattle for the French and bringing back salted meats and other sundry foodstuffs from Martinique for the Spanish residents

---

The Making of the Local Administrative Structure in Seventeenth-Century Buenos Aires," *HAHR,* LXVIII (1988), 784. For English and French examples, see Ernst Pijning, "A New Interpretation of Contraband Trade," ibid., LXXXI (2001), 735; Geoffrey J. Walker, *Spanish Politics and Imperial Trade, 1700–1789* (Bloomington, Ind., 1979), 20; Kenneth R. Maxwell, "Hegemonies Old and New: The Ibero-Atlantic in the Long Eighteenth Century," in Jeremy Adelman, ed., *Colonial Legacies: The Problem of Persistence in Latin American History* (New York, 1999), 81. For French privateerers' misusing their licenses, see Celestino Andrés Araúz Monfante, *El contrabando holandés en el Caribe durante la primera mitad del siglo XVIII,* I (Caracas, 1984), 165.

13. Adrian J. Pearce, "*Rescates* and Anglo-Spanish Trade in the Caribbean during the French Revolutionary Wars, ca. 1797–1804," *Journal of Latin American Studies,* XXXVIII (2006), 621; Mercedes M. Alvarez F., *Comercio y comerciantes, y sus proyecciones en la Independencia venezolana* (Caracas, 1964), 37–40; P. Michael McKinley, *Pre-Revolutionary Caracas: Politics, Economy, and Society, 1777–1811* (Cambridge, 1985), 44; Silvia Marzagalli, "Was Warfare Necessary for the Functioning of Eighteenth-Century Colonial Systems? Some Reflections on the Necessity of Cross-Imperial and Foreign Trade in the French Case," in Cátia Antunes and Amélia Polónia, eds., *Beyond Empires: Global, Self-Organizing, Cross-Imperial Networks, 1500–1800* (Leiden, 2016), 276. As discussed in greater detail in Chapter 3, the initial free trade decree ending the Cádiz monopoly occurred in 1765. Venezuela and Mexico were among the last Spanish territories to receive free trade, in 1789.

of Guyana. He defended the sparse and peculiar contents of his ship's cargo by explaining that the French provisioning official with whom he worked required Venezuelan cattle before he would send any products to Guyana. The French provided the gunpowder to ward off privateers, the boots as a personal gift from the provisioning official to his Spanish counterpart, and the liquor to sate the crew. Rexat even claimed that he had hidden the spirits so that the crew would not abuse them. Although Spanish authorities conceded that he had official permission to travel to the French colony, they doubted the sincerity of his intentions given that he had arrived in a French sloop, produced no papers of sale, and offered only a French letter of passage. They eventually released him, but a prize court judge confiscated and auctioned off as contraband the contents of Rexat's sloop.[14]

Given their insider knowledge of coastal geography and Spanish coast guard tendencies, prácticos were valuable assets. Foreign traders employed them to guide vessels passing anywhere near potentially guarded Venezuelan shores. Prácticos sometimes made payments or bribes in advance of foreigners' visits to the coast. Dutch traders recruited one práctico, a Havana native named Francisco Javier de Rosa, in 1763 to ferry Venezuelan cacao and mules from a contested spit of land known as Isla de Aves to Curaçao. Unlike the French who commissioned Salvador Rexat, Rosa's employers could not claim the veneer of legitimate business. Nevertheless, both trading interests depended on their Spanish middlemen for secure passage.[15]

For cautious and well-to-do foreign smugglers and traders, a safer tactic than hiring a middleman was simply to stay at home and wait for Spanish merchants to come to them. In the second half of the eighteenth century, a group of decrees in the English, French, and Dutch empires opened up some of their ports in the Caribbean to regulated trade with merchants from various empires. The laws permitted the import and export of certain enumerated products in limited quantities in the free ports, so as not to damage the shipping and mercantile systems of these empires. The rise of sanctioned trading entrepôts

14. Auto de Don Josef Farriles, Contador del Ejercito y Real Hacienda de la Provincia, and Don Andres de Oleaga, Thesorero y Administrator General, Guyana, July 24, 1779, AGNV, Comisos, XXXII, fols. 87–88; Confesión de Salvador Rexat, Guyana, Aug. 9, 1779, AGNV, Comisos, XXXII, fols. 91–93; Auto de Antonio de Pereda, Guyana, Aug. 11, 1779, AGNV, Comisos, XXXII, fols. 180–184.

15. Declaración del Capitán Francisco Javier de Rosa, Puerto Cabello, Oct. 3, 1763, AGNV, Comp Gui, XI, fols. 309–310. On prácticos more broadly, see Jeremy David Cohen, "Cultural and Commercial Intermediaries in an Extra-Legal System of Exchange: The *Prácticos* of the Venezuelan Littoral in the Eighteenth Century," *Itinerario*, XXVII (2003), 111–120.

led to an influx of Spanish buyers visiting from the South American mainland and Caribbean islands. The frequent lack of Spanish imperial permission to anchor in these ports did not diminish Spanish American traders' appetite for outside goods.[16]

Foreign colonial administrators nurtured this easy strategy for black market commerce with Spanish subjects. British colonial officials' attempts to lure Spanish American merchants to British shores illustrate how profitable these transactions were. As early as 1715, the governor of Barbados advocated opening the island to Spanish commerce in order to pry Caracas cacao sales away from Martinique, where Spanish subjects arrived in droves. In 1734, British royal officials continued to voice Barbadians' demands to allow Spanish cacao merchants onto the island without hassle. Jamaica became a free port in 1766, mostly to resuscitate trade with Spanish smugglers after the British capture of Havana in 1762 led to a ten-month trade fair that glutted Spanish markets with British goods. Farther north, an agent for the island of Bermuda asked that the island be made a free port in 1783 so that Spanish merchants could openly purchase British slaves and goods in return for cacao, indigo, and cash. One admiral documented a practice carried out by British officials in the late eighteenth century to help Spanish merchant interests trade in their Caribbean harbors. British ships distributed letters of passage from British governors to La Guaira, Havana, and other Spanish ports. Though the documents bore the governors' signatures, they left blank information about the vessels, crew, and captains. After Spanish merchants filled in these carte blanche letters, the papers protected them and their cargo from the risk of British seizure. For non-Spanish colonial interests, the gains of commercial integration produced by their merchants' interaction with Spanish traders outweighed the security of isolationism.[17]

As the previous discussion of smuggling methods and tactics has eluci-

16. The British free ports, for example, were opened in 1766 and finally ended in 1822. See Frances Armytage, *The Free Port System in the British West Indies: A Study in Commercial Policy, 1766–1822* (London, 1953), 1–12; Adrian J. Pearce, "British Trade with the Spanish Colonies, 1788–1795," *BLAR*, XX (2001), 242–243.

17. For examples from Barbados, see Governor Lowther to the Council of Trade and Plantations, Barbados, Dec. 30, 1715, NA, CO, 28 / 14, no. 47, 47i; Governor Lord Howe to the Council of Trade and Plantations, Barbados, Nov. 7, 1734, 28 / 24, fols. 114–121. For Jamaica, see Theodore C. Hinckley, "The Decline of Caribbean Smuggling," *Journal of Inter-American Studies*, V (1963), 117. For Bermuda, see Henry Tucker to Lord North, Bermuda, May 3, 1783, NA, CO, 37 / 38. For a description of fraudulent documents by British Caribbean officials, see Extract of a Letter from Admiral Sir Hyde Parker to Mr. Nefrean, Port Royal, Jamaica, Oct. 8, 1799, NA, PC, 1 / 45 / 163.

dated, contrabandists lived and died based on the networks they cultivated. Although the lone wolf smuggler might occasionally ferry goods across imperial lines without much in the way of contacts, sustained success demanded an array of foreign and domestic allies. Not all of a contrabandist's acquaintances would be long-standing and familiar. Yet even in these cases, buyers, sellers, and facilitators established trust relationships that encouraged future transactions. Merchants trafficking on the coast of Venezuela transcended imperial, religious, and ethnic barriers to cultivate trust and barter goods. Merchant confidence, however, might begin from categorical homogeneity with at least one partner in a larger network.[18]

18. A recent surge of interest in networks has led authors to examine nonnational merchant, intellectual, diasporic, and friendship conglomerations (to name just a few relationships). Sociologists Joel M. Podolny and Karen L. Page elegantly define a network as "any collection of actors . . . that pursue repeated, enduring exchange relations with one another and, at the same time, lack a legitimate organizational authority to arbitrate and resolve disputes that may arise during the exchange" (Podolny and Page, "Network Forms of Organization," *Annual Review of Sociology,* XXIV [1998], 59). David Hancock, in his far-reaching survey of the merchant linkages that enabled the Madeira wine trade, uses this definition extensively as the grounding for his discussion of commodity trading networks (Hancock, *Oceans of Wine: Madeira and the Emergence of American Trade and Taste* [New Haven, Conn., 2009], xxi, 145). On relationships between economic actors, Xabier Lamikiz argues, "Trust was of fundamental significance to the eighteenth-century trader. . . . Other elements such as supply, demand, capital, infrastructure, instruments of credit, and the law are seen as the main influences on the operation of trade. But it was trust that performed the role of combining all these elements, thereby constituting a prerequisite for the creation of trade" (Lamikiz, *Trade and Trust in the Eighteenth-Century Atlantic World: Spanish Merchants and Their Overseas Networks* [London, 2010], 182). See also Francisco Bethencourt, "The Iberian Atlantic: Ties, Networks, and Boundaries," in Harald E. Braun and Lisa Vollendorf, eds., *Theorising the Ibero-American Atlantic* (Leiden, 2013), 19.

Several scholarly works on networks have concentrated on how they coexisted with governments. For Fabrício Prado, networks were more durable than state initiatives and directives (Prado, *Edge of Empire: Atlantic Networks and the Revolution in Bourbon Río de la Plata* [Oakland, Calif., 2015], 47, 57). Lindsay O'Neill believes networks bridged public or governmental and private spheres (O'Neill, *The Opened Letter: Networking in the Early Modern British World* [Philadelphia, 2015], 8). Other literature has discussed what qualities defined networks in the first place. Nikolas Böttcher, Bernd Hausberger, and Antonio Ibarra emphasize the security and market incentives of merchant networks (Böttcher, Hausberger, and Ibarra, "Introducción," in Böttcher, Hausberger, and Ibarra, eds., *Redes y negocios globales en el mundo ibérico, siglos XVI–XVIII* [Orlando, Fla., 2011], 16). Eric Van Young characterizes networks as entities of "defensive exclusion" designed to keep out undesirables (Van Young, "Social Networks: A Final Comment," ibid., 293). Jonathan Israel stresses path-changing historical circumstances, such as the expulsion of Sephardic Jews from the Iberian Peninsula, as crucial to galvanizing a trading network (Israel, "Diaspora Jewish and Non-Jewish and the World Maritime Empires," in Ina Baghdiantz McCabe, Gelina Harlaftis, and

Notwithstanding the perceptual limitations posed by courtroom proceedings, smugglers' accounts allow for fleeting glimpses of criminalized commercial connections that nourished the economies of contested imperial spaces. Consolidating the brief and cagey declarations of interimperial contrabandists allows at least a peek into their networks with foreign businessmen and Spanish subjects in Venezuela. These linkages formed out of habitual trading relationships. Unlicensed traders labored outside the protection of imperial judicial structures, which generally considered an unlicensed trader's actions illegal and prosecutable by mercantile law. Smugglers relied instead on their own professional reputations and commercial norms to discourage and redress offenses committed against them by other trading parties. For non-Spanish contrabandists, networks signified sustained contacts in Spanish territories and a better chance for safe passage through unpredictable waters.[19]

If a Venezuelan smuggler wanted to thrive in the transimperial Caribbean, he first had to cultivate relationships with non-Spanish merchants. Attaining the right mix of goods for illicit importation into Spanish America sometimes required leaving one's home port and ranging farther afield. Even without the threat of Spanish coast guard forces, interimperial voyagers confronted constraints on their freedom of movement posed by war, shifting imperial alliances, privateers, and pirates. Contacts in foreign harbors helped to minimize risk.

Securing passports and letters of passage from multiple empires and ports helped avoid harassment and testified to a smuggler's influence over merchants and officials. One ship captured near Cumaná in eastern Venezuela in

---

Ioanna Pepelase Minoglou, eds., *Diaspora Entrepreneurial Networks: Four Centuries of History* [Oxford, 2005], 9–10). Francesca Trivellato conceives of the trust that produced networks as multifaceted, incorporating kinship, community, institutional support, correspondence, and reliable behavior (Trivellato, *The Familiarity of Strangers: The Sephardic Diaspora, Livorno, and Cross-Cultural Trade in the Early Modern Period* [New Haven, Conn., 2009], 16, 272). Finally, some of the historiography has focused on the functions of networks. Pierre Gervais highlights their role in quality control and verification of products and sellers for merchants (Gervais, "Neither Imperial, nor Atlantic: A Merchant Perspective on International Trade in the Eighteenth Century," *HEI,* XXXIV [2008], 467). Kenneth J. Banks sees networks as fonts of news and unregulated information (Banks, *Chasing Empire across the Sea: Communications and the State in the French Atlantic, 1713–1763* [Montreal, 2006], 158–162). For more on the advantageous nature of cross-imperial and cross-cultural in early modern trade, see the essays in Antunes and Polónia, eds., *Beyond Empires.*

19. Licensed traders in the early modern world also depended on norms and professional reputations to regulate business transactions, but also had the benefit of state and guild mechanisms as a fail-safe. See Ana Sofia Ribeiro, "The Evolution of Norms in Trade and Financial Networks in the First Global Age: The Case of Simon Ruiz's Network," in Antunes and Polónia, eds., *Beyond Empires,* 32, 37.

1762 had a passport from Dutch Curaçao and a trading license from what was then English Guadeloupe. The smuggling captain, who was born in the Canary Islands, and his multinational crew all confessed to undertaking the journey between the two islands multiple times on short trading voyages. Their claims that the British had forced them into this trade after capturing them and holding their original papers hostage failed to convince Spanish officials. The presence of English and Dutch papers implied the traders' familiarity with and willingness to engage in transimperial trade.[20]

In other cases, a suspected smuggler's personal ties to foreign dominions betrayed his guilt. For Francisco Javier de Rosa, the Dutch-employed Spanish middleman mentioned earlier in this chapter, family relationships were particularly damning evidence. Rosa, a sailor from Havana, had married a Dutch woman in Curaçao. Though the particular circumstances of his marriage remain unknown, his legal attachment to his foreign wife and the Dutch colony probably encouraged businessmen there to trust him. The governor of Venezuela seemed convinced of Rosa's foreign allegiances, sentencing him to four years of service in the king's fortifications at Puerto Cabello in Venezuela.[21]

Once a smuggler had used his contacts in foreign and domestic ports to put together cargo and crew, he then turned to Venezuelan associates to introduce merchandise into Spanish dominions. Routine trading partners helped foreign contrabandists maximize the efficiency of their voyages. Although some ships trawled the coast haphazardly searching for willing buyers and sellers, this strategy increased exposure to coast guard ships and militias. The well-connected illicit merchant sought security by reaching out to his connections on land. John Campbell, an English merchant who wrote of his experiences with clandestine commerce throughout Spanish America, described an orderly signaling process between ship and shore after which a "long-boat was sent off well manned, brought the merchants on board with their money, and carried them back with their goods." In Venezuela, several smuggling cases referenced signals exchanged either by torchlight or by cannon blasts. This communication implied previous organization by parties that recognized each other.[22]

20. Declaraciones del Capitan José Sicilia, 38, y marineros José Nicolás Altúne, 23, Andrés Paredes, 21, Antonio Rodríguez, 26, La Guaira, Feb. 12 y 13, 1762, AGNV, Comp Gui, VIII, fols. 112–121.

21. Instancia del Capitán Francisco Javier de Rosa, Puerto Cabello, Oct. 18, 1763, AGNV, Comp Gui, XI, fol. 318; Sentencia por Gobernador y Capitán General Don José Solano, Caracas, May 26, 1764, AGNV, Comp Gui, XIII, fol. 194.

22. Linda M. Rupert writes that smuggling required "extensive preparations, a high degree of coordination and communication between all parties involved, clear planning as to

A desire to maintain plausible deniability with authorities meant that, in many instances, contrabandists established recurring trading arrangements with Spanish subjects without learning much about them beyond their physical appearance. When asked to reveal his Venezuelan accomplices, one illegal trader captured aboard a Dutch vessel offered a few names but also declared that usually all identities were kept secret unless a Venezuelan merchant came aboard a foreign ship. Thus, for the purposes of accountability, foreign businessmen might force Venezuelan middlemen actually performing transactions to identify themselves but permit the owners of larger cargoes who employed these small peddlers to remain unnamed. A Dutchman known as Jan Bislick testified in 1761 to trading with Venezuelans "of all kinds whom we did not know" in several locales around eastern Venezuela. Taken at face value, Bislick's statement implies that coastal inhabitants were incredibly amenable to illicit trading, even with unconnected smugglers. However, given that Bislick found himself the captive of a prize court, his testimony might have been a concerted strategy to downplay his familiarity with the coast and keep his trading contacts away from further scrutiny.[23]

This is not to say that all relationships between foreign and Venezuelan smugglers were friendly. Conflicts arose from these business affiliations. The criminal nature of contraband partnerships added to their volatility. In 1734, for example, one middleman working for the Dutch stabbed a Venezuelan merchant to death in his own home. His impetus to murder the Venezuelan was an unpaid debt of twenty pesos. Close networks of trade and credit clearly had the capacity to endanger as well as enrich those involved in the black market.[24]

---

the site and time of the encounter, and a certain degree of mutual confidence between the participants" (Rupert, "Contraband Trade and the Shaping of Colonial Societies in Curaçao and Tierra Firme," *Itinerario*, XXX [2006], 39). My own sense is that contraband trade could be somewhat more spontaneous than she concedes. Numerous cases discuss smugglers following the coast aimlessly looking for buyers. See also Rupert, *Creolization and Contraband: Curaçao in the Early Modern Atlantic World* (Athens, Ga., 2012), 185. "Brought the merchants on board with their money": [John Campbell], *The Spanish Empire in America: Containing . . . a Full and Clear Account of the Commerce with Old Spain . . .* (1741; rpt. London, 1747), 313–314. For examples of signaling by smugglers, see Información de Gabriel Amengual, Puerto Cabello, Sept. 17, 1733, AGNV, Comisos, XIV, fols. 155–156; Declaraciones de Louis Lagarene, Capitan de "La Catharina," Caracas, Nov. 29, 1763, AGNV, Comp Gui, VIII, fols. 284v–290.

23. For obscured identities, see Información de Juan Pascual, Puerto Cabello, Sept. 18, 1733, AGNV, Comisos, XIV, fol. 160–161; Declaraciones de Capitán Jan Bislick, 25, Mercader Isaque Abenatar, 48, y el marinero Bartolomé Bode, 25, La Guaira, Apr. 18, 1761, AGNV, Comp Gui, VIII, fols. 10–13.

24. Auto de Joseph de Matos, Comandante General y Justicia Mayor, Puerto Cabello, Sept. 2, 1750, AGNV, Comisos, XXIV, fol. 3.

Acquaintances with corruptible Spanish imperial administrators also paralleled and enriched the connections that foreign smugglers developed with Venezuelan buyers. The colonial officer was not a rigid boundary between legal and illegal trade but a permeable membrane that allowed some smuggling into his realms and rejected other ventures. Official support for smuggling depended largely on the potential for officials to administer its exchanges. By the eighteenth century, illicit commerce had become so normalized in the overall patterns of exchange in the Americas that only the naïve or deluded official believed it could be completely halted. Instead, most authorities separated illicit business into two groups: that which they informally sanctioned and that which was completely outside of their control. Illicit traders operating in the former category got to know local officials and paid for a blind eye in enforcement matters. By contrast, smugglers who did not curry favor with port authorities might encounter vigilant opposition. Generally, foreign smugglers followed the advice of British smuggler Thomas Kinder: "To prevent your vessel being ordered out of harbour, you will likewise have to make a friend of somebody." The entangled worlds of permissive bureaucrats will be discussed more fully in Chapter 6. Here, it is important to simply note that royal officials represented yet another sphere of influence that the prosperous smuggler needed to cultivate.[25]

## THE IDENTITIES OF SMUGGLERS

The identities of interimperial smugglers were every bit as intricate and enigmatic as the tactics and networks they deployed in practicing their trade. As the cases above have implied, contrabandists came from a transimperial, multiracial, and multiethnic lot of seafarers. In describing non-Spanish smugglers, Spanish legal records first demarcated their nationality. After all, their first crime involved being an unlicensed foreigner in the Spanish colonies. Following this notation, Spanish American scribes often noted the race and religion of the defendants. Yet, in many ways, the occupational identity of "contrabandist" formed a more common denominator than any of these categories. Smuggling sustained large populations of rootless sailors in the eighteenth-century Caribbean. Humble social origins drew many maritime laborers into

25. Pijning, "A New Interpretation of Contraband Trade," *HAHR*, LXXXI (2001), 736. "Prevent your vessel being ordered out of harbour": Malyn Newitt, ed., *War, Revolution and Society in the Rio de la Plata, 1808–1810: Thomas Kinder's Narrative of a Journey to Madeira, Montevideo and Buenos Aires* (Oxford, 2010), 182.

the profession. Most entered the trade on their own account as a flexible way to make a living in the turbulent Caribbean basin. The act of smuggling shaped their aversion to rigid imperial formations. The interests of itinerant contrabandists sometimes overlapped with the imperial commercial and political projects of the Dutch, English, and French. However, it would be difficult to label the truly interimperial crews that plied the waters of coastal Venezuela as representatives of any empire.

Certainly, demarcated polities influenced the experiences and working routines of non-Spanish illicit traders. Their business flourished because legal boundaries separated mutually willing merchant interests. In general, most Dutch, English, and French traders shared their home empires' desire to consolidate trading posts and toeholds in the Antilles that their seventeenth-century predecessors had snatched from the Spanish. Most clandestine merchants also hoped to break open, whether by legal or illegal means, the declared Spanish monopoly on trade with New Spain, Central America, and Tierra Firme. Even the most autonomous smugglers fell back on empires for legal and military protection in times of trouble. In sum, allegiances between smugglers and their empires of origin were malleable and murky, even as they were impossible to disentangle.[26]

Given these ambiguous legal and political relationships, the national designations used by Spanish prize courts to identify foreign contrabandists seem reductive. In addition, the realities of finding sailors for illicit commercial ventures underscored the subjectivity in categorizing individual traders by nationality. Because contrabandists, by the very nature of their work, willingly disregarded restrictions on interimperial contact, they found nothing objectionable about international crews. A single vessel might have been made in one empire, owned in another, sailed by mariners from three or four empires, and endorsed by letters of passage from multiple ports. The question arising from

26. Early modern empires successfully co-opted a range of supposedly autonomous subjects and practices when it suited imperial purposes. Casey S. Schmitt demonstrates how both British naval and Spanish coast guard strategists effectively dabbled in interimperial black markets to supply imperial maritime forces (Schmitt, "Virtue in Corruption: Privateers, Smugglers, and the Shape of Empire in the Eighteenth-Century Caribbean," *Early American Studies*, XXXIII [2015], 80–110). Discussing religion rather than commerce or defense, Owen Stanwood's reexamination of Huguenot migration offers a similar example, wherein empires manipulated religious refugees to advance the former's expansionary aims more than these exiles were able to use empires to create ideal spiritual communities in the Americas (Stanwood, "Between Eden and Empire: Huguenot Refugees and the Promise of New Worlds," *AHR*, CXVIII [2013], 1321–1322).

such multi-imperial ventures is, What identity paradigm is most applicable to analyzing crews and voyages?

The case of the *Pitre,* a Danish sloop, highlights the inadequacies of nationality as a descriptive category for illuminating the social history of smugglers. Caracas Company patrols ranging far afield captured the *Pitre* off the southern coast of Puerto Rico and brought it back to Venezuela. The sloop had left from the Danish island of Saint Thomas (present-day U.S. Virgin Islands) in 1779 with an assortment of goods. Crew members claimed they put ashore in Spanish Puerto Rico only to secure water and firewood for their journey. The vessel itself was Danish. Among her crew were a pilot from Philadelphia, a Dutch Jewish scribe from Amsterdam, a ship's officer from Languedoc in the south of France, and a Venezuelan common sailor. Adding another transimperial wrinkle to the voyage, the sloop's ultimate destination was New England, where in 1779 war raged between the British and their former subjects. Though none of their testimonies mentioned it explicitly, the crew likely carried supplies from this part of the Caribbean to aid the American revolutionaries. The Dutch island of Saint Eustatius, a close neighbor of Saint Thomas, served as a key provider of smuggled matériel for the American cause in the war's early years.[27]

A letter written by the pilot and scribe of the *Pitre* to the intendant of Caracas demonstrated the multi-imperial crew's frustration at being detained for little more than their places of origin. They quoted chapter and verse of the navigational laws of the *Recopilación de Castilla* that allowed foreign vessels to land on Spanish shores in order to replenish provisions. Nonetheless, they believed that Spanish laws should not matter for their situation, as "there is no precept in natural law nor by the laws of man that impedes the free navigation of the seas or the common use of their wide open spaces." They added, "Human society requires this liberty to communicate." That two officers of a relatively unimportant vessel in the Caribbean would make such bold pronouncements indicates what little regard they had for imperial boundaries.[28]

27. For the case of the *Pitre,* see Documentos relativos al apreso de la balandra dinamarquesa "El Piter," Caracas, Mar. 13, 1779–Jan. 18, 1780, AGNV, Comp Gui, XX, fols. 161–230. For discussions of the place of St. Eustatius in Atlantic trade, see J. Franklin Jameson, "St. Eustatius in the American Revolution," *AHR,* XIII (1903), 683–708; Andrew Jackson O'Shaughnessy, *An Empire Divided: The American Revolution and the British Caribbean* (Philadelphia, 2000), 215–221; Peter Andreas, *Smuggler Nation: How Illicit Trade Made America* (New York, 2013), 55–56; Norman F. Barka, "Citizens of St. Eustatius, 1781: A Historical and Archaeological Study," in Robert L. Paquette and Stanley L. Engerman, eds., *The Lesser Antilles in the Age of European Expansion* (Gainesville, Fla., 1996), 225.

28. John Benemen and Manuel Enrique to the Intendant General of Venezuela, Caracas, Oct. 25, 1779, AGNV, Comp Gui, XX, fols. 203–210.

If foreign smugglers frequently did not identify with or conform to the imperial projects of their birthplaces, what commonalities characterized them? For many contrabandists, religion proved a powerful organizing principle. This is not to say that smugglers were a terribly religious group. Rather, many coalesced around the cultural bond of not being Catholics in Catholic kingdoms. Spanish interrogations of foreign prisoners nearly always asked defendants and witnesses to declare their religion. Smugglers of northern European descent frequently, though not exclusively, identified as Lutherans, Protestants, and Jews. Spanish Catholics swore in Protestants, who could not make the sign of the cross, by asking them to swear on a Bible or by "the evangelical saints." Judges commanded Jews to pledge to tell the truth "by the laws of Moses."[29]

Judaism formed an important bond for many smugglers. Many Jewish traders in the eighteenth-century Caribbean were the descendants of the great Jewish transatlantic trading houses centered in Portugal in the sixteenth and seventeenth centuries. Like these earlier commercial entities, Jews in the Caribbean often represented "a nation without a state, a collectivity dispersed across the seas."[30]

Dutch Curaçao, Venezuela's dominant illicit trading partner, contained an especially high number of Jews in its merchant ranks, as the Dutch Republic tolerated them in its colonies. What is more, the Dutch perceived them as a strategic commercial resource, given the Sephardim's ties to medieval Iberian empires and continuing with the Jewish expulsion from Spain in 1492. The Jews had populated Dutch ventures in Brazil and later migrated to the Dutch West Indies after the Portuguese had reconquered the colony. Multilingual capacities, a cultural fluency in the Hispanic world, and a history of underground activities made Jewish traders formidable illicit conduits for Spanish American wealth. In the seventeenth century, they had been slave dealers representing the Dutch West India Company in a host of ports. By some estimates, as much as one-third of eighteenth-century trade in Curaçao passed through Jewish hands, and the percentage was probably higher if the count included only commerce with Spanish America. Even the tiny and unofficial Dutch smugglers' settlement of Tucacas in the wilds of the Venezuelan west central coast had a synagogue.[31]

29. "The evangelical saints": Declaración de Capitán Juan Maddox, Mar. 16, 1764, AGNV, Comisos, XXVI, fols. 302–303. "The laws of Moses": Declaración del escribano de la balandra dinamarquesa, Manuel Enriquez, Caracas, Apr. 1, 1779, AGNV, Comp Gui, XXII, fols. 173–174.

30. Studnicki-Gizbert, *Nation Upon the Ocean Sea*, 5; see also 67–69, 92–94, 179.

31. For Jewish traders in Dutch Curaçao, see Jonathan I. Israel, "The Jews of Dutch

Many Jewish traders personally undertook voyages from Curaçao to the Venezuelan coast. In 1764, Spanish coast guard officials captured two Jewish smugglers, Manuel Taboada and Isaac Barugh, near a key contraband crossroad at the mouth of the Unare River with substantial quantities of cacao, hides, and beef tallow purchased from local merchants. Jewish merchants also hired middlemen to trade their wares for them. One wealthy Jewish trader from Curaçao employed a Spanish práctico to run circuits between Aruba, Curaçao, and the western Venezuelan port of Coro. He was to rake salt from barrier islands between these points, to trade merchandise with the Spanish, and to bring Venezuelan produce and the salt for further export. The merchant even manufactured fake Spanish trade licenses to help his middleman avoid capture.[32]

Though their numbers never approached the concentration in the Dutch West Indies, Jewish smugglers were also active in the British Caribbean. Jamaica, in particular, nurtured a thriving Jewish commercial community. By 1720, 18 percent of Kingston's population was Jewish. Some Jews probably entered into illicit trading arrangements because of restrictions placed on them by the Jamaican Council of Trade and Plantations. Additionally, Jewish financiers contributed to the development of colonies in the British Antilles by lending money both to merchants involved in clandestine trade and to plantation owners. Trust between coreligionists or members of a diaspora was not always self-evident or solely dependent on professed belief structures. As trade in northern South America demonstrates, the Caribbean Sephardim operated well outside of their faith community in their relationships with Catholic Spanish Americans. Allegiances fostered by religion, nevertheless, could provide important business advantages as well as networking capabilities across imperial boundaries.[33]

---

America," in Paolo Bernardini and Norman Fiering, eds., *The Jews and the Expansion of Europe to the West, 1450 to 1800* (New York, 2001), 339–346; Stanley J. Stein and Barbara H. Stein, *Silver, Trade, and War: Spain and America in the Making of Early Modern Europe* (Baltimore, 2000), 68; Wim Klooster, *Illicit Riches: Dutch Trade in the Caribbean, 1648–1795* (Leiden, 1998), 65–66; Rupert, *Creolization and Contraband,* 45; Aizpurua, *Curazao y la costa de Caracas,* 261–264. For the Jewish settlement in Tucacas, see Mordechai Arbell, *The Jewish Nation of the Caribbean: The Spanish-Portuguese Jewish Settlements in the Caribbean and the Guianas* (Jerusalem, 2002), 265; Araúz Monfante, *El contrabando holandés en el Caribe,* I, 65.

32. For Taboada and Barugh, see Declaraciones de Manuel Taboada, 42, mercader judio y Isake Barugh, 21, escribano, La Guaira, Mar. 6, 1764, AGNV, Comp Gui, XIII, fols. 91–93. For the Jewish trader sending a Spanish práctico to Coro, see Auto de Don Antonio Josef Romana y Herrera, Maracaibo, July 28, 1777, AGNC, Contrabandos, III, fols. 8–14.

33. Fortune, *Merchants and Jews,* 45–46, 131–139, 153; George H. Nelson, "Contraband

Demographic and socioeconomic circumstances, more than religion, led men into smuggling. In general, participants in clandestine commerce on the Venezuelan coast were young and single. Although men in their forties and fifties occasionally appeared in the crew registries of Spanish prize courts, sailing was a young man's trade. Ordinary seamen on smuggling ships were most commonly in the second decade of their lives; ships' officers, captains, and principal merchants might be in their thirties. A sampling of foreign contrabandists who disclosed their ages to Spanish officials confirms this breakdown. Of thirty-one contrabandists who gave their ages, 58 percent were in their twenties or younger, 23 percent were in their thirties, and only 19 percent were forty years old or older. Life expectancies in the Caribbean were low because of tropical diseases and natural disasters. Furthermore, sailing was a dangerous profession. With these caveats in mind, the evidence suggests that smugglers as an occupational group shared a common bond of youth.[34]

Smugglers also shared characteristics in their backgrounds and business size. Humble origins, as much as age, motivated many contrabandists to enter the business. Most illegal traders captured along the Venezuelan coast were petty traders, not wholesalers. Their profits depended on frequent transactions rather than large ones. Notwithstanding some outliers, this distinction was visible in the vessels they chose. Contrabandists chose small and maneuverable ships with shallow bottoms to hug the shore and reach areas where larger craft would run aground. Smuggling crews typically numbered fewer than ten men. They carried a mixed cargo of clothes, foodstuffs, and a few slaves meant to attract a range of buyers. These voyages hardly resembled the much larger endeavors of asiento slave purveyors or the legal commerce of the Spanish trade fleets. Coast guard patrols sporadically ensnared large-scale foreign trade operations and more frequently captured small vessels financed and provisioned by affluent merchants. Yet, ventures chartered by itinerant hawkers and peopled by small crews overwhelmingly comprised the norm.[35]

---

Trade under the Asiento," *AHR,* LI (1945), 62; Nuala Zahedieh, "The Merchants of Port Royal, Jamaica, and the Spanish Contraband Trade, 1655–1692," *WMQ,* 3d Ser., XLIII (1986), 580; Trivellato, *Familiarity of Strangers,* 9, 12; Ribeiro, "Evolution of Norms," in Antunes and Polónia, eds., *Beyond Empires,* 26–27.

34. The two large collections of documents on smuggling constituting my sample are from the Archivo General de la Nación de Venezuela. I did not record every case and testimony from the Compañía Guipuzcoana (42 volumes, 1726–1786) or the Comisos (36 volumes, 1691–1784) sections. Rather, these thirty-one cases are drawn from documents across the chronological range of the sections that I surveyed for this book. The sample size is further reduced by the fact that not every contrabandist was asked his age.

35. In his study of eighteenth-century British smuggling in coastal Colombia, Ernesto

Although contraband trade offered a subsistence occupation for foreign and domestic smugglers alike, it rarely provided profound riches for the rank-and-file sailor. He did, however, receive a wage for his voyage and an allotment of space on most boats for Spanish goods he hoped to trade privately. The English merchant John Campbell described a shares system of this kind that made "every private Man on board . . . a Proprietor" who "fights for his own Property."[36]

Defendants often explained that they had entered into clandestine commerce simply to make a living. Juan Piñero, the captain of a Curaçaoan schooner in the employment of a Dutch merchant, provided this rationale for his activities on the Venezuelan coast in 1778. Piñero claimed that he did not realize the severity of his actions. "It had not been my intent to violate the laws of the Spanish monarch," he explained, "but rather to care for my needs, and those of my family, wife, and children. These concerns impelled me, for the first time, to visit these shores." Piñero pleaded for clemency. The extent to which he understood the criminality of his actions is debatable. However, it is unlikely that he would have lied about using his trip to support his family. Piñero and others like him smuggled in Venezuela, not to strike a blow to Spanish commercial interests, but to put food on the table.[37]

---

Bassi writes, "While the Atlantic was a world of wholesalers, with a few big vessels carrying huge volumes and values, the Caribbean was a world of peddlers" (Bassi, *An Aqueous Territory,* 110). Frequent, short voyages served as a more profitable and risk-averse way to trade illegally than carrying large cargoes and staying in port for a long duration as wholesalers might.

One- or two-masted sloops and schooners *(balandras* and *goletas)* dominated records of contraband seizures. Even smaller craft such as crudely rigged canoes *(canoas)* might be sailed on short voyages. See Rupert, *Creolization and Contraband,* 167; I. C. B. Dear and Peter Kemp, eds., *The Oxford Companion to Ships and the Sea,* 2d ed. (Oxford, 2006), 495, 540.

36. [Campbell], *Spanish Empire in America,* 314.

37. For examples of smugglers stating their attempts to make a living, see Testimonio de Graham de Langhe, La Guaira, Apr. 30, 1731, AGI, SD, 781; Confession de Joseph de los Reyes, Caracas, May 6, 1732, AGI, SD, 782; Declaración de Guillermo Brundenbrug, Capitán de balandra "Guillermo Joven," Puerto de Patanemo, July 9, 1731, AGI, SD, 782; Declaración de Juan Piñero, Capitán de "La Perfecta," La Guaira, Aug. 19, 1778, AGNV, Comp Gui, XXXVIII, fols. 219–220. "Care for my needs, and those of my family, wife, and children": Juan Piñero to the Intendant General, Caracas, Apr. 24, 1779, AGNV, Comp Gui, XXXVIII, fols. 275–276. Although utterances of this sort sometimes reduced punishments for Venezuelans involved in petty illegal trading, they had no impact on the sentences prize court judges doled out to foreigners. Juan Piñero, for example, received a ten-year labor sentence in the castle of San Juan de Ulúa in Mexico. Foreign smugglers' networks of maritime

Venezuela was not alone in attracting those who practiced commercial crimes as a means of subsistence. Smuggling provided a livelihood to maritime workers throughout the Caribbean and particularly in ports considered peripheral to imperial interests. Caribbean-based petty merchants in the French Lesser Antilles, known as *commisionnaires,* trafficked goods to foreign colonies without royal sanction. In the British case, hybrid "merchant mariners" in Bermuda built a living around under-the-table trade. The dynamics aboard small ships, where everyone had a stake in a voyage's success, reduced hierarchies of labor on the water.[38]

Structural shifts in Caribbean economies transformed many free subjects at the bottom of the socioeconomic ladder into a relatively flexible and mobile maritime labor force. Starting in the mid-seventeenth century with the sugar revolution in the Antilles, planters holding large tracts of land and significant numbers of slaves came to dominate the politics, economics, and territory of the region. By the early eighteenth century, small landholders, frontiersmen, buccaneers, and other people of humble means had lost a meaningful place in the new plantation complex as they were neither slaves nor sugar planters. The monoculture dominance of sugar also concentrated legal trade in fewer hands. At the same time, war and displacement in the Caribbean and population pressures in Europe increased the ranks of transient men. As non-Spanish colonies in the Caribbean morphed from bases for buccaneering to centers of agricultural production, Antillean officials of multiple empires came to see sea raiders as a nuisance to stability. In the late seventeenth and early eighteenth centuries, they branded these men, who had helped to establish non-Spanish footholds in the Caribbean, as pirates and hunted them down. Many maritime workers who survived these changes in the region would become smugglers.[39]

---

knowledge would have informed them that pleading poverty as a catalyst for their crimes served no purpose. See Informe del Yntendente de Caracas en vista de los autos formados sobre el apresamiento de una goleta olandesa nombrada la Perfecta por los Guardacostas de la Compañia Guypuzcoana de aquella Provincia, Aug. 19, 1780, AGI, Caracas, 839.

38. For the French Lesser Antilles, see Banks, *Chasing Empire across the Sea,* 157. For Bermuda, see Jarvis, *In the Eye of All Trade,* 124–125, 152, 461–465.

39. For the rise of sugar and accompanying economic changes, see Richard S. Dunn, *Sugar and Slaves: The Rise of the Planter Class in the English West Indies, 1624–1713* (1972; rpt. Chapel Hill, N.C., 2000), 22–23, 156–162; Isaac Curtis, "Masterless People: Maroons, Pirates, and Commoners," in Stephan Palmié and Francisco A. Scarano, eds., *The Caribbean: A History of the Region and Its Peoples* (Chicago, 2011), 149; Philip D. Curtin, *The Rise and Fall of the Plantation Complex: Essays in Atlantic History* (Cambridge, 1990), 79–85; J. H. Parry and P. M. Sherlock, *A Short History of the West Indies* (London, 1956), 74–80, 92–94. For the effects of war and displacement, see J. S. Bromley, *Corsairs and Navies, 1660–1760* (London, 1987), 8.

Despite its questionable legality, interimperial trade provided employment opportunities and favorable terms of labor for seafarers displaced by Caribbean upheavals. Illicit commerce comprised part of a life course that might include privateering, legal shipping, naval service, and piracy. This is not to say that the flotsam and jetsam of the Antilles represented a cohesive and self aware protoproletariat. Maritime workers' interests and identities sometimes aligned with those of their empires and social betters. However, they sought out occupations on the margins of the plantation complex and usually defied mercantilist trade objectives. The conflicting imperial legal systems that Caribbean mariners passed through in their seaborne travels blurred the line between licit and illicit professions.[40]

## SMUGGLERS BEFORE THE SPANISH COURTS

Although the expansive international connections developed by smugglers made contraband trade seem like the normative mode of commercial exchange in the Caribbean, it was still a highly criminalized economic practice in Spanish America. If the testimonies of illicit traders remind the historian of how arbitrary national designations could be when applied to people and their material transactions, these documents also confirm that imperial commercial boundaries concretely shaped the destinies of many early modern subjects. Put differently, illicit trade was still illicit by someone's laws. The reason

---

For heightened imperial actions against raiders, see Robert C. Ritchie, *Captain Kidd and the War against the Pirates* (Cambridge, Mass., 1986), 135–159; Mark G. Hanna, *Pirate Nests and the Rise of the British Empire, 1570–1740* (Williamsburg, Va., Chapel Hill, N.C., 2015), 330–415; John Latimer, *Buccaneers of the Caribbean: How Piracy Forged an Empire* (Cambridge, Mass., 2009), 278–280; C. H. Haring, *The Buccaneers in the West Indies in the XVII Century* (Hamden, Conn., 1966), 200, 230–233; Kris E. Lane, *Pillaging the Empire: Piracy in the Americas, 1500–1750* (Armonk, N.Y., 1998), 168–172; Jesse Cromwell, "Life on the Margins: (Ex) Buccaneers and Spanish Subjects on the Campeche Logwood Periphery, 1660–1716," *Itinerario*, XXXIII (2009), 43–71.

40. Anne Pérotin-Dumon, "Cabotage, Contraband, and Corsairs: The Port Cities of Guadeloupe and Their Inhabitants, 1650–1800," in Franklin W. Knight and Peggy K. Liss, eds., *Atlantic Port Cities: Economy, Culture, and Society in the Atlantic World, 1650–1850* (Knoxville, Tenn., 1991), 58; Doris Bonet de Sotillo, *El trafico ilegal en las Colonias españoles* (Caracas, 1955), 23; Franklin W. Knight, *The Caribbean: The Genesis of a Fragmented Nationalism*, 2d ed. (1978; rpt. Oxford, 1990), 90–104; Latimer, *Buccaneers of the Caribbean*, 261. Peter Linebaugh and Marcus Rediker argue for the notion of a conscious Caribbean protoproletariat in *The Many-Headed Hydra: Sailors, Slaves, Commoners and the Hidden History of the Revolutionary Atlantic* (Boston, 2000), 26–35.

smugglers' testimonies survive today is because Spanish coastal forces ensnared some contrabandists in dragnets of commercial policing. In Venezuela, the Caracas Company's interest in protecting its monopoly on the cacao trade along with its private navy produced especially active enforcement structures. Coast guard forces stripped smugglers of their mobility and their wares. Investigators prodded them about their itineraries, trading patterns, connections, and intentions in Spanish waters. Prize court judges sentenced guilty contrabandists to exile, jail, and forced labor. To carry out these sentences, the Spanish military complex shipped them all over the Spanish-speaking world. The criminal prosecution of smugglers contradicts narratives of seamless intercolonial exchange and underscores the lasting human consequences to economic actors who transgressed imperial borders.

Foreign smugglers' first contact with the Spanish justice system came when coast guard patrols captured, impounded, and processed their ships. Spanish marine forces, whether under the auspices of the crown or the Caracas Company, followed the shoreline of Venezuela looking for suspicious vessels. Any ship captain that acquiesced to the boarding of his craft could expect maritime enforcers to review the crew's travel documents and search the ship's hold. By Spanish law, coast guardsmen had the right to stop ships of any nationality. They frequently searched Spanish vessels as well as those of foreign empires. Non-Spanish shipping, however, usually presented a more tempting target. As only special licenses or emergency circumstances legitimized the presence of foreign ships in Spanish territorial waters, higher authorities were more likely to declare them contrabandists. In general, foreign vessels also contained a richer cargo of commercial goods to impound.

When coast guard vessels appeared on the horizon, a contrabandist captain had several options. He could loose his sails and attempt to outrun the pursuers. If close to shore, he and his crew could abandon ship and try to hide on land. If he had a good claim to legitimate business or thought he could pay off a coastal patrol, he could allow his vessel to be boarded. Finally, he could stay and fight. This last option was usually a losing prospect, as the arms aboard Spanish privateering boats overwhelmingly dwarfed those of most smuggling ships.

The suddenness of a coast guard attack could precipitate fight-or-flight instincts and the breakdown of discipline among a ship's company. On October 10, 1784, the royal privateer *San Nicolás* overtook a Dutch smuggling schooner called the *San Josef*. The two ships entered into a brief artillery duel until the superior firepower of the *San Nicolás* forced the Dutch into submission. Some

Dutch sailors hid in the ship's hold; others jumped overboard. These panicked actions incriminated the *San Josef's* crew as smugglers and its cargo as illicit.[41]

Seizures like that of the *San Josef* served the interests of coast guard crews far better than instances in which illicit traders immediately surrendered. Spanish courts would bestow a portion of the spoils from convicted smugglers' cargoes upon the members of a patrol ship, making it beneficial for coast guardsmen to quickly establish the guilt of those they pursued.[42] Self-defense and flight were sure signs of a trader's culpability. Dead or absent foreign sailors could not defend their right to property in prize courts. Documents record case after case of fleeing smugglers and abandoned ships, raising suspicions of overzealous or even sinister enforcement. Might these unaccompanied contraband caches signal excessive levels of coast guard violence against smugglers? Foreigners had every reason to fear capture as it risked harsh punishments, but the number of documents cataloging abandoned vessels and merchandise imply that the fear of castigation alone could not have produced these results. It is little wonder that one royal accountant *(contador general)* admonished "the carelessness and malice of militias and coast guards in failing to apprehend any suspects" when they seized ships.[43]

If captive smugglers survived the ordeals of arrest, Venezuelan anticontraband patrols brought them to land for arraignment. Depending on their site of capture, accused contrabandists came before prize courts in La Guaira / Caracas, Puerto Cabello, or Maracaibo. Authorities in port drew up appraisal forms *(avaluos)* that identified all pertinent goods and supplies aboard a seized vessel. Officials then estimated the value of these items and the ship in which they arrived. In noting the minutiae of a boat's cargo, investigators meant to record evidence of illegal commerce and also to prepare products for auction if the court determined the voyage to be illicit. In the same formulaic manner, Spanish scribes also prepared crew lists, which enumerated the name, nationality, and occupation of each man aboard.

After these procedures, a sort of trial could begin. Although a procedural order of events existed in trying smugglers, individual cases could diverge from these informal norms, adding or omitting steps as they went along. The term "trial" helps to conceptualize the flexible series of arrest summaries, in-

41. Informe del Intendente de Caracas Don Francisco Saavedra sobre el apresamiento de una Goleta Holandesa nombrada San Josef por la Lancha del Real Corso San Nicolas del mando de Don Ygnacio Xavier Emazabel, Dec. 14, 1790, AGI, Caracas, 839; Cedula del Rey al Intendente de Caracas, San Lorenzo, Oct. 10, 1792, AGI, Caracas, 836.

42. Klooster, *Illicit Riches,* 150.

43. Informe del Contador General, Madrid, Nov. 24, 1790, AGI, Indif, 1835.

terrogations, prisoner and witness testimonies, and magisterial consultations that occurred in most contraband cases, but these legal proceedings lacked elements the modern observer would associate with fair criminal prosecution and defense. Smugglers usually received no legal counsel and could rarely call witnesses or present evidence on their own behalf. Prize court judges, with the council of governors and occasional outside officials, deliberated on the fates of the defendants. In some tricky cases with extenuating circumstances, magistrates made appeals to the viceregal court or peninsular judges for help with decisions.[44]

Prisoners' status as uninvited foreigners made for the presumption of guilt unless they could prove their innocence. This is not to say that prize courts presided over show trials. As this chapter will discuss later, anticontraband magistrates exonerated many accused smugglers. On the whole, though, captured contrabandists found the deck stacked against them in the courts.

The process of trying the accused began with the testimonies of several coast guard officials to provide eyewitness accounts of wrongdoing and of the arrest. After taking these statements, judges questioned prisoners one by one. Interrogators examined as many sailors from a ship's complement as they deemed necessary to establish guilt or innocence. Once they had sworn in a defendant, officials asked for his name, nationality, religion, and sometimes age and marital status. With these formulaic details out of the way, the interrogation became more particular to a given case. Mostly, suspects responded to a group of questions meant to establish where they had been, why they were on the Venezuelan coast, what they carried, and whether they knew that unlicensed trade in the Spanish Empire was a crime. In situations where coastal patrols had detected accomplices, judges often asked sailors about their associations with Spanish or other foreign contrabandists.

Authorities occasionally probed for deeper motivations for visiting

44. Obviously, the malleability of the trial was not unique to trials of smugglers but rather a feature of early modern Spanish American, and indeed European, judicial proceedings. Speaking generally about the administration of justice in seventeenth- and eighteenth-century Spanish America, Tamar Herzog relates, "The idea that judicial decisions were inherently just, or were not decisions at all, influenced the judicial system in a variety of ways. There was no clear typology of offenses, no legal definition of crimes, in the manner we have today. . . . There was no need to determine which law was breached and in what way because what was breached was a norm that was not only legal: it was also moral and social. Judges were not required to explain how they reached verdicts. . . . The legality of the decision was never at stake. Judges did not focus on the observance of certain rules, but only on the fitness of the solution" (Herzog, *Upholding Justice: Society, State, and the Penal System in Quito [1650–1750]* [Ann Arbor, Mich., 2004], 21).

Spanish dominions. Inquiries about raiding, potential settlement plans, or war movements were not out of the question. Particularly in wartime, officials grilled potential interlopers about strategic military developments in the Caribbean. During the War of Jenkins' Ear in 1741, magistrates pumped one predominantly English crew for news because these men had heard rumors during a stopover in French Guadeloupe of a potential English fleet heading for Cartagena.[45]

Although prize court records outline basic procedural patterns of smuggling trials, they remain silent about key elements of these legal undertakings. Documents usually include the signatures of a scribe and at least one official, but it is impossible to determine how many people were in the room or who was asking questions during an interrogation. In addition, prize court records almost never speak to how authorities conducted the sessions. Unlike inquisition documents, smuggling cases provide no mention of coercion or torture in order to produce testimony. Nevertheless, conventions of early modern justice make it difficult for the historian to rule out physical torment.

The conditions of captivity are a mystery, as well. Were the accused well fed, sheltered, and clothed? If not, did their corporal want influence their testimonies? Numerous cases mention prisoners' developing illnesses after their arrests owing to jail conditions. Sickness might have allowed for a transfer to better quarters and a means to escape. One sick Venezuelan smuggler named Pedro José de Echeverría requested and received a transfer from his jail cell to the Hospital of San Pedro. When he was found guilty, Echeverría fled from the hospital and successfully avoided recapture for several years.[46]

Another major analytical concern of prize court records is how to interpret the voices of suspects in captivity. Smuggling trial documents present virtually the only means to reconstruct the experiences of a group of people who purposefully destroyed any paper trail vouching for their existences. Furthermore,

45. Declaraciones del Capitán de la balandra apresada Daniel Haley, holandes, 3 marineros Johanis Michael Lusk, Alemán, 31, Thomas Case, inglés, 24, Joseph Ray, inglés, 22, La Guaira, June 19, 1741, AGNV, Comp Gui, I, fols. 190–193.

46. Echeverría's case can be found in Informe, El Intendente de Caracas Don Francisco de Saavedra, Sobre un comiso de 3915 pesos en plata 317 id. en generos y 30 dhos valor de una canoa, pertenentes a Pedro José de Echeberría, y Don Juan Andueza . . . , Dec. 22, 1790, AGI, Caracas, 839. For other examples of sick prisoners, see Memorial del Presidente interino de la Casa de la Contratacion al Sr. Intendente General de Marina, Aug. 12, 1754, AGI, Caracas, SD, 792; Representación de Don Felipe de Ugarte ante el Gobernado y Capitán General, Caracas, Oct. 12, 1752, AGNV, Comp Gui, III, fols. 283–285; Sentencia de los reos ultimos de Leon, Auto de Governador Don Phelipe Ricardos y Asesor Gen. Don Antonio de Liendo, Caracas, Sept. 28, 1752, AGI, Caracas, 421.

the ad hoc quality of interrogations meant that nothing was out of bounds in their testimonies. Though smugglers often proved reticent, magistrates allowed them to discuss virtually anything that came to mind in response to inquiries. Nevertheless, contrabandists' testimonies show the interlocution of the investigator and the scribe. An interrogator's queries led the illicit trader's narrative in certain directions and toward what a prize court hoped to learn. Most trial documents recorded the accused's utterances in the third person, potentially obscuring what he or she actually said. First-person letters and appeals to higher officials show up only in some cases.[47]

With these limitations in mind, smuggler interrogations permit a glimpse of the general strategies and counterstrategies employed by foreign contrabandists and Spanish legal officials in establishing maritime criminal behavior. From this cat and mouse game, both sides expressed their understanding of what was illicit trade. Defendants' first line of defense involved trotting out any explanation that might provide a legitimate air to their voyages. As mentioned previously, bad weather, ship repairs, the need for freshwater and provisions, and other emergencies came up early and often in foreign sailors' testimonies.

Captured traders also claimed to be just passing through commonly used sea lanes en route to legitimate business elsewhere. The crew of the *Prins Willem,* a Dutch ship, said they had left from Saint Eustatius with the intention of buying mules and horses in Curaçao and Bonaire. A coast guard vessel captured the sloop near Los Roques, a tiny group of Spanish islands off the coast of Venezuela, nearly thirty leagues (one hundred miles) from the South American mainland. Despite the believable rationale of the *Prins Willem*'s captain that the vessel engaged only in intra-Dutch commerce and had no intention of sailing for the Spanish coast, the La Guaira prize court pronounced them guilty of clandestine trade.[48]

Other smugglers feigned ignorance that the items they had loaded or unloaded were illegal. Considering the numerous and conflicting trade laws of the various empires transnational smugglers encountered, their claims of obliviousness were sometimes honest. Nevertheless, contrabandists strained

47. These correspondences present their own problems of representativeness and articulation as defendants who wrote them were normally literate and of a higher social class. Additionally, legal formalism dominated these letters and suppressed a smuggler's true voice.

48. Declaraciones de Juan de Silva, 44, Luise Harse, 21, Juan Henrique, 34, Capitán Mercader, y contramaestre de balandra presa, respectivamente, La Guaira, Oct. 31, 1763, AGNV, Comp Gui, XII, fols. 7–11; Sentencia de Gobernador Solano, Caracas, Feb. 9, 1764, AGNV, Comp Gui, XII, fol. 68.

their credibility with outlandish rationales. One foreign merchant disavowed knowledge of the entire Spanish commercial code, remarking that he "was not aware, nor had he heard it said, that a prohibition existed against trading on the coasts of this province."[49]

To defend themselves successfully in court, foreign smugglers had to employ these strategies while placing their voyages within the bounds of internationally agreed-upon sailing routes and commercial practices. Context mattered in a defendant's remarks. The trajectory of a ship's itinerary needed to be believable. In 1760, coastal patrols seized one Dutch craft that supposedly sought to replenish their water near Cumaná in eastern Venezuela. The Dutchmen stated that they had intended to fill their barrels after a voyage from Saint Eustatius to Grenada and before catching the circular Caribbean currents that would take them back to Saint Eustatius. However, Spanish authorities were skeptical of their need to go to the mainland because, as one investigator pointed out, they could have filled their water supplies on the uninhabited and offshore islands of Isla Blanca or Isla de los Testigos. The contents of a foreign ship's hold also factored into a story's believability. When coast guardsmen found vessels nearly empty or containing only noncommercial items, they usually allowed them to go free. Conversely, when Spanish authorities found "goods only produced in the Spanish dominions," they became incredulous of smugglers' stories.[50]

A defendant's actions during and immediately after his capture proved as important as the context surrounding his voyage. It was essential that a crew stick to their initial story, as multiple or changing narratives rarely convinced prize court judges. Furthermore, Spanish magistrates almost never exonerated foreign sailors who resisted or sought to flee from coast guard patrols. They believed that innocent men would face scrutiny willingly.[51]

49. Declaración de Juan Piñero, La Guaira, Aug. 19, 1778, AGNV, Comp Gui, XXXVIII, fols. 219–220.

50. For the Dutch ship headed back to Saint Eustatius, see Declaraciones de Francisco Santoyo, 35, Francisco Loreto Marín, 46, José Vincente Ameston, 22, marineros del "Aránzazu," La Guaira, Aug. 1, 1760, AGNV, Comp Gui, VIII, fols. 166–169; Declaraciones de Don José Joaquín Arriaran, Capitán del Jabeque "San Pablo," 45, Juan Cornelio Maris, 40, Vincente Suárez, 43, La Guaira, December 1760, AGNV, Comp Gui, VIII, fol. 190. For an example of Spanish officials' questioning cargo, see the case of the Dutch sloop the *Two Brothers,* whose cargo contained cacao, hides, and beef tallow (all products of Venezuela) in Representación del apoderado ante el Gobernador y Capitán General, La Guaira, Mar. 6, 1764, AGNV, Comp Gui, XIII, fols. 85–86.

51. In 1759, a group of Dutch mariners belonging to the sloop *John Paul* went missing from the temporary jail where officials held them following the ship's capture in Barcelona

When testimonies and deliberations concluded, prize court judges issued a verdict that set in motion the final phase of the legal process. If found guilty, smugglers received a criminal sentence and saw their cargo publicly auctioned off. The Spanish treasury, officials, and others affiliated with the ship's capture divided the proceeds from these sales.[52] If vindicated, defendants retook control of their ship and cargo and sometimes even received restitution for their inconvenience. Such was the case in 1762, when a Dutch crew carrying meat and cheese from Saint Eustatius to French Grenada fell into the hands of Caracas Company patrols. The sailors protested the seizure and argued that they had papers for the voyage and carried no contraband. They had followed a conventional route between the two islands, and were captured near Grenada. During the time of the crew's imprisonment, Spanish officials auctioned off some of their goods and supplies. In the end, the chagrined governor of Venezuela had to concede the sailors' innocence and to offer them 19,583 reales as indemnity for these lost products. The exact divisions of the money from these auctions varied from verdict to verdict.[53]

When trials neared their conclusions, a significant number of contrabandists ducked the verdicts of prize courts by escaping from custody. The case of one 1767 jailbreak illustrates this trend. Three penniless and nearly naked prisoners used a picklock to flee the royal jail in La Guaira while their guard took a smoke break. The cellmates consisted of two smugglers (one French and one English) taken from two separate voyages in March and April of that year and a

(eastern Venezuela). Their flight from justice was a key piece of evidence for prize court judges in declaring the Dutchmen's actions to be criminal and their cargo worthy of forfeiture. See Expediente No. 5, Expediente sobre el Apresamiento de la Balandra Olandesa nombrada Juan Pedro . . . , Caracas, Nov. 14, 1759, AGI, Ctdra, 1634.

52. For example, consider the division of the proceeds of a contraband haul from 1786. The total value of this large seizure represented 33,120 pesos. Royal taxes took 6,955 pesos. The costs of the trial subtracted another 3,538 pesos. One-sixth of the remaining sum went to the judge in the case (3,771 pesos) while 10 percent went to an informant who facilitated the arrest (1,885 pesos). The crew of the coast guard vessel received 8,484 pesos. The remaining money flowed into the coffers of a handful of senior officials and the Venezuelan treasury (Ynforme del Yntendente de Caracas en vista de los dos testimonios de Autos que remite causados en la aprehension de la lancha Santa Rita . . . , Sept. 19, 1786, AGI, Caracas, 839). Another case from 1721, which seized 9,181 reales of contraband, subtracted 643 reales in royal duties and then broke up the remaining sum more elegantly into payments of a third for the informant, a third for the judge, and a third for the king (Juan Bautista, Genoves, contrabando que se le aprehendió en Maracaibo y juicio a que fue sometido, 1721, AGNC, Contrabandos, II, fols. 811–869).

53. Autos sobre apreso entre Isla Margarita y Tierra Firme de una balandra holandesa nombrada "La Anna," 1760–1762, AGNV, Comp Gui, X, fols. 188–265.

Spanish prisoner jailed by the ecclesiastical tribunal for an unspecified offense. Pervasive mentions of suspects breaking out of jail suggest that some prisoners might also have had help from their captors. A 1787 contraband trade investigation on the island of Trinidad discovered and prosecuted one jailer who had received a bribe to help his prisoner escape. In another incident, Company officials, presumably bribed, did not even take smugglers to trial. Instead, the Venezuelan courts tried a coast guard sergeant who had allowed illicit traders aboard an English ship to go free, despite stopping their vessel. Official corruption played a key role in the criminal justice process and in facilitating transnational trade.[54]

For foreign sailors not fortunate enough to escape jail or to beat the charges against them, smuggling convictions carried stiff punishments. To modern observers, these penalties may seem draconian given that unlicensed trade was typically a victimless crime and a pillar of the coastal Spanish American economy. Nevertheless, the sentences emphasize that although smuggling represented an ordinary transgression in the minds of most merchants, the Spanish legal system remained convinced of the offense's severity and eagerly prosecuted it. Among the lesser punishments meted out to convicted contrabandists were fines, short stints in jail, and deportation from the Spanish colonies. More serious offenders received long labor sentences building the great eighteenth-century fortifications of Bourbon Spanish America. These punishments are all the more noteworthy because smugglers were among the only civil offenders to be conscripted into compulsory labor service in New World locales.[55]

54. Gerardo Vivas Pineda notes the incredibly high percentage of fugitives from Venezuelan prize court jails in the second half of the eighteenth century. Between 1762 and 1764, he claims that 90.9 percent of contraband cases ended with flight from prison. Between 1765 and 1770, that number stood at 58.1 percent. See Gerardo E. Vivas Pineda, "La Compañía Guipuzcoana de Caracas: Los buques y sus hombres," in Ronald Escobedo Mansilla, Ana María Rivera Medina, and Alvaro Chapa Imaz, eds., *Los vascos y América: Actas de las jornadas sobre el comercio vasco con América en el siglo XVIII y la Real Compañía Guipuzcoana de Caracas* . . . (Bilbao, 1989), 314–315. For the bribed jailer, see Declaración de Manuel Aparicio, La Guaira, July 8, 1767, AGNV, Comp Gui, XV, fols. 266–267; Auto del Conde Miguel Roncali, Theniente Coronel y Ingeniero, Commandante Castellano Theniente y Justicia de La Guaira y Declaración de Diego Lopez, alcalde de la carcel, La Guaira, July 8–9, 1767, AGNV, Comp Gui, XIX, fols. 370–371. For the compromised coast guard sergeant, see Governor Phelipe Ramirez to Don Julian de Arriaga, Caracas, July 1, 1763, AGI, Caracas, 892.

55. Defrauders of the tobacco monopoly might also receive sentences of compulsory labor in the Americas (Ruth Pike, "Penal Servitude in the Spanish Empire: Presidio Labor in the Eighteenth Century," *HAHR*, LVIII [1978], 23).

The imperial justice system also deposited the convicted in military posts that Spanish subjects would not willingly man. It shipped them away as free labor to presidios and forts, as sailors on transportation galleys and coast guard vessels, and as factory workers in peninsular arsenals. Spanish officials theoretically could order the death penalty for smuggling. However, judges rarely mandated the execution of smugglers, as capital punishment tended to provoke reprisals among rival governments holding Spanish subjects and to deplete able-bodied labor for the military arm of the empire.

Changes in sentencing of smugglers over time exemplified subtle shifts in Spanish legal attitudes toward contraband trade and foreigners. In Venezuela, the formation of the Caracas Company in 1728 began a period of strict prosecution of illicit traders. Corruption and bribery, of course, still flourished within anticontraband enforcement structures. Nevertheless, criminal sentences for foreign merchants from the 1730s until roughly the late 1770s tended to be harsh and long in duration. Normal penalties for smuggling between the 1730s and 1760s included four to six years of forced labor in the arsenals of Cádiz, the Spanish presidios of North Africa, or other peninsular fortifications. During the second half of the eighteenth century, Spanish governors increasingly diverted foreign criminals from Spanish peninsular work details to the expansive Bourbon military projects in the Americas. The 1762 British capture of Havana catalyzed intensive fort building and defensive preparations that relied heavily on coerced laborers and soldiers. Even before this, a royal order in 1754 discouraged shipments of prisoners to Spain.[56] Convicted contrabandists endured four- to ten-year work sentences building and manning fortifications in port towns like San Juan, Puerto Rico, Havana, Cuba, San Juan de Ulúa, Mexico, and Cartagena, Colombia. The crown specifically solicited convicts from Venezuela to repair Puerto Rican fortifications in 1765. Between the 1760s and 1790s, convict laborers *(forzados)* helped build or revamp enormous de-

56. For long labor sentences, see Informe de Don Francisco de Varas, Cadiz, Jan. 10, 1737, AGI, Indif, 1829; Tribunal de la Casa de Contratación to the King, Cádiz, Feb. 26, 1742, AGI, SD, 790; Memorial del Presidente interino de la Casa de la Contratación, Aug. 12, 1754, AGI, SD, 792; Sentencia de Don Gabriel de Zuloaga Mariscal, Caracas, Dec. 3, 1740, AGNV, Comisos, XX, fols. 311–312. Sentencing to Spanish peninsula arsenals increased throughout the empire in these years (Ruth Pike, *Penal Servitude in Early Modern Spain* [Madison, Wis., 1983], 66–67). For increased fort building after 1762, see Lauren Benton, *A Search for Sovereignty: Law and Geography in European Empires, 1400–1900* (Cambridge, 2010), 177; Pike, "Penal Servitude in the Spanish Empire," *HAHR*, LVIII (1978), 24. For the order restricting convict shipments to Spain, see Se ordena que no se envíen reos a los Presidios de España, dándoselos destino en los de la América, Madrid, Jan. 25, 1754, AGNV, RO, II, fols. 98–204.

fense works in these strategic points as well as in Portobelo, Callao, and Manila. In many instances, construction necessities or the safety of shipping lanes due to war dictated whether convicts ended up in Spain or the Americas.[57]

By the end of the Caracas Company's tenure in the 1780s and 1790s, the Spanish criminal justice system demonstrated increasing leniency for contrabandists. Long labor sentences gave way to fines. Though royal magistrates still threw the book at captains and head merchants of smuggling voyages, they tended simply to deport rank-and-file crewmembers back to their colonies of origin. These shifts demonstrate the seriousness of purpose and manpower that the Caracas Company had brought to prosecuting smuggling as well as its desire to cut out competition in the cacao trade. They also reveal how much Caribbean commerce opened up in the second half of the eighteenth century. With the development of free ports and limited free trade between Spanish harbors, interimperial commerce seemed more innocuous in the minds of Spanish jurists.[58]

Despite liberalizing attitudes toward the punishment of unlicensed trade at the end of the eighteenth century, smugglers had long experienced dislocation and misery as captives laboring in far-flung corners of the Spanish realm.

57. Convict labor was the most important labor source in revamping fortifications in Puerto Rico between 1763 and 1783 (Fernando Picó, *History of Puerto Rico: A Panorama of Its People* [Princeton, N.J., 2006], 141). Slave and convict labor built much of the infrastructure of late-eighteenth-century Havana (Sherry Johnson, *The Social Transformation of Eighteenth-Century Cuba* [Gainesville, Fla., 2001], 85). For the crown's request, see Pike, *Penal Servitude in Early Modern Spain*, 137. Examples of convict labor sentences can be found in Autos de apresamiento hecho por Cap. Don Vincente Crespo, Capitán de balandra corsaria "Santa Gertrudis" de la Compañía Guipuzcoana en la bahia de Cubullon en Puerto Rico en 26 Febrero 1779 de una goleta dinamarquesa "La Juana" . . . , AGNV, Comp Gui, XXXIX, fols. 183–283; Autos de apreso en Puerto de Guayanilla, Puerto Rico en 27 Febrero 1779 de una balandra dinamarquesa, AGNV, Comp Gui, XL, fols. 1–67. For convict labor at other strategic fortifications in the second half of the eighteenth century, see Nicolas Cabrillana, "Las fortificaciones militares en Puerto Rico," *Revista de Indias*, XXVII (1967), 157; Benton, *Search for Sovereignty*, 177–180.

58. Wim Klooster, "Inter-Imperial Smuggling in the Americas, 1600–1800," in Bernard Bailyn and Patricia L. Denault, eds., *Soundings in Atlantic History: Latent Structures and Intellectual Currents, 1500–1830* (Cambridge, Mass., 2009), 175. For examples of sentences, see Gobernación de Caracas, Comisos, y Presas, Ynformes sobre Expedientes de Presas y Comisos hecho en la Jurisdición . . . desde 1714 a 1809, AGI, Caracas, 839; Cedula del Rey al Intendente de Caracas, San Lorenzo, Oct. 10, 1792, and Cedula al Yntendente de Caracas, San Yldefonso, Oct. 6, 1783, AGI, Caracas, 836; Reales Cédulas, informes y expedientes sobre comisos y presas en Barinas, Maracaybo y Margarita, 1792–1796, AGI, Caracas, 837; Yntendente Estevan Fernández de León al Sr. Don Diego de Gardoqui, Caracas, Oct. 25, 1792, AGI, Caracas, 810; Resumen del Consejo de Yndias, June 31, 1782, AGI, Caracas, 835.

Their position as foreign observers and coerced laborers in a nominally isolationist empire offers a fascinating perspective on both criminal justice and transnational contact in the early modern Spanish Atlantic. The prisoner narratives that survive mention poor food, heavy labor, and extreme discomfort. These complaints might have been rhetorical tropes to avoid appearing overly friendly with the enemy or to engender sympathy from the convicts' own imperial officials. Even taken with a grain of salt, the narratives express how gravely the Spanish legal system might have perceived and punished commercial crime. In their 1792 trial, a group of Dutch mariners testified that they were "treated in a way that we would not treat a dog." They complained that the coast guard captured their vessel only to rob it, threw them in jail for three months without due process, and then coerced them into signing false confessions by threatening to "tie us to the church bell and have the executioner beat us with sticks." The crew even claimed that interrogators tried to force them to renounce their Jewish faith.[59]

Although Spanish authorities shipped convicted smugglers all over the empire, the Spanish military often lacked the money to pay for their sustenance. In 1742, one officer bemoaned not having enough food to send along with prisoners embarking for the House of Trade in Cádiz. A British sailor in 1737 wrote that, while awaiting transport from Havana to Cádiz, his only food consisted of "turked Beef and maggoty bread."[60]

Reaching their destinations did not end the men's hardships. The same anonymous British convict described his time in the infamous Cádiz arsenal, shipyard, and prison known as La Carraca. It was a place "where we are put in Gaol every night among all manner of Villains, such as Thieves, Murderers, Turks, Fellows that has committed all manner of Villany." One of his former shipmates wrote to his wife, informing her that their living quarters were "130 foot long and about 30 broad" and held "300 odd slaves with irons on and Chains," who were "as full of Vermin as you can think anybody else." Spanish trial records routinely mentioned attaching shackles to a convicted criminal's leg *(grillete a pie)* as a part of their punishment.[61]

59. Certificación de los marineros olandeses de la Goletta Esperanza sobre el apresamiento de esta, San Felipe, Sept. 17, 1792, AGI, Caracas, 810.

60. Manuel de las Casas y la Quadra to the Tribunal de la Casa de Contratación, San Sebastian, July 2, 1742, AGI, SD, 790. "Turked Beef and maggoty bread": Copy of a letter from Cadiz, Feb. 1, 1737, BL, Add. MSS, 32797, fol. 148.

61. "Put in Gaol every night among all manner of Villains": Copy of a letter from Cadiz, Feb. 1, 1737, BL, Add. MSS, 32797, fol. 148. "300 odd slaves with irons on and Chains": Copy of a letter from Cadiz, Feb. 6, 1737, BL, Add. MSS, fol. 150. For examples of shackles, see

Construction details were harsh. In making gun batteries in Cuba, one Englishman and his fellow prisoners awoke "every Morning to carry Stones, and cut Wood, which we were compell'd to do, with a Driver at our backs, for six Weeks. . . . In a Word, we were much worse used than their Negroes." Though these English accounts no doubt exaggerated the suffering of sailors as a propaganda tool around the time of the War of Jenkins' Ear, their descriptions give a sense of the captives' experiences.[62]

These forced labor terms proved incredibly hazardous to the health of captured smugglers. Few records survive from which to estimate mortality rates in the Spanish convict labor system. However, bad and insufficient food, harsh toil, overcrowding, and disease (especially in the Caribbean) certainly took their toll. Such was the case for Lucas Hanos, a Dutch ship captain sent to Cádiz. An official in the House of Trade interceded in 1754 on his behalf after he had worked and served less than a year in the royal jail. The toil had made him develop a respiratory ailment that caused him to cough up blood uncontrollably. Spanish authorities eventually gave Hanos passage back to the Netherlands on the condition that he would never smuggle again. The forts and presidios that received foreign criminals had continual shortages of Spanish manpower for many of the same grim reasons. Typhus, tuberculosis, scrofula, and scurvy ran rampant in peninsular and Caribbean outposts. In presidios such as San Juan, Puerto Rico, at least 10 percent of forzados were idle at any given time owing to illness. Convict labor was a necessary method for replenishing ranks ravaged by disease and desertion.[63]

---

Autos de apresamiento hecho por Cap. Don Vincente Crespo, AGNV, Comp Gui, XXXIX, fols. 183–283; Autos de apreso en Puerto de Guayanilla, Puerto Rico en 27 Febrero 1779 de una balandra dinamarquesa, AGNV, Comp Gui, XL, fols. 1–67.

62. Richard Copithorne, *The English Cotejo; or, The Cruelties, Depredations, and Illicit Trade Charg'd upon the English in a Spanish Libel Lately Published, Compared with the Murders, Robberies, Barbarities, and Clandestine Trade Proved upon the Spaniards* (London, 1739), 15. Copithorne's account is very suspect and filled with geographical inaccuracies. I use this quote only because it is representative of other testimonies and accounts of the working conditions at fortification construction projects during the period.

63. Lauren Benton has noted that little documentary evidence remains of convict laborers because they had almost no access to legal recourse (Benton, *Search for Sovereignty,* 220–221). For Hanos's case, see Memorial del Presidente interino de la Casa de la Contratacion to Sr. Intendente General de Marina, Aug. 12, 1754, AGI, SD, 792. For illness among laborers, see Pike, *Penal Servitude in Early Modern Spain,* 140; Pike, "Penal Servitude in the Spanish Empire," *HAHR,* LVIII (1978), 27–31. The diseased environment of La Carraca, the prison and arsenal in Cádiz, led to the death of the imprisoned Venezuelan independence fighter Francisco de Miranda in 1816 (Karen Racine, *Francisco de Miranda: A Transatlantic Life in the Age of Revolution* [Wilmington, Del., 2003], 250).

In an irony not lost upon Spanish magistrates, forced labor punishments converted enemies of the state into its soldiers and defenders. Foreign convict labor built and patrolled the walls of all the key strongholds of Spanish military power in the Caribbean basin and some in Spain. Spanish bureaucrats saw exiling clandestine traders to faraway defensive positions as a way to increase troop numbers and remove contrabandists from the original sites of their crimes. More surprisingly, imperial authorities conscripted captured contrabandists to serve on Spanish ships in the fight against smuggling. Coast guard duty represented a low-paying and thankless task that, like presidio garrisoning, drew from the dregs of society. In many ways, smugglers, as warm bodies with maritime training and insider knowledge of contraband trade, made strong candidates for coast guard service.[64]

Eighteenth-century Spanish officials were certainly weary of employing criminals to capture their brethren. A letter from the king's royal attorney (*fiscal)* from 1735 conscripted foreign prisoners into the king's ships, but only for use in Old World ports so they could not return to Caribbean smuggling. By 1738, the Council of the Indies opined that the risk of convicts' flight and recidivism proved too great to allow forced maritime labor to continue. Despite the council's warning, the practice of drafting smugglers into antismuggling operations continued throughout the eighteenth century. A royal cédula of Charles IV in 1793 directed his governors to send contrabandists to serve in the regular Spanish army or in the presidios of Africa and the Americas but forbade their conscription into naval or maritime forces. Their crimes made them "not apt" for these duties. Worries about espionage also drove colonial governors to restrict the number of foreign prisoners allowed to work on Pacific forts less familiar to outsiders.[65]

64. In 1793, plans to fill the ranks of Spanish naval ships in Puerto Cabello called for emptying the jails (Julius Sherrard Scott III, "The Common Wind: Currents of Afro-American Communication in the Era of the Haitian Revolution" [Ph.D. diss., Duke University, 1986], 91). The Caracas Company also put convicted contrabandists into service on their ships while the smugglers awaited transport to Spain (Gerardo Vivas Pineda, *La aventura naval de la Compañía Guipuzcoana de Caracas* [Caracas, 1998], 37). The Spanish treasury and local coffers continually underfunded coast guard operations (Lance Grahn, "Guarding the New Granadan Coasts: Dilemmas of the Spanish Coast Guard in the Early Bourbon Period," *American Neptune,* LVI [1996], 24–26).

65. Thomas W. Gallant points out the early modern "dilemma of setting a thief to catch a thief." He observes, "Brigandage flourished in the frontier zones and the security forces sent to control their depredations and guard the border were often indistinguishable from the outlaws." See Gallant, "Brigandage, Piracy, Capitalism, and State-Formation: Transnational Crime from a Historical World-Systems Perspective," in Josiah McC. Heyman, ed.,

The prosecution, conviction, and punishment of foreign smugglers in Spanish courts and penal systems illustrate how imperial boundaries still constrained transnational commerce in the eighteenth century. Despite endemic corruption in most facets of the legal process, Spanish judges approached contraband commerce as a pernicious offense and believed its proprietors deserved to suffer. The very real human costs of deportation and coerced labor contradict the perception that smugglers and their accomplices could disarm enforcement structures with a wink and a nod.

## A VIOLENT BUSINESS

Between the extremes of unfettered commerce and imperial regulation of trade and borders existed a range of economic interactions that were by turns open and bellicose. The Spanish imperial presence on the Venezuelan coast was simply too weak to monitor all commercial exchange taking place in the region. Autonomous violence between foreigners, Spanish subjects, and coast guardsmen filled this power vacuum. As a result, intermittent, undeclared, and unpredictable warfare represented a familiar hazard for unlicensed traders. Maritime combat in the commercial arena blurred distinctions between smuggling, privateering, and piracy in the minds of officials and traders in multiple empires.

Foreign merchants' very presence on Spanish shores put them in violation of Spanish commercial codes and legitimized potential violence inflicted upon them. As the many examples of run-ins with the coast guard have highlighted, outsiders who trafficked wares on the Venezuelan littoral might find themselves forcibly subdued. Spanish laws specified that coast guard patrols were to make every effort to stop foreign shipping peacefully and avoid extortion, exemplary punishments, or the unjustified use of force. Additionally, any mariner who wished to join a coast guard patrol had to receive a license *(patente de corso)* and post a small amount of money *(fianza)* as collateral against any abuses he might commit. Notwithstanding these regulations, the

---

*States and Illegal Practices* (New York, 1999), 47. See also Janice E. Thomson, *Mercenaries, Pirates, and Sovereigns: State-Building and Extraterritorial Violence in Early Modern Europe* (Princeton, N.J., 1994), 68. For the 1735 order for the conscription of foreign prisoners for royal ships, see Ynforme del Sr. Fiscal, Apr. 30, 1735, AGI, Indif, 1829. For the Council of the Indies' explanation of the drawbacks of convict labor, see Consulta del Consejo de Indias, Madrid, Jan. 15, 1738, AGI, Indif, 1829. For Charles IV's 1793 ruling, see *Real cedula de S.M. de 21 de agosto de 1793, en la que se manda que á los reos de contrabando, ó fraude, se les destine inmediatamente al servicio de las armas en los regimientos del exército*... (Madrid, 1793). For concerns about espionage, see Charles F. Nunn, *Foreign Immigrants in Early Bourbon Mexico, 1700–1760* (Cambridge, 1979), 18.

right to seize vessels imbued some Spanish coastal patrols with an appetite to rob or harm nonnationals.[66]

No doubt, some maritime forces violently overstepped their missions because of their zeal for the job or their hatred of Spain's rivals. The capture of two Dutch ships off the coast of Hispaniola in 1733 underscores this point. Although the vessels sailed peacefully toward Curaçao and had no discernible connection to contraband trade, the Spanish impounded them anyway. After his men roughed up the Dutch crews, a Caracas Company coast guard captain supposedly told one of his Dutch counterparts that "if he could seize twenty ships like yours he would." Dutch authorities protested incessantly to Spanish colonial officials that Caracas Company patrols had captured and injured their law-abiding subjects for traversing routine shipping lanes to Curaçao. In many cases, Spanish maritime forces acted as judge, jury, and executioner, disregarding prize court protocol. Several coast guardsmen found themselves on trial in 1732 for using excessive force, having killed several alleged Dutch smugglers in front of their Spanish American associates. A 1788 plea for protection written by a group of forty-seven merchants to the governor of Curaçao noted that very little had changed in previous five decades. It described how Spanish coast guard forces,

> like true pirates, confront the Dutch flag and treat the letters of passage granted [to these subjects] by the governor of this island with utter contempt. They throw subjects of our rulers, who believe themselves protected by the flag and these letters of passage, in dark, disease-ridden jails, and treat them worse than the slaves of Algiers, who at least have something to eat and can still work for themselves at least part of the day in order to acquire some drink or refreshment. Whereas, on the Spanish coast, they not only are made to work in an inhumane fashion, but they are forced to do it, like dogs, with the whip. For the petitioners to give all the examples would only detract from their point.[67]

66. See, for example, "Ordenanza para el Corso de particulares contra enemigos de la corona, fecha en El Pardo a 1 de Febrero de 1762," in Aizpurua, *Curazao y la costa de Caracas,* 349–354; Vivas Pineda, "La Compañía Guipuzcoana de Caracas," in Escobedo Mansilla, Rivera Medina, and Chapa Imaz, eds., *Los vascos y América,* 313.

67. "If he could seize twenty ships like yours he would": Traducion de Letra A de Samuel Wusseluis por la Corte de Holanda, Jan. 4, 1735, AGI, SD, 785. For the 1732 trial for excessive force, see Autos criminales contra Francisco de la Rosa, Juan Lorenzo, Juan de la Cruz por decomiso de una balandra en Manzanillo, Coro, Mar. 28, 1732, AGNV, Comisos, XIII, fols. 1–134. "Made to work in an inhumane fashion": Annexe Recu le 3 Mars 1788: A Mon-

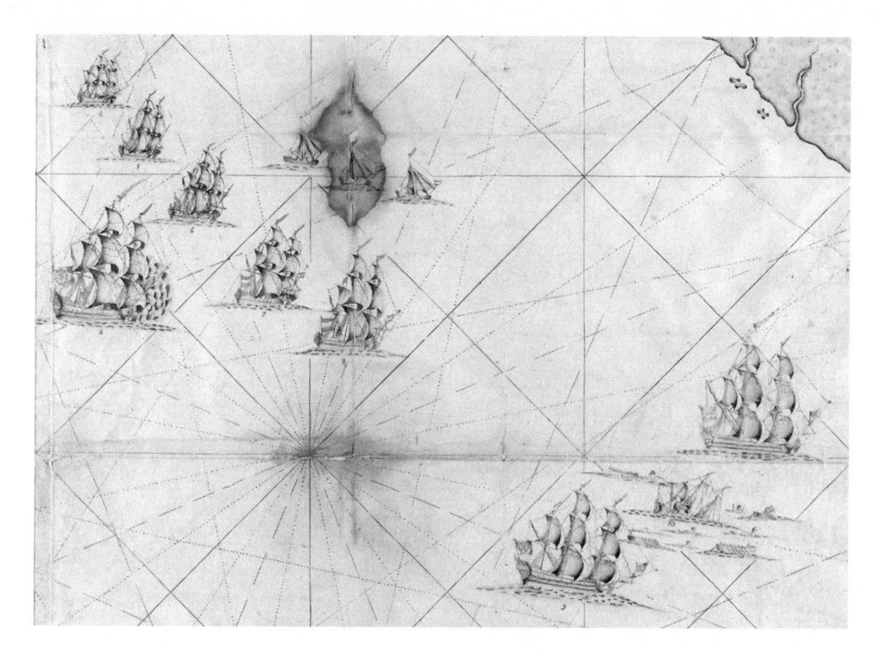

FIGURE 8. Fight between Spanish Coast Guard and Dutch Smugglers. Detail of *Plano y descripcion de un segmento de la costa de Caracas (en las Yndias occidentales), desde el Cauo de Cordera hasta la Punta de las Tucacas: Con las yslas adjazentes Curazao, Buenayre etc. en el qual ha demostrada la funcion que tubieron los de nauios Ynfante y Potencia guarda costas de S[u] M[a]g[estad]. Con cinco trantantes oland[e]s de los q[ue] apresaron 3. y uno echaron à pique.* By Domingo Antonio Pérez. 1727. *Courtesy of the John Carter Brown Library at Brown University*

In other cases, structural incentives overwhelmed the call of duty. The coast guard system, based on organized privateering, encouraged confrontation. As a group of British merchants explained, it was "the general custom and usage in the Spanish West Indies for all who engage in these cruising voyages to do it without any certain pay, each man being by agreement to depend entirely for his reward out of the captures they shall make." In their view, this incentive structure put Spanish coast guardsmen "on the same footing with freebooters and pirates." The merchants concluded that this maritime looting went hand in hand with wanton violence.[68]

seiur le Noble, et Venerable Jean de Veer Abz, Governeur de Curacao et des Distrcts de sa dependence de meme qu'a Messieurs les Nobles conseillers de cette Isle, Mar. 3, 1788, AGI, Caracas, 806. I wish to thank Nicolas Trepanier and Marc Lerner for help with translating the more idiomatic elements of this passage.

68. For privateering in the coast guard system, see Vivas Pineda, "La Compañía Guipuzcoana de Caracas," in Escobedo Mansilla, Rivera Medina, and Chapa Imaz, eds., *Los vascos y*

FIGURE 9. Spanish Coast Guard Ships Destroy a Dutch Smuggling Ship. Detail of *Plano y descripcion de un segmento de la costa de Caracas (en las Yndias occidentales), desde el Cauo de Cordera hasta la Punta de las Tucacas: Con las yslas adjazentes Curazao, Buenayre etc. en el qual ha demostrada la funcion que tubieron los de nauios Ynfante y Potencia guarda costas de S[u] M[a]g[estad]. Con cinco trantantes oland[e]s de los q[ue] apresaron 3. y uno echaron à pique.* By Domingo Antonio Pérez. 1727. *Courtesy of the John Carter Brown Library at Brown University*

The use of force against smugglers dovetailed with the contrabandists' own militancy. Those aboard smuggling voyages often bore arms and retaliated for Spanish cruelties visited upon their colleagues. As mentioned earlier, Spanish meddling with British shipping precipitated a strong British response in the 1730s, culminating with the War of Jenkins' Ear. Nevertheless, the British and French did not have the resources or interests in Venezuela to pursue regular reprisals.[69]

---

*América,* 314; [Campbell], *Spanish Empire in America,* 288. "Reward out of the captures they shall make": Memorial of the Merchants Interested in and Trading to H.M.'s Plantations and Colonies in America to the Duke of Newcastle, Feb. 9, 1738, NA, CO, 5 / 5, fol. 153B.

69. In his work on global smuggling, Alan L. Karras argues that smugglers rarely resorted to violence in practicing their trade. Yet numerous incidents on the Venezuelan coast contra-

Dutch smugglers, it appears, committed most freelance acts of revenge in Venezuela. Dutch aggression mostly took the form of raids against coast guard patrols. Spanish enforcement of anticontraband regulations had created friction since the Dutch took possession of Curaçao in the mid-seventeenth century. In 1689, a Dutch merchant ship opened fire on coast guard troops near Coro in western Venezuela. The troops were ferrying José Anieto, a former governor of Coro accused of illicit commerce with foreigners, to Caracas to stand trial. Raiders from the Dutch vessel quickly overwhelmed the Spanish patrol and took Anieto aboard their ship bound for Curaçao. Perhaps they sprang the fallen official from custody to defend him as their commercial ally or because he planned to expose their networks. Despite this foreign assistance, Spanish officials eventually recaptured Anieto and forced him to pay a 20,000-peso fine.[70]

The early years of the Caracas Company witnessed a surge in contraband arrests and an accompanying uptick in Dutch violence on the Venezuelan coast. Dutch merchants armed themselves as never before and sometimes outgunned their Spanish foes. The 1730s and 1740s saw bloody raids on Company ships and storehouses in retaliation for Company interference with Dutch trade. Spanish and British accounts discussed a 1737 fleet of Dutch privateers manned by more than one hundred sailors that picked fights with Caracas Company ships and looted cacao from their warehouses. According to the British governor of Saint Christopher, the privateers succeeded in killing an infamous Spanish coast guard official known for his viciousness toward foreigners. A year later, another Dutch raiding party seized a Company ship transporting brazilwood (a common dyestuff) to Santo Domingo. The aggressors settled scores with the Company by freeing two imprisoned contrabandists, burning the ship's registers, torturing the ship's captain until he disclosed the whereabouts of treasure aboard the vessel, and executing two Spanish crewmembers with pistols. The Dutch captain's brother was a well-known member of the Curaçaoan merchant community, which probably motivated his actions. Foreigners relished the opportunity to turn the tables on coast guard

---

dict this assessment (Karras, *Smuggling: Contraband and Corruption in World History* [Lanham, Md., 2010], 7). For British examples, see Sicilian Abbots to Waldegrave, May 26, 1738, NA, SP, 78 / 218, fols. 148–149; Eliga H. Gould, "Entangled Histories, Entangled Worlds: The English-Speaking Atlantic as a Spanish Periphery," *AHR,* CXII (2007), 777; Earl G. Sanders, "Counter-Contraband in Spanish America: Handicaps of the Governors in the Indies," *Americas,* XXXIV (1977), 79.

70. Declaración del Theniente Quiroz, Ocumare, Apr. 4, 1689, AGI, SD, 217.

assailants. In 1741, a group of Dutch vessels ganged up on a Caracas Company patrol ship that had run aground attempting to pursue them. They boarded the helpless craft, fired on those who jumped overboard in flight, and took as prisoners all those who could not swim. They beat the Company employees with sticks and swords and later burned their ship after ransacking it. One Spanish coast guardsman testified that the traders beat him, stabbed him, and forced him to work for eleven days after the confrontation.[71]

Such wanton bloodshed soured relations between Caribbean representatives of the two empires and ensured that contraband trade would continue to operate in a conflict zone. Dutch calls for restitution for improperly seized ships went unheeded. One Spanish bureaucrat wrote that "so many deaths, drownings, and home invasions on the coasts of Caracas, Cumaná and his majesty's other possessions" by Dutch seamen in the 1730s made restitution unlikely. The Dutch ambassador to the Spanish court, in turn, denied these accusations. He complained that the Spanish had captured at least five Dutch vessels illegally in the past year and noted that the Treaty of Utrecht (1713) forbade harassment of Dutch shipping "on the open sea."[72]

The Dutch also performed violence through comercio forzado. By this practice, smugglers used their maritime muscle to coerce Spanish subjects into exchange. In 1737, Venezuelan governor Gabriel de Zuloaga described an incident of forced trade like this: "They took the cacao violently after they made the cacao producers from whom they stole sign a bill of sale under duress. They also left European products on the beach corresponding to the value of the cacao taken." In another instance, smugglers supposedly ambushed a Venezuelan merchant in the central coast port of Higuerote who was loading his ship with cacao bound for La Guaira in 1759. According to the merchant, the Dutch crew, which was five times larger than his own, "against his will . . . took the cacao they wanted and then, by their own accord and despite his resistance, left

71. For examples of violent encounters with Dutch traders, see Araúz Monfante, *El contraband holandés en el Caribe*, I, 143; Gobernador Don Gabriel de Zuloaga to the King, Caracas, Nov. 14, 1737, AGI, SD, 785; Zuloaga to the King, Caracas, July 18, 1741, AGI, Caracas, 891; Auto de Sebastián de Arriola, condestable de la Galeota Corsaria de Compañía Guipuzcoana, Puerto Cabello, Apr. 11, 1741, AGI, Caracas, 891; Governor William Mathew to Council of Trade and Plantations, St. Christophers, June 14, 1737, NA, CO 152 / 23; Carta del Marques de San Gil, Traducido de la francesa por Miguel Joseph de Asiz, Feb. 17, 1738, AGI, SD, 785.

72. "So many deaths, drownings, and home invasions": Carta del Marques de San Gil, Feb. 20, 1738, AGI, SD, 785. "On the open sea": Van der Meer to the Marques de la Quadra, Madrid, Dec. 18, 1738, AGI, SD, 785.

him several little bundles and three cases" of goods. Filling these receptacles were European hats and bolts of cloth.[73]

Parsing out the intentions of both foreign and Spanish American subjects in such seemingly absurd transactions is difficult. A smuggling party that could take cacao producers captive could steal their cacao as easily as pay for it. Why go through the hassle of making the transaction and writing out a receipt? One Spanish royal attorney looked suspiciously upon a similar description, explaining, "The owners of the cacao attempt to buy the illicitly introduced effects under the pretext that they cannot be held responsible because of Dutch coercion." Dutch officials also recognized the subterfuge and wrote to their Spanish counterparts that, "to avoid the established penalties against prohibited commerce," Spanish subjects "pretend that they have been compelled [into trade] with violence, when at the same time it is they who have invited and persuaded other nations to do it." Spanish American traders certainly used the specter of forced commerce to justify their transactions at times and had Dutch participation in this ruse. A record of nine separate cases of coerced trade from 1763 lists the value of products left by the Dutch for each occasion. Amounts ranged from 300 to 5,008 pesos, sums presumably far too large for "captives" to have received in coercive situations. That this awkward arrangement of trade occurred nine times in one year on the Venezuelan central coast also casts doubt on the credibility of victims' accounts.[74]

Notwithstanding this skepticism, Venezuelans sometimes told the truth when they asserted that coerced commerce masked the theft of their possessions. Foreigners had good reason to give off the appearance of trade rather than unabashed theft. Leaving goods and receipts, even in instances where their actions approached outright robbery, shielded smugglers from receiving

73. "Took the cacao violently": Gobernador Don Gabriel de Zuloaga to the King, Caracas, Nov. 14, 1737, AGI, SD, 785. "By their own accord and despite his resistance": Declaración de Gerónimo de la Cruz, Puerto de Higuerote, May 21, 1759, AGI, Caracas, 892.

74. The French continental smuggler Louis Mandrin used similarly aggressive tactics of forced trade in mid-eighteenth-century France to compel the French royal tobacco monopoly to buy his contraband leaf. The presence of this practice across the ocean and in a different imperial group suggests that it was a ritualized practice common to eighteenth-century European extralegal commerce. See Michael Kwass, *Contraband: Louis Mandrin and the Making of a Global Underground* (Cambridge, Mass., 2014), 129–132, 148. "Cannot be held responsible because of Dutch coercion": El Fiscal al Consejo de Indias, July 29, 1732, AGI, SD, 781. "Pretend that they have been compelled": Extracto del Registro de la Resoluciones de sus Alti Potencias los Senores Estados Generales de las Provincias unidas, Oct. 14, 1739, AGI, SD, 785. For the nine cases from 1763, see Ynforme del Gobernador de Caracas, Madrid, Nov. 14, 1763, AGI, Caracas, 438.

the death penalty for piracy. In 1753, one Dutch expedition of three ships sent twenty-five armed men of color inland to find a cacao hacienda. Once there, they tied up the overseer of the farm, took thirty-five fanegas of cacao (roughly 3,850 pounds), and left a token sum of goods. The size of this force, their aggressive binding of the overseer, and the small amount of wares they discarded signal the unlikelihood of collusion between the trading parties.[75]

Provoked and emboldened by sporadically strict Spanish coastal policing, Dutch smugglers and, to a lesser extent, their foreign contemporaries accepted violence as part of their trade. If the Caracas Company's early patrols represented a shock to the status quo of lax enforcement, the raiding of the 1730s was the contrabandists' response. Violent engagements punctuated accounts of smuggling in Venezuela throughout the eighteenth century. Of course, many illicit merchants used stealth or a well-placed bribe to pass through Spanish territories unmolested. Yet contrabandists understood that in the event of confrontation, force, more than treaties, was the ultimate arbiter of their fate.

## CONCLUSION

Although smugglers, as quasi-stateless actors, sometimes collided with the state's enforcement mechanisms, on the whole they were essential agents of global trade, especially in neglected colonies. European empires in the Age of Sail grew not simply by following metropolitan blueprints but also through colonial actors who sometimes contradicted imperial will. In Venezuela, contrabandists aided the commercial development of the province, albeit in a manner that went against the wishes of peninsular Spanish authorities. Foreign smugglers became vital for the importation of European products and the exportation of Venezuelan produce. Their role as willing traders in a passed-over region, along with the early-eighteenth-century boom in cacao, revived the Venezuelan economy.[76]

More than simply improving the prospects of commerce in Venezuela, smugglers catalyzed free trade and merchant experimentation throughout the Americas. Particularly in peripheral locales, lax imperial control and di-

75. Expediente sobre los insultos de los Olandeses e Yngleses de Curazao, años 1753 a 1756, Consejo de Indias, Madrid, May 3, 1755, AGI, SD, 792.

76. Alison Games, *The Web of Empire: English Cosmopolitans in an Age of Expansion, 1560–1660* (Oxford, 2008), 11. Murdo MacLeod similarly identifies how smuggling resuscitated the economies of Central America, another peripheral region in the Spanish Empire, toward the end of the seventeenth century (MacLeod, *Spanish Central America: A Socioeconomic History, 1520–1720* [1973; rpt. Austin, Tex., 2008], lvii, 385).

rectives, local autonomy, and material scarcity combined to produce remarkably unrestricted trading patterns. As independent participants in the New World marketplace, smugglers cared little for imperially bound modes of trade and employed a range of commercial strategies in the struggle to provide for themselves. With the aid of willing Spanish American trading partners, foreign contrabandists' business developed into an important means by which many coastal subjects procured their daily wares.[77]

Supplying Spanish kingdoms put illicit traders at odds with enforcers of Spanish commercial law, as much because of what these contrabandists represented as their toll on the imperial treasury. The Spanish state, like most early modern governments, feared that smugglers' mobility and economic autonomy inspired insubordination among its subjects. Illicit merchants signified the spread of goods, information, and relationships that the state could not control.[78] Furthermore, their lifestyles evinced a weak allegiance to their home nations and a greater preference for independent, nonstate voyaging. This ethos evoked a long and painful history of piracy and raiding in Spanish dominions. Metropolitan imperial governors perceived smugglers not just as thieves of revenue but as a moral contagion. As the next chapter will show, Venezuelan subjects who contracted this social "disease" endured legal ambivalences similar to those experienced by foreign smugglers. They navigated between parallel moralities of permissiveness and scorn in their everyday interactions with the illicit commercial marketplace.[79]

77. Amy Turner Bushnell contends that these conditions in the Spanish American periphery encouraged low-intensity warfare throughout the seventeenth and eighteenth centuries but also "offered cover to smuggling, profiteering, and bold experiments in self-government" (Bushnell, "Gates, Patterns, and Peripheries: The Field of Frontier Latin America," in Christine Daniels and Michael V. Kennedy, eds., *Negotiated Empires: Centers and Peripheries in the Americas, 1500–1820* [New York, 2002], 23). In her work on colonial New Orleans, Shannon Lee Dawdy has argued that colonialism was, in many cases, a fundamentally experimental process carried out by independent agents seeking to develop successful survival strategies (Dawdy, *Building the Devil's Empire: French Colonial New Orleans* [Chicago, 2008], 5–20).

78. Banks, *Chasing Empire across the Sea*, 176.

79. Abraham and van Schendel, "Introduction," in van Schendel and Abraham, eds., *Illicit Flows and Criminal Things*, 9.

# 5

## *The Societal Ties of Smuggling*

### Venezuelan Merchants

Although Dutch, British, and French smugglers were resourceful bearers of unfettered trade, their livelihoods depended on the patronage of Spanish colonists. Traders from Spanish America responded to market inefficiencies or outright breakdowns in the imperial commercial system with independent commercial solutions. By trafficking directly with foreigners on their own shores, and occasionally abroad, they cut out layers of middlemen. It seems self-evident that Spanish American traders on the periphery would seek the broadest possible autonomy from laws created by metropolitan bureaucrats unexposed to Spanish American commercial conditions. They were also frustrated with the dominance of peninsular merchants in the Spanish Atlantic system. Nevertheless, the choices made by domestic merchants involved in interimperial trade were more complicated than this peninsular-creole divide reveals. Venezuelan coastal inhabitants' political and commercial identities operated on multiple registers. For them, being Spanish subjects, interimperial consumers, and local community members were not mutually exclusive positions. Unlike their itinerant, non-Spanish trading partners, Venezuelan merchants had to grapple with the distinct social contexts of conducting criminalized business in their own homeland.[1]

1. Geoffrey J. Walker nicely summarizes the worldview of colonial traders by pointing out, "Obviously the colonial merchant came to resent the Peninsular merchant. Of course he welcomed the smuggler. Naturally he sought as much freedom as possible from commercial domination by compatriots who lived in the mother country, and who, despite their economic impotence, thought they had the right to dictate the terms of trade" (Walker, *Spanish Politics and Imperial Trade, 1700–1789* [Bloomington, Ind., 1979], 14). In the context of neighboring Colombia, Ernesto E. Bassi Arévalo similarly finds that local affinity for

Spanish commercial law placed those who welcomed smugglers in a truly difficult position. Aside from the nationality of their trading partners, the commercial practices of Spanish American smugglers were similar to those of their counterparts who trafficked in legal wares. They studied market conditions and bought and sold the goods they needed at the best prices they could negotiate. By every conceivable metric, historians would call them merchants. Yet, in their correspondence, Spanish royal officials might describe their subjects who practiced unlicensed trading with outsiders as traitors and even rebels. One prize court justice in 1718 wrote to his superiors that Venezuela was "a land of uprisings . . . because every subject is friends with the Dutch and between the two groups there are a thousand entanglements" *(enredos)*. Nevertheless, a crucial circumstance separated these cohorts. Whereas foreign smugglers could sail from anchorage to anchorage conducting what Spanish authorities deemed illicit business and then return home, Spanish American contrabandists had to complete most of their transactions in the same legal jurisdictions where they lived.[2]

Internal contradictions attached to illegal exchange only added to the domestic smuggler's legal stigma. Particularly in Venezuela, the decrepit and exclusive state of commerce compelled merchants to trade illegally. These individuals either lacked legal trading partners or traded from a disadvantaged position because of the terms of licit exchange moderated by the state and the Caracas Company. By contrast, non-Spanish traders stood at the ready to sell their merchandise to frustrated Venezuelan merchants. Almost anyone, from habitual wholesalers to occasional peddlers, could do business with foreigners off the coast. The ubiquity and utility of smuggling in the neglected colony did nothing to decriminalize the practice in the minds of imperial bureaucrats. Royal authorities branded all those who engaged in commerce with nonnationals as "contrabandists." The term generalized what was, in reality, a nuanced group of traders and trading practices.

With these incongruities of legality and identity in mind, several questions

---

homeland (patria) commingled with Spanish imperial loyalty and commercial attachments to foreign Jamaica, Haiti, and Trinidad (Bassi Arévalo, "Between Imperial Projects and National Dreams: Communication Networks, Geopolitical Imagination, and the Role of New Granada in the Configuration of a Greater Caribbean Space, 1780s-1810s" [Ph.D. diss., University of California, Irvine, 2012], 65).

2. Salvador Pérez Guzmán to Governor y Capitán General Diego de Matos, AGNV, Diversos, VII, fol. 344, cited in Vicente de Amézaga Aresti, *Hombres de la Compañía Guipuzcoana* (Caracas, 1963), 11.

help to elucidate the experiences of Venezuelan black market merchants. What drove Venezuelans to smuggle? What distinctions separated smugglers from one another? How did these distinctions affect the way they were treated by the Spanish legal system? And finally, how did their connections in Venezuelan society facilitate their work?

A survey of criminal proceedings against domestic contrabandists in Venezuela demonstrates that they entered into commerce with foreigners for a variety of reasons in addition to simple profit motive. The backgrounds of smugglers were as diverse as the incentives that propelled them into the trade. Their lack of money and clout made them more susceptible to prosecution and assured that they would appear more often in prize court documents. Thus the connections engendered by social class, an often underappreciated determinant of the possibilities and limitations of colonial subjects, are important here.[3]

Illuminating the life courses of Venezuelan smugglers humanizes the trade and repositions it as social force in Venezuela. The reluctance to include Venezuelan contrabandists in the eighteenth-century history of the colony is particularly surprising given that, according to one study, Spanish American subjects made up the largest percentage by nationality (46 percent) of personnel aboard contraband ships seized by the Caracas Company. Most smugglers were, not full-time criminals marginalized from law-abiding society, but rather members of coastal communities. Their influence spread over many sectors of society including the Spanish royal bureaucracy, the Catholic Church, kinship groups, and, of course, criminal cliques. Strengthened by these networks, domestic smugglers often engaged in both legal and illegal commercial activities. Illicit business provided monetary gain and material sustenance. Covert commerce also drove Venezuelan merchants, albeit to a lesser extent than their foreign counterparts, into a world of violence and punitive legal action.[4]

3. Ann Laura Stoler and Frederick Cooper argue, "With the muting of political economy in recent colonial studies, class too has often been relegated to the sidelines, held constant, sometimes ignored." To them, class shaped empire by "constraining who came to the colonies, what visions they harbored" (Stoler and Cooper, "Between Metropole and Colony: Rethinking a Research Agenda," in Cooper and Stoler, eds., *Tensions of Empire: Colonial Cultures in a Bourgeois World* [Berkeley, Calif., 1997], 27).

4. The terminology here is worth discussing. I separate Venezuelan "smugglers," "contrabandists," and "illicit traders" from Venezuelan merchants when their interactions with contraband trade were more than just occasional. Certainly many, if not most, merchants engaged in some mix of legal and illegal commerce. For the examples I discuss in this chapter, smugglers were individuals who appear to have devoted significant resources and effort to smuggling and who faced criminal prosecution for their actions, rather than simply being

Venezuelan smugglers, along with foreign contrabandists and willing officials, formed the indispensable parts of a trade that held together the local economy, kept merchants in business, and drove the province toward commercial autonomy. Contraband commerce stocked Venezuelan cupboards

---

rumored to have traded illegally. The introduction and first chapter of this book offer a more complex discussion of terminologies regarding smugglers and merchants.

Scholarly works on the colony tend to focus on commercial actors only as they factored into resistance and loyalty to Spanish rule in the years immediately preceding the nineteenth-century independence wars. Coverage for the earlier eighteenth century emphasizes merchants' political activity, portraying them as a unified bloc opposed to the Caracas Company. Although these histories admit that unlicensed interimperial trade played a big part in the Venezuelan economy, they gloss over the details of domestic merchant participation in these exchanges, offering only an occasional anecdote. With a few notable exceptions, historians of the broader Spanish Atlantic world have analyzed cadres of legal commercial agents. Scholars have written deep histories of merchants' firms, finances, insurance policies, and credit arrangements. Similar portrayals of illicit commerce are scarcer. For works focusing on Venezuelan commerce and the independence movement, see Mercedes M. Álvarez F., *Comercio y comerciantes, y sus proyecciones en la independencia venezolana* (Caracas, 1964); P. Michael McKinley, *Pre-Revolutionary Caracas: Politics, Economy, and Society, 1777–1811* (New York, 1985). For more general works on this topic in late colonial Spanish America, see Sergio Villalobos R., *El comercio y la crisis colonial: Un mito de la independencia* (Santiago de Chile, 1968); John Fisher, *Commercial Relations between Spain and Spanish America in the Era of Free Trade, 1778–1796* (Liverpool, 1985). For works that offer commercial coverage but generally minimize Venezuelan merchant activity in contraband trade, see Roland Dennis Hussey, *The Caracas Company, 1728–1784: A Study in the History of Spanish Monopolistic Trade* (1934; rpt. New York, 1977), 122–149; Francisco Morales Padrón, "La Real Compañía Guipuzcoana de Caracas y la sociedad venezolana," in Ronald Escobedo Mansilla, Ana María Rivera Medina, and Alvaro Chapa Imaz, eds., *Los vascos y América: Actas de las jornadas sobre el comercio vasco con América en el siglo XVIII y la Real Compañía Guipuzcoana de Caracas . . .* (Bilbao, 1989), 217; Padrón, *Rebelión contra la Compañía de Caracas* (Seville, 1955), 33–34, 43. Examples of collective biographies of legal merchant groups in the early modern Spanish Atlantic include Jeremy Baskes, *Staying Afloat: Risk and Uncertainty in Spanish Atlantic World Trade, 1760–1820* (Stanford, Calif., 2013); Xabier Lamikiz, *Trade and Trust in the Eighteenth-Century Atlantic World: Spanish Merchants and Their Overseas Networks* (London, 2010); Susan Migden Socolow, *The Merchants of Buenos Aires, 1778–1810: Family and Commerce* (Cambridge, 1978). For a book treating the illicit side of merchant collectives, see Fabrício Prado, *Edge of Empire: Atlantic Networks and Revolution in Bourbon Río de la Plata* (Oakland, Calif., 2015). On Venezuelans aboard contraband ships seized by the Caracas Company, see Vicente de Amézaga Aresti, *Vicente Antonio de Icuza, comandante de corsarios* (Caracas, 1966), 200. Amézaga Aresti's numbers are mostly from the latter half of the eighteenth century. See also Ramón Aizpurua, *Curazao y la costa de Caracas: Introducción al estudio del contrabando de la provincia de Venezuela en tiempos de la Compañía Guipuzcoana, 1730–1780* (Caracas, 1993), 221. Aizpurua's work is one of the few produced by Venezuelan historians that pays close attention to domestic smugglers.

and closets. More important, contraband trade was not just economic but also political. It contributed to local self-identity. For Venezuelan merchants, participation in clandestine interimperial trade was an affirmation that they determined their own economic fate independent of privileged companies and imperial regulations.[5]

Spanish officials could temper this sentiment through enforcement of the law. Indeed, they made life challenging and criminally tinged for the ranks of merchants and peddlers who traded with foreigners. However, imperial bureaucrats realized that, by killing illegal trade, they would be crippling the economic activity of the society that had hosted it for generations. All but the most naïve officials acknowledged that smuggling was necessary for colonial provisioning and revenue. Royal authorities negotiated smuggling's place within imperial rule and settled for prosecuting its most flagrant or most humble domestic practitioners. The stories and circumstances of these unlucky individuals illuminate complex conflicts over everyday patterns of exchange and subjecthood in eighteenth-century Spanish America. Smuggling did not exist in a vacuum; despite engaging in an extracolonial behavior, its participants still lived within colonial structures of welfare, hierarchy, and social confluence.

## THE ECONOMIC AND POLITICAL RATIONALE FOR SMUGGLING

Venezuelan merchants chose to join the potentially dangerous business of smuggling for reasons that were sometimes self-evident and sometimes not. Basic convenience combined with economic practice and geopolitics to compel traders into below-boards exchange. Their contact with the Dutch, English, and French represented a practical solution to commercial deprivation.

At their core, Venezuelans' forays into illicit trade reflected aspirations for more equitable terms of exchange. Local merchants willing to risk criminal prosecution reaped economic rewards from the lower prices of unlicensed foreign trade. This was the case because of the onerous taxes that came with trading legally. Fees varied over time and were contingent on the goods traded and where a merchant entered port. Merchants from Spain paid these taxes up

5. As Christian J. Koot has demonstrated for the British Atlantic colonies, covert foreign trade gave domestic smugglers a "growing belief that local interests diverged from imperial concerns and that they, as locals, best understood the commercial needs and opportunities of their colonies" (Koot, *Empire at the Periphery: British Colonists, Anglo-Dutch Trade, and the Development of the British Atlantic, 1621–1713* [New York, 2011], 14).

front but passed the expenses on to Venezuelan merchants and consumers in the prices they charged for European goods.[6]

The Venezuelan merchants who subsidized all these additional costs could not hope to resell imported goods in the province at a competitive price. Though it is difficult to ascertain the exact prices of smuggled goods, the Dutch probably sold clothes an average of 20 percent cheaper than the Caracas Company's rates. The Company had a virtual monopoly on cacao going to Spain and could afford to offer the best prices on legitimately traded imports. Venezuelan merchants without such advantages probably had to charge even higher costs than these inflated sums to make a profit on the items they wished to resell. As Jorge Juan and Antonio de Ulloa reasoned in their famous critique of mid-eighteenth-century Spanish American corruption, "If [profits] were the same for both types of commerce, there would be no smuggling, for those who engage in it do so only to avoid royal taxes, and they would not take the risk if there were no advantages." Eliminating the overhead of paying taxes made seemingly circuitous trade routes more cost effective. As one intendant noted, smugglers were willing to pass through the countryside "by way of overgrown roads and mountain passes inaccessible on horseback" to avoid "royal duties that are paid . . . for the exporting [of goods] to America and importing into this province." This commercial detour "leaves the contrabandist a profit that allows him to sell his goods cheaper" than those legally imported to the central coast.[7]

Covert exchange also helped merchants sell Venezuelan exports effectively. Dutch traders offered better prices for cacao than Caracas Company officials. Over the course of the 1760s, Dutch traders paid an average of twenty pesos per fanega of cacao while the Company bought it at fourteen pesos per fanega. As discussed in Chapter 3, the Company's unchallenged position in the legal cacao market allowed its agents to depress prices to truly abysmal sums. Unless a Venezuelan merchant enjoyed a position in the Company's

6. These taxes and fees included the almojarifazgo, corso, avería, alcabala, and almirantazgo.

7. On estimated costs for smuggled goods, see Aizpurua, *Curazao y la costa de Caracas*, 105. "There would be no smuggling": Jorge Juan and Antonio de Ulloa, *Discourse and Political Reflections on the Kingdoms of Peru, Their Government, Special Regimen of Their Inhabitants, and Abuses Which Have Been Introduced into One Another, with Special Information on Why They Grew up and Some Means to Avoid Them* (1749), ed. John J. TePaske, trans. TePaske and Besse A. Clement (Norman, Okla., 1978), 62. "By way of overgrown roads": El Intendente General, Joachim Cubells da en globo una idea General del estado en que se hallan aquellas Provincias, la Real Hacienda, Agricultura, y Comercio, Caracas, Feb. 23, 1791, AGI, Caracas, fol. 809.

good graces, he depended on foreign intervention to help him profitably liquidate cacao.[8]

Smuggling aided merchants in sidestepping the Caracas Company's monopolization of provincial resources, as well. In a 1779 petition to the king, the Caracas city council argued that the first half of the eighteenth century had witnessed an explosion in contraband trade "born out of shortages and the poor arrangement of licit commerce." The council tied "the origin and crooked course of how cacao and other exports became illicit" to the Caracas Company's monopoly. The majority of the province's trade with the outside world "continues to be maintained by one hand alone," they complained, resulting in "rising prices for their merchandise and falling ones for our exports." Lacking other legitimate options, a Venezuelan merchant, in the council's opinion, had to choose between poverty and criminality.[9]

Throughout the eighteenth century, wartime privations further exacerbated problems in legal modes of trade and heightened contraband's appeal for Venezuelan merchants. As the colony lacked adequate naval forces to protect against foreign warships, its inhabitants endured blockades and ship seizures during a slew of conflicts. Bellicose geopolitics stalled already listless Spanish trade to Venezuela during the War of the Spanish Succession (1701–1714), the War of Jenkins' Ear (1739–1748), the Seven Years' War (1756–1763), the American Revolutionary War (1776–1783), and the conflicts of the French Revolution and Napoleonic Wars (1789–1815).[10]

These wars crippled licit merchant activity and import consumption in the province. Though Caracas Company forces and coastal militias helped to ward off a 1743 English invasion during the War of Jenkins' Ear, they could not break the blockades and end the misery of Venezuelan consumers. One Caracas Company director proposed to land goods in Santa Marta and Cartagena, Colombia, in 1743 because entering Venezuelan ports remained too dangerous.[11]

Wartime legal commerce further deteriorated in the second half of the eighteenth century, leading merchants to question Spanish imperial sover-

8. Aizpurua, *Curazao y la costa de Caracas,* 284.

9. El cabildo de la ciudad de Caracas hace presente al Rey la decadencia y portación de la agricultura, la ventajosa posicion geografica de la provincial y las bentajas que se derivarian de la libertad de comercio que solicita, Caracas, May 14, 1779, in Enrique Bernardo Nuñez, *Cacao* (Caracas, 1972), 264.

10. Antonio García-Baquero González, *Cádiz y el Atlántico (1717–1778): El comercio colonial español bajo el monopolio Gaditano,* I (Seville, 1976), 376; Baskes, *Staying Afloat,* 267.

11. Manuel de las Casas to the Juez de Arribadas de San Sebastian, May 10, 1743, AGI, Caracas, 927.

eignty in the Atlantic. Venezuelans smuggled brazenly with Dutchmen from Curaçao to supply slaves, in particular during the disruptions of the Seven Years' War. By 1779, superior British sea power harassed Spanish merchant shipping almost continuously as a series of conflicts blended into one another. The Napoleonic Wars showcased a commercial system in utter disarray. The intendant of Caracas in 1791 described Caraqueños driven to smuggling with the inhabitants of Cumaná, owing to a complete lack of underwear *(lencería)* in the capital. Contraband trade spiked in the late 1790s because Spanish American merchants lost confidence in the crown's ability to protect their interests from foreign navies and to govern commerce in a consistent manner. It took on complicated quasi-legal forms, as well. For example, Spanish and Spanish American merchants repurchased ships and cargoes taken as prizes during wartime and sold them in the British West Indies (known as *rescate).* Spanish authorities offered permits for this newly devised and technically legal commercial contrivance to favored merchants. Rescates sustained trade during wartime and served as a tacit toleration of illicit foreign trade. Merchant behavior during the Napoleonic Wars reveals a historical constant of the eighteenth century: smuggling increased during times of conflict-induced scarcity.[12]

Whether at war or at peace, a host of political factors also prompted merchants to engage in illicit commerce. Bureaucratic missteps in regulating the Mexico trade encapsulated how imperial politics hindered legitimate trade opportunities in the province. Overregulation, oligarchic meddling, and economic competition from elsewhere in the empire chipped away at this pillar of Venezuelan commerce. In 1722, the marqués de Torre Casa, a wealthy nobleman in Caracas, attempted to monopolize the cacao trade with New Spain by limiting the use of his ships for transport to favored individuals. Though the Council of the Indies quickly intervened to break Torre Casa's stranglehold on

12. On the smuggling of slaves, see Pedro Rodríguez Campomanes, *Reflexiones sobre el comercio español a Indias (1762)* (Madrid, 1988), 83. On British sea power, see Miguel Izard, "Contrabandistas, comerciantes e ilustrados," *BA,* XXVIII (1978), 79. Trade with Cumaná in 1791: El Intendente General, Joachim Cubells Da en globo una idea General del estado en que se hallan aquellas Provincias, la Real Hacienda, Agricultura, y Comercio, Caracas, Feb. 23, 1791, AGI, Caracas, 809. On the spike in contraband trade during the late 1790s, see Jeremy Adelman, "Commerce and Corruption in the Late Spanish and Portuguese Empires," in Emmanuel Kreike and William Chester Jordan, eds., *Corrupt Histories* (Rochester, N.Y., 2004), 438–448; Adelman, *Sovereignty and Revolution in the Iberian Atlantic* (Princeton, N.J., 2006), 5–10, 135–146. On rescates, see Adrian J. Pearce, "*Rescates* and Anglo-Spanish Trade in the Caribbean during the French Revolutionary Wars, ca. 1797–1804," *Journal of Latin American Studies,* XXXVIII (2006), 607–608, 621.

the Mexico trade, they did little when the Caracas Company sought to expand beyond its initial charter and into the Mexican market in the late 1730s. By 1741, the crown was convinced of Company rationales promising lower cacao prices for imperial consumers, made possible in part by the relative security of Company ships even during wartime in New Spain. The Company's permission to trade cacao in New Spain went into effect in 1742.[13]

Venezuelan merchants not closely linked to the Caracas Company viewed this development with consternation. They believed the Company would come to dominate the market and depress the prices of cacao exported to Mexico, just as they had done for supplies of the commodity headed to Spain. As one of the consequences of the Juan Francisco de León rebellion (1749–1751) against the Company, imperial authorities in 1753 forbade their presence in the Mexican market. However, the crown also placed strict regulations on the trade, including the formation of price lists for enumerated goods that could be bought with cacao.[14]

Venezuelan cacao merchants and producers not only coped with bureaucratic ambivalence regarding monopolization of the Mexican chocolate trade but also endured the crown's laissez-faire response to competition from Ecuador. Guayaquil was a fertile site for cacao production and a convenient Pacific shipping port to Acapulco, Mexico. Venezuelans resented Ecuadoran intrusion into their supposedly exclusive market. Although the king issued a royal order in 1724 outlawing Guayaquil cacao in New Spain, the empire invested few resources toward stanching the illicit flow of chocolate from Ecuador.

On this issue, Venezuelan merchants took a political position that was contradictory to the illicit actions of many of their number: they asked the state to regulate commerce more strictly. In doing so, they asserted their firsthand experience in imperial trading matters as justification for why they should have a voice in commercial policy. Frequent dispatches from merchants and governors complained that Guayaquil cacao had glutted the Mexican market and dramatically reduced legal cacao prices.[15]

13. Joseph Pérez, *Los movimientos precursores de la emancipación en Hispanoamérica* (Madrid, 1977), 35; Robert J. Ferry, *The Colonial Elite of Early Caracas: Formation and Crisis, 1567–1767* (Berkeley, Calif., 1989), 5–6. On expanded cacao trade with New Spain, see Real Cédula, El Pardo, Jan. 21, 1741, AGI, Caracas, 926.

14. Eduardo Arcila Farías, *Economía colonial de Venezuela* (Mexico City, 1946), 441.

15. Real Cedula que prohibe comercio de cacao de Guayaquil con Nueva España, Madrid, Jun. 27, 1724, in Nuñez, *Cacao,* 132; Sobre el bajo precio que tiene el cacao de esta provincial en Nueva España por la competencia que le hace el de Martinica y Guayaquil, Cabildo del 18 de junio de 1708, Caracas, Jun. 18, 1708, ibid., 124; Representación en que se pide al rey la prohibición de introducer cacao de Guayaquil en Veracruz, Cabildo del 23 de febrero de

Ironically, Venezuelan traders became the victims, rather than the beneficiaries, of smuggling in this case. Guayaquil continued to be the thorn in the side of Venezuelan cacao producers throughout the century. The crown gave the Ecuadorian port the right to comercio libre sooner than Caracas. Because Ecuadorian cacao producers could ship unlimited quantities of cacao to New Spain while Venezuelan exports were limited by quotas, they held a significant commercial advantage over their Venezuelan competitors from 1774 to 1789. The difficulties with the Mexican cacao trade as a viable means of aboveboard commerce provided yet another impetus to sell Venezuelan produce to foreign markets.[16]

Even the late-eighteenth-century commercial reforms credited with reinvigorating the Venezuelan economy pleased some merchant groups while upsetting others. The formation of the Caracas Consulado (merchants' guild) in 1793 satisfied elite merchants as it rationalized trade and production. However, this organization excluded traders of more humble means, driving them away from legitimate business. More locally, several governors and intendants sought to clean up the physical space of Caracas's central market (on the *Plaza Central*). This initiative contented merchants who desired a more orderly space to sell their wares but irked purveyors who saw their stalls shut down because they sold contraband.[17]

Competitive advantages, simple circumstances, and complex political transformations all attracted Venezuelan merchants to smuggling. In the province, legitimate trade consistently proved prohibitively expensive, inconvenient, unavailable, or dangerous. Although it could be a risky proposition to enter the criminal world of illicit exchange, the lackluster conditions of legal commerce presented just as much uncertainty but comparatively smaller opportunities for profit. The more appropriate question when analyzing Venezue-

---

1767, Caracas, Feb. 23, 1767, ibid., 211; Ynforme del gobernador de Caracas, Madrid, Feb. 29, 1776, AGI, Caracas, 438; Michael L. Conniff, "Guayaquil through Independence: Urban Development in a Colonial System," *Americas*, XXXIII (1977), 391.

16. Guillermina del Valle Pavón, "Cacao de Guayaquil y apertura commercial: La promoción del comercio de cacao y azúcar a través del Consulado de México," in Nikolaus Böttcher, Bernd Hausberger, and Antonio Ibarra, eds., *Redes y negocios globales en el mundo ibérico, siglos XVI–XVIII* (Orlando, Fla., 2011), 239–240, 262; Eduardo Arcila Farías, *Comercio entre Venezuela y México en los siglos XVII y XVIII* (Mexico City, 1950), 249–278.

17. On the Caracas Consulado, see Manuel Lucena Salmoral, *Vísperas de la independencia americana: Caracas* (Madrid, 1986), 208, 366; Rosario Salazar Bravo, *El comercio diario en la Caracas del siglo XVIII: Una aproximación a la historia urbana* (Caracas, 2008), 72–74; McKinley, *Pre-Revolutionary Caracas*, 78. On the central market, see Salazar Bravo, *El comercio diario en la Caracas*, 66, 74, 194.

lan merchant motivations is, not "Why did they smuggle?" but rather, "How did smuggling intermingle with the structures of their lives?"

## CLASS AND THE DIVERSITY OF SMUGGLERS

For the purposes of outlining the dire conditions of legal trade in Venezuela, it has made sense to speak of domestic merchants as a unified bloc, but they did not act as such. Local traders separated into many different strata. Their business interests, advantages, liabilities, and connections varied greatly. The factors animating one merchant to exchange goods with a foreign smuggler kept another within the fold of legitimate commerce.[18]

Overwhelmingly, participants in smuggling at the lower end of the class hierarchy found themselves more frequently targeted for arrest and prosecution. This reality reflected their lesser ability to bribe or buy their way out of trouble. It also illustrated colonial administrators' decision to pursue easy convictions, given their limited resources. When authorities needed to punish someone to show compliance with their duties, they prosecuted merchants who contributed the least to bureaucratic pocketbooks and imperial coffers. Sentencing of Venezuelan residents could be every bit as severe as that of non-Spanish subjects described in the previous chapter, although in practice judges tended to soften Venezuelans' punishments, since they did not represent dangerous foreign agents.

The term "merchant" provides a convenient designation for those who bought and sold goods in coastal Venezuela, but it fails to express the gradations of commercial participants. This diversity was particularly evident for domestic businessmen and even casual consumers involved with clandestine commerce. Career Spanish American smugglers existed in the province, but they surely comprised a small portion of the total body of practitioners. In the less specialized commercial society of Venezuela, defining an individual exclusively as a merchant or contrabandist is difficult. The lack of imperial shipping made for greater material need among all classes but smaller degrees of wealth separating them. Therefore, trading partners of non-Spanish smugglers could be career merchants, opportunists, agricultural producers, clergy

18. For Sanjay Subrahmanyam, identifying a collective merchant identity in any early modern context is nearly impossible because "the sense of 'community' and the sense of class or stratum militated against one another. Merchant society was prone to factionalism based on community, and this was thus the characteristic of any great mercantile city" (Subrahmanyam, "Introduction," in Subrahmanyam, ed., *Merchant Networks in the Early Modern World* [Brookfield, Vt., 1996], xix).

members, or just independent-minded consumers formally employed in other occupations.[19]

The echelons of those subjects technically known as merchants, though not representative of all who engaged in smuggling, included a number of class designations. At the top of the heap were *comerciantes.* To be a member of this group, a merchant needed 30,000 pesos in wealth. Comerciantes oversaw their firms, which dealt in European imports, but did not directly buy or sell anything themselves, as they considered this activity beneath their station. Their agents bought and sold in quantities befitting wholesalers and were most active in transatlantic trade. In Venezuela, the comerciantes usually numbered only about 100 to 120 individuals. Most were noblemen and of Basque origin, given the Caracas Company's dominance over the colony. Beneath the comerciantes, a group of primarily Spanish-born, large-scale retailers called *mercaderes* bought and sold European imports they received from comerciantes. Although they did not own storefronts, they personally sold most dry goods and cloth and often traded in Spanish intercolonial markets. Further down the socioeconomic ladder were the *bodegueros,* who mainly sold imported food. Unlike comerciantes and mercaderes, they maintained retail stores in towns. They developed close business relationships with the mercaderes. The *pulperos* were the lowest merchants to own their own shops. In contrast to the bodegueros, they sold mostly native *(criollo)* foodstuffs. At the bottom of the merchant ranks existed the *buhoneros,* who made a living as street vendors without fixed retail space.[20]

Adding to this diversity, planters and agriculture producers also partici-

19. Separating "merchants" from "smugglers" proves difficult throughout history. Merchants in a range of times and places might dabble in the illegal economy and use profits from this space to add to their legal finances and public credit (Alexandra Harnett and Shannon Lee Dawdy, "The Archaeology of Illegal and Illicit Economies," *Annual Review of Anthropology,* XLII [2013], 42). In his survey of two hundred years of interimperial smuggling, Wim Klooster writes, "The term 'merchant' may be misleading: on the receiving end, there was no prototypical smuggler. People from all walks of life participated in illicit trade with foreigners" (Klooster, "Inter-Imperial Smuggling in the Americas, 1600–1800," in Bernard Bailyn and Patricia L. Denault, eds., *Soundings in Atlantic History: Latent Structures and Intellectual Currents, 1500–1830* [Cambridge, Mass., 2009], 142).

20. Mercedes M. Alvarez F., *Comercio y comerciantes, y sus proyecciones en la independencia venezolana* (Caracas, 1964), 48–50; Jay Kinsbruner, *Petty Capitalism in Spanish America: The Pulperos of Puebla, Mexico City, Caracas, and Buenos Aires* (Boulder, Colo., 1987), 61; Manuel Lucena Samoral, *Vísperas de la independencia americana: Caracas* (Madrid, 1986), 207–215; Salazar Bravo, *El comercio diario en Caracas,* 110–111; Catherine Lugar, "Merchants," in Louisa Schell Hoberman and Susan Migden Socolow, eds., *Cities and Society in Colonial Latin America* (Albuquerque, N.M., 1986), 47–48; Socolow, *Merchants of Buenos Aires,* 14.

pated in trade and smuggling. Many large-scale planters (known as the *grandes cacaos,* or mantuanos) could afford the overhead costs that came with trading legally with Spain or New Spain or smuggling through an intermediary. Smaller producers (the *cosecheros)* lacked the financial means to interact with overseas markets or with smugglers by proxy and often carried out trade directly with foreigners. Convenience also played a role in the direct trading, as cacao plantations often were located very close to the coast. Cosecheros, along with overseers for large plantation owners *(mayordomos),* sometimes stole cacao from the mantuanos to trade with foreigners.[21]

It was not uncommon for subsistence farmers and coastal residents employed in other occupations to trade with foreigners to increase the quantity and variety of goods coming into their communities, making them "merchants" of a sort. Immigrants from the Canary Islands, in particular, conducted brisk business with non-Spanish smugglers. The Isleños's affinity for smuggling stemmed from their fiercely independent and self-made character in Venezuela, as well as the marginal lands they had received upon arriving in the colony at the end of the seventeenth century. As a disadvantaged group living outside the main routes of the Caracas Company's legal trade, the Canary Islanders used contraband commerce as an important bridge to transatlantic markets. Their proclivities toward unlicensed foreign trade, as well as Company attempts to disrupt this commerce, would make the Isleños the catalytic population of the León Rebellion of 1749–1751.[22]

Within the hierarchy of domestic smugglers, elite merchants maintained the most ambivalent relationship with the business. Many comerciantes and mercaderes had one foot in legitimate commerce and the other in clandestine trade. These individuals possessed no ideological affiliation to the official Spanish transatlantic system, foreign contrabandists, or the Caracas Company. Instead, they made calculated business decisions regarding which means of trade would maximize their profits in volatile times. Many of the Venezuela merchants and producers who made up "the illustrious families known in Europe" supported León's rebellion against the Caracas Company's abuses in 1749. These same patricians became partners in the Company when the crown

21. Morales Padrón, "La Real Compañía Guipuzcoana de Caracas y la sociedad venezolana," in Escobedo Mansilla, Rivera Medina, and Chapa Imaz, eds., *Los vascos y America,* 217; Aizpurua, *Curazao y la costa de Caracas,* 272–273.

22. John Lynch, "Spanish America's Poor Whites: Canarian Immigrants in Venezuela, 1700–1830," in Lynch, *Latin America between Colony and Nation: Selected Essays* (New York, 2001), 60–64; Lucas Guillermo Castillo Lara, *La aventura fundacional de los Isleños: Panaquire y Juan Francisco de León* (Caracas, 1983), 10–12, 164–166.

granted Venezuelans partial ownership of the venture in 1751. One of the Bolívar family's personal slaves had read the news of the Company's temporary expulsion to a cheering crowd in 1749, but the Bolívars numbered among the many prominent Caracas names inscribed as shareholders in Company ledgers several years later. Following a common pattern in the Bourbon-led Americas, many of the first mantuano families of Caracas even married into Basque merchant lineages in order to extend their connections into the Iberian Peninsula and the Spanish court during the second half of the eighteenth century.[23]

Throughout the Americas, elite merchants who benefited from the rigid fleet and register ship systems often bristled at commercial reforms. Many Mexican merchants, for instance, continued to advocate for the flota and annual trade fairs even though they had no personal stake in the success of these institutions. These traders had become master manipulators of the status quo, purchasing and spreading contraband items throughout New Spain and Central America in advance of the fairs to ensure deeply discounted prices on officially licensed goods. Likewise, many of the top merchants in Venezuela loathed comercio libre because it lessened their control over producers, who gained more options for shipping their cacao.[24]

Wealthy merchants rejected attempts to open up legal trade with foreigners because non-Spanish traders threatened their dominant influence over the licit cacao market. The elite-controlled Real Consulado de Caracas of the late eighteenth century took a strict stance against foreign trade in its pronouncements and actions. Thomas Kinder, a British trader in Argentina at the end of the eighteenth century, confirmed a similar sentiment in Buenos Aires, where "every Merchant here is a decided enemy to the establishment of free

23. "The illustrious families known in Europe": Joseph Luis de Cisneros, *Descripción exacta de la Provincia de Venezuela* (1764) (Caracas, 1981), 121–122. On the Bolívars, see Diligencia del Escribano Gregorio del Portillo, Caracas, Apr. 23, 1749, AGNV, León, fol. 1, 33–39, in Augusto Mijares, ed., *Documentos relativos a la insurrección de Juan Francisco de León* (Caracas, 1949), 55; Montserrat Gárate Ojanguren, *La Real Compañía Guipuzcoana de Caracas* (San Sebastián, 1990), 87. Alejandro Cardozo Uzcátegui labels politically and commercially powerful offspring of mantuano and Basque marriages "neo-mantuanos" (Uzcátegui, *Los mantuanos en la Corte española: Una relación cisatlántica, 1783–1825* [Bilbao, 2013], 21; see also 142–143, 157, 171–175, 266). The general pattern of elite creole families' marrying their daughters to peninsular merchants is outlined in D. A. Brading, *Miners and Merchants in Bourbon Mexico, 1763–1810* (Cambridge, 1971), 306–312, and Lugar, "Merchants," in Hoberman and Socolow, eds., *Cities and Society in Colonial Latin America,* 63–64.

24. On trade fairs, see Baskes, *Staying Afloat,* 50–53; Allyn C. Loosley, "The Puerto Bello Fairs," *HAHR,* XIII (1933), 330–332; Walker, *Spanish Politics and Imperial Trade,* 214. On merchant critiques of comercio libre, see Arcila Farías, *Economía colonial de Venezuela,* 365.

trade, and to Englishmen being permitted to settle as Merchants. They see therein the downfall of these rich profits for which they cannot hope honestly to compensate themselves."[25]

In contrast to wealthy wholesalers, peddlers depended on covert commerce because they frequently did not have the fiscal resources and connections to conduct business on both sides of the legal divide. One small-time smuggler named Dionysus Black (Dionisio Negra) made ends meet by trading with foreigners near the city of Coro. Black was an Irish immigrant and a self-described "laborer" who had lived in the isolated west central Venezuelan hamlet of Capadare for many years. After coastal authorities caught him exchanging tobacco for flour and a little imported cloth in 1736, they insinuated that he regularly bought and sold with the Dutch. Black denied the charge, claiming that his business with the Dutch was a singular event. Regardless of whether or not his illicit trading was habitual, the negligible amount of goods he received suggests he probably smuggled as a means to supply himself, his friends, and possibly a few consumers in a region passed over by licit merchants.[26]

Others relied on smuggling to keep their jobs. In a late-seventeenth-century case, a parda servant named Beatriz traded with foreigners, not to clothe herself, but to dress the family of her employer. According to an informant, Beatriz went aboard a Dutch ship in 1693 to buy finished clothes like shirts and dresses, fabric such as taffeta silk, and even a pearl choker on behalf of Juana Agras, her boss. Spanish officials called her a "contrabandista," charging that she had a history of covert trading with foreigners. Unlike Dionysus Black, she smuggled because her employment with Agras depended on it. Still, for both of these small-time "traders" (if such a word is applicable), black market commerce represented the most efficient, and perhaps only, means of

25. On the consulado's stance, see Lucena Samoral, *Vísperas de la independencia,* 365–366. "Decided enemy to the establishment of free trade": Malyn Newitt, ed., *War, Revolution, and Society in the Rio de la Plata, 1808–1810: Thomas Kinder's Narrative of a Journey to Madeira, Montevideo, and Buenos Aires* (Oxford, 2010), 162–163.

26. Edward P. Pompeian contends that the more humble traders and peddlers were, in turn, more vulnerable to risk and uncertainty than those of major merchant houses. Their relative fragility made it necessary to seek out riskier enterprises where greater profits were to be had. Small-time merchants engaged, perhaps with greater frequency than their wealthier associates, in transimperial commerce (Pompeian, "Mind the Global U-Turn: Reorienting Early American History in a Global and Commercial Context," *Journal of the Early Republic,* XXXVI [2016], 739–740). On Dionysus Black, see Confession de Dionisio Negra, Caracas, May 6, 1737, AGNV, Comisos, XVII, fols. 51–55, and Auto de Don Martin Lardizabal, Caracas, Oct. 13, 1736, fols. 42–44.

entering the European textile market. Their cases also reveal the difficulties faced by subjects illicitly trading in the same location where they lived: personal relationships intruded into covert business transactions.[27]

Although both rich and poor traders engaged in smuggling, individuals of humble means became convenient and disproportionate targets for law enforcement officials. People like Dionysus Black and Beatriz appear more frequently in documents cataloging contraband arrests. Black received a three-year term of exile from his town and the threat that any further offenses would trigger banishment to one of the Spanish presidios in Africa. No sentence against Beatriz exists, and it is telling that authorities pursued no legal actions against her boss.[28]

Sometimes authorities arrested even seemingly innocent domestic traders with no discernible connection to foreign contrabandists. The Caracas Company was particularly guilty of such overzealousness. In 1757, even the governor of Cumaná protested that the Company had "cruelly menaced" a group of "poor laborers who brought plantains and other produce from the coastal valleys for their internal trafficking in the province." Their vessel had permission to trade these foodstuffs along the coast. Similarly, the Company boarded a tiny Venezuelan ship in 1768 near La Guaira, whose cargo held nothing more than mules and a license to trade. Juan Vicente Bolívar, the father of Simón Bolívar, objected to this seizure from his position as a prize court judge but could not overturn the verdict to confiscate and auction off the vessel and its contents.[29]

Lower-class merchants felt the severity of the law more frequently than their wealthy peers for a number of economic, social, and logistical reasons. First and foremost, well-to-do comerciantes and mercaderes had the money and power to buy their way out of the consequences of criminality. Bribes and kickbacks to royal officials were exceedingly common. Appeals to the colo-

27. Carta de Francisco Cáceres que denuncia parda Beatriz como contrabandista, Caracas, Feb. 12, 1693, AGNV, Diversos, II, fol. 176. As will be explored in Chapter 7, the use of slaves to perform illicit commercial tasks for their masters was quite common.

28. Wim Klooster argues for stricter enforcement against lower-class smugglers across several imperial legal systems from 1500 to 1830 (Klooster, "Inter-Imperial Smuggling in the Americas," in Bailyn and Denault, eds., *Soundings in Atlantic History,* 158). For Black's sentence, see Sentencia contra Dionisio Negra, Caracas, Sept. 17, 1737, AGNV, Comisos, XVII, fols. 146–148.

29. "Cruelly menaced": Carta de Justicia del Gobernador y Capitán General de Cumaná Don Mateo Gual al Gobernador y Capitán General de Venezuela, Cumaná, Aug. 10, 1757, AGNV, Comp Gui, V, fol. 164. La Guaira seizure: Documentos relativos apreso balandra española de Juan de Espinosa, Caracas, Aug. 25, 1769, AGNV, Comp Gui, XVII, fol. 70.

nial bureaucracy based on personal connections also allowed rich merchants to avoid punishments for smuggling. Upper-class purveyors might even pay for pardons. Joseph Vincente Rodríguez was a trader from Maquetía (near La Guaira) suspected of illicit foreign commerce on numerous occasions. He paid 250 pesos to forgive the large, 400-peso haul of unlicensed merchandise authorities seized from him in 1752.[30]

Royal officials could ease an administrative dilemma by showing leniency or feigning ignorance to instances of contraband trade. Bureaucrats tasked with policing Spanish American trade had to provide tangible results to demonstrate that they were doing their jobs. However, their enforcement resources were too scarce to prevent all covert commerce. Furthermore, material necessities compelled officials to allow some illicit trade so that supplies would reach Venezuela. Smuggling smoothed over the market failures produced by exclusivist commercial systems. The illicit trade with foreigners also brought down consumer prices throughout the Americas, mitigating unrest that might incite uprisings among the masses. It was unsurprising, therefore, that royal officials situationally offered pardons (indultos) instead of punishments in an attempt to keep the colonial peace and recoup some of the money lost through illicit commerce.[31]

Sheltering the rich from prosecution concealed the societal range of smuggling and safeguarded imperial revenue from the colony. Wealthy merchants' involvement in smuggling helped them accrue vital funds that eventually trickled down into crown coffers through taxes on these businessmen's licit commercial incomes. To throw the book at upper-class brokers would have decimated the pantries and wardrobes of the colony while simultaneously depleting the royal income these men produced.[32]

More selfishly, many Spanish officers declined to investigate wealthy merchants because these royal representatives participated in smuggling themselves. Whereas punishing the poor carried little risk, prosecuting elite mem-

30. Autos de Joseph Vincente Rodriguez y Marques de la Torre, Caracas, Aug. 12, 1771, AGNV, Comisos, XXVIII, fol. 228–230.

31. Alan L. Karras, "'Custom Has the Force of Law': Local Officials and Contraband in the Bahamas and the Floridas, 1748–1779," *Florida Historical Quarterly,* LXXX (2002), 287.

32. Zacarías Moutoukias points to the pivotal role of elite Buenos Aires merchants who smuggled in funding defense subsidies (the *situado).* Officials were loath to arrest these men and damage payments for much-needed imperial revenue streams like the situado (Moutoukias, "Power, Corruption, and Commerce: The Making of the Local Administrative Structure in Seventeenth-Century Buenos Aires," *HAHR,* LXVIII [1988], 771–772). In Venezuela, elite taxes paid for the upkeep of similarly important services like coast guard forces, consulados, fleets, and the funding of costly wars.

bers of colonial society (and potential business partners) might bring forth testimonies damning to a bureaucrat. Royal administrators negotiated with these groups informally and enforced smuggling prohibitions inconsistently.[33]

In addition to a selective policing of the various strata of merchants who engaged in smuggling, Venezuelan officials had to decide what to do with another prominent faction that trafficked in illicit goods: the clergy. Their role as contraband brokers and accomplices was well known to administrators on both sides of the Atlantic. Tomás Ortiz de Landázurri, a member of the Special Junta convened in Spain to establish the first laws of comercio libre in 1765, reminded his colleagues that "convents and clergymen's homes are often warehouses for smuggled goods, and refuge for smugglers." Belonging to one of the most powerful branches of Spanish colonial society, priests, friars, and missionaries usually found their way into lucrative New World enterprises. A plethora of cases and royal orders regarding smuggling committed by Venezuelan clergymen attests to this pattern of clerical entrepreneurship in consequential colonial industries. Their participation underscored contraband trade's centrality in the province's economy. The priesthood's success in the business also illuminates the jurisdictional difficulties in prosecuting spiritual authorities.[34]

Some branches of the Catholic Church were more prone to smuggling than others. In Venezuela and throughout the Americas, the Jesuits accrued a particularly noteworthy reputation for illegal trading. Members of this order usually did not originate from Venezuela and therefore worried less than locally born clergy about the repercussions of potential prosecution for nearby family and kin networks. They traded heavily in both the legal and illegal cacao markets. In the end, the Jesuits' commercial proclivities were as much a determining factor as their theological and political convictions in the crown's decision to expel them from the empire in 1767.[35]

33. Lance R. Grahn, "Cartagena and Its Hinterland in the Eighteenth Century," in Franklin W. Knight and Peggy K. Liss, eds., *Atlantic Port Cities: Economy, Culture, and Society in the Atlantic World, 1650–1850* (Knoxville, Tenn., 1991), 169. Alan L. Karras comes to a similar conclusion regarding enforcement of elite smuggling between British Grenada and the French Lesser Antilles in the eighteenth century (Karras, "Smuggling and Its Malcontents," in Jerry H. Bentley, Renate Bridenthal, and Anand A. Yang, eds., *Interactions: Transregional Perspectives on World History* (Honolulu, 2005), 140.

34. Stanley J. Stein and Barbara H. Stein, *Apogee of Empire: Spain and New Spain in the Age of Charles III, 1759–1789* (Baltimore, 2003), 76.

35. Several scholars have noted the Jesuit presence in illicit trade across the Americas. See Celestino Andrés Araúz Monfante, *El contrabando holandés en el Caribe durante la primera mitad del siglo XVIII*, I (Caracas, 1984), 136; Lance Grahn, *The Political Economy*

Just like other Venezuelan contrabandists, the clergy had a range of motives for trafficking in foreign wares. Sometimes, simple profit motive drove their actions. Two priests in 1726 attempted to take ownership and sell off the unlicensed goods of a dead Galician named Joseph Basadre, who had brought Flemish products to Maracaibo (western Venezuela) illegally by smuggling them aboard register ships coming from Cádiz. After Basadre passed away in Maracaibo, the governor there caught wind of the priests' plan and attempted to stop the sale. Although the governor protested to the bishop about the rogue actions of the two clerics, the bishop favored his subordinates and refused to reprimand them. In a letter to the king, the exasperated governor expressed his suspicions that many priests wielded their spiritual authority to protect worldly criminal activities.[36]

In some cases, churchmen's interactions with clandestine commerce were more benign. In 1734, a group of Jesuit missionaries in the Orinoco River delta sent one of their own out in a canoe carrying a cargo of knives and money in the hopes of securing much-needed foodstuffs for their communities from unspecified foreigners. Officials claimed that the goods the Jesuits' representative carried back to the missions came from contrabandists. The Jesuits escaped punishment by pleading ignorance of this fact and insisting that blame for any criminal actions lay with the Venezuelan merchant with whom they had traded.[37]

Officials faced jurisdictional roadblocks in trying to bring clergymen to justice. First, priests were technically allowed to visit Curaçao freely, as it was a part of the Venezuelan diocese. This situation provided clergy, like the Jesuit missionaries, cover for a range of illicit commercial activities. It also tied the hands of contraband prosecutors. Second, in many instances the Spanish legal system rigidly separated secular and spiritual courts. Priests and friars enjoyed a wide range of privileges and exemptions from prosecution owing to a medi-

---

*of Smuggling: Regional Informal Economies in Early Bourbon New Granada* (Boulder, Colo., 1997), 134–136; Sophie D. Coe and Michael D. Coe, *The True History of Chocolate,* 3d ed. (London, 2013), 143; George H. Nelson, "Contraband Trade under the Asiento, 1730–1739," *AHR,* LI (1945), 58–59; Prado, *Edge of Empire,* 29. On the Jesuits' commercial violations and expulsion, see Richard M. Morse, "Toward a Theory of Spanish American Government," *Journal of the History of Ideas,* XV (1954), 77; Lugar, "Merchants," in Hoberman and Socolow, eds., *Cities and Society in Colonial Latin America,* 61.

36. Gov. Manuel Fernandez de las Casas to the King, Maracaibo, Dec. 20, 1726, AGI, SD, 654.

37. Exposición por los Padres Ignacio Ferrer y Carlos Nigri, religiosos Jesuítas sobre la imputación de haber introducido ropa de extranjería, Caracas, Feb. 6, 1737, AGNV, Diversos, XX, fols. 331–336.

eval legal franchise (the *fuero)* granted to them by the Spanish kings. Under the fuero, only separate ecclesiastical courts could try the clergy for crimes. Authorities could not enter their religious buildings and domiciles without Church permission, making these structures safe havens for many types of people in trouble with the law. A 1757 case in the town of Nirgua, in the western interior of Venezuela, underscores the complications that could arise from investigating clerical crime. A local judge named Joaquín Rivera accused the priests of his parish of harboring smuggled items in their residence and ordered a search of the premises. When residents refused their request, Rivera's men broke down the door and confiscated the contraband goods. The priests complained bitterly to Rivera that the unauthorized intrusion represented "a sin against God." Although the case ends without a verdict, Rivera apparently incurred no censure for the destruction of Church property.[38]

To avoid infuriating the Catholic Church and risking the retaliation of excommunication, Spanish officials trod lightly when reining in clerical excess. One of the simplest means to contain smuggling by Church representatives was to be proactive and prevent them from traveling routes known for illicit commerce. One governor of Venezuela denied a clerical request in 1728 for a license to navigate the Yaracuy River near Caracas. The Capuchin friars claimed that they hoped to cut wood on the riverbanks and to ease the transportation of iron to their monasteries by utilizing the waterway. The governor refused their appeal on the grounds that the Dutch were currently very active in the area. Similarly, Venezuelan governor Phelipe Ricardos declined to allow a priest in 1751 to take wood from Venezuela to Curaçao in order to refurbish the church on that island. Ricardos opined, "This concession would equal an open door for contraband."[39]

Even the king proceeded cautiously when acting against clerical smug-

38. On the mobility of Jesuit missionaries, see Linda M. Rupert, *Creolization and Contraband: Curaçao in the Early Modern Atlantic World* (Athens, Ga., 2012), 190. For the Nirgua case, see Auto Joaquin de Rivera, Theniente de Justicia Mayor de Nirgua, Valle de Alpargattón, Sep. 13, 1757, AGNV, Comisos, XXVI, fols. 55–56. "A sin against God": Fray Juan Pablo, Religioso Presbiterio del sagrado corazón, to Señor Theniente de Justicia, Valle de Alpargattón, Sept. 15, 1757, AGNV, Comisos, XXVI, fols. 57–58.

39. For the Capuchin request, see El gobernador Don Lope Carrillo informa a S.M. sobre los inconvenientes que tiene la permisión de hacer navegable el Río Yaracuy, como solicitan los religiosos capuchinos misioneros de aquella provincial, Caracas, 1728, AGI, SD, 701, in Enrique Marco Dorta, ed., *Materiales para la historia de la cultura en Venezuela, 1523–1828: Documentos del Archivo General de Indias de Sevilla* (Caracas, 1967), 139. "Open door for contraband": Governor of Venezuela Don Phelipe Ricardos to Marques de la Ensenada, Caracas, Nov. 14, 1751, AGI, Caracas, 366.

gling. A royal cédula in 1730 began by stating that Philip V hoped churchmen understood what constituted smuggling. He believed that clerical exemption from secular justice made convents and monasteries hotbeds of illicit trade where subjects perpetrated offenses against the Spanish commercial codes "with greater liberty." Philip threatened exile from the Indies for any clergy member caught smuggling. However, by 1748, Philip's successor, Ferdinand VI, had softened this stance. In another cédula, he merely asked the archbishops and bishops "to remedy the disorder experienced by the introduction of goods and products of illicit commerce" by warning their subordinates and parishioners about the criminality of smuggling. Some royal officials in the Americas even nudged churchmen to punish their parishioners for these secular crimes. Authorities in Puerto Rico, for example, asked bishops to excommunicate unrepentant contrabandists.[40]

The incredible diversity of Venezuelan traders who engaged in illicit commerce prompted Spanish commercial enforcers to vary their treatment of offenders. The wealthy, the well connected, and the jurisdictionally exempt usually escaped severe punishment because prosecuting them presented social challenges and because smuggling, on the whole, was necessary for a peripheral colony like Venezuela to function. Instead, the burden of domestic criminality in foreign commerce fell unduly on poor and small-time traders.

## CONTRABANDISTS IN SOCIETY: HABITS, CONNECTIONS, AND THE SMUGGLING RING OF LUCIANO LUZARDO

The practices and networks of domestic smugglers played a large part in determining their success or failure in criminal undertakings. Venezuelan merchants' methods mostly mirrored those performed by non-Spanish contrabandists. However, the isolationism of Spanish commercial policy imposed restrictions on mobility and navigation far in excess of those that foreign purveyors had to contend with in their own empires. These constraints forced domestic illicit traders to hone their relationships within Venezuelan merchant and political communities. Such connections spread the influence of smugglers past the marketplace and into governmental, religious, and kinship structures of colonial society.

40. "With greater liberty": Contrabando de los eclesiásticos, Real Cédula, para que se evitara y sancionara, El Soto de Roma, May 7, 1730, AGNC, Contrabandos, VII, fols. 658–659. "To remedy the disorder": Real Cédula, San Lorenzo, Nov. 6, 1748, AGI, Caracas, 23. On religious punishment for contrabandists, see Fernando Picó, *History of Puerto Rico: A Panorama of Its People* (Princeton, N.J., 2006), 118.

Venezuelan contrabandists conducted business by utilizing a similar, if simplified, set of tactics to those employed by Dutch, English, and French commercial interlopers. Given that the Spanish Empire permitted less inter-Caribbean trade than these nations, ranging freely across islands and jurisdictions proved difficult for many Venezuelan merchants. Instead, foreign contrabandists had to come to them in most cases. Merchants and agricultural producers alike often pooled the cacao and tobacco of a group of planters and brought it to the coast. Trading occurred on the beach or aboard foreign ships. The receiving party often served liquor as a show of hospitality and good faith.[41]

Another way of avoiding restrictions placed on travel involved a liberal interpretation of Spanish trading licenses. Merchants often used officially approved voyages to visit unauthorized locales. Cuban authorities in 1784 granted one Spanish captain a license to bring slaves, foodstuffs, tools, and cash from Havana to La Guaira in exchange for cattle. On the return trip to Havana, the merchant stopped off in Danish St. Thomas, returning to Havana with 15,000 more pesos' worth of goods than had been on his ship when he disembarked from Cuba. In 1780, two merchants (one Venezuelan and one Puerto Rican) went so far as to forge licenses that they then disobeyed. The fraudulent documents, which provided cover for their voyage, supposedly allowed the two men to conduct reciprocal trade between Venezuela and Santo Domingo. Instead, they visited Curaçao, buying contraband items to sell back in Venezuela. Trips like these to foreign islands ultimately fostered relationships of both debt and trust as Spanish subjects bought items on credit from foreign sellers.[42]

More than foreign affiliations, domestic merchant networks connected smugglers to other licit and illicit traders, bureaucrats, and clergymen.[43] Smug-

41. Declaracion de Marcos Jacobo, Puerto Cabello, Dec. 20, 1735, AGI, Indif, 1829.

42. Colin Palmer, *Human Cargoes: The British Slave Trade to Spanish America, 1700–1739* (Urbana, Ill., 1981), 128; Lamikiz, *Trade and Trust,* 9-11; Klooster, *Illicit Riches,* 130. For the unauthorized visit to St. Thomas, see Cedula al Yntendente de Caracas, Aranjuez, Apr. 11, 1788, AGI, Caracas, 836. For examples of fraudulent documents, see Informe, el Yntendente de Caracas, Sobre los Autos seguidos contra Don Francisco Ygnacio de Areizaga Capitan y Maestre de la Goleta titulade Nsa. Sra. de la Candelaria, y Don Josef Escovar, y Lazcano, por haber extraviado el viage, y destino con que salieron de Puerto Cavello, fingido la Tornaguia, y otros delitos que cometieron para ocultar la furtiva negociacion que practicaron con los Olandeses de Curazao, Caracas, Apr. 14, 1780, AGI, Caracas, 839.

43. In studying how military, bureaucratic, and commercial sectors bonded in the Spanish American port town of Puerto del Carmen, Mexico, Claudio Vadillo López has characterized smuggling as "the social nexus that united and identified them in the presence of outsiders" (Vadillo López, "Las contradicciones del orden colonial en el Puerto y presidio del

glers formed complex rings *(sindicaciones)* that wielded significant power, especially in relatively autonomous provinces like Venezuela. The sindicaciones commanded influence in politics and threatened the authority and safety of officials who tried to stop them. Although the sindicaciones could be antagonistic to individual magistrates, these groups' activities were not illustrative of some broader revolution against Spanish colonial power. Instead, they represented the streamlining and synergy of a parallel economy. For contrabandists, these informal unions helped pool resources, establish reliable trading ventures with foreign clients, and avoid prosecution.[44]

The smuggling ring of Luciano Luzardo offers a specific case study into the normally veiled and nebulous relations that aided the proliferation of criminalized commerce in the province. Luzardo was serving as a second lieutenant (alférez) of Maracaibo in 1715 when authorities began to discover his group of smugglers. The royal official might not have been the leader of this decentralized conglomeration. In fact, the questionable veracity of typical defendant testimonies and the informal nature of many sindicaciones make locating their heads of operations nearly impossible. However, the investigation of the smuggling ring revolved around the prosecution of Luzardo, so positioning him at the center of analysis gathers together many narrative strands of this lengthy case.

After making a series of arrests, authorities in Maracaibo began to diagram the linkages between seemingly isolated criminals. Rumors of Luciano Luzardo's illicit trading had first led the governor of Maracaibo, Francisco de la Rocha Ferrer, to summon him in June of 1715. Officials hauled in Luzardo, along with his trading partner, Nicolás Rodríguez, for questioning. They alleged that Luzardo had served as a broker, assembling the cacao of many producers into a sufficient quantity for Rodríguez. Presumably, Luzardo also used his royal office to smooth over potential inquiry into their illicit dealings. Rodríguez, a merchant and ship owner in the register ship trade between the Spanish colonies, provided a vessel for their partnership as well as an air of legitimate business. With wholesale quantities of cacao coming from Luzardo, Rodríguez could trade raw chocolate in Curaçao for a range of products to im-

---

Carmen, 1732–1766," in Johanna von Grafenstein Gareis, ed., *El Golfo-Caribe y sus puertos*, I [Mexico City, 2006], 362).

44. I agree with analogous arguments regarding authority and hierarchy in networks made by Shannon Lee Dawdy about colonial Louisiana (Dawdy, *Building the Devil's Empire: French Colonial New Orleans* [Chicago, 2008], 137) and Francesca Trivellato about Livorno (Trivellato, *The Familiarity of Strangers: The Sephardic Diaspora, Livorno, and Cross-Cultural Trade in the Early Modern Period* [New Haven, Conn., 2009], 273–276).

port into Venezuela. For his role in pooling cacao, Luzardo received a share of Rodríguez's foreign goods to resell.[45]

Luzardo and Rodriguez's arrangement enjoyed the support of at least one clergyman. Friar Alonso de Galvez, the head of a monastery, allegedly allowed Rodríguez to store his Dutch goods in the sacred space and refused to divulge the merchant's illicit activities to authorities. In early July 1715, Luzardo made a formal statement claiming that he and many others had consigned small amounts of cacao to Rodríguez but had no idea that the trader was bound for Curaçao. He instead believed that Rodríguez planned to sell the cacao in Santo Domingo. After testifying, Luzardo abruptly fled to the safety of Galvez's monastery. Displaying his culpability in the ring, the friar who had protected Rodríguez now sheltered the merchant's partner from prosecution.[46]

The verdicts of the investigations reflected the differing manners in which the men defended themselves. Whereas Luzardo immediately fled to the monastery, Rodríguez stayed put and marshaled many witnesses to testify to his good character and innocence. These developments led Governor Francisco de la Rocha Ferrer to conclude that the crimes of Rodríguez and the producers who sold him cacao were trifling compared to those of Luzardo. The alférez not only had smuggled but also had tried "to obscure the justification for his crime with a fabricated deposition" that shifted blame onto others. Rocha Ferrer acquitted Nicolás Rodríguez but sentenced Luzardo in absentia to a four-year term of service in the dismal Castillo de Santa María de Gálvez in Pensacola, Florida.[47]

A month after the verdict, additional branches of the Luciano Luzardo smuggling ring came to light. In September 1715, Maracaibo coast guard officials stopped the ship of Bernardo Guillén de Saavedra. He was a merchant, a deacon, and the cousin of Luciano Luzardo. His vessel contained a sizable amount of merchandise from Curaçao. Among the items confiscated from his ship, authorities found letters meant for Luzardo. In them, Guillén de Saavedra detailed how he planned to import the foreign wares into Maracaibo. The letters also expressed his incorrect hunch that Governor Rocha Ferrer would

45. Decreto de Don Francisco del Rocha Ferrer, gobernador y capitán general de Maracaibo, Maracaibo, June 21, 1715, AGNC, Contrabandos, XIV, fol. 815; Governador Don Francisco de la Rocha Ferrer to the Fiscal, Maracaibo, May 30, 1716, AGI, SD, 652.

46. Declaración del Alfarez Luciano Luzardo, Maracaibo, Jul. 1, 1715, AGNC, Contrabandos, XIV, fol. 821; Auto de Don Francisco de la Rocha Ferrer, Maracaibo, Aug. 1, 1715, AGNC, Contrabandos, XIV, fol. 894–895.

47. "A fabricated deposition": Auto de Don Francisco de la Rocha Ferrer, Maracaibo, Aug. 29, 1715, AGNC, Contrabandos, XIV, fols. 928–929.

allow him to import illegal merchandise because previous governors had done so. The remark revealed Guillén de Saavedra's perception of the Venezuelan bureaucracy as a familiar institution that his family business could bribe.[48]

The governor's wary management of the Guillén de Saavedra case reflected the limits of administrative power in early-eighteenth-century Spanish America. The governor eventually prosecuted the smuggler but sent him to the House of Trade in Spain for final sentencing. In Rocha Ferrer's words, avoiding public pronouncements of punishment for Guillén de Saavedra was essential "so that there will be no occasion for rebellion against me or my ministers."[49]

The power of the contrabandist's family and the instability of the empire during this period informed Rocha Ferrer's reluctance to act. The tumultuous transition from Habsburg to Bourbon rule had left the colonies unsettled. Many prominent subjects still held loyalties to the old dynasty. One of these colonists was Guillén de Saavedra's uncle, Agustín Caizedo, an Augustinian friar who traveled back and forth between Maracaibo and Curaçao and participated in his nephew's smuggling ventures. Rocha Ferrer feared that Caizedo acted as a Habsburg fifth column who "no doubt sows in the hearts of inhabitants of both places a pernicious rift that could cause immense unrest." The friar's political leanings and his familial connection to Guillén de Saavedra signified dangerous threats to Rocha Ferrer's rule. As most governors in the early eighteenth century commanded no standing armies, Rocha Ferrer knew he would be ill equipped to put down insurrection if a sentence against Guillén de Saavedra aroused the populace.[50]

It is telling that the victor of this factional conflict was the Luzardo smuggling ring. Luciano Luzardo stayed in the monastery for almost three years while family members and acquaintances made appeals to the royal judiciary on his behalf. In 1718, his fortunes improved when authorities conducted an appraisal *(residencia)* of Rocha Ferrer's governorship. Ironically, and perhaps with the aid of factional investigations, they found that the executive himself

48. Governador Don Francisco de la Rocha Ferrer to the Fiscal, Maracaibo, May 30, 1716, AGI, SD, 652.

49. Ibid.

50. John Lynch has investigated the many Habsburg plots circulating in early Bourbon Spanish America. In particular, he notes that Austrian and Flemish Jesuit missionaries were sympathetic to the Habsburgs and established contacts with Dutch contrabandists in Cumaná, Caracas, and Maracaibo (Lynch, *Bourbon Spain, 1700–1808* [Oxford, 1989], 53). On Caizedo, see Araúz Monfante, *El contrabando holandés en el Caribe,* I, 102. "A pernicious rift": Governador Don Francisco de la Rocha Ferrer to the Fiscal, Maracaibo, May 29, 1716, AGI, SD, 652.

had been involved in smuggling. This discovery nullified his verdicts on commercial crime and left Luzardo a free man. Despite his offenses, Rocha Ferrer eventually became governor and president of the colony of Santo Domingo.[51]

The complexities of sindicaciones underscore that the criminal methods of contraband trade not only facilitated the business's success but also connected various branches of civil society in eighteenth-century Venezuela. Luciano Luzardo belonged to a smuggling ring that typified illicit merchant organization in many coastal municipalities. Prosecutors traced only the most cursory sketch of what was undoubtedly a much larger association of traders.

Yet investigators' discoveries offer clues to the critical linkages that made such illicit associations viable. First, smuggling rings courted governmental support. Luzardo held a royal office. His cousin, Bernardo Guillén de Saavedra, assumed that his sindicación could buy off officials like Francisco de la Rocha Ferrer. Likewise, the smuggling ring allied itself with representatives of the Church. One friar protected two smugglers from prosecution while another's rebellious leanings hindered judicial efforts to punish his nephew. Kinship connections cemented trust within these otherwise unregulated criminal affiliations, just as legal ones did. It was no accident that the blood-related trio of Luzardo, Guillén de Saavedra, and Friar Agustín Caizedo all played roles in the ring's operations. Most important, sindicaciones allowed individual smugglers who might have been easy prey for law enforcement officers to amplify their power and enter the political arena. When confronting an association of smugglers, even governors like Rocha Ferrer feared that they operated from a comparatively weak position.[52]

## CONCLUSION

Without Spanish subjects willing to smuggle, foreign contrabandists would have had no clients and, therefore, no reason to cross imperial boundaries in the first place. However, domestic smugglers were more than passive buyers

51. On Luzardo's long stay in the monastery, see Petición de Dona Mauricia Gertrudis Luzardo Balues, vecina de Maracaibo, hermana de Luzardo, Maracaibo, Feb. 25, 1718, AGNC, Contrabandos, XIV, fols. 937–940. On his release, see Juan Vincente Sanchez de Leon, procurador de esta Real Audiencia presenta instrumentos en parte del Sr. Fiscal, Santa Fe de Bogotá, Jan. 17, 1719, AGNC, Contrabandos, XIV, fols. 946–948. On his later career in Santa Domingo, see Sentencia del consejo dada en la residenzia tomada al Coronel Don Francisco de la Rocha Ferrer del tiempo que sirvio los empleos de Presidentte Gobernador y Capitán General de la Ciudad e Ysla de Santo Domingo, Mar. 3, 1739, AGI, Esc, 1194.

52. Prado, *Edge of Empire,* 132.

of foreign goods or skilled professional traders. The pervasiveness of clandestine commerce in Venezuela meant that they came from all walks of life. Agricultural producers, clergymen, wholesale merchants, and itinerant peddlers all embodied the label of "contrabandists" bestowed upon them by Spanish officials.

A range of economic, material, and political conditions favored Venezuelan domestic smugglers. Onerous taxes and overregulation meant that prices for foreign contraband merchandise undercut those of officially licensed items, while foreign merchants tendered much better offers for Venezuelan exports than their Spanish competitors. Scarcities of even the most common goods produced ready markets for domestic traders. Moreover, the Bourbons' promotion of the Caracas Company as virtually the only legitimate outlet for Venezuelan cacao allowed the organization to dictate the terms of trade to ordinary merchants. Privileges extended to the Company overturned a status quo of benign neglect and unprosecuted smuggling to which subjects had grown accustomed. Company primacy and the late arrival of comercio libre kept Venezuelan traders working in the shadows.

Venezuelan smugglers compensated for the dearth of profitable legal commerce by employing a range of tactics to avoid prosecution. Like foreign contrabandists, they utilized stealth in their trading practices and manipulated existing commercial regulations for their own benefit. Domestic smugglers organized networks that stretched across many sectors of society to maximize their collective influence and minimize risk. Although conducting business close to home made them less vulnerable than outsiders to the severity of Spanish justice, it also raised their profile.

Not all Venezuelan illicit traders faced the same challenges or possessed the same advantages when confronting obstacles to commerce. The rich and powerful might accomplish more and suffer less. The empire needed smuggling to keep its peripheral subjects fed and clothed and to maintain revenue-producing merchant communities in the colony. At the same time, its bureaucrats had to demonstrate their vigilance against foreign commercial intrusion. The result was that smugglers of humbler origins bore the brunt of commercial enforcement. Nevertheless, the unequal process by which the Spanish legal system prosecuted its own subjects demonstrates an empire in limbo between idealized exclusivism and fluid commercial realities. In the same way, the trading practices of Venezuelan smugglers illustrate how deeply the roots of illegal commerce penetrated into every facet of the economic and social activities of the colony.

It was the job of Spanish American royal officials to ameliorate these contradictory tendencies of commercial law and practice in communities infiltrated by smuggling. Their experiences form the subject of the next chapter. Just as colonial authorities determined, to a significant extent, who and what passed through the Spanish imperial dragnet, they, in turn, were bound to informal standards of acceptable criminality. As stakeholders in the trade and society they regulated, bureaucrats alternated between roles of enforcement, facilitation, and profiteering. The illicit economy depended on this ambiguity of purpose.

# 6

## "Men of Good Will Who Will Harm No One"

### Venezuelan Officials

Royal officials were mediators between Spanish commercial law and the colonial Venezuelan populace. Contradictions abounded in how they carried out this role. Tasked with enforcing trade exclusivism and punishing transgressors of it, many administrators also became economic actors in the world of illicit commerce. Through active and passive means, officials served as gatekeepers between foreign smugglers and their Spanish American counterparts. The extent to which coastal communities perceived bureaucratic permissiveness as harmful, advantageous, or even outside the norm informs our multivariate understanding of corruption.

Writings from colonial Spanish America dramatize how uncoupled officials could be from the strictures of Spanish trade law. In 1749, nearly fourteen years after first embarking for the Americas, naval officers Jorge Juan and Antonio de Ulloa wrote a scathing portrayal of the pervasive political corruption that dominated South America. They devoted an entire chapter of their jeremiad, *Discourse and Political Reflections on the Kingdom of Peru,* to illicit trade. The two lamented,

> Officials who allow the trade to go on in return for payment of a bribe for each fardo are called "men of good will who will harm no one." Obviously these functionaries do nothing to remedy the abuses which deprive the royal treasury of revenue. Although the king absolutely prohibits illicit trade, his officials tolerate the smuggling. Although tax revenues belong solely to the king, his agents appropriate them as

> if they were their very own. Not only do they fail to stop smuggling but they also give rise to a cynicism among the people within their jurisdiction when they fail to enforce the law. Confident that the penalty for their offense will be commuted to payment of a tolerable fine, merchants see the tremendous opportunities for personal gain and are never constrained from pursuing them. It is very rare to find any merchant, large or small, who has not been involved in illicit trade at one time or another.[1]

Juan and Ulloa's description emphasized that the complicity of colonial officials was essential to the success of illicit trade. Authorities actively smuggled goods themselves, participated as shareholders in contraband ventures, communicated directly with foreign merchants, and received bribes to ignore the black market dealings of others. Administrators used kinship and professional connections to create and sustain intricate smuggling rings spanning multiple empires. These functionaries recognized that breakdowns in the licensed system of trade would produce alternate understandings of what was legal or not.[2]

Authorities' pivotal support to smugglers made the evasion of Spanish commercial law standard operating procedure within Venezuelan society. Their actions encouraged subjects to break the law themselves. Mighty governors and lowly coast guardsmen alike ignored or participated in the illicit commerce taking place around them. For both foreign and domestic smugglers, partnerships with or bribes for coastal authorities mitigated the threats of imprisonment, loss of goods, and exile. Emboldened by the example of their public servants and the knowledge that enforcement of commercial statutes was uneven, smugglers and buyers of smuggled goods felt themselves to be above the law.

Desirous of the material benefits of unrestricted exchange, colonial subjects overlooked covert agreements between smugglers and officials up to a

1. Jorge Juan and Antonio de Ulloa, *Discourse and Political Reflections on the Kingdoms of Peru, Their Government, Special Regimen of Their Inhabitants, and Abuses Which Have Been Introduced into One and Another . . .* (1749), ed. John J. TePaske, trans. TePaske and Besse A. Clement (Norman, Okla., 1978), 50.

2. Catherine Tracy Goode, "Merchant-Bureaucrats, Unwritten Contracts, and Fraud in the Manila Galleon Trade," in Christoph Rosenmüller, ed., *Corruption in the Iberian Empires: Greed, Custom, and Colonial Networks* (Albuquerque, N.M., 2017), 190–191; Alan L. Karras, "'Custom Has the Force of Law': Local Officials and Contraband in the Bahamas and the Floridas, 1748–1779," *Florida Historical Quarterly*, LXXX (2002), 294.

point. Authorities' complacency with smuggling merely facilitated the transition of goods to a population undersupplied by legal Spanish trade. In the majority of cases, locals welcomed the participation or complicity of willing officials in filling the void left by Spanish commercial inadequacies.

Nonetheless, subjects' patience for their officials' extralegal behavior had its limits. Despite the seemingly symbiotic and prosperous relationship between bureaucrat and colonist, Venezuelan governors frequently appeared in colonial documents as defendants in extensive imperial investigations into their illicit dealings. Complaints about governors usually came from one of three sources: fellow bureaucrats with an ax to grind, the Caracas Company, or colonists themselves. Whereas the motivations of the first two groups are more straightforward, the interests of locals are more difficult to disentangle. Why would subjects with everything to gain from smuggling turn on governors involved in the trade?[3]

Venezuelan merchants and producers negotiated commercial thresholds, calculating the amount and sort of contraband corruption they would tolerate from officials. These subjects took into account several considerations when evaluating authorities. They had few qualms about administrators who enriched themselves and opened trade to Venezuela by violating commercial regulations. However, in evading detection and prosecution, bureaucrats could be vindictive, duplicitous, and ruthless with their subjects. In those instances, the same merchants and producers would seek to overturn governors who lined their pockets at the expense of the community—or did violence to it. When officials breached this line of excess, smuggling transformed, in the eyes of Venezuelan subjects, from an essential or tolerable legal infraction into an unacceptable transgression.[4]

3. Source material for an analysis of bureaucratic corruption comes from public investigations (residencias), trials, sentences, official correspondence, citizen petitions and testimonies concerning more than thirty Venezuelan officials. The cases presented here are particularly rich, but still representative, examples of governmental diffusion into all aspects of smuggling. Of course, many of these sources contain distinct biases. Residencias were open inquiries into the conduct and actions of bureaucrats conducted at the end of their terms in office. As such, they were usually rife with partisan speculation and struggle between rival administrative and commercial groups seeking to discredit one another's representatives (C. H. Haring, *The Spanish Empire in America* [1947; rpt. New York, 1963], 141–142; Kenneth J. Andrien, "Corruption, Inefficiency, and Imperial Decline in the Seventeenth-Century Viceroyalty of Peru," *Americas*, XLI [1984], 1–2).

4. Various authors have stressed that understanding limits of tolerable corruption between authorities, merchants, and the general populace is more crucial than pointing out where corruption did or did not exist. See Anne Pérotin-Dumon, "The Pirate and the Em-

Within this spectrum of perceived right and wrong, space existed for parley between shady functionaries, the Spanish legal system, and colonial subjects. A corrupt official's conduct, scale of operations, and leniency toward smugglers all depended upon variables outside the law. Likewise, extrajudicial factors often determined the success or failure, evasion or detection, exoneration or conviction, and punishment of government functionaries. An officer's connections to networks of fellow officials, kin, and smugglers, his rank, and the amount he stole from the imperial bureaucracy and the Caracas Company might affect his legal impunity. Most important for Venezuelans and their transactions, these dynamics determined the degree to which authorities would enforce commercial law.

The role of bureaucratic corruption in facilitating smuggling and commercial fraud helps to explain alternate formations of authority in eighteenth-century Venezuela. This chapter first outlines the dynamics of bureaucratic engagement with illicit trade by focusing on the criminal actions of low-level magistrates and military men. The means by which officials broke commercial law are important for understanding how they interacted with foreign and domestic purveyors in the illicit economy. Next, two case studies of smuggling governors in early-eighteenth-century Venezuela show how smuggling influenced the relationships of these senior officials with the subjects they governed, their colleagues, and key sections of the Spanish imperial government. These gubernatorial case studies underscore that the violation of unspoken rules and agreements with the community could undermine an official's regime. Finally, this chapter traces the course of both groups of officials within the legal systems of Spain and the Americas to reveal the negotiation between Spanish bureaucrats, colonial officials, and local interest groups over contraband trade. Key variables such as factionalism, rank, and the recovery of crown revenues determined the fate of extralegal administrators and the enforcement of mercantile law.[5]

---

peror: Power and the Law on the Seas, 1450–1850," in C. R. Pennell, ed., *Bandits at Sea: A Pirate Reader* (New York, 2001), 47; Kris Lane, "From Corrupt to Criminal: Reflections on the Great Potosí Mint Fraud of 1649," in Rosenmüller, ed., *Corruption in the Iberian Empires*, 56; Frances L. Ramos, "Custom, Corruption, and Reform in Early Eighteenth-Century Mexico: Puebla's Merchant Priests versus the Reformist Bureaucracy," ibid., 155.

5. I use Kenneth Andrien's definition of corruption as "the conscious violation of legally prescribed modes of behavior by public officials in order to advance their own well being or that of some particular interest group" (Andrien, "Corruption, Inefficiency, and Imperial Decline," *Americas* [1984], 1). I also agree with Horst Pietschmann and Christoph Rosenmüller that the term "corruption" should be used as an analytical tool for a political process, not a moral judgment (Pietschmann, "Burocracia y corrupción de Hispanoamérica colo-

The terminology used to describe personalistic government and extralegal bureaucratic influence over commerce matters. Just as "smuggling" and "smuggler" are weighted words, so, too, are "corruption" and "corrupt." Connotations of deviancy hang over them. In a twenty-first-century context of civil service, corruption appears harmful, wasteful, and potentially dangerous. Yet, from an early modern perspective, corruption was so intertwined with government in the form of patronage, patrimonialism, and factionalism that one can scarcely speak of functioning states without it. This book still uses the term "corruption," as a shorthand to discuss practices that enriched individuals and groups in government instead of the state and diverted resources away from enforcement of commercial law. But its focus is on how this process occurred, not the moral judgments the legal system attached to such divergences. For that same reason, this book shies away from the adjective "corrupt," as this word carries the judgment of an individual's ethical deviance in addition to an acknowledgment of his or her simple participation in a set of customs. Instead, it uses the more neutral "extralegal" to denote that these men were acting outside the law, but not necessarily offending moral sensibilities.[6]

By uncovering bureaucrats' engagement with illicit trade and deciphering

---

nial: Una aproximación tentative," *Memorias de la Academia Mexicana de la Historia,* XXXVI (1993), 9–11, 35–36; Rosenmüller, *Patrons, Partisans, and Palace Intrigues: The Court Society of Colonial Mexico, 1702–1710* [Calgary, Alb., 2008], 32).

6. Recent works delving into the political thought of the eighteenth century have cautioned against the use of the term "corruption" to describe administrative practices in societies where official behavior considered venal by modern standards was the norm. These studies have emphasized that the pervasive infiltration of merchant and bureaucratic networks and patron-client relations into Spanish American government made deciphering what "corruption" was all but impossible. See, for example, Jeremy Adelman, "Commerce and Corruption in the Late Spanish and Portuguese Empires," in Emmanuel Kreike and William Chester Jordan, eds., *Corrupt Histories* (Rochester, N.Y., 2004), 428–460; Arnold J. Heidenheimer, "Perspectives on the Perception of Corruption," in Heidenheimer, Michael Johnston, and Victor T. LeVine, eds., *Political Corruption: A Handbook* (New Brunswick, N.J., 1989), 149–163; Alejandro Cañeque, *The King's Living Image: The Culture and Politics of Viceregal Power in Colonial Mexico* (New York, 2004), 13, 175; Pietschmann, "Burocracia y corrupción de Hispanoamérica colonial," *Memorias de la Academia Mexicana de la Historia,* XXXVI (1993), 9–36. For non-Iberian literature that generally agrees with these studies, see Ann Laura Stoler and Frederick Cooper, "Between Metropole and Colony: Rethinking a Research Agenda," in Cooper and Stoler, eds., *Tensions of Empire: Colonial Cultures in a Bourgeois World* (Berkeley, Calif., 1997), 24; Shannon Lee Dawdy, *Building the Devil's Empire: French Colonial New Orleans* (Chicago, 2008), 135. Rosenmüller backtracks a bit from these authors, stating that although "these insights on the flexible nature of corruption are important, perhaps historians have overstated the issue a bit" ("Introduction: Corruption, Abuse, and Justice in the Iberian Empires," in Rosenmüller, ed., *Corruption in the Iberian Empires,* 3).

how subjects encouraged, coped with, or rejected these enterprises, this chapter adds depth to the existing body of Spanish American literature on corruption. The symbiosis between pliable administrators and smugglers, shopkeepers, and coastal dwellers destabilized official Spanish trade policy and nurtured a culture of illegality. In place of the law's rigid dictums, authorities and subjects settled on their own rules to regulate the black market and thus normalized it within the colonial economy. As central players in circum-Caribbean contraband networks, Spanish American officials not only facilitated smuggling but also exemplified the power of corruption to inadvertently energize lagging provincial economies, accentuate factionalism, and shape community norms.[7]

7. Early studies confirmed that medieval governmental legacies of personalistic politics and patrimonial relations carried over into early modern states, slowing the emergence of dispassionate, impartial bureaucracies. Some revisionist arguments have contended that corruption even served a positive function in Spanish American government, allowing for greater flexibility in what otherwise would have been a brittle and unwieldy administrative system. By contrast, other historians debated whether fraud, deception, and the purchase of offices by Spanish American bureaucrats tipped the balance of political power and wealth toward the provincial elite or the monarchy in the seventeenth and early eighteenth centuries. Scholars interested in late-eighteenth-century Bourbon responses to this corruption have documented how reformers' efforts to eliminate practices such as the sale of offices and the appointment of creoles to high positions in the imperial bureaucracy brought political unrest to the empire. For early works, see Magali Sarfatti, *Spanish Bureaucratic-Patrimonialism in America* (Berkeley, Calif., 1966); Frank Jay Moreno, "The Spanish Colonial System: A Functional Approach," *Western Political Quarterly*, XX (1967), 308–320; John Leddy Phelan, *The Kingdom of Quito in the Seventeenth Century: Bureaucratic Politics in the Spanish Empire* (Madison, Wis., 1967). For arguments about smuggling and governmental flexibility, see Casey S. Schmitt, "Virtue in Corruption: Privateers, Smugglers, and the Shape of Empire in the Eighteenth-Century Caribbean," *Early American Studies*, XIII (2015), 82–83; Anthony McFarlane, "Political Corruption and Reform in Bourbon Spanish America," in Walter Little and Eduardo Posada-Carbó, eds., *Political Corruption in Europe and Latin America* (New York, 1996), 41–63; Lance Grahn, *Political Corruption and Reform in Cartagena Province: 1700–1740*, Center Discussion Paper no. 88 (Milwaukee, Wis., 1995); Zacarías Moutoukias, "Power, Corruption, and Commerce: The Making of the Local Administrative Structure in Seventeenth-Century Buenos Aires," *HAHR*, LXVIII (1988), 771–801. For debates on whether smuggling increased or decreased provincial power, see Andrien, "Corruption, Inefficiency, and Imperial Decline," *Americas*, XLI (1984), 1–20; and Christoph Rosenmüller, "'Corrupted by Ambition': Justice and Patronage in Imperial New Spain and Spain, 1650–1755," *HAHR*, XCI (2016), 1–37. For efforts to suppress corruption and the unrest they produced, see Mark A. Burkholder, "From Creole to *Peninsular:* The Tranformation of the Audiencia of Lima," ibid., LII (1972), 395–415; Leon G. Campbell, "A Colonial Establishment: Creole Domination of the Audiencia of Lima during the Late Eighteenth Century," ibid., 1–25; McFarlane, "Political Corruption and Reform," in Little and Posada-Carbó, eds., *Political Corruption in Europe and Latin America*, 41–63.

In this analysis of the symbiosis of contraband, I agree mostly with Zacarías Moutou-

## THE BASICS OF BUREAUCRATIC SMUGGLING

In the contraband-rich world of eighteenth-century Venezuela, the existence of an honest official was often more remarkable than that of a compromised one. The complaints of Agustín Fernández de Verastegui confirm the challenges facing those administrations that refused to acquiesce to contraband trade in their area. In 1701, Fernández de Verastegui testified before a Venezuelan criminal court, claiming that six men with knives had accosted him on a dark country road and tried to take his life. Luckily for him, he fought off his attackers and escaped unharmed. As a judge in Caracas's prize courts, Fernández de Verastegui had enforced anticontraband policies and convicted those guilty of trading with foreigners. He believed that his assailants' hatred of his office had precipitated this attempted murder. In the early eighteenth century, before the arrival of the Caracas Company and its enforcement muscle, the greater impunity given to contrabandists suggested he was correct.[8]

Particularly for local officials, following the letter of the law won neither popular support nor material gains. Ensconced in small towns with little administrative aid, many Venezuelan bureaucrats had no desire to toe the line of Spanish mercantile law. A martinet might provoke threats on his life like those Fernández de Verastegui received. Many officials concluded that it was better to tap into the booming interimperial trade than to oppose it. In this way, colonial officials in the lower rungs of imperial bureaucracy leveraged their offices for personal and familial enrichment. Most of the time, Venezuela's smugglers and producers and foreign merchants were all too happy to accept this bargain. Moreover, smuggling served at the local level as a means to assert autonomy from imperial structures of government.[9]

---

kais, who argues that low official salaries are not sufficient to explain corruption in commercial enforcement. Officials belonged to large networks of smugglers and had more complex arrangements of business in mind than simply an economy premised on graft. Moutoukias argues, "We should ask ourselves up to what point the representatives of the crown, charged with carrying out its legal dispositions, constituted an element separate from the dominant nucleus of smugglers, whose activities they were supposed to repress" (Moutoukias, "Power, Corruption, and Commerce," *HAHR*, LXVIII [1988], 775).

8. Of course, Fernández de Verastegui's testimony was the only one from that night. It is possible that this was a deal gone wrong and he was merely covering his tracks. However, either possibility highlights the violence that might accompany enforcement of commercial statutes. See Testimonio de Agustín Fernández de Verastegui, Ocumare, Apr. 17, 1701, AGNV, Comisos, I, fols. 140–144.

9. On cultivating autonomy through illicit trade, see Ana Crespo Solana, *Mercaderes atlánticos: Redes del comercio flamenco y holandés entre Europa y el Caribe* (Córdoba, 2009), 258;

The actions of local officials help uncover the simple mechanics of contraband corruption in Venezuelan ports and towns. Compared to more senior, salaried officials such as governors and viceroys, local officials who participated in illicit trade had some distinct advantages. Lower-level bureaucrats attracted less attention from the crown and their superiors because they skimmed smaller quantities of goods and money from royal balance sheets and maintained less contact with imperial centers. Minor civil and military officials such as *alcaldes* (town magistrates), prize court judges, militia corporals, and coast guardsmen were often the only governmental representatives in far-flung outposts. The number of officers in Caracas diluted each other's power, whereas functionaries placed in Venezuela's coastal hamlets often possessed immense authority over their jurisdictions. The disadvantage was that it usually bound lower bureaucrats to one locality and one manner of smuggling. These circumstances make their stories analytically easier to comprehend and establish the daily corruption of officials at the lowest rungs of government.

What motivated administrators to participate in contraband? From the start, gaining an appointment drove authorities' desire to profit from illicit trade. Since the mid-sixteenth century, the sale of colonial offices served as a crucial moneymaker for the royal treasury. A would-be administrator often faced heavy costs associated with waiting years for the opening of a position, paying for his appointment, crossing the Atlantic, and establishing himself and his family in the Americas. Thus, local offices, unlike positions with longer tenures, greater supervision, or consistent salary from the crown, almost always became entrepreneurial endeavors. The crown recognized the inherent corruption in this system and the lessened accountability of local officials to the monarchy, even going so far as levy a tax known as the *media annata*. This tax on the annual salary of officials functioned as a means to regain revenue lost to authorities' indiscretions.[10]

---

Linda M. Rupert, *Creolization and Contraband: Curaçao in the Early Modern Atlantic World* (Athens, Ga., 2012), 175, 182. In his wide-ranging work on global smuggling, Alan L. Karras writes, "Corruption helped to relieve tension between those who governed and those who consumed in many societies, in a sense restoring their governability" (Karras, *Smuggling: Contraband and Corruption in World History* [Lanham, Md., 2010], 113).

10. Barbara Hadley Stein and Stanley J. Stein, "Financing Empire: The European Diaspora of Silver by War," in Jeremy Adelman, ed., *Colonial Legacies: The Problem of Persistence in Latin American History* (New York, 1999), 57; J. H. Parry, *The Spanish Seaborne Empire* (1966; rpt. Berkeley, Calif., 1990), 207–211; Pietschmann, "Burocracia y corupción," *Memorias de la Academia Mexicana de la Historia,* XXXVI (1993), 27–28; Andrien, "Corruption, Inefficiency, and Imperial Decline," *Americas,* XLI (1984), 6–9. On the media annata, see McFarlane, "Political Corruption and Reform," in Little and Posada-Carbó, eds., *Political*

Poor salaries exacerbated the strain on administrators' funds and contributed to their involvement in illegal activities. Pedro José de Olavarriaga, whose *Instrucción general y particular del estado presente de la provincia de Venezuela en los años de 1720 y 1721* revealed the depths of corruption in eighteenth-century Venezuelan bureaucracy, complained that lesser officials

> lack salaries corresponding to the offices they hold. Although many of them have paid between two hundred and three hundred pesos to obtain these positions, after a year a corporal will have one thousand or two thousand pesos in reserve. Certainly these men could not eat, nor maintain themselves, nor amass wealth in such a short time from their legitimate wages. Thus, it is impossible for them not to have stolen publicly and permitted trade with foreigners. From this they have enriched themselves and from this they pay and have paid the governors for their offices.

Contraband trade represented one of the most common and profitable crimes in colonial Venezuela, and it is no surprise that bureaucratic participation in the business was widespread.[11]

Traditions of bureaucratic graft also predisposed government functionaries to corruption. Local officials encountered relatively little oversight, allowing them the flexibility to participate in illicit schemes. Higher authorities at the provincial level frequently appointed lesser officers with the mutual understanding that the chain of command would keep its secrets and share its ill-gotten profits. To reinforce this patronage, governors allowed their subordinates to keep a share of captured contraband spoils.[12]

Venezuelan authorities found many ways to penetrate mercantilist trade restrictions and siphon off for themselves a portion of the enormous foreign trade passing through the region. At one extreme, some bureaucrats took on the role of smugglers, engaging in the direct buying and selling of contraband goods from non-Spanish traders or their Venezuelan accomplices. This was

---

*Corruption in Europe and Latin America,* 51–52; Pietschmann, "Burocracia y corrupción," 25–28.

11. See Ramón Aizpurua, *Curazao y la costa de Caracas: Introducción al estudio del contrabando de la provincia de Venezuela en tiempos de la Compañía Guipuzcoana, 1730–1780* (Caracas, 1993), 55–56; Wim Klooster, *Illicit Riches: Dutch Trade in the Caribbean, 1648–1795* (Leiden, 1998), 133. "Lack salaries corresponding to the offices they hold": Pedro José de Olavarriaga, *Instrucción general y particular del estado presente de la provincia de Venezuela en los años de 1720 y 1721* ([1722]; rpt. Caracas, 1981), 18.

12. Robert J. Ferry, *The Colonial Elite of Early Caracas: Formation and Crisis, 1567–1767* (Berkeley, Calif., 1989), 116–118.

risky, owing to both the frequent violence that characterized illicit commerce and the higher level of exposure an official might incur in the direct perpetration of a crime. However, this tactic was the most efficient means for bureaucrats to profit, for it eliminated the middlemen. It also suited the circumstances of lower officers. Unlike more senior officials, local authorities usually could afford to keep a higher profile, as they governed areas with few other royal representatives to oversee their actions.

Judge Ambrosio Bello exemplified this type of trader. Bello served as a militia corporal and prize court judge in Morón, a small town near Puerto Cabello in north central Venezuela. In 1733, higher officials charged him with conducting illicit trade with foreigners. Caracas Company agent Domingo Arosteguí specifically accused Bello of doing business with a known Irish smuggler named John White (also referred to as "Juan Blanco"). Usually such trade went undetected, but anticontraband patrols caught White bartering with Bello.

According to White's testimony, the corporal had used his office to orchestrate a complex arrangement of trades with White and other Spanish merchants. Bello asked White to procure gunpowder, musket balls, shotguns, and European foods including cured ham, bacon, wine, and liquor from Curaçao on credit. When White arrived with these items and requested payment, Bello arranged for one hundred *zurrones* of cacao (a zurrón being about a satchel-sized package, often wrapped in animal skin) to be sold to him at the very favorable price of two pesos per zurrón. White received his payment fifteen days later. Bello subsequently brought Catalan merchants in to sell an additional 150 zurrones to White. It seems that Bello and his men kept a portion of the goods to resell in town and gave the rest to the merchants as payment for their cacao. It is unclear whether Bello and his men worked as agents of the Catalans, as independent traders, or both. White admitted that Bello and his soldiers had received commercial benefits from his voyages in the past, indicating a long-standing relationship.[13]

Ambrosio Bello's connections to merchants, his military appointment, his reputation for discretion, and his willingness to accept propositions all inspired trust from foreign smugglers and Spanish American buyers. His familiarity with an Irish smuggler and Catalan merchants allowed him to arrange favorable trades, given his knowledge of circum-Caribbean commercial conditions. In a small town such as Morón, the complacency of an authority such as Bello

13. Información de Juan Blanco, Puerto Cabello, Sept. 17, 1733, AGNV, Comisos, XIV, fols. 157–160.

almost assured impunity. Juan Pascual, one of the traders captured with White, admitted that he and the other merchants traded with White only because they knew that Bello was complicit in the trade. Bello could keep a secret. Pascual stated that the terms of trade established by Bello mandated that the names of all merchants involved remain undisclosed to limit their exposure.[14]

The smuggler White's willingness to sell goods to Bello and his soldiers on credit and wait fifteen days for payment also signaled the trust he placed in the corporal. Even if a deal went awry, as this arrangement did, smugglers were confident in their ability to placate virtually any royal representative with cash. Several soldiers involved in capturing White and Bello recounted how their ambush astounded the smuggler. White, assuming these guards were as amenable as Bello, was shocked to learn that they would not take a bribe of two thousand pesos to let him go. Though records of the case end without a verdict for Bello, Pascual received a two-year sentence serving on defensive works in Cádiz, and one of Bello's foot soldiers received a reasonably stout fifty-peso fine. The presence of Caracas Company employees in the province had established a backbone to commercial policing, even if their targeting of smugglers was uneven.[15]

Like Bello, Felipe de Ugarte used his position as corporal to enrich himself through direct commerce. Despite two decades of Company patrolling by the time of Ugarte's 1756 case, direct trading was still lucrative enough for some officials to warrant the risk of prosecution. Over the course of his tenure in the Valle de Capaya immediately east of Caracas, Ugarte became friendly with Dutch smugglers and, by local accounts, traded frequently with them. He was rumored to have boarded Curaçaoan ships on numerous occasions to do business and travel. As evidence of these deals, prosecutors presented receipts, confiscated from his belongings, that listed goods he had purchased from his foreign friends and letters from them, "signed with very distinct gratitude." This evidence made Ugarte's defense, that he had curried the favor of the Dutch smugglers to eventually ambush and overwhelm their ship, ring hollow.[16]

Though hands-on illicit trade was the most direct means to accumulate wealth from smuggling, a more passive approach to extralegal commerce was

14. Ibid., fols. 160–161.

15. Informaciones de Gabriel Amengual and Joseph Maní, Puerto Cabello, Sept. 17, 1733, AGNV, Comisos, XIV, fols. 156–157; Sentencia de Martin Lardizabal, Jan. 28, 1734, AGNV, Comisos, XIV, fols. 280–281.

16. Confesión de Felipe Ugarte, Caracas, Oct. 27, 1756, AGNV, Comisos, XXIV, fols. 134–135.

more common. In this scenario, authorities from the viceregal level down to the lowliest corporal might accept bribes and kickbacks for looking the other way when contraband goods came through their jurisdictions. For some officials, tolerating smuggling was a small side business; for others, it was an elaborate enterprise. Connivance with smugglers, although just as damaging for imperial trade revenues as direct exchange, was more difficult to pin on an offending bureaucrat. Although anticontraband forces would have been insufficient to handle the sheer volume of contraband passing along the coast in the best of circumstances, it was administrators' complacency with illicit exchange, not breakdowns in imperial defense, that enabled the business to flourish.[17]

Some lower-echelon administrators nibbled at the edges of the contraband trade by ignoring the small-time smuggling of those around them. In 1719, officials in Caracas prosecuted corporal Rodrigo Álvarez, who operated in the Valle de Caruao, east of Caracas. They denounced him for his associations with both foreign and domestic illegal traders. Álvarez allegedly had ignored the presence of illegal Dutch slaving vessels from Caruao to La Guaira and allowed them to anchor offshore and unload their human cargoes. In addition to facilitating Dutch commerce, he supposedly aided the trade in illicit cacao within Caruao. The corporal owned a store that carried, according to authorities, stolen cacao. This product came to Álvarez's *pulpería* by way of enslaved people who, in violation of both slave codes and commercial law, swiped discrete amounts of the crop from their masters. Prosecutors suspected Álvarez of involvement as a middleman in both of these smuggling infractions, but their only evidence, other than circumstantial witness testimonies, was the presence of tiny amounts of cacao and foreign liquor in his home. A fine of twenty pesos and the costs of his trial were the most that these prosecutors could muster as punishment against the corporal.[18]

17. For a concise history of the monetary shortcomings and problems of implementation that beset honest efforts at patrolling contraband, see G. Earl Sanders, "Counter-Contraband in Spanish America: Handicaps of the Governors in the Indies," *Americas*, XXXIV (1977), 59–80. Contrary to this chapter, the author argues that structural limitations in anticontraband forces hindered governors' attempts to stop illicit trade more than their own venality.

18. Auto de D. Marcos Francisco de Betancourt y Castro, Gobernador y Capitan General de Venezuela, Caracas, July 22, 1719, AGNV, Diversos, VIII, fol. 452; Declaración de Rodrigo Alvarez, Cabo de Guerra de valle de Caruao, Caracas, Aug. 7, 1719, AGNV, Diversos, VIII, fols. 456–457; Declaración de Luis Joseph de Aguilera, soldado pagado de La Guaira, Caracas, July 22, 1719, AGNV, Diversos, VIII, fol. 454; Auto de D. Marcos Francisco de Betancourt, Caracas, Sept. 2, 1719, AGNV, Diversos, VIII, fols. 464–465.

Some officials extracted much more substantial and habitual enrichment from smugglers. Sebastián Medrano, the prize court judge of Maracaibo in 1722, tolerated the presence of an elaborate smuggling ring that dwarfed the modest dealings allegedly perpetrated by Rodrigo Álvarez. Medrano appointed his nephew Miguel de Medrano and his friend Francisco Puche as his lieutenants. Miguel's familial connections to the prize court judge and Puche's knowledge of the trade in contraband clothing made the two effective smugglers. With Sebastián Medrano's cooperation, they traveled widely throughout the regions surrounding Maracaibo, collecting cacao from many separate producers and selling it for illegal textiles. The governor of Maracaibo noted that Miguel de Medrano and Francisco Puche's job was "to be vigilant and guard the roads against clothing introduced through illicit commerce." In practice, they did just the opposite. Though the viceroy had appointed Sebastián inspector of the royal treasury *(visitador de las reales cajas)*, the governor remarked, "It was notorious and publicly acknowledged that he has done nothing in service to his Majesty" except collect his daily ten-peso salary. Having been appointed by Sebastián Medrano, his nephew and Francisco Puche believed that they could simply sail their ships into port in broad daylight without declaring their cargoes.[19]

In addition to the family connection that cemented the Medranos' smuggling enterprise, their business benefited from administrative and popular support. The governor of Maracaibo believed that the Medranos could still count on the viceroy's backing. His supposition was well founded, as the viceroy of New Granada, Jorge de Villalonga, was also involved in illegal trade and later faced charges of defrauding the royal treasury. The clan's relative immunity to conviction provided further evidence of their bureaucratic favor. Miguel de Medrano presumably escaped numerous prosecutions over the years, given that documents produced in 1740, some eighteen years after initial suspicions about the Medrano family, detailed his arrest for colluding with smugglers as a lieutenant in Maracaibo's fort.[20]

19. Carta del Theniente D. Juan de Olivares al Gobernador y Capitan General y Declaración de Juan de Orosco, Maracaibo, Oct. 3, 1721, AGI, SD, 653; Gobernador de Maracaibo Guillermo Thomas de Roa to the King, Maracaibo, Nov. 22, 1722, AGI, SD, 653.

20. On the governor's estimation of Medrano's support, see Gobernador de Maracaibo Guillermo Thomas de Roa to the King, AGI, SD, 653. On Villalonga's own smuggling, see Sentencia dada en visito de la residencia tomada a Don Jorge de Villalonga, Virrey Gobernador y Capitan General de el nuebo Reyno de Granada y Presidente que fue de la Real Audiencia de Santa Fe, Apr. 19, 1730, AGI, Esc, 1194. On Miguel de Medrano's eventual prosecution, see Casal y Ferreira, Antonio Benito del. Capitán de infantería española,

Popular sentiment most likely favored the Medranos as they provided a much needed, if illegal, service to the region. The governor observed that, before their smuggling, "this city and its province were so lacking and exhausted of goods that not for any price could olive oil, paper, iron, wax, and cloth be obtained." Since "the arrival of Don Sebastián de Medrano and his judges to this city, there has been an abundance of quality products that would not have existed otherwise." The governor's backhanded compliment dramatized how the Medranos' commercial misdeeds brought desired products to the area.[21]

As the Medrano uncle-nephew smuggling partnership demonstrates, local officials often had the easiest time overlooking offenses committed by family members. Corrupt administrators not only placed relatives in office but also disregarded smuggling by kin not on the payroll. In small towns where one family member held an administrative position, a family business in smuggling might prosper. Such was the case with Andrés de Tovar, who held the post of sheriff (teniente) in the militia of Nuestra Señora de Pilar de Zaragoza, an inland village west of Puerto Cabello in western Venezuela. Tovar's son Martín ran a store that sold illicit goods, but Tovar failed to shut down the shop and ignored his son's frequent trips to transport illegal tobacco to the larger city of Carora, where a Spanish merchant arranged for its passage to Curaçao. The Tovars' actions clearly ran counter to Spanish strictures in Venezuela, which tightly licensed the growth and trade of tobacco, the province's other prominent cash crop, and forbade officers from participating in tobacco production. Tovar's reluctance to enforce the law stemmed from loyalty to his son, certainly, but also because—as one resident of the area flatly stated—"it is said publicly that all of the tobacco collected in this jurisdiction is bought by Don Andrés de Tovar."[22]

Another strategy for officials looking to turn a profit involved embargoing and misappropriating contraband cargoes rather than ignoring them. After seizing a ship's cargo and judging it to be contraband, military and civilian officials would sell the goods at public auction. After port duties, sales taxes,

---

gobernador que fue de Maracaibo, causas que le siguió por contrabando a Miguel Suárez Medrano, Maracaibo, 1740, AGNC, Contrabandos, IV, fols. 1–93.

21. Gobernador de Maracaibo Guillermo Thomas de Roa to the King, Maracaibo, Nov. 22, 1722, AGI, SD, 653.

22. "All of the tobacco collected in this jurisdiction is bought by Don Andrés de Tovar": Dec. de Luis Eznal and Nicolas Menendez de Elizondo, San Phelipe, Sept. 22, 1736, AGNV, Diversos, XVIII, fols. 386–387. For an example of the ways that military and civil government intermingled with family and patronage structures to form units of power that were nearly impenetrable to outside authorities, see Margarita Gascón, "The Military of Santo Domingo, 1720–1764," *HAHR*, LXXIII (1993), 434, 449–452.

and the judge had all been paid (around one-third of the total sum), between one-half and two-thirds of the remaining prize would go to the royal treasury, and the crew of the anticontraband patrol would divvy up the rest. Local officials who either failed to report a ship seizure or pilfered a portion of a vessel's contents before declaring them significantly affected royal revenues. In some areas, goods and money from captured ships were among the only sources from which the Spanish state could recoup income lost to illicit trade and tax evasion.[23]

The imperial bureaucracy rigorously investigated this type of fraud, as it cut into an important revenue stream. Prosecutors accused several of the authorities described above of embezzling from embargoed contraband hauls. The Medranos took illegal cuts from seized stockpiles of contraband. Corporal Felipe de Ugarte of Capaya faced charges of misappropriating seized Dutch contraband goods in 1750. Rather than registering a detained foreign sloop and its cargo, Ugarte took it to port, stripped the vessel of its contents, and distributed the loot between himself and his men. Don Julián de Arriaga, the governor of Venezuela, revealed that an inventory of Ugarte's house and boat turned up goods as diverse as cloth, candles, Castilian soap, stockings, knives, glass, and gin. Also in the inventory were two enslaved women. Arriaga recommended that these impounded items be carefully watched, as he feared that the Dutch might seek to reclaim them by force.[24]

Though prosecutors often tolerated embezzlement of small amounts of foreign contraband by officials, they were less likely to countenance functionaries who stole from Spanish American producers. In the case of Felipe de Ugarte, what caught the governor's attention in the first place was, not Ugarte's embezzlement of foreign prizes, but rather his robbery of his neighbors under the guise of suppressing illicit trade. In 1750, Juan Antonio Rodríguez de Sosa testified that Ugarte had violently robbed him of 50,600 pounds of cacao. The *hacendado* claimed that he had stored the cacao in a shed on his

23. For the neighboring colony of New Granada, Lance Grahn has deduced that ship seizures and other contraband-derived income accounted for 20 percent of Cartagena's locally generated revenue between 1713 and 1763. In Rio de la Hacha, funds from ship seizures more than doubled the revenue obtained from import duties between 1743 and 1765 (Grahn, *The Political Economy of Smuggling: Regional Informal Economies in Early Bourbon New Granada* (Boulder, Colo., 1997), 193; see also 25.

24. Celestino Andrés Araúz Monfante, *El contrabando holandés en el Caribe durante la primera mitad del siglo XVIII,* I (Caracas, 1984), 102. For Ugarte and Arriaga's case, see Auto de Don Julian de Arriaga, Gobernador y Capitan General de Venezuela, Caracas, Aug. 23, 1750, AGNV, Comisos, XXIV, fols. 267–268; Carta de Gob. Don Julián de Arriaga y Ribera al Ten. Just. de Capaya D. Juan de Silva, Caracas, Aug. 22, 1750, AGNV, Comp Gui, III, fol. 227.

property bordering the Tuy River while awaiting a merchant who would take it to be legally sold. According to Rodríguez de Sosa, Ugarte came to his rancho during this period aboard one of two Dutch vessels. Without provocation, the ships opened fire on Rodríguez de Sosa's property, causing him to flee into the woods. As he hid, he saw Ugarte and the Dutchmen carting off his crop and burning his rancho. Ugarte and his accomplices stole from a Galician hacendado as well, bringing the total amount appropriated to somewhere between 66,000 and 77,000 pounds of cacao. The corporal acquired this large sum, not through graft, but by outright robbery.[25]

Felipe de Ugarte pointed to his duties as a corporal to explain his presence at Rodríguez de Sosa's property. He testified that he and his men had arrived at the rancho after the Dutch intruders and rallied to capture the ship. Ugarte's men added that Rodríguez de Sosa was not the victim at all but a contrabandist himself who had sold his cacao to the Dutch. They believed that Rodríguez de Sosa sought to settle the score with Ugarte because the latter had embargoed his ill-gotten goods in the past and jailed several of his friends and relatives. Furthermore, they stated that Ugarte had been transporting the cacao to La Guaira for proper registration when Caracas Company patrols stopped his ship and accused him of the robbery.[26]

For prosecutors, Ugarte's excuses did not hold water. The collaboration of a Spanish corporal and Dutch smugglers in the bombardment of a Venezuelan hacendado was intolerable, even within administrations given to extralegal activities. The lawyer for the audiencia of Santo Domingo accused Ugarte's men of perjuring themselves to pay off their debts to him. Governor Felipe Ricardos decried the audacity of an "assistant of the foreigners to take the produce of the inhabitants of this province by force in order to make trade with these foreigners." The auctioning of Ugarte's ship and slaves as a legitimate seizure suggested that his legal position was untenable.[27]

Whether they served as smugglers, brokers, facilitators, or accessories to the contraband trade, local officials used their unique positions in the mili-

25. Declaración de Juan Antonio Rodríguez de Sosa, Caracas, Oct. 12, 1750, AGNV, Comisos, XXIV, fols. 329–331.

26. Declaraciones que rinden en Caracas por ante el Alcalde Ordinario Doctor Gabriel Martín de Ibarra, los testigos José Clemente Fernández Valladares, de 45 años, José Luciano de la Santa, de 32, Julián Hipólito Mejías, de 19, y Juan Isidro de Liendo, de 37 años, Caracas, January and March, 1751, AGNV, Comp Gui, IV, fols. 2–5.

27. Carta de Licenciado Don Fernando Thamaris, abogado de la Real Audiencia de Santo Domingo to the Gobernador y Capitan General, Caracas, July 16, 1751, AGNV, Comisos, XXIV, fols. 225–228; Confesion de Don Felipe Ugarte, Caracas, Oct. 27, 1756, AGNV, Comisos, XXIV, fol. 133.

tary and political apparatuses of small-town Venezuela to aid illicit foreign commerce. In the process, they enriched themselves and their families and strengthened smuggling rings. Subjects in undersupplied Venezuelan localities usually approved of the increased economic interaction with the outside world brought by pliable officials more than they disapproved of these authorities' criminal actions. Collusion in smuggling at the gubernatorial level featured many of the contraband trading processes used by local officials.

## SMUGGLING GOVERNORS AND THEIR COMMUNITIES: JOSÉ FRANCISCO DE CAÑAS AND SEBASTIÁN GARCÍA DE LA TORRE

Governors of Venezuela were significant conduits for illicit trade, even as their actions made them lightning rods for controversy in Venezuelan society. Governors could enjoy far more influence in the smuggling business than local officials because of their power and prestige. But they were only as powerful as their connections to governmental, familial, and commercial networks. Caraqueño subjects, specifically the merchant class, ousted governors who threatened community norms or monopolized the contraband trade for themselves. In the 1730s, the Caracas Company rose to prominence and wrestled this oversight capacity from local creoles. The Company based its intrusion into Caracas politics on the need to eliminate contraband in the province. Its intervention endangered a long-standing symbiosis between smugglers and officials and engendered the hatred of all classes of Caraqueños.[28]

This section offers two case studies of corrupt governors of Venezuela. The transgressions of José Francisco de Cañas y Merino (1711–1714) and Sebastián García de la Torre (1730–1732) are representative of many of their peers. Their experiences with smuggling also illustrate changes in the commercial and political fabric of the province as a result of the arrival of the Caracas Company.

Governors like Cañas and García de la Torre pursued more diverse courses in their circumvention of Spanish trade law than their subordinates. Gubernatorial enrichment through the black market was just as common as commercial crime at the lower levels of government and often employed the same processes. However, governors ruled over larger geographic areas, participated in more branches of governmental affairs, and had more discretionary powers than local officials. The amount of money an individual governor might skim off the top from imperial trade revenue was also much greater than that of

28. Francisco Morales Padrón, *Rebelión contra la Compañía de Caracas* (Seville, 1955), 27.

a local functionary. As a result, investigations of their infractions, when they were caught, left an immense paper trail in the documentary record. Although the diffusion of authority in Caracas meant that there were more crown and city representatives to monitor a corrupt governor, his wide-reaching authority allowed him to participate in more parts of the contraband business.[29]

One form of gubernatorial smuggling involved direct buying and selling from contrabandists. Governors in Venezuela sometimes bartered face-to-face with illegal foreign merchants, but they engaged in this practice less frequently than their subordinates. It was dangerous to appear on the coast presumably trading with outsiders. One governor unafraid to engage in such trading was Cañas, who served a stormy term from 1711 to 1714. The son of a presidio sergeant in northern Africa, Cañas came from a middling military background. During his reign, he irritated the cabildo, elites, ordinary citizens, clergy, and virtually anyone else not within his inner circle.[30]

Cañas was a prolific smuggler. Of the thirty charges enumerated against him by royal prosecutors at his 1716 sentencing, sixteen were linked in some way to illicit trade. Several sources catalogued his brazen trading with the French under the cover of the asiento. Cañas used this institution, which allowed appointed foreign contractors to legally import slaves into the Spanish colonies, as a pretext to bring in ships from the French Caribbean that sold him contraband flour and other goods. He bought flour from the asiento ships for seven pesos per barrel, then sold them in Caracas's starved markets for twenty-eight pesos each. As the royal treasurer in Caracas remarked, "He has introduced so much clothing by way of the French that there is not a shop in town that is not full to the rafters with the clothing and flour of the governor." Cañas also convinced the director of the asiento to send Cañas's cacao aboard asiento ships to Spain, even though it was illegal for these vessels to carry extraneous goods back to Europe. The cacao, along with profits from his illicit trading, crossed the Atlantic under the name of a notary public in Caracas to conceal the governor's involvement in the extralegal shipments. In addition to crooked trafficking under the asiento, Cañas also carried on friendly commer-

29. In archival documents, references to pliable local officials are numerous but often terse. In the best of cases, investigations lasted a few dozen pages. Given their high status and the amount of money they were accused of stealing, governors figured much more prominently in the archival record. My research found both a multitude of governors accused of commercial crimes and significant investigations into their conduct (many continuing on for hundreds of folios).

30. Luis Alberto Sucre, *Gobernadores y capitanes generales de Venezuela* (1928; rpt. Caracas, 1964), 207.

cial relations with the Dutch governor of Curaçao. This exchange was particularly brazen given that the two colonies were formally at war during Cañas's term in office.[31]

Cañas did not limit his commercial crimes to transactions with foreigners. He also purchased several oceangoing vessels and transported his own cacao to Veracruz. Though certain Venezuelan merchants received this privilege, Spanish law forbade royal authorities from directly participating in such trade.[32]

For governors like Cañas, collusion formed a more sensible and low-profile path to wealth than direct exchange. The hush money paid to provincial executives by contrabandists helped the latter evade capture, escape from custody, and avoid indictment. Cañas made it abundantly clear that he would offer safe passage to foreign merchants willing to pay for the convenience. His trial identified two Frenchmen and a Valencian from Martinique that he had allowed to trade in La Guaira in exchange for sizable bribes. One smuggler, a Monsieur Buscarons, sold the enormous sum of 20,000 pesos of clothing to traders in Caracas. For permitting the transactions, Cañas received a payment of 3,000 to 4,000 pesos. Though Cañas withheld arrest and prosecution for these paying salesmen, he vigorously extorted those who would not pay his kickbacks voluntarily. Caracas's cabildo accused him of squeezing nearly 1,600 pesos in fines from the merchants of the city after threatening them with confiscation of their goods, which he believed to be contraband from China or New Spain.[33]

In addition to taking bribes from foreign and domestic smugglers, colonial governors also profited illegally from defense and antismuggling efforts.

31. Sentencia en vista de la Causa y Pesquisa contra Don Joseph Francisco de Cañas Governador y Capn. General que fuese la Provincia de Venezuela y otros Complices, Madrid, June 12, 1720, AGI, Esc, 964. "He has introduced so much clothing by way of the French": Consejo, Resumen de diferentes cartas y un memorial sobre la vacante de Plaza de contador de la Cajas de Caracas, Caracas, Nov. 19, 1713, AGI, SD, 751. For Cañas's cacao exports, see Declaracion de D. Julio Chourío, Director del Real Asiento de Negros, Caracas, Oct. 7, 1714, AGI, SD, 751. For Cañas's ties to the Dutch governor, see Sentencia en vista de la Causa y Pesquisa contra Don Joseph Francisco de Cañas, Madrid, June 12, 1720, AGI, Esc, 964.

32. El Cabildo Secular de Caracas to the King, Caracas, June 24, 1712, AGI, SD, 751; Sentencia en vista de la Causa y Pesquisa contra Don Joseph Francisco de Cañas, Madrid, June 12, 1720, AGI, Esc, 964.

33. For Cañas's trial, see Sentencia en vista de la Causa y Pesquisa Contra Don Joseph Francisco de Cañas, AGI, Esc, 964. For the city council's accusations against him, see El Cabildo Secular de Caracas to the King, Caracas, June 24, 1712, AGI, SD, 751; Oficiales Don Juan de Urbina y Don Andres Alonso Gil contra Don José Francisco de Cañas y Merino, Caracas, Nov. 23, 1714, AGNV, Comisos, II, fols. 45–81.

Governors could perpetrate this type of graft in ways that lower officials could not, because they exerted control over the distribution of military funds in the province. Royal investigators accused Cañas of stealing gunpowder meant for the protection of La Guaira against foreign enemies and selling it to private merchants. Furthermore, he lined his pockets from imperial endeavors to suppress the contraband trade. One method of diverting these attempts at enforcement involved embezzling portions of a captured contraband stockpile (comiso) before prize court judges could lawfully appraise and sell it at auction. Cañas allegedly skimmed a considerable haul of 10,200 pesos' worth of goods from various comisos over a period of years.[34]

Cañas's extensive bribery, fraud, embezzlement, and smuggling brings the issue of impunity to the fore. How did bureaucrats get away with such blatant violations of the law? Who covered their tracks, and what relationships developed out of the inclusion of royal administrators into the structure of Venezuela's illicit economy? Imperial functionaries rarely acted as lone wolves in smuggling. Instead, they were aware of their social surroundings. Governors used their accumulated familial, collegial, and community connections to avoid detection and prosecution. These executives' ability to evade prosecution through alliances, judicial power, and appeasement of their subjects' commercial desires determined their fortunes as contrabandists and officials. Governors given to participation in illicit trade greatly simplified the process of extralegal enrichment for themselves if they found like-minded authorities with whom to enter into symbiotic relationships. Cañas, for example, paid two treasury officials, the Urbina brothers, to falsify records as he skimmed off the top of contraband seizures.[35]

Cañas's interventions in the judicial process sought to strike against his Caraqueño competitors. Many of the most animated complaints against Cañas came as a result of the scandal in which he became embroiled in 1712. That year, he ordered the summary executions of eleven mule drivers *(arrieros)* who had been smuggling cacao and tobacco from the hinterlands around Caracas. Though the law allowed for contrabandists to receive the death penalty, this punishment was exceptionally rare in the colonial period. These

34. Sentencia en vista de la Causa y Pesquisa contra Don Joseph Francisco de Cañas, AGI, Esc, 964; Testimonio de D. Diego Reynaldos, vecino de Caracas, Caracas, Sept. 30, 1714, AGI, SD, 751.

35. D. Gaspar Caldo, receptor de la Pesquissa de D. Jorge Lozano Peralta, Sept. 12, 1713, AGI, SD, 751; Ynforme que hace el Ministro de Campo D. Julio Primo Ascamó a S.M. Catholica de las operaciones del Governador de Caracas, D. Joseph de Cañas, La Guayra, Feb. 15, 1713, AGI, SD, 751.

men were essentially poor, ignorant middlemen, but Cañas ordered them all to be hanged after a mere three-day trial. That three of the arrieros were minors only increased the infamy of this sentence. The governor overruled an appeal from the men's legal counsel to spare them, threatened the lawyer with physical violence should he continue to question Cañas's will, and executed the mule drivers that day. In doing so, Cañas violated judicial procedure not only for the right of the accused to make appeals but also concerning the proper interval after sentencing when the guilty could be executed.[36]

Cañas's newfound zeal for prosecuting contrabandists to the full extent of the law came, not from a sudden change of heart, but from a more straightforward motivation: these mule drivers carried the goods of his competitors. Various accounts credited him with efforts to tamp down illicit commerce throughout his tenure. The governor's leniency only applied to those traders who had cooperated with him. Smugglers not willing to go into business with Cañas experienced his strict adherence to the law. As the citizens of Caracas made clear in a petition to the crown, "Without more cause than the desires of his absolute will, he has treated many of the noble vassals of this republic with public contempt, imprisoning and incarcerating them with shackles and chains in this city and in La Guaira."[37]

Whether out of a desire to deflect attention from his crimes or merely a petty sense of vindictiveness, the governor was given to playing the martinet in his public persona. He railed against contraband trade and claimed it sprang from the moral depravity of subjects. He warned of the "grave harm and disorder originating from the many vagrants and people without residence" who converged in the hinterlands of Caracas and of the "unmarried women capable of causing scandal." Mobility and indecency, in his mind, were powerful inducements to smuggle.[38]

After linking moral vices to commercial crime, Cañas sought to get to the problem's roots. He advocated a twofold solution. First, he would resettle immoral and itinerant subjects. Then, more bizarrely, he would launch a sporadic series of morality campaigns that involved questioning young women about their sexual habits. Cañas claimed the authority to enter homes and then haul

36. El Cabildo Secular de Caracas to the King, Caracas, June 24, 1712, AGI, SD, 751; Blas José Terrero, *Teatro de Venezuela y Caracas* (Caracas, 1967), 190.

37. D. Joseph Melero to the King, Caracas, Oct. 30, 1711, AGI, SD, 751; Sucre, *Gobernadores y capitanes generales de Venezuela,* 211. "Treated many of the noble vassals of this republic with public contempt": El Cabildo Secular de Caracas to the King, Caracas, June 24, 1712, AGI, SD, 751.

38. Bando de D. Joseph Fran. de Cañas, Cocorote, Mar. 3, 1712, AGI, SD, 751.

away and punish wayward young ladies. Most shocking, the governor insisted on administering virginity tests to determine these women's virtue. As one citizen petition to the king stated,

> He removed a measure from his pocket and invoking the name of Your Majesty in such an obscene action, and told them: "This is a measure that the king grants us governors to learn who is not a maiden *(doncella)*. Thus, [even] if she refuses, I will measure the lady to find out." Fearful, as they were ignorant people, they thought it would be an execrable crime to refuse after having heard the sovereign name of His Majesty mentioned. And they began confessing their weakness and abuses.

Although it is difficult to identify exactly what Cañas hoped to gain from these perverse procedures, he most likely aimed to shift scrutiny away from his illicit trade and simultaneously indulge his carnal appetites. It is likely that the tests were mere subterfuge for his sexual abuse of the women. That Cañas successfully executed these lewd actions demonstrated the power a governor held over marginal provinces such as Venezuela.[39]

Despite his authority, outraged subjects skillfully and forcibly argued for Cañas's removal. The petitions of the Caracas cabildo and citizens of the city emphasized Cañas's commercial fraud and judicial meddling long before they turned to his sexual abuses. The writers of such appeals undoubtedly understood that crimes against the king's money and legal order mattered more to the Council of the Indies than abuses against individual subjects. The petitioners stressed the violence wrought on the collective good. In their view, the governor's virginity tests and public questioning of ladies had done significant harm to the social order and public credit of the city. His conduct threatened the marriage prospects and respectability of these women who, "having been taken before by popular belief for maidens, now were defamed and without credit and took from this occasion such an undignified label."[40]

39. The original text is as follows: "Esta es una medida, que el Rey nos da a todos los Governadores, para que por ella sepamos, la Mujer, que no es donzella, y assi la que me negase, la medire para saberlo, a cuia propocizion atemorizadas, como Gente ignorante, discurriendo al oir mentar, el Soberano nombre de Vsa. Magd. que era Cometer, execrable delicto, si lo negaban fueron confesando su flaqueza los atropellamientos" (Los Vasallos de Caracas to the King, Caracas, May 10, 1714, AGI, SD, 751). It is possible that the "medida" mentioned by Cañas was a euphemism for his penis. I wish to thank Asunción Lavrin for her help in translating this particularly opaque passage.

40. "Defamed and without credit": AGI, SD, 751. For a similar pattern, see Matthew Restall, "The Telling of Tales: A Spanish Priest and His Maya Parishioners (Yucatán, 1573–90),"

Cañas fought back against these accusations and tried to turn the tables on his opponents. The governor opined that his anticontraband operations had been received "very sensitively by the residents of this province, especially the cabildo and vecinos of this city, because they have not been able to carry on their commerce seeing as they have been charged with this and other evils and offenses." He attributed his initial imprisonment in Caracas to the malevolent hatred of Don Luis Arias, who had petitioned for a royal order to take him into custody. This, he argued, was revenge for the governor's seizure of the assets and slaves of Arias's sister during the prosecution of her husband, whom the governor believed to have defrauded the king for nearly twenty years.[41]

Cañas's sentencing demonstrated his contentious relationship with Caracas's illicit merchants. In spite of his counterarguments, a secret investigation eventually resulted in the governor's removal, many thousands of pesos in fines, and his imprisonment in Spain. He only narrowly escaped a death sentence when a royal birth resulted in a general pardon. Though Cañas acquired some friends from his involvement in covert commerce, he clearly alienated much larger portions of the province. That the secret investigation into Cañas came about as a result of the incessant complaints of Caracas's cabildo, rather than imperial authorities, highlights the rancor he had incited in the capital. His ruthless intimidation, unlawful arrests, and sexual violation of Caraqueñas overshadowed his utility as a functionary complicit with the contraband trade. Moreover, in attempting to intrude into every aspect of extralegal commerce and viciously cutting out his competition, Cañas threatened the lifeblood of the economy.

Like Cañas, Sebastián García de la Torre also excelled at profiting from direct illicit trading while occupying high office. García de la Torre served as governor of Venezuela nearly twenty years after Cañas. During his brief tenure from 1730 to 1732, he built an equally large retinue of illegal traders that allowed him to profit from Venezuela's covert commerce. His principle offense, in the eyes of his royal superiors, was, not his flagrant violation of the law, but rather his tendency to do nothing. The residencia and trial of García de la Torre outlined numerous cases in which he and his son, who oversaw military and port operations at La Guaira's fort, declined to prosecute their friends and associ-

---

in Richard Boyer and Geoffrey Spurling, eds., *Colonial Lives: Documents on Latin American History, 1550–1850* (New York, 2000), 18–31. There the economic crimes of priest Andrés Mexía were highlighted by his Yucatecan Maya parishioners before they detailed his sexual transgressions against young women in the community.

41. D. Joseph Francisco de Cañas to the King, Caracas, Dec. 9, 1714, AGI, SD, 751; Sucre, *Gobernadores y capitanes generales de Venezuela*, 212–213.

ates for trafficking illicit goods. Of the fifty charges leveled against García de la Torre in his trial, thirteen concerned instances in which he had let known contrabandists pass through his jurisdiction or freed them from prison without trial.[42]

García de la Torre was an equal pardoner, forgiving foreigners, Venezuelans, Canary Islanders, Indians, and fellow corrupt officials alike. According to reports, numerous ships coming into port in 1731 and 1732 with unlicensed goods from Spain, the Canaries, and non-Spanish Caribbean islands dropped anchor and sold their cargoes in broad daylight. In one case, Caracas Company officials seized a ship arriving by way of Trinidad with a cargo of illicit slaves and dry goods originally from Martinique. Though many witnesses testified to the illegal nature of the cargo, García de la Torre overruled the Company, released the ship's goods, and allowed its captain to sell them under the pretext that the ship came licensed from Puerto Rico. In return, the captain compensated the governor's son with gifts and purchased one thousand pesos of his cacao. García de la Torre maintained similarly friendly relations with compromised lower officials, in one case withholding damning documents in a smuggling investigation against his lieutenant in San Felipe.[43]

For his tendency toward legal forgiveness, García de la Torre built allegiances and received thousands of pesos' worth of handsome compensation. The García de la Torre clan became notorious for their role in these pursuits. "It is said that captains of ships bring gifts to the captain of the fort [García de la Torre's son] so that he will tolerate the entrance of prohibited goods," one resident of Caracas explained. "With the help of the captain, there was abundant commerce in cacao sent to New Spain, Spain, and the Canary Islands." García de la Torre even released a suspected murderer. Don Francisco de Aguiar, likely one of the governor's business associates, was a known smuggler. Aguiar negotiated with a corporal in the Valley of Cata to send an assassin to murder his business rival, Don Eustachio Galindo. The killer carried out the homicide, yet the corporal and Aguiar both walked from jail without trial.[44]

42. Residencia de Sebastián García de la Torre, Gobernador de la Provincia de Venezuela, por Martín de Lardizabal, Comandante General, Caracas, 1735, AGI, Esc, 727A.

43. Ibid.; Auto de Revista del Consejo dado en vista de los autos de la Pesquisa de D. Sevastian Garcia de la Torre, Gov. y Cap. Xral que fue de la ciudad de Caracas, Juez, D. Martin de Lardizaval, Caracas, July 7, 1742, AGI, Esc, 964.

44. Residencia de Sebastián García de la Torre, Gobernador de la Provincia de Venezuela, por Martín de Lardizabal, Comandante General de ella, Caracas, 1735, AGI, Esc, 727A. "Captains of ships bring gifts to the captain of the fort": Testimonio de D. Francisco Antonio Emasavel, residente de Caracas, Caracas, July 9, 1733, AGI, Esc, 727A. For Fran-

Under García de la Torre, official funds had a tendency to disappear. He had a proclivity for incorrectly evaluating and reporting the value of captured goods. This deceit undermined efforts to curb contraband because it siphoned from the meager revenue that the crown was able to recover from illegal trade. Likewise, García de la Torre pilfered money meant to pay the salaries of soldiers patrolling the coast and instead gave these wages to his family members. For an official who did very little to halt illicit trading, García de la Torre requested plenty of support to pay for questionable anticontraband measures. Ironically, the governor who declined to imprison so many alleged smugglers took money from the royal treasury, without prior consultation, to pay for repairing Caracas's jail.[45]

In certain cases, García de la Torre's less-than-honest use of defense subsidies even compromised the security of the colonial edifice in Venezuela. During his tenure, authorities questioned García de la Torre's conduct with respect to a major trade rebellion. In 1730, Andresote, a slave of mixed African and Indian origins (zambo), started an uprising. Aided by Dutch arms and supplies, Andresote led fellow runaways and more than a few white Venezuelans in a three-year fight against the Caracas Company, its involvement in the slave trade, and Spain's commercial monopoly. Shortly after the rebellion began, García de la Torre took the exorbitant sum of four thousand pesos from the royal treasury without authorization to pay for a raid against the zambo chief. After a short and ineffectual sojourn into the country, García de la Torre returned to Caracas empty-handed but presumably with a fatter wallet. He also dipped into the Caracas Company's funds to pay for the fortification of the Yaracuy River, a key point of supply for the Andresote rebels, but investigations into his conduct concluded that he had not constructed useful defenses there. It is possible that García de la Torre was simply a poor military budgeter and not an embezzler of funds in these instances. However, the pattern of expensive outlays and few tangible results suggests the latter.[46]

---

cisco de Aguiar, see Auto de Revista del Consejo dado en vista de los autos de la Pesquisa de D. Sevastian Garcia de la Torre, AGI, Esc, 964.

45. Auto de Revista del Consejo dado en vista de los autos de la Pesquisa de D. Sevastian Garcia de la Torre, AGI, Esc, 964; El Marques del Valle de Santiago D. Miguel de Verroteran to El Comandante General, Caracas, Aug. 26, 1735, AGI, Esc, 727A.

46. El Marques del Valle de Santiago D. Miguel de Verroteran to El Comandante General, Caracas, Aug. 26, 1735, AGI, Esc, 727A; Cabildo de Caracas to the King, Caracas, July 20, 1732, AGI, SD, 782; Carlos Felice Cardot, *La Rebelión de Andresote (Valles del Yaracuy, 1730–1733)* (Caracas, 1952), 43–45; Petición de D. Pedro Joseph de Olavarriaga, Director de los Navios de la Real Compañía Guipuzcoana, La Guaira, Mar. 24, 1733, AGI, Esc, 727B.

Owing to the highly personalized nature of politics of early modern Spanish America, family relations were as pivotal as bureaucratic connections for many governors involved in contraband trade. Abnormally, no evidence points to Cañas's using familial connections to advance his extralegal aims. In contrast to his predecessor, García de la Torre attempted to mold Venezuela's customs administration into his family's personal domain. The governor's appointment of his son Antonio as captain *(castellano)* of the fort at La Guaira stirred conflict in certain Caraqueño merchant circles that thought the twenty-six-year-old vastly underqualified. Despite complaints, Antonio García de la Torre proved amenable to smugglers and maintained his father's cover for contrabandists. He accepted massive bribes and plucked his allies from the clutches of prosecution. He also used his advantageous position in La Guaira to arrange for the sale of cacao acquired by his family to merchants who then transported it to markets in New Spain.[47]

Sebastián García de la Torre's appointments did not stop with his son. He placed other family members in salaried positions as soldiers, though these men never showed up for muster. His personal family fiefdom of customs enforcement was completely ineffectual in preventing smuggling but a valuable enterprise for his clan. Over the course of his brief tenure, García de la Torre's nepotism was embraced by most Venezuelan traders and loathed by Caracas Company officials.[48]

Yet there were limits: pliable colleagues and familial relations could ease the legal pressures on a governor only so much. The support of Caraqueños, specifically local merchants with whom he traded, was paramount to maintaining good standing within the Spanish imperial bureaucracy. Unfavorable testimonies of locals could sour the evaluations of governors at the end of their terms or lead the imperial government to open secret investigations into a bureaucrat's conduct during his reign. Heavy fines and even jail time could result from such measures. Thus, governors like García de la Torre and Cañas needed the approval, or at least silence, of the men with whom they traded and connived. The same thresholds of corruption and smuggling set by Venezuelans for their lower officials applied also to their tolerance of governors' offenses. As García de la Torre's and Cañas's tenures show, the citizens of Caracas, led by the commercial class, powerfully influenced the outcomes of official inquiries into bureaucratic corruption.

47. Testimonio de D. Francisco Antonio Emasavel, Caracas, June 9, 1733, AGI, Esc, 727A; Petición de D. Pedro Joseph de Olavarriaga, AGI, Esc, 727B.

48. Testimonio de D. Francisco Antonio Emasavel, Caracas, June 9, 1733, AGI, Esc, 727A.

García de la Torre never undermined the covert business of others nor sought to monopolize the smuggling trade for himself. On the contrary, he was quick to provide an improper ship license or release contrabandists from the grasp of the law for the right price. His allegiance to Venezuelan traders was so strong that he even protected them when their interests interfered with critical government business. García de la Torre intervened in merchant affairs only to procure bribes from black market transactions. In one such case, he failed to prosecute Pablo Bernardo Enríquez, a hacendado who had been trading directly with Andresote, the leader of the failed 1730 slave uprising. Though this cacao producer's commerce with the rebel chief helped fund an insurgency that brought significant upheaval to the province, the governor gave him a free pass. Relatively few traders appeared in the records to speak ill of García de la Torre. This absence underscores the passive and mutually beneficial role that he played in the underground commerce of these merchants.[49]

As Sebastián García de la Torre was, on the whole, a less quarrelsome and more discreet governor than José Francisco de Cañas, he accumulated fewer enemies. Unfortunately for him, the main adversary he made, the Caracas Company, became a powerful player in Venezuelan politics. The Company exercised broad control over the seas, prize courts, laws, and finances of the province from 1728 onward. Fights over jurisdiction frequently broke out between government officials and Caracas Company employees because both groups wanted the spoils from captured goods and kickbacks. Adding to this struggle, Company employees were involved in significant smuggling of their own, motivating them to challenge royal officials for prizes. Company representatives used their considerable clout to advocate for the removal of corrupt officials who threatened their interests. Such efforts overpowered the Caracas cabildo and the subjects' preferences or petitions regarding a particular governor. Peninsular authorities began to prosecute bureaucratic corruption, not when it offended creole thresholds, but rather when it irritated the commercial whims of the Company.[50]

García de la Torre, who no doubt saw the Company as meddlesome to the interests of his smuggler friends, became a general nuisance to its operations. His men searched Company ships in port. His complacency also enraged

49. Auto de Revista del Consejo dado en vista de los autos de la Pesquisa de D. Sevastian Garcia de la Torre, AGI, Esc, 964.

50. Aizpurua, *Curazao y la costa de Caracas,* 204–208; Gerardo Vivas Pineda, *La aventura naval de la Compañía Guipuzcoana de Caracas* (Caracas, 1998), 18, 64–66; Alejandro Cardozo Uzcátegui, *Los mantuanos en la Corte española: Una relación cisatlántica, 1783–1825* (Bilbao, 2013), 159.

Company officials. The governor granted licenses to Venezuelan merchants to transport cacao to New Spain, the Canary Islands, and Spain, all in direct violation of the Caracas Company's rights. These merchants even formed the beginnings of a parallel trading company with García de la Torre's blessing. Encouraging direct competition in what was supposed to be a monopoly market naturally enraged the Basque company and hastened García de la Torre's demise. It was no accident that, after an investigation forced him to flee to a Caracas convent in 1732, García de la Torre's successor, Martín de Lardizabal, served as the first of a string of Basque-born governors of Venezuela.[51]

The expulsions of Cañas and García de la Torre by two very different authorities expressed how much had changed in Venezuelan politics in the twenty years between their appointments. Though the two approached Caraqueño society in very different manners, both men served only short tenures in office followed by ignominious exits. It was the cabildo and residents of Caracas that had had the last word in dismissing Cañas. Conversely, and despite subjects' favorable impression of García de la Torre twenty years later, his ouster for smuggling came from outsiders to the colony. The Caracas Company, owing to its promise to make Venezuela economically productive for Spain, possessed surprising judicial clout for a recently formed institution. It easily removed García de la Torre and went on to install two Basque governors whom locals almost universally detested. These moves came to signify an infuriating power grab by a foreign entity. The Company's meddling in the compact between officials on the make and colonists sustained by smuggling fed a creole anger that questioned the organization's right to rule Venezuelan commerce.[52]

## DEFENDING AND JUDGING EXTRALEGAL OFFICIALS

For administrators unlucky enough to get caught practicing or tolerating illicit trade, the Spanish legal system proved to be a deeply malleable apparatus. Suspect functionaries based their defenses around demonstrating personal service to the crown and discrediting their accusers, often by making their own allegations of smuggling. Their trials embodied the hyperpartisan and personalistic nature of early modern governing structures.

51. García eventually left the convent and returned to Spain in 1736 (Auto de Revista del Consejo dado en vista de los autos de la Pesquisa de D. Sevastian Garcia de la Torre, Caracas, July 7, 1742, AGI, Esc, 964; Sucre, *Gobernadores y capitanes generales de Venezuela,* 247–261).

52. Ferry, *Colonial Elite,* 5.

Administrative groups linked by patronage, friendship, and kinship sought to dishonor rival bureaucratic clusters. For the guilty, sentencing depended upon connections within the legal system and the amount they had stolen from royal revenues. In punishing the guilty, the royal government focused primarily on recouping lost funds. Its ability to differentiate between normal graft and extraordinary corruption also showed that, to some extent, it expected and tolerated the former. The Spanish legal system's subjective treatment of offending officials, like the illicit actions of these administrators themselves, reinforced contraband trade as a standard commercial practice in Venezuelan society.

In their trials and interrogations, public servants employed two well-worn defenses to exonerate themselves. Their most important argument was to portray themselves as fervent guardians against illicit trade. Most functionaries could list a few examples when they had hauled in the guilty. From these instances, officials hoped to emphasize their zealous enforcement of commercial law and detract from criminal accusations. Juan de la Tornera Sota, the governor of Cumaná, used this strategy to downplay the claims made against him between 1726 and 1730.

According to his accusers, Tornera Sota had soured the close trading relations between the province of Cumaná and nearby island province of Margarita. They claimed that in 1726, Tornera Sota had published an order that prohibited trade and shipping with Margarita because he claimed the island was in the midst of a smallpox epidemic. He insinuated that the epidemic had arrived via Dutch vessels. Despite Tornera Sota's warnings, numerous officials from Margarita testified that no such epidemic existed. The governor's accusers charged him with intentionally keeping subjects of Margarita from passing to Cumaná to discourage outsiders from discovering Tornera Sota's illicit commerce with foreigners. Additionally, they claimed he used the smallpox excuse to avoid seizing and properly evaluating Dutch ships. Tornera Sota even imprisoned and quarantined anticontraband patrols from Margarita who had battled Dutch smugglers.[53]

Tornera Sota denied these accusations and quickly pointed to his record of service in the "extinction of illicit commerce with foreigners." He claimed to

53. Auto de Don Juan de Vera, Gobernador y Capitan General de Margarita, Margarita, Nov. 8, 1726, AGI, SD, 635; Declaracion de Miguel de Vetancurt Margarita, Nov. 9, 1726, AGI, SD, 635; Veneficiado D. Antonio de Ugas, Cura Rector de la Sta. Yglesia Parroquial de Margarita, Margarita, Nov. 11, 1726, AGI, SD, 635; Auto de D. Juan de Vera, Margarita, Nov. 26, 1726, AGI, SD, 635.

have stopped Juan de Olea, a Venezuelan smuggler, from going to Martinique with his cargo. Two legal briefs *(autos)* that he presented to the king revealed that he had captured two known British smuggling ships during his tenure. In particular, Tornera Sota pointed to his prosecution of Bernabé Angel de Toledo, a merchant who had stolen goods from official register ships. With these examples of dedicated service, he hoped to vindicate his character.[54]

José Francisco de Cañas had also proffered his deeds as an enforcer in an attempt to nullify charges against him. From Cañas's point of view, Caraqueño society was rife with contraband. The patricians of the city had made a mockery of the law, trafficking with the Dutch from La Guaira whenever possible. Cañas estimated that as much as 25,000 fanegas of cacao, half the amount that left Venezuela every year, did so illegally. From this, he deduced that the crown lost around 100,000 pesos annually from duties not paid in Venezuela and Veracruz, the principle departure and arrival points of this cacao.[55]

To combat these excesses, Cañas stressed his numerous initiatives to fight smuggling. He had put his own money into contraband patrols and outfitted four sailing ships with a crew of three hundred men to guard the coast. He championed the formation of a pardo militia to suppress contraband. He even journeyed into the field to personally capture Dutchmen in the town of Barquisimeto. The governor extolled capital punishment of homegrown contrabandists, including the execution of the eleven arrieros describer earlier, as a means of sending a message to those who would break the law. There was some validity to several of Cañas's claims. He isolated the neighboring island of Tucacas, a hotbed of contraband, so that the Dutch momentarily abandoned it. During his tenure, legal cacao shipments out of Venezuela doubled. For this vigilance, he found himself chained up in Caracas's jail for eighty days because it was, in his opinion, "everyone's business to destroy me."[56]

54. "Extinction of illicit commerce with foreigners": Auto de Juan de la Tornera Sota, Cumaná, May 27, 1730, AGI, SD, 635. See also Auto de Juan de Vera, Margarita, May 26, 1730, AGI, SD, 635; Auto de D. Juan de la Tornera Sota, Gobernador de Cumaná, contra D. Bernabe de Toledo y otros sobre comercio, Cumaná, Apr. 15, 1730, AGI, SD, 635. The case record ends without a verdict regarding Tornera Sota's actions. The judgmental tone of documents commenting on the case from Spain, however, suggests that high-placed Iberian officials thought Tornera Sota culpable.

55. Don Joseph Francisco de Cañas al Rey, Caracas, Dec. 9, 1714, AGI, SD, 751.

56. For Cañas's coast guard force, see ibid. For his pardo militia, see Bando de Don Joseph Francisco de Cañas y Merino, Gobernador y Capitan General de Venezuela, Turmero, Feb. 27, 1712, AGI, SD, 751. For his foray to Barquisimeto, see Gobernador Don Joseph Francisco de Cañas al Rey, Caracas, May 28, 1712, AGI, SD, 751. For his views on capital punishment, see Gobernador de Caracas, D. Francisco de Cañas al Rey, Caracas, Aug. 20, 1711, AGI, SD,

To reinforce their personal claims of zeal and hardships in defending royal commercial revenues, officials marshaled their friends and cohorts to testify to their meritorious service. Such corroboration was a key element of a bureaucrat's legal defense. It also revealed the ways that functionaries courted the loyalty of their peers. Juan de la Tornera Sota brought captains of the Cumaná militias to testify to his sense of duty. These men acknowledged that "they had neither seen nor made such considerable foreign ship seizures as in the time of Governor Juan de la Tornera Sota." The captains' favorable remarks probably came as a result of the preferential treatment Tornera Sota gave to the militias. His accusers believed that Tornera Sota had showered these military units with the spoils of his trading with the Dutch. What's more, he allowed them to buy from his personal stores on credit. Rank-and-file irregular soldiers and coast guardsmen had endured precarious financial situations throughout the colonial period. As late as 1784, one official document spoke of the need to regularize coast guard forces by hiring more competent men, paying them higher wages, and encouraging them to catalogue more thoroughly their captured contraband. These measures would change a long-standing state of affairs wherein "the commander, his troops, and subordinates are those who agree to smuggle or cover it up." More regulated and compensated anticontraband forces would be "so much more than a few poor people on short assignments and with no obligations as are currently employed in coastal patrols." Given these lackluster descriptions of coast guard employment, it is no wonder that Tornera Sota's monetary incentives secured positive testimony from the militias.[57]

Corporal Felipe Ugarte showed a similar generosity to the armed forces. As discussed earlier in this chapter, Ugarte stood accused of using Dutch firepower to rob cacao hacendados in his jurisdiction. According to his detractors,

751. See also Araúz Monfante, *El contrabando holandés en el Caribe*, I, 145–150; Arbell Mordechai, *The Jewish Nation of the Caribbean: The Spanish-Portuguese Jewish Settlements in the Caribbean and the Guianas* (New York, 2002), 264. "Everyone's business to destroy me": Don Joseph Francisco de Cañas al Rey, Caracas, Dec. 9, 1714, AGI, SD, 751.

57. "Considerable foreign ship seizures": Declaración del Escribano Publico de Cumaná, Don Martin Pellon, Cumaná, Apr. 18, 1730, AGI, SD, 635. For accusations of Tornera Sota's preferential treatment of the military, see Declaracion de Capitan Don Domingo Bermudez, Alcalde Ordinario de Cumaná, Margarita, Apr. 30, 1730, AGI, SD, 635; Declaración del Fray Domingo Rubio Menendez, Cumaná, May 12, 1730, AGI, SD, 635. On the conditions of coast guard and militia forces, see Moutoukias, "Power, Corruption, and Commerce," *HAHR*, LXVIII (1988), 788; Grahn, *Political Corruption and Reform*, 11; Grahn, *Political Economy of Smuggling*, 78. "Who agree to smuggle or cover it up": Reglamento de los Resguardos de Mar y Tierra, Caracas, Apr. 28, 1784, AGI, Caracas, 784.

Ugarte had liberally gifted portions of his contraband seizures to the soldiers he commanded and bought their loyalty. The soldiers corroborated Ugarte's denial of the robbery, testified to his bravery in various skirmishes with smugglers, and confirmed that his accuser, Juan Antonio Rodríguez de Sosa, was a contrabandist.[58]

The second method of defense employed by besieged bureaucrats was to smear the reputations of their accusers. The most popular means of doing this involved hurling counterclaims of smuggling upon their opponents. In this way, corrupt officials made hypocrites of their enemies. Furthermore, as contraband trade was rife in Venezuela, counteraccusations were sometimes true. Factional considerations prompted much of the mudslinging. Networks of corrupt officials defended their shared interests, protected themselves from conviction, and distributed the riches of smuggling in Venezuela throughout their ranks. Members of rival groups of bureaucrats often accused one another of facilitating illicit commerce.

The trial of Governor Diego Portales y Meneses underscores administrative tribalism's importance in smear operations and legal defense in colonial Venezuela. Partisan politics generated fierce animosities during Portales's twice-interrupted term as governor from 1721 to 1728. Animosities began in 1720, when the viceroy of New Granada, Jorge de Villalonga, sent Pedro José de Olavarriaga and Pedro Martín Beato to Caracas. As discussed in Chapter 3, the crown had appointed these men as special judges of commercial affairs *(jueces comisionarios)* to investigate the state of the treasury and suppress contraband trade. Their inquiries led to the dismissal of the previous governor, Marco de Betancourt y Castro, in 1721 for his incessant smuggling. Portales replaced Betancourt in the post.[59]

Portales's reign was even more conflict-laden than that of his predecessor. In his first stint as governor, he alienated both the viceroy and the Caracas cabildo. Not wanting the viceroy's investigators to meddle in his affairs, Portales jailed Beato and Olavarriaga and then liberated the deposed Betancourt against the viceroy's orders. Faced with direct disobedience, Viceroy Villalonga ordered Portales's arrest in 1723 on account of his rough treatment of

58. Auto de Don Julian de Arriaga, Caracas, Aug. 23, 1750, AGNV, Comisos, XXIV, fols. 263–264; Declaraciones que rinden en Caracas por ante el Alcalde Ordinario Doctor Gabriel Martín de Ibarra, Caracas, January and March 1751, AGNV, Comp Gui, IV, fols. 2–5.

59. Arantzazu Amezaga Iribarren, "La Real Compañía Guipuzcoana de Caracas: Crónica sentimental con una vision historiográfica, los años áuricos y las rebeliones (1728–1751)," *Sancho el Sabio,* XXII (2005), 178; Ferry, *Colonial Elite,* 114–116.

Beato and Olavarriaga. Yet a royal cédula freed Portales from jail shortly after his imprisonment.[60]

Portales continued to stoke partisan rancor after his first arrest. He appointed the Bishop of Caracas as his temporary successor, gaining a powerful ally in the clergyman, and began a legal vendetta against members of the cabildo and the viceregal government. After the viceroy's men rearrested Portales, he served one month in jail in 1724 before fleeing and taking refuge in the bishop's house. At this point, both Portales's and the cabildo's supporters seemed ready to take up arms against one another to decide who would govern Caracas. After a brief period in exile, Portales returned to the governorship with the authority of another royal cédula in 1726. He governed unopposed until 1728.[61]

For nearly a decade (1720–1728), those partial to the Caracas cabildo, the viceroy, and his agents Beato and Olavarriaga had fought a legal battle for control of Caracas against the forces of Portales and the bishop of Caracas. Throughout this struggle, both cadres used accusations of contraband trading as weapons to weaken and discredit their opponents' right to rule. Investigators Olavarriaga and Beato accused Governor Portales of a host of infractions, most involving some form of illicit commerce. In addition to being insubordinate to the viceroy, Portales, they alleged, had used presidio troops in La Guaira for his own business purposes. He had also illegally participated in cacao trading. Finally, Portales associated with known smugglers, including the former governor Betancourt, and had let captured contrabandists go without trial.[62]

Olavarriaga and Beato pointed to their reputations and unjust imprisonment as proof that Portales was tangled up in extralegal trade. Both agents had records of incorruptibility. Olavarriaga, quite literally, had written the book on smuggling with the 1722 publication of *Instrucción general y particular del estado presente de la provincia de Venezuela.* The two men had been integral in bringing down Betancourt, and now they sought to depose Portales. For this, Portales imprisoned them, "pleasing the illicit merchants . . . with the violences done

60. Sucre, *Gobernadores y capitanes generales de Venezuela,* 231–236; Ferry, *Colonial Elite,* 114–116.

61. Ferry, *Colonial Elite,* 114–116.

62. Don Pedro Martin Beato y Don Pedro Olavarriaga al Rey, Caracas, June 16, Oct. 11, 1722, AGI, SD, 759; Sentencia de Visita del Consejo dada en las demandas puesttas por Don Ruy Fernandez de Fuenmayor y ottros, a Don Diego Porttales y Meneses Governador que fue de al Prov.a de Caracas, Nov. 11, 1732, AGI, Esc, 1194.

unto us because we had almost extinguished the foreign trade." Numerous testimonies from Olavarriaga, Beato, and others reinforced the agents' impeccable credentials. During their time in Venezuela, they had fought in pitched battles against Dutch contrabandists and recovered an astonishing 115,049 pesos in seized goods.[63]

Diego Portales y Meneses, for his part, brought forth allegations of Olavarriaga and Beato's misconduct in an attempt to discredit the two prize court judges. He accused them of embezzling more than eight thousand pesos from their contraband seizures and distributing this money among their fellow officers. Portales also alleged that they had received bribes to write pardons for masters who had brought unregistered slaves into the colonies. The governor enlisted the help of the bishop of Caracas, who testified in his favor and stated that Olavarriaga, Beato, and a number of other officials were "united and congregated to wipe out and destroy the authority and respect of the king's ministers, putting up litigious impediments to the observance of their duties." Despite Portales's arguments, he was unable to sway judicial opinion on Olavarriaga and Beato's credibility or escape viceregal censure upon termination of his term in office.[64]

Occasionally, factional divides broke down, not by governmental branch, but by province. As the case of Juan de la Tornera Sota in Cumaná demonstrated, rival provinces could use accusations of illicit trade to damage the fortunes of one another. Tornera Sota's trumped-up rumors of a smallpox outbreak on Margarita no doubt discouraged trade to that island. Margarita's governor, Juan de Vera, stressed Tornera Sota's proclivity toward smuggling and aiding foreign merchants in his complaints about his island's forced isolation. The allegations exchanged by these warring governors suggested the tension between their provinces.

Partisanship and personalism marked the sentencing of corrupt officials, just as it affected their legal defenses. Those found guilty received inconsistent punishments dependent on a host of factors. No codified manual determined how the culpable would pay. Instead, those officials with the fewest connec-

63. "Pleasing the illicit merchants": Don Pedro Martin Beato y Don Pedro Joseph de Olavarriaga al Rey, Caracas, Oct. 11, 1722, AGI, SD, 759. See also Auto de Pedro Joseph de Olavarriaga, Caracas, Jan. 20, 1721, AGI, SD, 759; Don Pedro Martin Beato y Don Pedro Olavarriaga al Rey, Caracas, Jan. 23, 1723, AGI, SD, 759.

64. "Destroy the authority and respect of the king's ministers": El Obispo de Caracas al Rey, Caracas, Apr. 21, 1726, AGI, SD, 774. See also Sentencia de Visita del Consejo dada en las demandas puesttas por Don Ruy Fernandez de Fuenmayor y ottros, a Don Diego Porttales y Meneses, Nov. 11, 1732, AGI, Esc, 1194.

tions in high places and the most enemies often received the harshest sentences. Lower-level officials convicted of anything more than petty smuggling frequently endured harsh punishments because of their lack of influence. Justice was often more consistent and summary at the lowest rungs of the administrative ladder. Conversely, those with friends and allies at the viceregal and imperial levels might see stiff punishments diluted into mere slaps on the wrist.[65]

Nowhere was nepotism and inconsistency more evident than in the contradictory punishments doled out by colonial and imperial courts. Surprisingly, sentencing for contrabandist officials was often harsher in colonial courts than in the appeals stage in Spain. It may be that officials whose cases reached the desks of the Council of the Indies had reason to believe this body would treat them leniently. That the Council chose to step in at all meant, in some instances, these men had friends protecting them in Madrid.[66]

Portales, the governor who disobeyed the viceroy and prosecuted officials who might inform upon him, possessed these connections in the Spanish court. The viceroyalty of Santa Fe had suggested that Portales be fined 300 pesos for not confirming autos and expedientes against contrabandists, 10,000 reales for illegally taking cacao from Venezuelan producers, 15,000 reales for his insider trading, 2,500 reales for letting various contrabandists walk away from prosecution, and 2,000 reales for not confiscating the assets of several prize court judges. Despite the numerous testimonies against Portales, the Council of the Indies perceived the jail time he had served during two separate interruptions of his term as punishment enough and nullified or lessened most of the fines against the governor.[67]

The Council of the Indies' apathy also lightened the sentences doled out to bureaucrats. The council primarily cared about the balance sheets of colonial trade and preventing unrest. Smuggling, in many cases, lubricated the ad-

65. For an enlightening case study of an official and merchant (Cipriano di Melo) that confirms analogous patterns of bureaucratic partisanship in the prosecution of smuggling in the Río de la Plata estuary, see Fabrício Prado, *Edge of Empire: Atlantic Networks and the Revolution in Bourbon Río de la Plata* (Berkeley, Calif., 2015), 131–152.

66. Official patronage in the larger early modern world was often transatlantic. Influence at imperial courts might be traded for on-the-ground connections and knowledge in the periphery. See Kenneth J. Banks, "Official Duplicity: The Illicit Slave Trade in Martinique, 1713–1763," in Peter A. Coclanis, ed., *The Atlantic Economy during the Seventeenth and Eighteenth Centuries: Organization, Operation, Practice, and Personnel* (Columbia, S.C., 2005), 232.

67. Sucre, *Gobernadores y capitanes generales de Venezuela,* 236; Sentencia de Visita del Consejo dada en las demandas puesttas por Don Ruy Fernandez de Fuenmayor y ottros, a Don Diego Porttales y Meneses Governador, Nov. 11, 1732, AGI, Esc, 1194.

ministrative, military, and commercial parts of the colonial apparatus and prevented friction between them. Thus, officials who skimmed a little off the top of contraband seizures or accepted bribes from foreign smugglers in a petty fashion tended not to arouse the interest of administrators in Madrid, who had bigger fish to fry.

Contrarily, in cases linked to widespread embezzlement from the royal treasury or where officials siphoned off large sums destined for imperial coffers, the Council of the Indies took notice. Only bureaucrats from the gubernatorial level and upward on the administrative chain possessed the clout to misappropriate such amounts of money, so the council rarely dealt with the crimes of local functionaries. Of the cases consulted in this chapter, only a handful of the rulings on local officials came from Madrid. The vast majority of council sentences made by the Council of the Indies concerned governors and viceroys.

As their first priority, officials in Madrid sought to recover lost funds from wayward colonial administrators. After confirming the guilt of the accused, prosecutors attacked the assets and private funds of corrupt functionaries. The paper trail of these financial inquiries sometimes stretched longer than the trial itself. The case of Sebastián García de la Torre, the governor of Venezuela in the 1730s, demonstrates this money chase. Much like modern police detectives investigating a mob boss's offshore bank accounts, prosecutors extensively documented where García de la Torre kept his money in both Venezuela and Spain. His diverse geographic holdings probably originated from García de la Torre's myriad connections to illicit merchant networks.[68]

Similarly, investigators in Caracas and Madrid traced the path of José Francisco de Cañas's assets and seized what they could. For example, Cañas had sent between 900 and 1,000 pesos aboard an asiento ship consigned under the name of a French merchant with orders to remit them to a contact in Madrid. Cañas also sent his associate 59,000 reales worth of cacao to Spain to be deposited in an account for his wife and three daughters. The detection of these far-flung funds indicated the Spanish imperial government's priorities in the prosecution of major smuggling officials.[69]

Repairing the social and commercial damages wrought by corrupt officials

68. Residencia de Sebastián García de la Torre, Gobernador de la Provincia de Venezuela, por Martín de Lardizabal, Comandante General, 1739, AGI, Esc, 727A.

69. Declaracion de Don Julio Chourío, Director del Real Asiento de Negros, Caracas, Oct. 7, 1714, AGI, SD, 751; Auto de Don Jorge Lozano Peralta, Madrid, May 14, 1715, AGI, SD, 751.

in the colonies was more of an afterthought for the Council of the Indies. The governing body applied few physical punishments such as prison terms, forced labor, or exile. It often removed these castigations entirely from viceregal sentences. Instead, fines predominated as a sort of retroactive recuperation of the money lost through smuggling. With Sebastián García de la Torre, for instance, the council upheld 6,000 of the 8,000-peso fine charged to him but canceled a four-year labor sentence at the Spanish presidio in Ceuta. In the sentencing of José Francisco de Cañas, the council allowed the "fathers, mothers, wives, children, and heirs" of thirteen arrieros and private traders he had executed for possession of illicit goods to sue Cañas for damages. It did not, however, directly concede any benefits to them. The body also permitted two men whom Cañas had falsely imprisoned for a period of years to seek restitution.[70]

Only in exceptional cases, when the corruption of a governor left a lasting scar on the social fabric of a community, might the Council of the Indies award damages. Virtually every testimony and town petition summoned against Cañas spoke of his infamous sexual abuse of and malice toward the young ladies of Caracas. For six charges ranging from his virginity tests to the beating, kidnapping, shaming, and possible rape of the young women, the council forced Cañas to pay a five-hundred-peso fine. To put this in perspective, he garnered the same five hundred-peso penalty for illegally sending one shipment of cacao to Spain via the asiento. Given the damage done to the community, the financial penalty exacted of Cañas was light.[71]

Nonetheless, Cañas's offenses were heinous enough that the council initially sentenced him to ten years of presidio labor in Ceuta, perpetual loss of office and exile from the Indies, and the fines. All this came after he had spent several years in jail in Madrid. As stated earlier, ministers even debated the death penalty for Cañas before a royal birth during his imprisonment secured him a general pardon with other prisoners. By 1720, the year of Cañas's sentencing, his notoriety had spread. In a directive sent to the Audiencia de Filipinas, the Council of the Indies used his case as an example for how to proceed against a governor in Manila. This official, among other offenses, had threat-

70. Moutoukias, "Power, Corruption, and Commerce," *HAHR,* LXVIII (1988), 796; Auto de Revista del Consejo dado en vista de los autos de la Pesquisa de D. Sevastian Garcia de la Torre, July 7, 1742, AGI, Esc, 964. "Fathers, mothers, wives, children, and heirs": Sentencia en vista de la Causa y Pesquisa contra D. Joseph Francisco de Cañas, Madrid, June 12, 1720, AGI, Esc, 964.

71. Sentencia en vista de la Causa y Pesquisa contra D. Joseph Francisco de Cañas, Madrid, June 12, 1720, AGI, Esc, 964. Cañas's total fines amounted to between two and three thousand pesos.

ened his subjects, engaged in insider trading, and seized several ships violently, resulting in unnecessary loss of life. The legal directive suggests both the Cañas case's importance as a legal precedent for dealing with smuggling governors—and also its exceptionality.[72]

What, then, were the most common sentences issued to wayward administrators by legal bodies in the Americas and Spain? Fines played the largest part in the punishment of offending bureaucrats. The quantities varied dramatically. Rodrigo Álvarez, who had been accused of buying and selling goods stolen by enslaved people from their masters, paid just 20 pesos for a few questionable items found in his store. At the other end of the spectrum, colonial authorities bled Juan de la Tornera Sota dry for inventing a smallpox scare to keep his illicit trade private. Officials in Cumaná forced Tornera Sota to pay 8,000 pesos to the province's treasury for personal trading that he did with merchants in Veracruz and the Canary Islands aboard register ships, 3,500 pesos to the treasury for unspecified "excesses committed during the time of his government," and 4,000 pesos to the royal chamber of Castille *(real cámara)* for falsely denouncing Bernabé Angel de Toledo, who was later acquitted. Fines could also take the form of the confiscation of an official's property, particularly when the effects themselves were suspected to be contraband.[73]

Prosecutors of crooked administrators usually removed the guilty from the office and location in which they committed their crimes. One member of Maiquetía's coast guard suspected of tolerating and arranging illicit transactions lost his office and his privilege to go within four leagues of the coast or La Guaira in 1758. Though these penalties were the soldier's only punishment, forced removal from one's community in early modern Spanish America rep-

72. Sentencia en vista de la Causa y Pesquisa contra D. Joseph Francisco de Cañas, Madrid, June 12, 1720, AGI, Esc, 964; Sucre, *Gobernadores y capitanes generales de Venezuela,* 212–213. For the use of Cañas's example in Manila, see Consulta del Consejo de Indias informando de la nueva notificación de auto de la junta de indultos del Consejo de Castilla al relator del Consejo de Indias para que haga relación de la causa de José Francisco de Cañas, Madrid, Oct. 19, 1720, AGI, Filipinas, 94.

73. Auto de Don Marcos Francisco de Betancourt, Caracas, Sept. 2, 1719, AGNV, Diversos, VIII, fols. 464–465; Demanda puesta por la Real Contaduria de esta Ciudad de Cumaná al Señor Don Juan de la Tornera Sota Governador y Capitan General que fue de esta Provincias por las multas y cosas en que por reales provisiones se le condeno, June 7, 1735, AGI, Esc, 727B; Autos del consejo dado en los autos seguidos por el Sr. Fiscal, contra el Capt. Don Bernave Angel de Toledo, sobre diferentes excesos y otras cosas, Madrid, Feb. 20, 1737, AGI, Esc, 964. "Excesses committed during the time of his government": Testimonio de los autos hechos sobre cantidad de pessos que deve el Sargento Mayor Don Juan de la Tornera Sotta a las Reales Caxas de Cumana, Caracas, 1737, AGI, Esc, 727B.

resented a significant hardship. Exile might be temporary or permanent depending on an official's misdeeds, but prohibition from holding office was usually perpetual. Officeholding and its illicit benefits were a significant source of income for many men, one they could scarcely afford to lose.[74]

Sentences of the guilty resulted in physical confinement and control less frequently than fines or exile. Officials' more selective use of this punishment probably had to do with its potentially lethal nature. Jails in this period were mainly temporary and insecure holding pens meant only for use over the course of a trial, so incarceration for long durations occurred rarely. Instead, prosecuting authorities invoked forced labor drafts to castigate many offenders. Just as foreign smugglers frequently found themselves toiling away on the construction of forts and manning military garrisons in inhospitable parts of the New World, Spain, and Africa, so did the corrupt officials initially tasked with stopping them. Backbreaking labor in malarial locales of the Caribbean, violent Spanish beachheads in Africa, and fetid fortifications along the Spanish coast, when combined with poor living conditions and inadequate diet, produced high mortality rates. The Spanish judicial system was hesitant to bestow such a fate on its own functionaries.[75]

Officials deciding the fortunes of their former colleagues, perhaps mindful of being castigated for their own potential infractions, probably reserved this punishment for the most unconnected officials and egregious offenders. For Andrés de Tovar, discussed above, and Andrés Martinez, lower-level smuggling soldiers, a lack of higher authorities willing to soften their sentences probably doomed the two. In retribution for giving safe passage and info to Dutch smugglers, Martinez, a coast guard official, received an eight-year term at Ceuta. Tovar, a sheriff in the militia of the inland hamlet of Nuestra Señora de Pilar de Zaragoza, faced the prospect of two years of service in Ceuta before he escaped from jail.[76]

Though capital punishment figured as the most serious punishment an official could receive for facilitating smuggling, its use in practice was exceedingly rare. Royal cédulas of 1706 and 1724 allowed officials to invoke the death

74. Sentencia de Don Phelipe Ramirez, Caracas, Oct. 11, 1758, AGNV, Comisos, XXVI, fols. 99–100.

75. Ruth Pike, "Penal Servitude in the Spanish Empire: Presidio Labor in the Eighteenth Century," *HAHR*, LVIII (1978), 27–36.

76. Sentencia en vista de la Causa y Pesquisa contra D. Joseph Francisco de Cañas, Madrid, June 12, 1720, AGI, Esc, 964; Sentencia de Martin de Lardizabal, Caracas, June 4, 1737, AGNV, Comisos, XV, fol. 165; Auto de Martin de Lardizabal, AGNV, Diversos, XVIII, fols. 399–400.

penalty for those found guilty of smuggling, but only a handful of executions were ever carried out. The frequency with which smuggling took place and its nature as primarily a commercial crime made capital punishment excessive in the eyes of most administrators.[77]

Overall, the Spanish legal system prosecuted or ignored officials involved in smuggling with the same mix of personal politics and factionalism that characterized these corrupt functionaries' illicit transactions in Venezuela. Investigations, prosecutions, defenses, and sentences all built on loyalties and connections running through the administrative chain of command. Both the accusers and the accused talked a good game about the ill effects of contraband trade upon the province of Venezuela and the evils of the men who allowed it.

Yet, for all this bluster, the cases examined here and the numerous administrators that evaded detection suggest that the business ventures of officials in Venezuela far outstripped the ability or will of Spanish Atlantic judicial administrators in either Spain or the colony to punish them. In practice, many parties negotiated commercial trade law and the penalties for those who broke it. As a result, the entrepreneurial bureaucrat, like foreign smugglers and their Venezuelan accomplices, continued to feature as an integral and regular member of the province's smoothly running illicit trade system.

## CONCLUSION

Bureaucratic engagement in smuggling was as integral to illegal trade as it was to the financial well-being of officials. Perhaps no amount of policing could have brought smuggling in Venezuela to a halt. The Jesuit Antonio Julián confessed as much about the northern coast of South America when he wrote, "The sea is wide and the coast is long. Along it there are many points and capes, and at certain places numerous inlets. It is, as we frequently say, a great sea *[mare magnum]* and if I wished to arrive [on its shores], I would have to cut a path through all the foreign purveyors." But a fully functioning and incorruptible system of customs enforcement and prosecution would have slowed the business. Illicit trading perpetrated by foreigners in the dead of night or out of isolated coves would have been more difficult. The category of brazen smuggling that took place in broad daylight or through official apparatuses of trade

77. Governador de Caracas, D. Francisco de Cañas al Rey, Caracas, Aug. 20, 1711, AGI, SD, 751; Autos contra el Alcalde Provincial Don Francisco Figueredo y Juan Nicholas de Lugo, arriero, por haber amparado en la casa que tienen en el sitio que llaman El Desembocadero, Jan. 4, 1765, AGNV, Comisos, XXVIII, fol. 77.

such as the asiento or register ships would have been nearly impossible. This never came to be.[78]

Instead, governmental corruption's role in the fluid operation of illicit commerce proves that local connections and networks greatly influenced not just commercial exchanges but also bureaucratic actions in colonial Spanish America. If the early modern state merely legitimated existing human interactions, administrative divergence from Spanish commercial policy should be seen as a corrective to the juridical code rather than the sabotage of it. As these Venezuelan cases make clear, most officials could scarcely be expected to maintain loyalty and fidelity to the commercial policy of Spanish rulers an ocean away when their local sphere of influence pushed them in the opposite direction. With bribes and business partnerships, Spanish American functionaries removed the greatest potential obstacle toward integration within international markets and enriched themselves in the process.[79]

In navigating this atmosphere of flexible government, eighteenth-century Venezuelans had developed, in collaboration with officials, acceptable norms of corruption. Keeping their operations within these boundaries could ensure a corrupt administrator's longevity in office. Most of Caraqueño society perceived no moral wrong in smuggling nor in their governors' use of the office to turn a profit. Furthermore, extralegal international trade benefited these subjects by opening up necessary markets to Venezuelan cacao.

Documents detailing the prosecution of corrupt officials for their complicity demonstrate that most Venezuelans found collusion in the everyday business of illicit trade to be tolerable and resisted attempts to punish it. Payoffs, business arrangements, and judicial impunity in colonial Venezuela confirms that illegal traders saw monetary kickbacks to officials as a standard operating cost in their business. When authorities like Governor José Francisco de Cañas crossed the thresholds of tolerable vice, locals quickly turned upon the abuser and used their open channels with higher authorities and the king to circumvent his authority and remove him from office. Yet, as the paucity of such cases reveals, in most instances Venezuelans accepted the complicity of their administrators.[80]

78. Antonio Julián, *La perla de la America: Provincia de Santa Marta, reconocida, observada y expuesta en discursos historicos* (Madrid, 1787), 251.

79. As Cañeque has claimed, the early modern state was just interpersonal relationships manifested in governmental forms (*King's Living Image*, 6). See also Schmitt, "Virtue in Corruption," *Early American Studies*, XIII (2015), 93.

80. In his examination of social responses to extralegal government, Arnold J. Heiden-

The Spanish legal system, in its inconsistency, legitimized contraband corruption as well. Though authorities at the regional and imperial levels sometimes doled out fines and other punishments in the prosecution of colonial officials, the administration of justice was deeply factional and nepotistic. Those who stole large sums via their smuggling might pay a heavy price, but corrupt officers mostly received only token punishments. Lacking the capacity or will to crack down on administrators, Spanish courts inadvertently regularized the informal exchange between bureaucrats and smugglers. With their entrance into the illicit economy, bureaucrats became arbiters between the legal intent of the state, the commerce of the populace, and the interconnectedness of the market.

Pliable bureaucrats, foreign smugglers, and domestic contrabandists hashed out the rules and practices of covert commerce in eighteenth-century Venezuela and altered the social and political culture of the colony through their trading. In the final two chapters, this book shifts from the granular aspects of how smuggling took place toward a more wide-ranging examination of how it affected key elements of Venezuelan society. Contraband trade and its suppression influenced the labor and legal status of Afro-Caribbean maritime workers and enslaved cargoes, shaped the day-to-day consumer culture of coastal inhabitants, and stirred up political unrest in the province. It is to these inadvertent yet powerful consequences of the parallel economy that we now turn.

---

heimer divides public acceptance of corruption into three categories: black, gray, and white. Black corruption signifies a majority consensus between elites and the masses of a society that a given corrupt practice is objectionable and that the offender should be punished on principle. In gray corruption, elites would like to see a crooked act punished, but at least some portion of the masses view it more ambivalently. With white corruption, the majority of elites and commoners resist attempts to punish a corrupt practice they find tolerable (Heidenheimer, "Perspectives on the Perception of Corruption," in Heidenheimer, Johnston, and LeVine, eds., *Political Corruption,* 160–163. See also Alexandra Harnett and Shannon Lee Dawdy, "The Archaeology of Illegal and Illicit Economies," *Annual Review of Anthropology,* XLII [2013]), 39.

# 7

## *Contrabandists or Cargo?*

### People of Color, Smuggling, and the Illicit Slave Trade

On the afternoon of April 21, 1763, Spanish corsairs captured a Dutch trading sloop off the coast of Cuyagua, a small port west of Caracas on the central coast. The Dutch captain and his fellow white officers escaped to land while three sailors of African descent stayed aboard. With the contraband vessel boarded and brought to port in Puerto Cabello, Spanish officials began the routine business of appraising and selling the prize. They then questioned and sentenced the prisoners taken from the sloop.[1]

Government functionaries learned from the declaration of one of the crew members, a black sailor named Juan Pedro Antonio, that the vessel came from Curaçao with a Dutch license to trade and a cargo of clothing and textiles belonging to a Curaçaoan merchant. The ship had exchanged goods freely with residents of the central Venezuelan littoral until the Spanish patrol had captured it. As a sailor guilty of illegally trafficking foreign wares in the Spanish overseas kingdoms, Juan Pedro Antonio received a year and a half of forced labor in the royal factory (Real Fábrica) of the fort at Puerto Cabello. Upon completing his sentence, he lived as a free man in Venezuela.[2]

1. It is unclear from the documents whether the Afro-Dutch mariners chose to stay aboard the ship or were ordered to do so by the captain. See Declaraciones de Don Juan Antonio Usabaraza, Don Miguel Antonio Larruleta y Joaquín Petriarza, Puerto Cabello, Sept. 26, 1763, AGNV, Comp Gui, XI, fols. 189–190.

2. Declaraciones de tres negros holandeses, Puerto Cabello, Sept. 27, 1763, AGNV, Comp Gui, XI, fol. 190; Declaración del negro Juan Pedro (Carlos Antonio Méndez), Caracas, Sept. 15, 1768, AGNV, Comp Gui, XI, fol. 220. The Dutch government in Curaçao commonly

People of African descent often took to the seas between empires, navigating the short distances and immense political and legal divides separating colonies. In the early modern Caribbean, they represented essential elements of society as both a socioracial section of the populace and the primary engine of the region's wealth through slavery and the slave trade. Smuggling, which infiltrated all aspects of Caribbean and Venezuelan society, had consequences for Afro-Caribbean people as laborers and as human beings in search of autonomy and self-determination. Interimperial trade offered Africans an unstable means to flee to freedom or to avoid harsher labor conditions. On illicit voyages between the Spanish, French, Dutch, and English Antilles, both free blacks and slaves found some degree of independence and freedom of movement. As mariners, porters, supercargoes, traders, and go-betweens, they became integral, if not always voluntary, participants in extralegal seafaring commerce.

Men of African descent involved in contraband trading encountered enormous dangers on top of those their white counterparts faced. Black contrabandists took on the risks of capture, enslavement (or re-enslavement), and forced labor while negotiating overlapping societies that generally shared a belief in white supremacy and held independent people of color under suspicion. The seizure of their vessels in Spanish waters brought into question nonwhite mariners' status, citizenship, occupational identity, and ties to contrabandists and masters. It was the crossing of imperial boundaries and legal regimes that made the experiences of free and enslaved maritime contrabandists unique among the majority of their land-based Afro-Caribbean peers.

A consistent demand for enslaved laborers to work cacao plantations brought people of African descent to Venezuela in the hulls of ships as smuggled goods themselves rather than the bearers of illicit cargo. Difficulties in the legal procurement of Africans motivated Venezuelan planters to search for illicit sources of enslaved workers. Unlicensed foreign traders met this need but rarely specialized in slave trading. Although they considered slaves just another type of product in their holds, the legal and conceptual challenges of illicitly trafficking human beings became apparent for both sellers and buyers when Spanish authorities discovered their transactions.

To understand the gradations between bondage and liberty that black contrabandists and slaves faced, it is useful to dig deeper into Juan Pedro Antonio's case. The documentary record of Antonio's story might have ended

---

provided trading licenses to its subjects visiting Spanish colonies even though it knew that Spain forbade commerce between Spanish subjects and foreigners.

with his labor sentence had his past not caught up with him. Five years after his arrest, a letter arrived in Caracas from a French subject of Martinique named Juan Antonio Marión. Marión claimed that Antonio belonged to him, provided papers proving ownership, and asked that Antonio be returned. Officials in Caracas hauled in Antonio, who had resided in Caracas and Puerto Cabello for the past three and a half years doing odd jobs and living as a free man. Authorities questioned him about how he had come to Venezuela.[3]

Inconsistencies between Juan Pedro Antonio's two testimonies began to emerge. In his initial statement of 1763, he claimed to be the slave of José Garabato, a Frenchman who had left Martinique for Curaçao with Antonio in tow to avoid the brief 1762 English occupation. Garabato had hired Antonio out for ten pesos per month to the Dutch sloop on which he was captured. Antonio also stated in his first testimony that his name was actually Carlos Antonio Méndez and that Juan Pedro Antonio was the name of his father. In his second testimony, in 1768, Antonio claimed to be the slave of Marión, not Garabato. The story of his migration and employment aboard the Dutch sloop remained largely the same.[4]

Santiago Francine, Marión's lawyer in Caracas, seized on the contradictions in Antonio's declarations. According to Francine, Antonio had not found employment aboard the Dutch sloop with his master's consent. Rather, he had fled Martinique alone, changed his name, and passed himself off as a free man aboard the Dutch ship. Francine chastised the Caracas Company for selling the fugitive into forced labor when they should have returned him to his master. In Francine's opinion, "The slave should not be believed in the testimony he gives against his legitimate master because he is his master's mortal enemy." To smooth over the legal conflict, Marión's lawyer suggested that his client would be willing to buy Antonio back at the going market rate in Caracas.[5]

Royal officials arbitrated the case by offering Juan Pedro Antonio an unconscionable ultimatum. In response to his accusations that Marión had cruelly mistreated him, the governor of Venezuela gave Antonio six days to find himself another buyer. If he could not find a new master within this time frame, the governor would sell him back to Marión. With no other option,

3. Instancia de Juan Antonio Marión ante el Gobernador, Caracas, June 21, 1768, AGNV, Comp Gui, XI, fol. 208.

4. Declaración del negro holandés, Puerto Cabello, Sept. 27, 1763, AGNV, Comp Gui, XI, fol. 204; Declaración del negro Juan Pedro (Carlos Antonio Méndez), Caracas, Sept. 15, 1768, AGNV, Comp Gui, XI, fol. 220.

5. Carta de Don Santiago Francine to Gobernador y Captain General, Caracas, Sept. 28, 1768, AGNV, Comp Gui, XI, fols. 223–225.

Antonio, a formerly free man, began the process of selling himself back into slavery. An appraisal by court authorities put his value at nearly half that of a healthy male slave owing to an unspecified injury. Exactly six days after the governor's order, Antonio produced a local Caracas merchant willing to purchase him.[6]

Despite his seemingly expedient solution to the dispute, Antonio's maneuverings came to nothing. Marión's lawyer was not satisfied. Whether out of spite or some other reason, Francine petitioned the governor not to accept the Caracas merchant's proposal and also withdrew his client's offer to purchase the slave. Instead, he asked that Antonio be remanded to Caracas's port to work on the construction of fortifications there. The governor accepted Francine's petition and ordered what was probably a death sentence for the injured Antonio, sending him to an indefinite labor term in La Guaira.[7]

The case of Juan Pedro Antonio speaks to the many contradictions inherent in conceptualizing Afro-Caribbean seamen as both the practitioners of contraband trade and bondsmen capable of being converted into contraband goods themselves. Free and enslaved black contrabandists are vibrant examples of "Atlantic creoles." The term's nod to the transformational culture produced through Atlantic encounters certainly characterizes the nonnational and cooperative tenets of smuggling. Smugglers of African descent experienced a wide breadth of Atlantic customs and legal cultures and adaptively attempted to better their place in societies prone to corrosive white supremacy. Afro-Caribbean involvement in illicit trade also emphasizes the precarious position of the semiautonomous Atlantic creole before courts, kidnappers, and planters that sought to brutalize blacks into submission.[8]

6. Instancia del esclavo ante el Gobernador, Caracas, July 28, 1769, AGNV, Comp Gui, XI, fol. 248.

7. Instancia de Francine ante el Gobernador, Caracas, Aug. 14, 1769, AGNV, Comp Gui, XI, fol. 249; Auto del Gobernador, Caracas, Aug. 14, 1769, AGNV, Comp Gui, XI, fol. 249.

8. The term "Atlantic creole" was coined by Ira Berlin to interpret the lives of people of color before the rise of great plantation societies and extreme racial differentiation (Berlin, "From Creole to African: Atlantic Creoles and the Origins of African-American Society in Mainland North America," *WMQ*, 3d Ser., LIII [1996], 254). Scholars such as Jane G. Landers have extended the term into the later colonial period in the Americas, when the plantation system flourished (Landers, *Atlantic Creoles in the Age of Revolutions* [Cambridge, Mass., 2010], 2–13). Paul Gilroy's interpretation of ships as the literal objects that rupture nationalist frameworks of history has informed my understanding of Atlantic creoles (Gilroy, *The Black Atlantic: Modernity and Double Consciousness* [Cambridge, Mass., 1993], 12, 16–17). On the effects of this traumatic instability for black consciousness and legal standing, see Stephanie E. Smallwood, *Saltwater Slavery: A Middle Passage from Africa to American Diaspora* (Cambridge, Mass., 2007), 7; Alan Gregor Cobley, "That Turbu-

This chapter first discusses the social history of non-Spanish free black mariners and smugglers trading in Venezuela. It then turns its attention to the slaves and free blacks who aided Venezuelan masters on the Spanish American side of contraband dealings. Finally, it transitions to an assessment of Venezuela's thriving eighteenth-century black market slave trade, a business that converted people of African descent into contraband property. Several works have dealt with seafarers of color in the Anglo-maritime world or enslaved laborers in Venezuela, but scholars have not substantially examined the role of Afro-Caribbean sailors and slaves in the Spanish American smuggling trade. The occupational histories of these traders are just as fascinating as the legal ambiguities they faced.[9]

Illicit commerce between foreign colonies and Venezuela made flexible work arrangements possible for men of color in the southern Caribbean. These jobs were simultaneously autonomous, empowering, and dangerous. Trading along the northern coast of South America could lead to freedom, some degree of personal wealth, or more negotiated forms of human bondage. It also

---

lent Soil: Seafarers, the 'Black Atlantic,' and Afro-Caribbean Identity," in Jerry H. Bentley, Renate Bridenthal, and Kären Wigen, eds., *Seascapes: Maritime Histories, Littoral Cultures, and Transoceanic Exchanges* (Honolulu, 2007), 157.

9. For literature on African American seamen, see W. Jeffrey Bolster, *Black Jacks: African American Seamen in the Age of Sail* (Cambridge, Mass., 1997); and David S. Cecelski, *The Waterman's Song: Slavery and Freedom in Maritime North Carolina* (Chapel Hill, N.C., 2001); Charles R. Foy, "Eighteenth Century 'Prize Negroes': From Britain to America," *Slavery and Abolition,* XXXI (2010), 379–393. For enslaved mariners, see Michael J. Jarvis, "Maritime Masters and Seafaring Slaves in Bermuda, 1680–1783," *WMQ,* 3d Ser., LIX (2002), 585–622; Stephanie E. Smallwood, "African Guardians, European Slave Ships, and the Changing Dynamics of Power in the Early Modern Atlantic," ibid., LXIV (2007), 679–716; Emma Christopher, *Slave Ship Sailors and Their Captive Cargoes, 1730–1807* (New York, 2006); Mariana P. Candido, "Different Slave Journeys: Enslaved African Seamen on Board of Portuguese Ships, c. 1760–1820s," *Slavery and Abolition,* XXXI (2010), 395–409; Kevin Dawson, "Enslaved Ship Pilots in the Age of Revolutions: Challenging Notions of Race and Slavery between the Boundaries of Land and Sea," *Journal of Social History,* XLVII (2013), 71–100. For an excellent work on Venezuelan slaves, see Miguel Acosta Saignes, *Vida de los esclavos negros en Venezuela* (Havana, 1978). The few studies that investigate contrabandists of color analyze their stories with an eye toward the apparent contradiction in legal history represented by enslaved or subordinated people practicing unbound commerce. Although this chapter concurs with Linda M. Rupert's assessment of the robust role of people of color in Caribbean smuggling, it does not share Rupert's belief that free trade and slavery were contradictory impulses in the early modern world (Rupert, *Creolization and Contraband: Curaçao in the Early Modern Atlantic World* [Athens, Ga., 2012], 104, 155; Rupert, "Marronage, Manumission, and Maritime Trade in the Early Modern Caribbean," *Slavery and Abolition,* XXX [2009], 367–368).

left people of color subject to capture, imprisonment, forced labor, and enslavement. Added to this misery, interimperial slave smuggling brought thousands of Africans to Venezuela. To the early modern mind, free trade and all its liberties were not incompatible with slavery. Though men of African descent might carry illegal cargoes across the Caribbean, their rights within one empire often dissolved as they crossed into another.[10]

## FOREIGN AFRO-CARIBBEAN CONTRABANDISTS IN VENEZUELAN SMUGGLING

Throughout the eighteenth century, English, French, and Dutch merchants bound for the Venezuelan coast widely employed Afro-Caribbean sailors to man their ships. Both slaves and freemen served aboard small vessels trading for cacao, tobacco, and hides. They labored side by side with whites on watercraft usually crewed by no more than twenty men and averaging closer to twelve. The substantial presence of Afro-Caribbean mariners aboard these vessels complicated the socioeconomic logic of the plantation economy in Caribbean colonies, which envisioned rigidly controlled African labor as a mainstay of large and lucrative agricultural systems. Why would societies that saw populations of African descent as the natural enemies of white men and sought to exert total control over their labor and mobility allow these men the latitude to take to the sea, drop anchor in foreign lands, and exchange white men's precious cargo virtually unsupervised?

The answer to this question involves a discussion of Caribbean demographics, economic production, and the nature of the contraband trade. A boom in African populations in the seventeenth and eighteenth centuries on Caribbean islands, particularly areas not dominated by sugar production, left colonial officials looking for ways to employ nonwhites. In Curaçao, Venezuela's most prominent contraband supplier, people of color were a majority by the 1660s. By 1789, the free black population on the island outnumbered that of its white inhabitants. Shipping and the slave trade powered the economy of the Dutch colony. Bereft of fertile soils yet blessed with a prosperous transit trade, Curaçao's whites began to introduce freemen and slaves as sailors

10. Gregory E. O'Malley points out, "Instead of landing in a busy entrepôt on a bustling afternoon, many captives reaching French or Spanish territory climbed into harbor dinghies in the dead of night. Others landed in hidden bays in sparsely populated areas, away from the prying eyes of officials. Little is known about the transit of these contraband peoples from the water's edge into French or Spanish colonial society" (O'Malley, *Final Passages: The Intercolonial Slave Trade of British America, 1619–1807* [Chapel Hill, N.C., 2014], 65–66).

onto contraband ships to make productive use of the island's labor force. By 1741, two-thirds of sailors residing in Curaçao were either slaves or free people of color.[11]

Like their Dutch counterparts, English merchants operating in the Atlantic and Caribbean similarly introduced people of color into maritime trade. In the eighteenth century, the British colony of Bermuda experienced a comparable increase to Curaçao in its African-descended population as it grew into a shipping colony. Bermuda came to depend on maritime trade for its economic sustenance and had one of the highest percentages of nonwhite sailors in its fleet at one in four by the 1740s. Like many other eighteenth-century colonies in the bellicose circum-Caribbean, Bermuda's inhabitants sent Afro-Caribbean men to sea in part because white men were needed to stay home as militiamen. Even among islands reliant on plantation agriculture, Afro-Caribbean sailors became a common sight in the eighteenth century. Edward Long, the eighteenth-century historian of Jamaica, estimated in 1774 that 15 percent (25,000) of Jamaica's 170,000 slaves were tradesmen, sailors, fisherman, and domestic employees.[12]

Ease of recruitment also factored into the decision to hire Afro-Caribbean sailors. Unlike whites, who generally saw sailing as a dishonorable profession, most men of color regarded it as a step up from jobs on land. The famous narrative of Olaudah Equiano, a slave who traversed the Caribbean and Atlantic worlds in the eighteenth century, offers a rationale for this preference. Though his master initially forced Equiano, like many enslaved people, into sailing, he grew to enjoy the profession's itinerant nature. He described a stint working on a plantation as "a new slavery; in comparison of which, all my service hitherto [as a sailor] had been perfect freedom." Seafaring placed Equiano in harm's way (in his years at sea, he fought in naval skirmishes, fell victim to kidnapping by slavers, and got into fights with sailors and port dwellers that left him beaten and bloodied), but it also offered him the means to buy his freedom. Equiano

11. For population factors, see Linda M. Rupert, "Contraband Trade and the Shaping of Colonial Societies in Curaçao and Tierra Firme," *Itinerario,* XXX (2006), 43; Wim Klooster, "Subordinate but Proud: Curaçao's Free Blacks and Mulattoes in the Eighteenth Century," *NWIG,* LXVIII (1994), 286, 288. For shipping and sailors, see Johannes Menne Postma, *The Dutch in the Atlantic Slave Trade, 1600–1815* (Cambridge, 1990), 27–51; Klooster, *Illicit Riches: Dutch Trade in the Caribbean, 1648–1795* (Leiden, 1998), 68.

12. On Bermuda, see Michael J. Jarvis, *In the Eye of All Trade: Bermuda, Bermudians, and the Maritime Atlantic World, 1680–1783* (Williamsburg, Va., and Chapel Hill, N.C., 2010), 148; Jarvis, "Maritime Masters and Seafaring Slaves," *WMQ,* 3d Ser., LIX (2002), 599. On Jamaica, see Edward Long, *The History of Jamaica; or, General Survey of the Antient and Modern State of That Island . . . ,* I (London, 1774), 496.

earned a wage and also made money by buying glassware and other trinkets on one Caribbean island and then selling them for profit on another.[13]

For both free and enslaved mariners of color, pay was a crucial impetus for joining a contraband voyage. In contrast to agricultural work where compensation, if it existed at all, often came in the form of credit for provisions and shelter, sailing put a man of color in control of coin, lessening the influence of slaveholders. To counteract this freedom, masters forced bondsmen to surrender around two-thirds of their earnings. Bringing enslaved sailors aboard was attractive for ship captains; their cheap labor allowed them to undercut shipping costs of the competition. Even though seafaring wages for men of African descent were below those of their white counterparts, monetary compensation at any rate attracted men like Olaudah Equiano to work under the masts.[14]

Yet the promise of a sailor's pay was never certain. Duplicitous captains sometimes lured free black mariners aboard the ships, only to use them for the most dangerous jobs and cheat them of their earnings. White contrabandists often sent sailors of color ashore rather than putting themselves at risk. In 1771, a coast guard ship captured four free blacks from a nearby Dutch ship on the coast near Puerto Cabello. The smuggling ship's supercargo, a white man identified as Miguel el Mallorquin, had sent the men ashore to trade for cacao. When interrogated, all four sailors claimed Miguel had tricked them into serving on the vessel by offering a wage of eight pesos per month to fish. The mariners accepted the positions only to find out, once under sail, that their ship was full of clothing and other wares to trade in Venezuela. They professed their ignorance as to the ship's itinerary along with their regret at signing up for the journey, but the governor of Venezuela was not swayed. After an extremely brief hearing, he condemned the sailors to five years of hard labor in the presidio of Puerto de Varcón.[15]

In addition to monetary compensation, Afro-Caribbeans labored at sea for a host of nonmaterial reasons. Why many free laborers stayed in the profession and many slaves did not run away from ships are difficult questions to answer. Investigators asked captured sailors about the composition, destinations, and trading ventures of a voyage, but rarely about their motivations.

13. Bolster, *Black Jacks,* 4. "A new slavery": Olaudah Equiano, *The Interesting Narrative of the Life of Olaudah Equiano* (1791) (Boston, 1995), 86; see also 103.

14. Jarvis, "Maritime Masters and Seafaring Slaves," *WMQ,* 3d Ser., LIX (2002), 599, 606; Jarvis, *In the Eye of All Trade,* 150, 464–465.

15. Klooster, "Subordinate but Proud," *NWIG,* LXVIII (1994), 286; Diligencias contra Pedro Mascaro, Juan Ventura llamado Luis, Juan Pedro Ventura y Juan Espera en Dios, Puerto Cabello, May 7, 1771, AGNV, Comisos, XXVIII, fols. 231–243.

Although documents fail to record more nuanced reasons seamen of color remained aboard trading vessels, some evidence about advantageous labor conditions and lesser racial discrimination comes to the fore. We can do little more than speculate about familial or romantic connections in ports, trust relationships with known masters and captains, or wanderlust that kept Afro-Caribbeans going to sea with smugglers.

Afro-Caribbean seamen serving on covert trading voyages encountered work arrangements that were among the most autonomous available to men of color in the eighteenth century. Sailors of color received a wage for their labor (although masters of enslaved sailors were entitled to take all or some portion of it) and sometimes worked without an overseer. Although some masters took their slaves with them to sea, others hired off their charges to merchants or ship captains. At sea, men of color labored under minimal supervision. In part this was due to the regional and short-haul nature of circum-Caribbean trade. Seafaring and illicit trading were certainly not the only permutations of slavery in the Americas characterized by negligible surveillance. Some control over one's work was, nevertheless, a draw for the enslaved.[16]

The case of eleven men of African descent seized in Los Roques in 1775 underscores the flexible labor relations in contraband trade. An English captain deposited the men on the chain of islands off the Venezuelan coast to fish and gather salt. They included seven enslaved laborers and three freemen from Curaçao and one enslaved worker from the island of Saba. English and Dutch merchants, as well as the widow of an Englishman residing in Curaçao, lent their human property to the ship's complement. For a week, the Afro-Caribbean sailors worked on Los Roques under the supervision of one unarmed white mariner. This arrangement shows that the owners of the slaves clearly had no reservations about leaving them. As Spain had laid claim to Los

16. For examples of how people of African descent used maritime occupations to fashion labor autonomy for themselves as riverboat men *(bogas)*, sailors, and pilots, see Aline Helg, *Liberty and Equality in Caribbean Colombia, 1770–1835* (Chapel Hill, N.C., 2004), 67–68; Randy J. Sparks, *The Two Princes of Calabar: An Eighteenth-Century Atlantic Odyssey* (Cambridge, Mass., 2004), 86–87; Candido, "Different Slave Journeys," *Slavery and Abolition*, XXXI (2010), 404; Dawson, "Enslaved Ship Pilots in the Age of Revolutions," *Journal of Social History*, XLVII (2013), 71–100. Slaves worked in a generally unsupervised capacity as retailers, produce hagglers, barber surgeons, and faith healers, just to name a few professions. See James H. Sweet, *Domingos Álvares, African Healing, and the Intellectual History of the Atlantic World* (Chapel Hill, N.C., 2011), 123–146; David Geggus, "The Slaves and Free People of Color of Cap Français," in Jorge Cañizares-Esguerra, Matt D. Childs, and James Sidbury, eds., *The Black Urban Atlantic in the Age of the Slave Trade* (Philadelphia, 2013), 116; Mariza de Carvalho Soares, "African Barbeiros in Brazilian Slave Ports," ibid., 207–230.

Roques and wished to prevent the archipelago from becoming a hotbed of contraband, officials captured and promptly deported the sailors back to Curaçao with a stern warning never to return.[17]

The independent work arrangements available to Afro-Caribbean sailors opened up opportunities to seek their freedom. Engaging in contraband commerce added wrinkles to the quest for liberty because of the business's inherent legal pluralism across empires. Illicit commerce not only separated slaves from their masters but also allowed them to cross into foreign waters where a slave owner's previous jurisdiction did not necessarily apply. Between 1680 and 1764, the Spanish monarchs promulgated at least seven royal cédulas giving colonial officials in Spanish America the right to manumit runaways from Protestant colonies who were baptized and converted to Catholicism. Venezuela was not unique in offering religious refuge to runaways. Non-Spanish slaves in the Caribbean took advantage of this "Spanish Sanctuary" policy in Cuba to escape plantations in Jamaica and in Puerto Rico to flee slavery in the Dutch Lesser Antilles. These provisions provided a legal path to freedom, even if Spanish officials frequently failed to distinguish between runaways and Afro-Caribbean smugglers.[18]

The autonomy of smuggling caused Afro-Caribbean seafarers to be defined more by their occupation than their status as freemen or slaves. The enslaved toiled next to free blacks and whites. In rare instances, free blacks even became leaders of their ships. One mulatto captained a ship in 1742 that sailed as part of a larger convoy of Curaçaoan smuggling ships trading on the central coast. In another case, an Afro-Dutch captain named Guillermo Cunche (also identified as "Conch") was in charge of a vessel whose crew consisted of fifty people of color and a white merchant and his scribe in 1756. Cunche appeared in the documentary record twice more as a smuggling captain and as an accomplice to Felipe Ugarte, the royal official discussed in Chapter 6

17. Declaraciones de negros prisioneros, La Guaira, Aug. 22, 1775, AGNV, Comp Gui, XXX, fols. 90–99; Carta de Joseph de Amenabar to Gobernador y Capitan General, La Guaira, Aug. 22, 1775, AGNV, Comp Gui, XXX, fol. 100.

18. Bolster's scholarship on African American mariners concludes, "The very vessels that carried Africans to New World slavery not infrequently became a pipeline to freedom for slaves on the lam" (Bolster, *Black Jacks,* 232). See also Julius Sherrard Scott III, "The Common Wind: Currents of Afro-American Communication in the Era of the Haitian Revolution" (Ph.D. diss., Duke University, 1986), 92–109; Sparks, *Two Princes of Calabar,* 87–88. For explanations of the Spanish Sanctuary policy, see ibid., 93–102; Rupert, "Marronage, Manumission, and Maritime Trade," *Slavery and Abolition,* XXX (2009), 362; Jane Landers, "Spanish Sanctuary: Fugitives in Florida, 1687–1790," *Florida Historical Quarterly,* LXII (1984), 296–313.

who attacked the riverine property of his fellow subjects to steal their goods. Another Afro-Dutch smuggler led a crew that "violently extracted" cacao and hides from a sea-venturing Venezuelan merchant in exchange for an assortment of cloth in 1760.[19]

Though men of color only occasionally became ship captains or merchants and no doubt faced discrimination from white seamen, they transcended many of the color lines dividing black from white in the Caribbean. Seafarers were often more tolerant of a racially integrated workforce than their terrestrial counterparts. Men of African descent worked as crew aboard slave ships, and whites almost certainly differentiated these fellow, if unequal, sailors from the shackled human beings populating the ship's hold. Paradoxically, however, black mariners reinforced racialized labor hierarchies on land by transporting captive Africans to and around the Americas. On many slaving vessels, even unfree mariners of color received the authority to discipline enslaved cargoes.[20]

The shipboard conflict between racial division and the common bonds of seafaring can be seen in Olaudah Equaino's narrative. Although this iterant African sailor met unscrupulous sailors, captains, and dock dwellers who attempted (in some cases successfully) to kidnap him into slavery, Equiano still remembered fondly the compassion of fellow tars who said goodbye to him with oranges and small presents. He reflected that Richard Baker, a white sailor, became "a faithful friend; who, at the age of fifteen, discovered a mind superior to prejudice." Despite his color, Baker "was not ashamed to notice, to associate with, and to be the friend and instructor of one who was ignorant, a stranger, of a different complexion, and a slave."[21]

Life aboard the *Esperanza,* the Dutch schooner captured by a patrol boat of the Caracas Company (discussed above), confirms how rigid racial and

19. For the free mulatto captain, see Declaración de Juan Domingo, marinero y mulato criollo de Curaçao, San Felipe, Dec. 21, 1742, AGI, Esc, 671B. For Guillermo Cunche, see Declaracion de Joseph Pablo Silbera, pardo libre vecino de este Puerto y pasagero que venia en la Goleta, Caracas, July 3, 1756, AGI, Caracas, 891; Documentos relativos al apreso de 2 goletas holandesas "La Fortuna" y "La Chipirola" al mando de Caps. Guillermo Cunche y Capiche Enrique, Caracas, July 4, 1765, AGNV, Comp Gui, XIV, fols. 1–63; Declaracion de Juan Antonio Rodriguez de Sosa Juron, Caracas, Oct. 12, 1750, AGNV, Comisos, XXIV, fols. 328–334. "Violently extracted": Testimonio de Autos sobre extraccion violentta echa por negro olandes nombrado Yayi y Gente de su goletta . . . , Valle de Choroní, July 4, 1760, AGI, Caracas, 892.

20. Smallwood, "African Guardians," *WMQ,* 3d Ser., LXIV (2007), 683–711; Christopher, *Slave Ship Sailors,* 87.

21. "A faithful friend": Equiano, *Interesting Narrative,* 61–62; see also 87.

status divisions might soften before the demands of maritime work. Three white Dutchmen, three enslaved Afro-Dutchmen, one Venezuelan ex-slave, and a French captain comprised the *Esperanza*'s crew. Venezuelan freedman Juan Livorro had fled to Curaçao for unspecified reasons with a fellow runaway aboard a Dutch ship three years before the *Esperanza*'s capture. Confiscation of the ship and its contraband cargo assured that Spanish officials would return Livorro to his master. Livorro testified that aboard the schooner "no one knew him as a slave." Two of his fellow sailors stated that their manumission was pending, but their masters let them serve as freemen aboard the *Esperanza*. There was a hazy understanding on the decks of the ship as to who was enslaved and who was free.[22]

Such ambiguity was not unique to the *Esperanza*. In a separate case in 1737, a free black Curaçaoan mariner told royal officials that he was ignorant of the number of slaves working aboard his vessel. "We don't treat them as such, but rather as sailors," he explained. "They come aboard with a license from their masters and for this reason we write nothing more about them in our rolls than their names." The practice of temporary manumission further complicates this testimony. Especially among Curaçaoans, documented cases exist where slaveholders drew up legal papers to make their slaves free while at sea trading. These "pro forma manumissions" gave masters a better chance of keeping their enslaved mariners should Spanish officials capture them. Prize court judges might deport free people back to their place of origin, but they rarely returned captured slaves, instead classifying them as contraband property. Temporary manumission also allowed slave owners to skirt increasingly strict eighteenth-century Dutch regulations that sought to limit the number of enslaved sailors serving on Dutch ships. Regardless of these legal gymnastics, a deeper truth about labor emerged in the statements of smugglers who shared a ship's confines with Afro-Caribbean seafarers. No one at sea could deny that these men—whether slave or free—were sailors and integral parts of the vessels they served. For the duration of a voyage, their toil, side by side with white crewmen, minimized rigid racial boundaries in the eighteenth-century Caribbean.[23]

22. Declaraciones de los quatro esclavos, Caracas, Mar. 31, 1775, AGNV, Comp Gui, XXVIII, fols. 114–116.

23. "But rather as sailors": Declaracion de Francisco Agustin, La Guaira, Jan. 22, 1737, AGI, Indif, 1829. One 1791 document complained that Dutch slaveholders, "at the time when their slaves leave for illicit trading, give them freedom papers." It was up to coast guard officials "to discover who is really free. Those that are not will never gain their freedom and will be sold among Spaniards to work in agriculture or the mines never to return to their home islands" (Ynstrucciones para los Guarda costas de Caracas, Caracas, July 28, 1791, AGI,

Despite the more egalitarian nature of race relations in contraband maritime labor, the seizure of a ship in Spanish waters could quickly separate freemen from slaves and blacks from whites. Capture threw Afro-Caribbean sailors' legal status into chaos. Proving freedom or a master's consent to sail was exceedingly complicated from a Venezuelan jail cell. Likewise, Spanish officials had difficulty determining whether a foreign mariner of African descent was free, enslaved, party to smuggling missions, property of the ship, or even part of its cargo. In some cases, prize court judges returned runaways to their masters, whereas in other instances they forced the fugitives to serve as cheap labor for the state. Conflicts over jurisdiction and prize money between Venezuela's provincial government and the Caracas Company only added to this uncertainty.

Although no printed regulations existed for Spanish judges concerning what to do with enslaved sailors, circumstances usually guided magistrates' actions. If the owner was not involved in smuggling and could be found, government functionaries usually returned the slave. If a master was complicit in the trafficking of contraband merchandise, possession of the enslaved usually reverted to Spanish authorities. The Caracas Company might force enslaved contrabandists into manual labor on coastal fortifications or sell them at auction, with proceeds of the sale benefiting the Company. Spanish officials were not alone in this practice; Dutch magistrates in Curaçao often auctioned off as slaves the men of color in Spanish crews they happened to capture, regardless of these captives' legal status in Spanish dominions.[24]

As in many arenas of the Atlantic world, free blacks found their legal standing the least stable. This was a truism throughout the colonial period, but particularly in the latter half of the eighteenth century, when laws began to limit manumissions. Equiano, who had passed many times between being free and enslaved, went so far as to state that free blacks "live in constant alarm for their liberty; which is but nominal, for they are universally insulted and plundered, without the possibility of redress; for such is the equity of the West Indian

Caracas, 784). See also Noticia de las embarcaciones que la Real Compañia Guipuzcoana de Caracas mantenia en aquella Provincia para el resguardo de la Costa, Madrid, May 9, 1783, AGI, Caracas, 784. "Pro forma manumissions": Rupert, "Marronage, Manumission, and Maritime Trade," *Slavery and Abolition,* XXX (2009), 372–374. See also Rupert, *Creolization and Contraband,* 156–160.

24. Ynforme de la Contaduría ejecutado en vista de una Carta y testimonio de autos obrados por el Gobernador de Cumaná con motibo del arribo a la costa del Rio Caribes, Cumaná, Jan. 16, 1755, AGI, Ctdra, 1662. For a Dutch example, see Expediente sobre los insultos de los Olandeses e Yngleses de Curazao años 1753 a 1756, Madrid, May 3, 1756, AGI, SD, 792.

laws, that no free Negro's evidence will be admitted in their courts of justice."[25] Equiano's experiences agree with the historiography regarding freemen's woes within slave societies. Spanish courts, however, unlike those of many other empires, often allowed enslaved men of color to testify.[26]

In contrast to their circumstantial deliberations over the enslaved, Venezuelan judges followed no distinct precedent in sentencing free blacks convicted of illicit trading. The arbitrariness of such decisions is evident in the case of Juan Tomás, a freeman of color from Curaçao. In 1755, a Caracas Company patrol ship captured the boat Juan Tomás was working on in the midst of a trading voyage to the western coast of Venezuela. Several days before his arrest, anticontraband forces had seized an unrelated Dutch trading canoe manned by an enslaved mariner named Nicolás. Officials at the prize court in Puerto Cabello tried the cases of Juan Tomás and Nicolás together. Though magistrates of the prize court observed the distinction between the two sailors, Juan Tomás probably suffered from the fact that he was tried at the same time as Nicolás. The cultural assumptions associated with their shared skin color perhaps trumped their disparate legal designations. The judge confirmed Nicolás's slavery and gave him to the Compañía Guipuzcoana as a slave; Juan Tomás faired little better as the judge remanded him to the Castillo de Puerto Cabello to work as a personal servant for company officials.[27]

Other cases demonstrate a similar tendency on the part of Spanish colo-

25. "Live in constant alarm for their liberty": Equiano, *Interesting Narrative,* 107. For the legal standing of free blacks and manumission laws, see David W. Cohen and Jack P. Greene, "Introduction," in Cohen and Greene, eds., *Neither Slave nor Free: The Freedmen of African Descent in the Slave Societies of the New World* (Baltimore, 1972), 17; David Barry Gaspar and Darlene Clark Hine, "Introduction," in Gaspar and Hine, eds., *Beyond Bondage: Free Women of Color in the Americas* (Urbana, Ill., 2004), xi; Sweet, *Domingos Álvares,* 229; Landers, *Atlantic Creoles,* 138–174.

26. For several examples of Spanish American people of color's use of the courts, see Herman L. Bennett, *Africans in Colonial Mexico: Absolutism, Christianity, and Afro-Creole Consciousness, 1570–1640* (Bloomington, Ind., 2003), 2–3; María Elena Díaz, *The Virgin, the King, and the Royal Slaves of El Cobre: Negotiating Freedom in Colonial Cuba, 1670–1780* (Stanford, Calif., 2000), 15–17; Landers, *Atlantic Creoles,* 7; Rupert, "Marronage, Manumission, and Maritime Trade," *Slavery and Abolition,* XXX (2009), 365. For people of color before British courts, see Roger N. Buckley, "Admission of Slave Testimony at British Military Courts in the West Indies, 1800–1809," in David Barry Gaspar and David Patrick Geggus, eds., *A Turbulent Time: The French Revolution and the Greater Caribbean* (Bloomington, Ind., 1997), 227; Elsa V. Goveia, *The West Indian Slave Laws of the 18th Century,* Chapters in Caribbean History, II ([Barbados], 1970), 34; Jarvis, *In the Eye of All Trade,* 176.

27. Auto del Gobernador y Capitan General Ricardos, Puerto Cabello, Jan. 21, 1755, AGNV, Comp Gui, IV, fol. 167.

nial officials to try captured foreign seamen of color together regardless of their legal status. In 1738, a storm shipwrecked Sebastián Atorneo, a free black mariner, and Manuel, an enslaved fellow crewman, as they piloted a rowboat in a desperate attempt to save a sailor who had fallen overboard. Spanish officials doubted Atorneo's repeated claim "that he is free." After deducing that the two sailors were part of a Curaçaoan contraband expedition, the governor of Venezuela sold the slave Manuel to Spanish America's licensed slave provider, the British Real Asiento. The documentation does not reveal Atorneo's punishment, but a notation where the case cuts off says that Manuel's penalty would likely apply to him also.[28]

In contrast to these cases, in which freemen found themselves treated like slaves, Spanish prize commission judges sometimes doled out the same sentence to men of color as their white counterparts, regardless of their citizenship status or race. The entire multiracial crew of the *Esperanza,* referred to earlier, received the sentence of four years' hard labor on Puerto Cabello's fortifications.[29]

In the majority of cases, nevertheless, justice was anything but colorblind. Men of color found themselves rushed through trial and without appropriate legal resources. Spanish officials allowed people of African descent to make statements in court but sometimes condemned and sentenced hastily and without proper evidence. Afro-Caribbean sailors gave shorter testimonies than their white shipmates. White lawyers, such as Santiago Francine, discredited the defendants' statements based on their race. In the end, contrabandists of color usually received longer and harsher sentences than their white counterparts. Although crossing the political and legal lines between empires aboard smuggling ships offered opportunities for work, wages, dignity, and freedom, the authority of Spanish coast guards and judges negated many of these hard-won gains.

## VENEZUELAN MIDDLEMEN OF COLOR ON THE COAST

Men of color not only brought illicit cargoes from sea to shore but also participated in the transfer of goods on land from seller to buyer. Colonial documents regarding the prosecution of domestic contrabandists reveal a significant num-

28. Testimonio de Sebastián Atorneo, Coro, Aug. 22, 1738, AGNV, Diversos, XXII, fols. 52–53; Auto de Gobernador y Capitán General, Don Gabriel de Zuloaga, Caracas, May 25, 1739, AGNV, Diversos, XXII, fol. 56.

29. Autos del apreso en el 19 de Julio de 1744 de la goleta holandesa "La Esperanza," Caracas, Apr. 6, 1775, AGNV, Comp Gui, XXVIII, fols. 36–144.

ber of Afro-Venezuelan slaves and free people complicit in commerce with foreigners. Many Afro-Venezuelans transported producers' harvests to port to exchange for foreign goods. Others functioned as security details for hacendados looking to protect their products from the vagaries of contraband trade. Like non-Spanish Afro-Caribbean sailors plying the wares of foreign merchants off the coast, Venezuelan people of color sometimes participated in riverine and coastal illicit trade to gain more independent labor arrangements. However, their involvement in covert commerce usually had more to do with their masters' wishes than their own volition. Regardless of their motivations, they played a critical role in the smooth performance of complex coalitions of Spanish American smugglers and producers involved in interimperial trade.

Venezuelan slaves and freemen frequently toiled as porters, ferrying planters' exports to the homes of Venezuelan smugglers or down to the docks for direct exchange with foreigners. As the governor of Cumaná, José Diguja y Villagómez, lamented in 1761, Dutch contrabandists could usually count on "Spaniards or inhabitants of these provinces, including blacks, mulattoes, and mestizos (many of these three groups being runaways)" as partners. Producers of cacao usually traded with outsiders through a broker; when a grower came to an agreement on price with the broker, he sent his crop via one of his slaves. Fear of being caught trading outside of the official Spanish cacao market and contempt for this menial labor compelled cultivators to send their slaves alone with their cargos.[30]

The use of slaves for product transportation implies not only the trust that Venezuelan planters and smugglers bestowed on their slaves not to run away or steal but also a belief that they were unlikely to inform on their masters' illegal activities. In 1734, Spanish officials broke up an extensive coastal smuggling rendezvous comprising more than thirty cargos of cacao from many haciendas around Higuerote, a town east of Caracas. Among the testimonies of suspected smugglers and producers involved in illicit cacao trading were two slaves named Joseph and Vincente. The pair belonged to Juan Sánchez de Yelamos, a Caracas merchant and planter who had brought together the cacao harvests of many hacendados for sale to French contrabandists. Sánchez de Yelamos loaned out Joseph and Vincente, along with a mule driver and several

30. Comercio Ilícito en la Gobernación de Cumaná, Cumaná, Dec. 22, 1761, in Antonio Arellano Moreno, ed., *Documentos para la historia económica en la Epoca colonial: Viajes e informes* (Caracas, 1970), 320. For an argument about the success of the Compañia Guipuzcoana in hampering hacendados' ability to sell cacao on the contraband market, see Eugenio Piñero, "The Cacao Economy of the Eighteenth-Century Province of Caracas and the Spanish Cacao Market," *HAHR*, LXVIII (1988), 91–92.

mules, to planter Sebastián de la Oliva so that they might collect Oliva's cacao and bring it to the French ship. Sánchez de Yelamos's slaves testified that they helped Oliva bring his crop to port, forcing the cultivator to confess his guilt in the case, but they remained silent about their master. Oliva was sentenced to four years' exile from the coast and assessed a seven-hundred-peso fine.[31]

Transporting contraband products was both similar to and distinct from other slave duties. Like any other aspect of bondage, a slave's compliance with the illegal assignments presented to them was obligatory. But hauling illicit items allowed slaves to travel sizable distances with minimal supervision. In this regard, smuggling was more akin to special tasks of the enslaved, such as going to market, selling labor for a wage, or toiling as an artisan than to working in the fields. Independent production, artisan labor, and market interaction provided a range of benefits for enslaved people, including greater control over labor processes and organization, more access to material goods and cash, a healthier standard of living, and even increased opportunities to purchase their freedom. Venezuelan slaves almost assuredly reaped some of these gains through their participation in contraband trade.[32]

Despite the benefits enslaved people might incur transporting illicit goods, this commerce necessitated an agile mind and a stout heart to overcome its logistical challenges. Venezuelan slaves navigated complicated smuggling rings. Satisfying the needs of producers, merchants, and foreigners re-

31. Auto de Don Juan Augustin Henrique de Almeida, Caracas, Sept. 6, 1734, AGNV, Comisos, XVI, fol. 97; Declaración de Sebastian de la Oliba, Caracas, Sept. 18, 1734, AGNV, Comisos, XVI, fols. 108–111; Sentencia de los reos por Don Martin de Lardizabal, Gobernador y Capitan General, Caracas, June 2, 1736, AGNV, Comisos, XVI, fols. 304–307. After Oliva later fled from jail, the governor discussed condemning him to death if authorities could recapture him. The slaves' unwillingness to implicate Yelamos, along with his connections to Caracas's merchant elite, probably accounted for his lighter punishment.

32. Ira Berlin and Philip D. Morgan, "Introduction: Labor and the Shaping of Slave Life in the Americas," in Berlin and Morgan, eds., *Culture and Cultivation: Labor and the Shaping of Slave Life in the Americas* (Charlottesville, Va., 1993), 20–41; Jorge Cañizares-Esguerra, Matt D. Childs, and James Sidbury, "Introduction," in Cañizares-Esguerra, Childs, and Sidbury, eds., *Black Urban Atlantic,* 4; David Wheat, "*Nharas* and *Morenas Horras:* A Luso-African Model for the Social History of the Spanish Caribbean, c. 1570–1640," *Journal of Early Modern History,* XIV (2010), 121. For regional studies of the effects of wage labor and independent production on slave autonomy, see Robert Olwell, *Masters, Slaves, and Subjects: The Culture of Power in the South Carolina Low Country, 1740–1790* (Ithaca, N.Y., 1998), 141–180; John Campbell, "As 'a Kind of Freeman'? Slaves' Market-Related Activities in the South Carolina up Country, 1800–1860," in Berlin and Morgan, eds., *Culture and Cultivation,* 243–274; Mark W. Hauser, *An Archaeology of Black Markets: Local Ceramics and Economies in Eighteenth-Century Jamaica* (Gainesville, Fla., 2008), 2–12, 64–66.

quired multiple exchanges. Enslaved workers were their masters' middlemen and representatives on these missions. A lone slave might take the gathered cacao of many hacendados downriver to the coast to give it to a broker. In turn, this broker would send the slave back with a variety of goods to pay each of these planters. Slaves could also fill the role of broker themselves. One Dutch trader familiar with the Venezuelan coast revealed in 1737, "The majority of the people who come aboard to trade have been mulatos, blacks, or Indians. One does not ask them for their names and in this way, they remain anonymous." Cloaked arrangements like these were standard practice in contraband trade.[33]

Slaves not only executed transactions but also protected their owners and goods. In the uncertain world of contraband trade, masters employed the enslaved as muscle to avoid being robbed or to perpetrate theft themselves. Slaves became ad hoc forces if deals with foreigners turned violent. Conversely, other men of color bore arms to suppress as well as to protect illicit trade. Both free and enslaved Afro-Venezuelans filled the ranks of pardo militias that enforced Spanish trade restrictions and captured contrabandists. Though the work of colored militias in fortifying Spain's late-eighteenth-century imperial defenses has been documented, their participation in anticontraband patrols remains more obscure. The captain of one pardo militia detachment, Nicolás Gutiérrez, was instrumental in prosecuting a smuggling ring consisting of Venezuelan merchants, planters, slaves, and mule drivers as well as Dutch smugglers. Gutiérrez, as a militia captain roaming the valley of Valencia, became familiar with the trading patterns of two of the principle Venezuelans engaged in commerce with the Dutch; his testimony helped prove the suspects' guilt in court.[34]

Blacks necessarily had intimate contact with officials who took part in illicit trade, sometimes even living with them or profiting from their misdeeds. The transgressions of Diego de Matos Montañez confirm the level to which both free and enslaved Africans became involved in the misdeeds of compro-

33. "Glossary," in Klooster, *Illicit Riches;* Sumaria contra un negro llamada Andrés, esclavo de Pascual Nuñez de Aguilar, por llevar varias fanegas de cacao de su amo a boca del Rio de Tuy a comerciar con los holandeses. Caracas, Jan. 3, 1752, AGNV, Comisos, XXV, fols. 244–248. "They remain anonymous": Declaracion de Francisco Agustin, La Guaira, Jan. 22, 1737, AGI, Indif, 1829.

34. Allan J. Kuethe, "The Status of the Free Pardo in the Disciplined Militia of New Granada," *Journal of Negro History,* LVI (1971), 105–109; Peter Blanchard, *Under the Flags of Freedom: Slave Soldiers and the Wars of Independence in Spanish South America* (Pittsburgh, 2008), 12–14; Ben Vinson III, *Bearing Arms for His Majesty: The Free-Colored Militia in Colonial Mexico* (Stanford, Calif., 2001), 1–84. For the Gutiérrez case specifically, see Declaración de Captain Nicolás Gutiérrez, Valle de San Esteban, Nueva Valencia, Sept. 14, 1734, AGNV, Comisos, XIV, fols. 28–30.

mised authorities. He held the office of prize court judge in 1718 when a group of his men, including six free pardos and one free black, attacked a Dutch ship trading for cacao off the coast of Puerto Cabello. In the process, they killed two unresisting officers and a cabin boy aboard the foreign vessel. Rather than take the ship's goods through the proper legal channels of appraisal and resale, Matos Montañez's soldiers lined their pockets with the vessel's cargo of arms, gold work, money, and clothing. These men of color claimed that the killings had occurred in their struggle to subdue the ship's crew, but the testimonies of officials and Matos Montañez's neighbors painted a different picture. One alcalde described how "Don Diego lives with his sons, soldiers, and slaves in a house that is a refuge for delinquents indifferent to any concept of justice." Investigators found a sum totaling more than four thousand pesos in the house of one of Matos Montañez's underlings three years later, suggesting that the robbery of the Dutch ship was not an isolated incident. Matos Montañez also regularly used nonwhites in under-the-table deals. In 1723, he sent a lone mulatto slave to shepherd nine mules burdened with cacao, liquor, and clothes to trade with the Dutch near the inland town of Nirgua, west of Puerto Cabello. When finally prosecuted, Diego de Matos Montañez attempted to blame the transaction on his slaves, but the questions of an examining alcalde forced him to admit that "a master was responsible for his slave's actions."[35]

Private citizens, like authorities, employed their slaves to perform acts of violence and robbery to protect their contraband trade. Soldiers found the cacao of Juan Tirado and Simón Marcano in the central coast town of Ocumare just as contrabandists were about to load it onto a Dutch smuggling vessel in 1727. Authorities deciphered that the cacao belonged to Tirado and

35. Matos Montañez accumulated an infamous record for smuggling. For the incidents described here, see Cargos de autos por Pedro Joseph de Olavarriaga, Caracas, Apr. 25, 1721, AGNV, Comisos, V, fols. 177–185; Testimonio de Juan Francisco Carrasquer, vecino de Puerto Cabello, Nueva Valencia, Oct. 5, 1723, AGNV, Comisos, V, fol. 219; Testimonio de Benito de la Calle, Caracas, Apr. 25, 1721, AGNV, Comisos, V, fols. 189–201. For other incidents, see, for example, Auto de Salvador Pérez, Teniente de Puerto Cabello, Nueva Valencia, Aug. 22, 1721, AGNV, Comisos, V, fol. 319. Though he acted violently toward some factions of Curaçaoan merchants, he sheltered others; see Testimonio de Domingo Viera, Valle de Moron, May 24, 1718, AGNV, Comisos, V, fols. 171–173. "Refuge for delinquents": Auto de Francisco Andres de Peñalosa, Alcalde Ordinario, June 26, 1718, Nueva Valencia del Rey, AGNV, Comisos, III, fols. 221–222. "A master was responsible for his slave's actions": Confesion de Don Diego de Matos Montañez, Caracas, June 25, 1720, AGNV, Comisos, V, fols. 183–187. Matos allowed Curaçaoan Jew "Coche Perreira" to trade openly and illegally with Venezuelan producers for eight months in Puerto Cabello around 1720. See Wim Klooster, "The Jews in Suriname and Curaçao," in Paolo Bernardini and Norman Fiering, eds., *The Jews and the Expansion of Europe to the West, 1450 to 1800* (New York, 2001), 366.

Marcano only after the suspects and several of their accomplices attacked three guards protecting the impounded cacao on the first night after the seizure. The assailants employed as muscle by Tirado and Marcano — whites, free people of color, and slaves — stabbed one of the guards to death and made off with their illicit goods after the rest of the guards retreated. (Though authorities took this brazen attack on anticontraband forces seriously and promised grave punishments for the culprits, they arrested no one from the smuggling party.)[36]

Given the obvious and immediate connections between white Venezuelan contrabandists and their slaves and workers, Spanish authorities prosecuting smugglers regularly confiscated their slaves along with other assets. An enslaved worker who had contributed to a smuggler's means of production could became, in punitive legal terms, just another piece of property. Spanish policymakers had long been aware of the centrality of Afro-Venezuelan slaves in illicit commerce. In 1678, Carlos II reminded his governor in Venezuela that many of those transporting cacao to foreigners were of African descent and that he should "make an example out of both master and slave if they are found guilty." A century later, in 1772, contraband had reached such proportions that the governor issued a proclamation guaranteeing freedom and monetary compensation for any bondsmen that offered information leading to the arrest of their master for this "abominable vice." A slave named Manuel Cabrera tested this guarantee thirty-one years later, when he went aboard a coast guard vessel and provided information leading to the capture of a ship unloading contraband on Margarita Island. Although Cabrera's master fled the scene, Cabrera received his freedom for denouncing him and, presumably, the satisfaction of hearing his master sentenced in absentia to six years of hard labor at the fortifications of San Juan de Ulúa in Veracruz. In spite of the deep racial anxieties characteristic of a society with a substantial slave population, like Venezuela, the governor's bold measure signaled that officials were keenly aware of the centrality of Afro-Venezuelans in the extralegal activities of white merchants and planters.[37]

36. Auto de Diego Portales Meneses, Gobernador y Captain General de Venezuela, Caracas, Mar. 11, 1727, AGNV, Diversos, XII, fols. 161–162.

37. "Make an example out of both master and slave": "No. 49 — Sobre negros esclavos complicados en comercio ilícito–27 noviembre 1687," in Ermila Troconis de Veracoechea, ed., *Documentos para el estudio de los esclavos negros en Venezuela: Selección y estudio preliminar* (Caracas, 1969), 224. "Abominable vice": Auto de Don Joseph Carlos de Aguero, Gobernador y Capitan General, Puerto Cabello, Mar. 24, 1772, AGNV, Diversos, XLII, fols. 198–199. Cabrera's freedom and his former master's sentence are documented in Cedula al Yntendente de Caracas, San Yldefonso, Sept. 4, 1803, AGI, Caracas, 836.

Smuggling cut both ways in the life courses of the enslaved; although both Venezuelan and non-Spanish owners sent their slaves to labor in nonlicensed trade, providing these men with opportunities for greater working autonomy, the contraband trade in Venezuela also transported thousands of Africans into bondage. The illegal slave trade along the Venezuelan littoral was distinctive among contraband activities. Contraband slavers in the region usually sold mundane goods in addition to their human cargoes. Enslaved Africans, however, were the only wares aboard a ship that might cease to be cargo. Unlike holds full of cloth, liquor, or foodstuffs, African captives confined within smuggling vessels were capable of betraying their carriers. They might rebel aboard ship. If captured by Spanish coastal patrols, slaves who spoke a European language often testified in court to being contraband. Even slaves whom smugglers successfully managed to traffic onto Venezuelan haciendas sometimes revealed their illegal entry to Spanish authorities and thus invalidated a master's claim to them. Despite their high value among contraband goods, when detected by anticontraband forces, slaves left an indelible record of a smuggler's activities.

Underground slave trafficking in Venezuela was influenced by the dynamics of Venezuelan slavery and the legal slave trade to the colony. By one estimate, more than 101,000 captives arrived on Venezuelan shores over the course of the colonial period. Notwithstanding these importations, slave populations never exceeded 10 percent of the total population in Venezuela. Though not a "slave society" like many of the Caribbean islands it traded with, the province still had a sizable number of forced laborers and a majority mixed-race *(casta)* population. In addition to their labor within the contraband trade, Venezuelan slaves also worked as domestic servants and artisans in Caracas, Puerto Cabello, and several other, smaller towns and as field hands on the cacao, tobacco, and indigo plantations that dotted the coast. The production of cacao required manual labor to cultivate and pick cacao pods but little specialized equipment or skill. By the late seventeenth century, cacao cultivation came to dominate slave labor in the region. Planters continually desired more slaves than they could reasonably procure. Indeed, unmet demand for enslaved Africans was common throughout the circum-Caribbean. As a result, illicit human trafficking often stimulated other types of black market trade.[38]

38. Alex Borucki's estimates include both legal and illegal shipping of slaves between 1526 and 1811. He points out that the *Trans-Atlantic Slave Trade Database* only lists 11,500 slaves

Much of the difficulty planters faced with securing sufficient slave labor in Venezuela came from the inefficiency of the slave trade to the province. Since the end of the sixteenth century, slaves entering Spanish America had come from the Asiento de Negros. To overcome Spain's lack of African territorial possessions or trading forts from which to extract slaves, the asiento allowed private traders and companies to enter into contracts with the Spanish crown for exclusive rights to supply Spain's New World dominions with Africans. Though the king initially gave the asiento to private traders of both Spanish and foreign nationalities, by the beginning of the eighteenth century, English and French state companies replaced private traders in competing for this monopoly.

The asiento assured Spanish America some supply of enslaved laborers, but Spanish regulations and quotas made slave transportation, distribution, and sale cumbersome. Before entering Caracas, asiento captives originating from foreign Caribbean ports had to pass first to Cartagena or Portobelo and then be re-exported. Spanish laws meant to prevent the smuggling that often accompanied asiento ships set rigid terms for purchasing slaves that handicapped both buyer and seller. Until the late eighteenth century, payment for enslaved workers could occur only in specie. This proved burdensome to Venezuelan planters, who were frequently cacao rich but cash poor. Slaves came to these planters at costs much higher than the going rate throughout the non-Spanish Caribbean, owing to Spanish royal tariffs and transportation costs. For

---

entering Venezuela via direct importation from Africa. Therefore, transshipped slaves made up the overwhelming majority of imports into the province (Borucki, "Trans-Imperial History in the Making of the Slave Trade to Venezuela, 1526–1811," *Itinerario,* XXXVI [2012], 29). A partial census of Venezuela in 1787 counted 147,564 "libres de color" and 53,055 slaves. In 1810, another survey of the demographics of the coastal region of the province of Venezuela revealed that 40 percent of its inhabitants were free people (castas), 30 percent were whites, 20 percent were slaves, and 10 percent were indigenous people. The higher percentage of slaves on the coast (20 percent) was balanced out by other areas in the province where slave populations were much lower. For 1787, see Frederick P. Bowser, "Colonial Spanish America," in Cohen and Greene, eds., *Neither Slave nor Free,* 37. For 1810, see P. Michael McKinley, *Pre-Revolutionary Caracas: Politics, Economy, and Society, 1777–1811* (Cambridge, 1985), 9–11. See also Angelina Pollak-Eltz, *La esclavitud en Venezuela: Un estudio histórico-cultural* (Caracas, 2000), 8. For shortages of slave labor, see Robert J. Ferry, "Encomienda, African Slavery, and Agriculture in Seventeenth-Century Caracas," *HAHR,* XL (1981), 635; Pollak-Eltz, *La esclavitud en Venezuela,* 45; Acosta Saignes, *Vida de los esclavos negros,* 65, 129. For the situation on nearby islands, see, for example, Kenneth J. Banks, "Official Duplicity: The Illicit Slave Trade in Martinique, 1713–1763," in Peter A. Coclanis, ed., *The Atlantic Economy during the Seventeenth and Eighteenth Centuries: Organization, Operation, Practice, and Personnel* (Columbia, S.C., 2005), 231–233.

foreign asiento traders, legal profits nevertheless remained small as a result of Spanish strictures on where they could trade and a crown order mandating that their ships depart from Spanish American ports empty, save for cash payments. The crown also frequently abrogated asiento contracts with companies as a result of European wars.[39]

In addition to these restrictions on trade, companies holding the asiento compounded the problems of hacendados by failing to comply with their contractual obligations. Asiento companies rarely imported the full number of slaves they promised to the Spanish government. Even when companies honestly tried to meet specified numbers, the vagaries of procuring and transporting human beings from Africa complicated the trade. Slave acquisition in Africa and the Caribbean was not an exact science by any means. Political conditions in Africa, European naval wars, and local market conditions all affected the supply of Africans. Disease aboard insalubrious slave ships decimated the slave populations available for trade. Numerous customs declarations spoke of quarantining or refusing entry to Africans infected with smallpox.[40]

Most asiento companies did not even make such good faith efforts. The English factors in charge of the South Sea Company's asiento contract (1713–1739) had a much greater interest in opening up both legal and contraband trade with Spanish America than in providing human cargoes. Between 1730 and 1739, as much as 90 percent of illicit goods entering Spanish America might have come through the asiento. Spain gave the English asiento the privilege of taking one thousand tons of nonslave shipping each year. These so-called annual ships, along with goods smuggled aboard slaving vessels, became a backdoor method to flood Spanish markets with English goods and contributed to the destruction of the Portobelo trade fairs so pivotal to the Carrera de Indias trade fleet. British contraband trade forced Spain eventually to revoke the South Sea Company's contract and served as a key impetus for the War of Jenkins' Ear in 1739. Though the English asiento, like the many agreements before and after it, brought enslaved Africans to the Americas, foreign slaving

39. Pollak-Eltz, *La esclavitud en Venezuela,* 41–42.

40. For unfulfilled asiento quotas, see Colin Palmer, *Human Cargoes: The British Slave Trade to Spanish America, 1700–1739* (Urbana, Ill., 1981), 20. For disease, see "Resoluciones del Cabildo de Cumaná acerca de los negros enfermos de viruelas traídos en la nave de Nicolás de Sosa," Cumaná, Oct. 25, 1620, Academia Nacional de la Historia, 6-Der-5, Residencia Juan de Aro, fols. 300–301, 310–311, in Troconis de Veracoechea, ed., *Documentos para el estudio de los esclavos negros,* 173–174; Autorización a la Compañía de Caracas para introducir 2000 esclavos en esa provincia y en la de Maracaibo, El Rey, Madrid, Oct. 31, 1765, Archivo de Colombia, Reales Cedulas, 1744–1807, Arch. V, vol. XII, tomo VI, fols. 59–63, ibid., 263–264; Acosta Saignes, *Vida de los esclavos negros,* 38.

companies neglected their full contractual obligations in favor of more lucrative, illegal pursuits.[41]

These factors greatly constricted the availability of legal slaves in Venezuela throughout the colonial period and led to a number of Venezuelan governmental pleas for slaves as cacao production flourished in the eighteenth century. In 1707, the sergeant major of the island of Margarita urged the captain general of Trinidad to comply with the king's orders and allow the French asiento to bring more slaves to Margarita. Little changed in the subsequent decades; in 1773, the governor of Cumaná wrote, "One of the major impediments to the development of these provinces has been the lack of slaves to work the land and cultivate agricultural products." The Caracas Company even tried its hand as an intermediary between foreign slave depots and Venezuelan buyers between the 1750s and 1770s, but with little success.[42]

The same conditions of material scarcity and insufficient trade that made colonies like Venezuela central locales for foreign contrabandists trading in general goods also provided a ready market for smugglers who sought to supplant the asiento and break Spanish slave trade regulations. Since the famous voyages of Sir John Hawkins to Tierra Firme in the 1560s and 1570s, slave traders had come ashore in Venezuela to peddle their human cargoes. Accurate counts of illegally introduced slaves are impossible to come by, but as many as half of the slaves imported to Venezuela might have been contraband.[43]

41. Adrian Finucane, *The Temptations of Trade: Britain, Spain, and the Struggle for Empire* (Philadelphia, 2016), 44–52; Curtis Nettels, "England and the Spanish-American Trade, 1680–1715," *Journal of Modern History,* III (1931), 8, 31; Vera Lee Brown, "Contraband Trade: A Factor in the Decline of Spain's American Empire," *HAHR,* VIII (1928), 179; O'Malley, *Final Passages,* 142; George H. Nelson, "Contraband Trade under the Asiento, 1730–1739," *AHR,* LI (1945), 63–66; Palmer, *Human Cargoes,* 94, 136.

42. On additional slaves for Margarita, see Petición hecha al Capitán General de Trinidad, Don Phelipe de Artieda por el sargento mayor Don Cristobal de la Villa Herrera, Margarita, Nov. 16, 1707, AGNV, Diversos, II, fols. 103–113. "Lack of slaves to work the land": Miguel Acosta Saignes, *La trata de esclavos en Venezuela* (Caracas, 1961), 18. For the Caracas Company's attempts to traffic slaves, see Eduardo Arcila Farías, *Economía colonial de Venezuela* (Mexico City, 1946), 400–402; Borucki, "Trans-Imperial History," *Itinerario,* XXXVI (2012), 39.

43. This calculation of smuggled slaves is based on Angelina Pollak-Eltz's estimate of 50,000 slaves imported legally into Venezuela between the sixteenth and eighteenth centuries, with 6,596 imported in the sixteenth century, 10,147 in the seventeenth, and 34,099 in the eighteenth. The calculation puts the total number of slaves imported through legal and illegal means into Venezuela as high as 100,000. The 100,000-slave total is close to Borucki's number of 101,000 slaves. See Pollak-Eltz, *La esclavitud en Venezuela,* 39; Borucki, "Trans-

Venezuela's proximity to formidable slave trading centers further eased the introduction of unlicensed slaves into the colony. Slave depots in Jamaica, Barbados, Martinique, Saint-Domingue, and Curaçao were all nearby. The Netherlands' dominance in the slave trade from the mid-seventeenth century onward depended on control of the asiento by individual Dutch merchants (on and off from 1662–1701), eager Spanish markets, and less legal means. Curaçao became a free port in 1675, making it legal under Dutch law for Venezuelan ships to make the forty-mile journey to the island. When not in control of the asiento themselves, the Dutch functioned as middlemen, supplying foreign contract-holders with slaves to take to Spanish America. Between 1662 and 1714, 90 percent of slaves disembarking in Curaçao went to Spanish America. From 1662 until 1700, 25 percent of all captives passing from the island to Spanish America arrived illegally in Venezuela. At the peak of Dutch imports, during the War of the Spanish Succession, that number reached 50 percent, even though Spain and Holland were technically belligerents. Additionally, a settlement of Dutch Jews in Tucacas, a formerly uninhabited island off the coast of western Venezuela, played an active role in illegal slave trafficking until Venezuelan authorities made an effort to eradicate the colony in the mid-eighteenth century. French merchants joined in this illicit trade at midcentury, shipping slaves from Saint-Domingue, Martinique, and Guadaloupe in exchange for Venezuelan mules to power sugar mills. Thus, Venezuelan planters used a mix of legal imports from asiento providers and the Caracas Company and a richer stream of illegal imports from foreign colonial merchants to purchase slaves as never before in the eighteenth century.[44]

Colonial authorities and the king of Spain noted the prevalence of the illegal slave trade between Venezuela and these foreign ports and enacted legis-

---

Imperial History," *Itinerario,* XXXVI (2012), 29. See also O'Malley, *Final Passages,* 115; Harry Kelsey, *Sir John Hawkins: Queen Elizabeth's Slave Trader* (New Haven, Conn., 2003), 81.

44. For Dutch dominance of the slave trade, see H. Hoetink, "Surinam and Curaçao," in Cohen and Greene, eds., *Neither Slave nor Free,* 65; Cornelius Ch. Goslinga, *The Dutch in the Caribbean and on the Wild Coast, 1580–1680* (Gainesville, Fla., 1971), 310, 338; Postma, *Dutch in the Atlantic Slave Trade,* 40–51; Klooster, *Illicit Riches,* 117–118. The Treaty of Utrecht, which ended the War of the Spanish Succession and provided the English South Sea Company with the asiento, finally unseated Dutch dominance over the Venezuelan slave market. Between 1715 and 1783, Venezuelan merchants purchased 35,617 slaves (about 516 per year). This was a 15 percent increase from the period from 1641 to 1714. See Borucki, "Trans-Imperial History," *Itinerario,* XXXVI (2012), 36–40. On Jews in Tucacas, see Celestino Andrés Araúz Monfante, *El contrabando holandés en el Caribe durante la primera mitad del siglo XVIII,* I (Caracas, 1984), 66; Borucki, "Trans-Imperial History," *Itinerario,* XXXVI (2012), 35.

lation to curb it. In 1705, Philip V, at the behest of the French Royal Guinea Company, issued a royal cédula lamenting "the ease with which the English and Dutch fraudulently introduce their slaves from the islands of Jamaica and Curaçao into Caracas as well as all the coasts of Venezuela." As a deterrent to potential buyers, the king ordered a three-hundred-peso fine and confiscation for each contraband slave a master owned. Recognizing how deeply embedded Venezuelans were in the contraband slave trade, Philip V also offered a means to legalize illicitly introduced slaves. For one hundred pesos, an owner could buy an indulto to legalize a slave. This pardon extended legalization at no additional cost to any children of that slave. Finally, the king encouraged his subjects to abide by the laws of trade by offering monetary compensation for freemen and freedom for enslaved people who denounced owners for keeping illegally trafficked slaves. The severity of punishments and the date of the 1705 royal order (almost seventy years before the governor of Venezuela would promise freedom for slaves who informed on their masters for general contraband trading) revealed the seriousness of the illicit slave trade in the king's eyes. The embarrassment and financial obligation associated with his own subjects' breaking binding contracts he had signed with foreign companies no doubt compelled Philip V to enact the order.[45]

The indulto system of slave legalization was a pragmatic means to cope with the influx of contraband slaves into Venezuela. By offering a way to purchase amnesty, the royal treasury actually recouped money from slave owners' contraband purchases, something it rarely accomplished through punitive measures. Furthermore, the self-confession of slave masters required none of the costly naval patrols, militias, or court cases commonly used to reduce illicit trading. The legislation also became a useful tool for slaves, who could use the legal process to inform on their masters. Records of indultos show that the procedure was used frequently in Venezuela. Between 1716 and 1719, ninety-one slaves were legalized in Caracas. Only Panama and Portobelo had a higher number of indultos among Spanish possessions where the pardon existed. The willingness of slave owners to use this system perhaps speaks to a dearth of legal slaves for purchase rather than their reluctance to buy slaves through legal means.[46]

45. Real Cédula de la instancia hecha por la Compañía Real de Guinea por la introducción fraudulenta de negros de Jamaica y Curazao a Venezuela y Portobelo, Madrid, Oct. 25, 1705, in Troconis de Veracoechea, *Documentos para el estudio de los esclavos,* 240–242.

46. Acosta Saignes, *Vida de los esclavos negros,* 68. For comparative indulto rates, see Palmer, *Human Cargoes,* 91–93.

Beyond legislation and softer measures designed to contain the contraband slave trade, Spanish officials employed the same *guarda costa* patrols and Compañía Guipuzcoana ships that chased regular contrabandists to hunt slave smugglers. In the 1730s, the right of the Company to stop, search, and impound smuggling vessels came into conflict with the desire of English asiento ships not to be disturbed in their trade. As noted earlier, English slave merchants participated in substantial amounts of smuggling under the banner of the asiento. It was little wonder, then, that they complained about Company officials' searching their holds. Not wanting to alienate either side, the king issued two orders in July and October 1731, specifying that Company vessels had the right to stop any ship but could not search asiento vessels. This contradictory policy diluted the authority of Company patrols to combat English smuggling.[47]

Leaving aside asiento merchants, the slave smugglers who sought to evade Spanish coastal patrols differed little in their methods from other contrabandists on the Venezuelan coast. Unlike the asiento companies' large ships, independent slave smugglers sailed brigs, small sloops, and coastal schooners and usually carried no more than twenty slaves. Contrabandists involved in the slave trade rarely sailed solely with human cargo. To appeal to the widest possible market, a trader might combine slaves with whatever European goods would fetch a decent price along the coast.[48]

A textbook case of this sort of multipurpose smuggling is the story of the *Catalina*. The Spanish coast guard stopped this small craft in 1770. The ship's crew, composed mostly of Venezuelans, had purchased ten creolized slaves in

47. Acosta Saignes, *La trata de esclavos*, 14.

48. The size of Venezuela's illicit slaving voyages appear consistent with those elsewhere in the Caribbean. O'Malley, in his exhaustive study of the intercolonial slave trade, found that most voyages contained between two and twenty captives per voyage (O'Malley, *Final Passages*, 49). This is far fewer than in the transatlantic slave trade. Ernesto E. Bassi Arévalo reveals a similar pattern of small-scale slave trading as part of larger smuggling voyages for late-eighteenth-century Colombia. He finds that between 1784 and 1817, 60 percent of ships carrying captive Africans between the much larger and more commercially important ports of Kingston and Cartagena held ten or fewer slaves (Bassi Arévalo, "Between Imperial Projects and National Dreams: Communication Networks, Geopolitical Imagination, and the Role of New Granada in the Configuration of a Greater Caribbean Space, 1780s–1810s" [Ph.D. diss., University of California, Irvine, 2012], 97). To use one non-Spanish empire as an example, the Dutch had virtually no ships made specifically for slave trading. Slaves were put in the middle decks, rather than the hold, of multipurpose cargo vessels. After the Dutch announced free trade in slaves from Curaçao in 1730, ships tended to be smaller and more numerous (Postma, *Dutch in the Atlantic Slave Trade*, 144).

Curaçao from their Dutch masters with the intent to sell them in La Guaira. The slaves, a mix of men, women, and children, were only part of the ship's wares. The *Catalina* also brought European cloth to sell covertly. Authorities in port saw slaves as just another part of the captured cargo, auctioning off the people of color side by side with the impounded fabrics and the vessel. However, contrary to the rest of the goods in the ship's hold, the slaves could testify and linked the Venezuelan crew of the ship to Dutch traders in Curaçao. Given the incriminating details these slaves knew of the smugglers' habits, it is hardly surprising that the contrabandists jumped ship before the Spanish could come alongside the *Catalina*.[49]

Contraband slaving differed from the legal transatlantic slave trade in its routes and priorities. Illicit traders engaged in trafficking slaves almost never went directly from Africa to the Venezuelan coast. Most slavers brought their ships first to Caribbean way stations like Jamaica, Curaçao, or Martinique before proceeding to Spanish America. The dangerous and disease-ridden Middle Passage necessitated time to refresh captives, crew, and ship in a friendly port before proceeding covertly along the coasts of Tierra Firme. Interimperial slaving was often part of larger, multipurpose commercial ventures. Smugglers also might bring excess consumer goods to barter and sell off a portion of their slaves in non-Spanish Caribbean ports before entering Spanish territory. In 1730, Captain Fernando Francisco of Curaçao ferried liquor and small arms to the coast, as well as African slaves. The six men and one woman who comprised Francisco's enslaved human cargo all belonged to Curaçaoan residents. Aside from the female slave, whom the traders clearly brought to sell in Venezuela, the planned destinations of the confiscated slaves and their legal status under Spanish law remained uncertain. Upon capture, Francisco noted that the slaves' owners intended an unspecified number to be sold, whereas others were to "be loaned out and earn wages for their masters who permit them to sail." Francisco, like many of his fellow contrabandists, was an opportunist and an improviser when it came to slave trading.[50]

Slave smugglers needed an extensive knowledge of market conditions in many corners of the Atlantic world and the flexibility to adapt to the unforeseen circumstances that human trafficking presented. The experience of John

49. Remate de bienes, Sept. 7, 1770, AGNV, Comp Gui, XXII, fols. 196–197; Declaraciones de cinco esclavos, Puerto Cabello, Aug. 13, 1770, AGNV, Comp Gui, XXII, fols. 184–187.

50. Testimonio de Fernando Francisco, Capitán de la balandra holandesa, Puerto Cabello, Sept. 6, 1730, AGI, SD, 781.

Maddock, an English slaving captain captured in 1764, sheds light on these challenges. A Caracas Company cruiser overtook Maddock's frigate near Tortuga, an island off the eastern Venezuelan coast. Company authorities accused Maddock of going toward Venezuela to trade his cargo of twenty slaves and European clothes from Barbados. Maddock claimed merely to be refreshing his supplies of freshwater before sailing the slaves to Maryland. Parceling out whether Maddock told the truth is difficult, based on available documentation. However, when pressed by interrogators, Maddock revealed an itinerary of startling complexity. He had left London a year earlier with wheat to drop off in Tenerife. He exchanged the wheat for wine. From Tenerife, he steered toward Senegal, where he off-loaded the wine and took on provisions. After several stops along the Gambia River trading European guns and liquor, Maddock had amassed one hundred enslaved Africans to bring to Barbados. He arrived in the Caribbean with seventy. Of these, he sold fifty in Barbados. According to Maddock, the remaining twenty slaves were destined for Maryland plantations. The inventory of his frigate's hold contained a laundry list of goods, including sugar, cotton, tobacco, añil, ginger, brazilwood, rice, naval timbers, copper, gunpowder, and hats. In addition to his human cargo, Maddox possessed wares to peddle for nearly any situation, demonstrating his ability to judge the value and trade a range of commodities in many different locales. Maddox's back-and-forth transactions also illustrated the complexity of Atlantic human trafficking and the ways it transitioned between legality and illegality.[51]

Spanish prize court judges rarely believed smugglers' rationales. Contrary to the court experience of black contrabandists, whose testimonies were often brief, forgettable affairs in the eyes of Spanish interrogators, the words of slaves being transported as cargo frequently carried more weight than those of their white captors. Enslaved individuals, unlike contrabandists, had no reason to lie about their voyages. Even so, a slave's ordeal aboard a confiscated ship usually ended much the way his or her life in bondage had begun: with evaluation, appraisal, and sale at public auction. Depending on who had caught the smuggler, proceeds from the sale of contraband slaves went to either the provincial treasury or the coffers of the Compañía Guipuzcoana. In a few cases, the slaves

51. Declaración de Juan Maddock, La Guaira, Mar. 24, 1764, AGNV, Comisos, XXVI, fols. 313–314; Traducción de papeles ingleses, La Guaira, Mar. 17, 1764, AGNV, Comisos, XXVI, fols. 308–310. Of these goods, it seems likely that only the gunpowder and hats would have been useful to sell in Venezuela. The rest of the goods might have been intended for English markets.

themselves served as a sort of currency, being given to labor on the Company's fortification projects as the Spanish state's payment for services rendered by the Company.[52]

Despite investigations, seizures, and confiscations, the efforts of coastal patrols and pardons to stem the tide of illegal importation of African slaves were ultimately ineffectual. Venezuelan planters and contrabandists reacted to slave scarcities and anticipated, by their illicit transactions, the policy changes to come. By the last quarter of the eighteenth century, the Spanish crown began to reduce tariffs on slaves entering Venezuela and the rest of Spanish America through the asiento. In 1777, Carlos III issued a royal order allowing Venezuelan merchants to export all agricultural products except cacao in exchange for slaves from foreign colonies. Cédulas in 1789 and 1791 finally ended the asiento along with fixed pricing on slave imports and opened up the slave trade in most of Spanish America to all nations.[53]

Ironically, the free trade in slaves came too late to be useful for many Venezuelan producers. Venezuelan planters had prefigured the royal decree opening the slave trade through more than two hundred years of illicit trade with foreigners. By the time of the cédula, many hacendados had already begun the transition to peasant *(peon)* labor for cacao production. Some historians believe that free labor had become a cheaper alternative to procuring and caring for slaves. Other historians dispute this, instead emphasizing the damage done to slavery by continuous warfare (which disabled the slave trade from the 1790s onward) and the fear of slave rebellions (produced by a rash of high-profile uprisings in the last quarter of the eighteenth century). The cédula came a generation too late for planters and officials traumatized by the upheaval of the Haitian Revolution. Slave imports waned in many Caribbean colonies as a result of the long shadow cast by the only successful slave revolt in the Western Hemisphere. In 1792, the intendant of Caracas prohibited the buy-

52. On dividing up spoils, see, for example, Ynforme del Yntendente de Caracas en vista de los dos testimonios de Autos que remite causados en la aprehension de la lancha Santa Rita, Sept. 19, 1786, AGI, Caracas, 839; Juan Bautista, Genoves, contrabando que se le aprehendió en Maracaibo y juicio a que fue sometido, 1721, AGNC, Contrabandos, II, fols. 811–869. For slaves used as spoils, see Autos sobre el apreso de la goleta "La Buena Esperanza" con siete negros esclavos, La Guaira, Dec. 20, 1759, AGNV, Comp Gui, appendice III, fols. 9–291.

53. For tariff reduction, see Pollak-Eltz, *La esclavitud en Venezuela,* 65. For Carlos III's 1770 order, see Arcila Farías, *Economía colonial de Venezuela,* 407. For the cédulas of 1789 and 1791, see David Eltis, *Economic Growth and the Ending of the Transatlantic Slave Trade* (New York, 1987), 36; Notificando la resolución de S.M. de que solo se cobre a los españoles y extranjeros el 6 por ciento de los frutos y dinero que extraigan, asi para, la compra de negros, Aranjuez, Apr. 22, 1791, AGNV, RO, X, fols. 281–282.

ing or selling of French slaves, even if they were recently arrived Africans on French ships. To Spanish officials, the Haitian contagion presented a threat not to be taken lightly. Similarly, he turned away a cargo of thirty-one creolized slaves from Curaçao because he believed that "creole slaves or those educated in the foreign colonies are prejudicial to these provinces." Fears of a second Haiti stunted slave sales for a time, but many Caribbean polities actually used Saint-Domingue's downfall to fuel a wave of "Second Slavery" in the nineteenth century. Well before these developments, the circumvention of Spanish mercantile trade policy through the contraband slave trade acknowledged the sad essentiality of forced African labor within emerging Caribbean plantation societies.[54]

## CONCLUSION

Whether mariners aboard foreign ships, porters of goods for their masters, soldiers in anticontraband operations, or captive cargoes in the holds of outlaw slave ships, freemen and slaves of African descent formed an integral part of the thriving illicit trade and contributed to the formation of a Venezuelan economy that was distinct from that of the Spanish Empire. Through their experiences with commonplace yet dangerous transactions, men of color understood far better than colonial policymakers that profit trumped patriotism in matters of international commercial exchange and could shake up legal status and subjecthood.

Venezuela's flourishing contraband trade created contradictions between freedom and slavery that challenged rigid distinctions of work, enslavement, and property rights in the circum-Caribbean. The illicit and informal nature of

54. On the transition to peon labor, see Federico Brito Figueroa, *La estructura económica de Venezuela colonial* (Caracas, 1963), 304–305, 366–368. White agriculturalists continued to struggle to fix itinerant pardo laborers in one place and provide sufficient peonage labor despite its economic benefits over slavery by the end of the eighteenth century. See Pollak-Eltz, *La esclavitud en Venezuela,* 44; McKinley, *Pre-Revolutionary Caracas,* 19. For an interpretation that emphasized, instead, war's disruption to slavery, see Borucki, "Trans-Imperial History," *Itinerario,* XXXVI (2012), 42. For restrictions against French ships, see Sr. Intendente del Ejercito a Joseph María Chacon, Caracas, Sept. 1, 1792, AGI, Caracas, 23. "Prejudicial to these provinces": Acosta Saignes, *La trata de esclavos,* 39. Curaçao's milder slavery was a result of greater face-to-face contact between masters and slaves; the island thus developed a reputation in the eighteenth century for undisciplined and unruly slaves. See also H. Hoetink, "Surinam and Curaçao," in Cohen and Greene, eds., *Neither Slave nor Free,* 67–69; Scott, "Common Wind," 81. "Second Slavery": Ada Ferrer, *Freedom's Mirror: Cuba and Haiti in the Age of Revolution* (New York, 2014), 12, 36.

the business allowed for working arrangements of greater autonomy for men of color both in Venezuela and at sea. Nonwhites of Spanish, French, Dutch, and English origins toiled at jobs in which they were entrusted with valuable cargo and bargaining power. As a plethora of cases involving runaways demonstrates, these responsibilities frequently defied the desires and expectations of white slave masters. Moreover, the criminality of unregulated trade sometimes worked in favor of the enslaved, winning them their freedom when the colonial justice system punished masters for illegally purchasing unlicensed slaves.

At the same time, Venezuela's illicit commerce presented thorny legal questions for men of African descent caught up in it. Royal officials were inconsistent in their prosecution of nonwhite contrabandists and smugglers. Capture by Spanish anticontraband forces might throw to the wind the carefully cultivated freedom of seafaring men of color. For other enslaved sailors, confiscation of their vessels merely exchanged a foreign master for a Spanish one. Though Spanish American officials might capture cargoes of illegally trafficked Africans, these seizures rarely halted their sale to hacendados. Creolized Venezuelan slaves often morphed from smugglers' accomplices into seized assets in the eyes of the Spanish authorities who caught their masters. This difficulty in separating contraband participant from human property defined the uneasy status of black contrabandists in the imperially fluid early modern Caribbean.

Slave trading and the struggles of Afro-Caribbeans for autonomy, like most aspects of illicit trade, were imbued with political considerations. Coastal inhabitants could not overtly advocate for smuggling to Spanish officials, but they could defend the economic practice when it came under attack. When the Caracas Company achieved political and economic dominance over the colony from the 1730s onward, disrupting long-held routines of interimperial extralegal trade, colonists in Caracas and its surrounding areas reached a breaking point. The 1749 rebellion of Juan Francisco de León united diverse classes and races behind the desire to demolish the Caracas Company and return to an earlier status quo of mostly unchecked contraband trade.

# 8

# *The Political Power of Covert Commerce*

## The Rebellion of Juan Francisco de León, 1749–1751

An upsetting name from decades past reappeared in Spanish imperial documents in 1773. After nineteen years of forced service in the presidio of Oran in Spanish North Africa, Nicolás León requested his freedom to return to Venezuela. Nicolás was the surviving son of Juan Francisco de León, whose thwarted rebellion in 1749 began this book's introduction. Having served time for his role in his father's revolt, Nicolás asked the Spanish secretary of state for clemency. But he never apologized for his father's actions and, instead, lionized Juan Francisco's role in the foundation of the family's hometown of Panaquire. Nicolás emphasized the respectability of the family line, bragging that relatives held prestigious positions as priests and army captains. He most likely mentioned such honorable occupations to erase any perceived stain to the family legacy caused by the punishments visited upon his father. Nicolás received permission to leave and to regain his family's lost land. In spite of the time that had passed, the connections he had lost, and the opportunity to make a fresh start in Spain, Nicolás de León chose to return to his boyhood home in 1773.[1]

Although most Venezuelans would identify themselves as Spanish in the grand scheme of empires, like Nicolás they maintained corporate identifications bound more to province and ethnicity than to the mother country. A

1. Extracto de la carta de Nicolás León, San Lorenzo, Nov. 15, 1773, AGI, Caracas, 421; A Don Francisco Nuñez Ybañez, July 16, 1774, AGI, Caracas, 421.

slack grip on Spanish imperial possessions had allowed the monarchy to contain the worrisome potential ramifications for loyalty that this multivalent subjecthood raised. Under the Habsburgs' commercial regime, for example, smuggling in the province of Venezuela had been almost an unwritten fuero. However, with the Bourbon imposition of the Caracas Company, coastal subjects had been, in effect, ordered to align their fiercely independent commercial agendas with that of the crown. After two decades of Company control over the province, the rebellion of Juan Francisco de León tapped into Venezuelan resistance to this line of thought. León's rebels had a simple demand that masked their more complicated sentiments: the expulsion of the Compañía Guipuzcoana and its employees from the province.

The León Rebellion brings into sharp focus the interplay between community standards of economic fair play and contraband trade. Protesters in the León Rebellion acted out against a disruption in their common understanding of legitimate and illegitimate economic practices. León's supporters took up arms because they lacked other means to rectify their grievances, and they showed restraint in their public attempts to legitimize their cause. The protesters sought to legitimize their actions as a defense of traditional economic customs, like smuggling, that had been outlawed by the state. This put them in an awkward and ambivalent position: the livelihoods of many coastal Venezuelan subjects went against the laws of their cherished sovereign. The protesters' attempts to rationalize or minimalize this bedrock truth of their uprising offer a window into the ideological potency of early modern contraband trade. The León rebels wanted local control over their commercial choices but sought to use wide-ranging interimperial trade to attain it.[2]

2. The uprising followed many patterns consistent with the riots described by E. P. Thompson. Most important, it was a fight for local control of the economy. Two major points in the rebellion's ideology diverge from Thompson's eighteenth-century English bread riots and help expand the concept of the moral economy. First, my argument departs from Thompson's contentions that the social contract of the moral economy militated, in some ways, against the free market and individual liberty and that authorities and individuals agreed upon proper and legitimate economic functions for members of a society. Although the León rebels protested the state's intervention in the marketplace, their demands differed from those of Thompson's bread rioters in that they implicitly supported freer and more diverse markets by way of illegal interimperial commerce. Second, the indisputable criminality of the smuggling encouraged by the León rebels according to Spanish commercial law filled them with considerably more indecision than English rioters about how to best state their case. See E. P. Thompson, "The Moral Economy of the English Crowd in the Eighteenth Century," *Past and Present*, L (1971), 78–79, 86. For a work that similarly extends Thompson's moral economy beyond its ideological confines, in this case toward the spiritual world, see Kevin Gosner, *Soldiers of the Virgin: The Moral Economy of a Colonial Maya Rebel-*

The uprising's causes, events, and consequences are complex and demand multifaceted coverage. The first part of this chapter delves into several earlier protests against Caracas Company dominance, predating the León Rebellion. These smaller and more localized uprisings expose a common undercurrent of frustration with Company privilege lurking just beneath the surface of colonial politics. The second section examines the events of the León uprising itself. The course of this trade rebellion allowed Venezuelan subjects, via popular protest, to participate in the colonial political arena. The final part of the chapter analyzes petitions and correspondence of the insurgents to reveal elements of their sense of justice, commercial thought, and communal identities.[3]

---

*lion* (Tucson, Ariz., 1992). Jani Marjanen argues that the moral economy cannot be confined to subaltern classes and that Thompson's model can be used to describe patriotic actions of elite eighteenth-century European social engineers (Marjanen, "Moral Economy and Civil Society in Eighteenth-Century Europe: The Case of Economic Societies and the Business of Improvement," *Journal of Global Ethics,* XI [2015], 205–217).

3. The historiographies of Venezuela and Spanish America have neglected the León Rebellion and its connections to illicit trade. Scholarship on the major late-eighteenth-century rebellions in Spanish America mostly ignore León's revolt or reference it obliquely. Anthony McFarlane's three articles on the comparative history of the Quito, Comunero, and Túpac Amaru rebellions refer to the León Rebellion only once. See McFarlane, "Rebellions in Late Colonial Spanish America: A Comparative Perspective," *BLAR,* XIV (1995), 313–338; McFarlane, "Civil Disorders and Popular Protests in Late Colonial New Granada," *HAHR,* LXIV (1984), 17–54; McFarlane, "The 'Rebellion of the Barrios': Urban Insurrection in Bourbon Quito," ibid., LXIX (1989), 283–330. The rebellion is entirely absent from five major monographs on late colonial unrest: Sergio Serulnikov, *Subverting Colonial Authority: Challenges to Spanish Rule in Eighteenth-Century Southern Andes* (Durham, N.C., 2003); Sinclair Thomson, *We Alone Will Rule: Native Andean Politics in the Age of Insurgency* (Madison, Wis., 2002); Ward Stavig, *The World of Túpac Amaru: Conflict, Community, and Identity in Colonial Peru* (Lincoln, Neb., 1999); John Leddy Phelan, *The People and the King: The Comunero Revolution in Colombia, 1781* (Madison, Wis., 1978); Carlos de la Torre Reyes, *La Revolución de Quito del 10 de Agosto 1809* (Quito, 1990). Only Joseph Pérez seems to acknowledge the León Rebellion in any substantial way, though he devotes only 13 pages out of a 156-page book to it (Pérez, *Los movimientos precursores de la emancipación en Hispanoamérica* [Madrid, 1977], 31–44). To my knowledge, only two English-language works devote more than a couple of sentences to the uprising. Ronald Dennis Hussey and Robert J. Ferry each spend a chapter of their respective books on the Caracas Company and the elites of Caracas discussing the rebellion, focusing on the rebellion as an economic consequence of Company rule (Hussey, *The Caracas Company, 1728–1784: A Study in the History of Spanish Monopolistic Trade* [1934; rpt. New York, 1977]; Ferry, *The Colonial Elite of Early Caracas: Formation and Crisis, 1567–1767* [Berkeley, Calif., 1989]).

Many Venezuelan scholars have investigated the León Rebellion as part of their broader projects, but only a handful have made it the central theme of their studies. Among Venezuelan historians, the traditional interpretations of the rebellion's causes have emphasized it as a protonationalist struggle, a battle between Basques and Canary Islanders for control

Illegal commerce affected more than the pocketbooks of those who partook in it. Otherwise loyal Spanish subjects, such as the León insurgents, benefited from everyday illegal trade. They used popular protest to defend it against commercial concessions that encroached upon contraband's central position in their economy of makeshifts. As previous chapters have demonstrated, smuggling and its suppression were commonplace nodes of conflict along the coast. These seemingly inconsequential struggles molded the character of the León Rebellion. As such, smuggling was consistent with larger ideologies of self-sufficiency and extra-statism held by inhabitants of colonial peripheries.[4]

Contraband commerce also influenced colonial politics. Though illegal traders were not a formal political faction themselves, they heavily influenced how provincial elites reacted to metropolitan orders. Those who smuggled or benefited from smuggled goods were equal parts political reactionaries, in their wish to reinstitute a Habsburg period of salutary neglect, and forward thinkers, in their desire to create free trade from the bottom up. Neither vision completely fitted with midcentury Bourbon designs.

Finally, clandestine trade was a strong indicator of colonial autonomy and

---

of the province, a result of economic hardships, or a fight strictly over the fate of the Caracas Company. For the idea of the rebellion as a protonationalist movement, see Luis Alberto Sucre, *Gobernadores y capitanes generales de Venezuela*, 2d ed. (1928; rpt. Caracas, 1964); Mercedes Álvarez de Ramos Marquez, *Aspectos de nuestros orígenes patrios (Historia interpretativa de Venezuela): Para uso de los liceos y escuelas normales de Venezuela*, Biblioteca femenina venezolana, no. 9 (Caracas, 1944); Augusto Mijares, "Prologo," in Mijares, ed., *Documentos relativos a la insurrección de Juan Francisco de León* (Caracas, 1949), 14–18; J. A. de Armas Chitty, prologue, in Chitty, ed., *Juan Francisco de León (Diario de una insurgencia), 1749* (Caracas, 1971); Enrique Bernardo Nuñez, *Miranda; o, El tema de la libertad / Juan Francisco de León; o, El levantamiento contra la Compañía Guipuzcoana* (1950; rpt. Caracas, 1979).

Arguments for the uprising as a conflict between Basques and Canary Islanders can be found in Vicente de Amézaga Aresti, *Hombres de la Compañía Guipuzcoana* (Caracas, 1963); Ramón de Basterra, *Los navios de la ilustración: Una empresa del siglo XVIII* (Madrid, 1970); Lucas Guillermo Castillo Lara, *La aventura fundacional de los Isleños: Panaquire y Juan Francisco de León* (Caracas, 1983). Works prioritizing the economic dimensions of the rebellion include José Estornés Lasa, *La Real Compañía Guipuzcoana de Navegación de Caracas* (Buenos Aires, 1948); Analola Borges, "Los Canarios en las revueltas venezolanas del siglo XVIII (1700–1752)," *BANHV*, XLVI (1963), 128–140; John V. Lombardi, *Venezuela: The Search for Order, the Dream of Progress* (New York, 1982). Francisco Morales Padrón emphasizes the rebellion as strictly a struggle against the Caracas Company (Padrón, *Rebelión contra la Compañía de Caracas* [Seville, 1955]). None of these treatments has emphasized sufficiently the role of contraband trade in the rebellion's development.

4. I am drawing on the ideas of Serulnikov, who has written about "the forms whereby routine dissension at the local level shaped the nature of mass rebellion" (Serulnikov, *Subverting Colonial Authority*, 4).

networks of association. Venezuelan contrabandists and their accomplices were notoriously hostile to outsiders' attempts to enforce antismuggling ordinances. They identified most strongly with their Venezuelan homeland, although, in the mid-eighteenth century, very few harbored any desire to be politically independent of Spain. Venezuelan traders, producers, and consumers looked to Spain for many of their cultural and political allegiances, but they reached out to non-Spanish traders to fill their shopping baskets and bring their produce to market. The tension in this dichotomy of colonial character manifested itself in the actions and words of León and his insurgents.

The León Rebellion of 1749–1751 was neither politically nor ideologically inert. Like the later and better-known Quito, Comunero, and Túpac Amaru rebellions in late-eighteenth-century South America, the León uprising was not just a spontaneous outbreak of violence bred from utter desperation. Rather, basic political beliefs grounded the insurgents' defense of consumption patterns and community rights. The uprising shed light on characteristics of Venezuelan society shaped by illicit trade. In the León Rebellion and the popular protests that preceded it, smuggling transcended its simple definition as an illegal economic exchange and became a pivotal building block for political expression and local identity formation.[5]

## THE CARACAS COMPANY AND ITS MALCONTENTS ON THE EVE OF REBELLION

In the two decades preceding the León Rebellion, many sectors of Venezuelan society found common cause in their rancor for the Compañía Guipuzcoana. Venezuelans found their governmental autonomy curtailed by the Caracas Company's political influence, their control over the colony's primary cash crop transferred largely to the Basques, and their hopes for more substantive Spanish provisioning of the colony dashed by Company neglect. Most important, the Company's suppression and surveillance of interimperial trade along the coast struck many colonists as greedy and hypocritical. These grievances spurred two short anti-Company rebellions that shared the goals of the León uprising and fueled the indignation of its participants.

When the Caracas Company clamped down on and simultaneously monopolized extralegal commerce for its own benefit, it tightened a safety valve

5. McFarlane makes the most forceful argument about the ideological power of the Quito, Comunero, and Túpac Amaru rebellions. See his "Civil Disorders and Popular Protests," *HAHR*, LXIV (1984), 52–53, and "'Rebellion of the Barrios,'" LXIX (1989), 327.

that had helped to relieve pressure from the colonial compact between subjects and the state for centuries. Colonial subjects often declined to rebel against the economic order because their grievances could be soothed by retreating to the autonomy of peripheral spaces or by engaging in illegal trade. Whereas British American subjects protested unpalatable elements of colonial rule by boycotting British imports, their Spanish American counterparts resisted metropolitan authority by enthusiastically engaging in illicit commerce. The Caracas Company's intrusion into the underground economy hindered these modes of passive resistance to Spanish commercial regulations. Subjects cloaked their complaints in the appropriate language of lost legal trade opportunities, but it was the Company's antismuggling operations that animated their claims for redress and eventual revolt.[6]

In order to protect its image in Spain, the Compañía Guipuzcoana parried Venezuelans' criticism with its own perspective on the previous twenty years of history. Numerous letters to royal officials offered a full-throated defense of Company patrols as "the brake on illicit trade" and the only real military measure against foreign invasion. At the height of the León Rebellion, several senior Company officials, led by director Joseph de Yturriaga, published *Manifiesto, que con incontestables hechos prueba los grandes beneficios, que ha producido el establecimiento de la Real Compañía Guipuzcoana de Caracas* defending the Company's continued presence in Venezuela. The document is notable for its measured tone and orderly arguments, which contrasted sharply with the impassioned pleas of creole petitions. It minimized the rebellion's importance, claiming that a few bad apples (mostly elite Caraqueño merchants and

6. On modes of comparative colonial resistance to imperial trade policy, see Aline Helg, *Liberty and Equality in Caribbean Colombia, 1770–1835* (Chapel Hill, N.C., 2004), 72; J. H. Elliott, *Empires of the Atlantic World: Britain and Spain in America, 1492–1830* (New Haven, Conn., 2006), 316–317. In interpreting Venezuelan frustrations with the Caracas Company, I agree mostly with Hussey. Hussey's argument emphasizes the anticontraband operations of the Caracas Company as their original sin in the minds of Venezuelans. Though I concur that the Company's enforcement of contraband restrictions played a prominent role in colonial complaints, even if they could not be articulated as such, Hussey's argument is moralistic and overly determinist in its belief "that monopoly and all-inclusive governmental regulation were evil principles upon which to found an economic system" and its overriding assumption that colonists single-mindedly wanted free trade (*Caracas Company,* viii; see also 99). Mercedes Álvarez de Ramos Marquez also agrees with Hussey's contention that Company crackdowns on contraband caused the León Rebellion (Álvarez de Ramos Marquez, *Aspectos de nuestros orígenes,* 106–109). However, this interpretation almost entirely lacks supporting documentation. I have attempted in this chapter to provide documentation and a more nuanced analysis than this previous literature.

foreigners) had led an otherwise loyal populace astray. In the view of these Company men, the minority that hated the Basque merchant venture did so because it enforced antismuggling prohibitions. The manifesto rejected the idea of the Company as a malevolent monopoly, reasoning that colonists could legally trade with Mexico, the Canary Islands, and the interior provinces outside of the Company's control. Moreover, the Company had benefited the region. The authors pointed to increased cacao production, the construction of forts and deep harbors, and defensive outlays of 15,000 pesos annually as proof that the Compañía Guipuzcoana had Venezuela's best interests in mind. These gains were not, as petitioners had misconstrued them, the result of "*tyranny, oppression, mistreatment, or poverty,* but rather advantages that gave *help, assistance, opportune aid,* and *fecundity* to the province."[7]

This rubicund portrayal to Madrid notwithstanding, coastal Venezuela was the scene of frequent unrest before the 1749 uprising. Venezuela's coastal inhabitants had voiced their dismay through two previous tumults. The first of these civil disorders, the Andresote Rebellion, flared up in 1730, soon after the Caracas Company's installation. Named after Andrés Lopez de Rosario, a former slave of African and indigenous descent (zambo), the amorphous uprising lasted nearly two years. It consisted of sporadic skirmishes in the inland western towns of Nirgua and Barquisimeto. Andresote led sophisticated smuggling rings that traded from the coast near Puerto Cabello deep into these interior towns to the southwest by way of the Yaracuy River. According to the governor of Venezuela, Andresote was an agitator for Dutch interests and the unlawful aims of powerful Venezuelans; he had "agreed to foment this uprising to further their illicit commerce." The rebellion comprised many slaves and free blacks and a few whites. His followers fired on Company officials and troops and destroyed the homes and property of several authorities and planters loyal to the Basques. Andresote's men received arms and logistical support from the Dutch, who were his trading partners and stood to gain from the destruction of the Company. He used Dutch ships to hop over to Curaçao, where he was "received with great applause and satisfaction by the residents and especially their governor who bestowed on him magnificent hospitality at

7. "The brake on illicit trade": El Yngeniero Don Juan Gayangos, Puerto Cabello, May 19, 1749, AGI, Caracas, 418; Los Directores de la Compañía de Caracas to Marques de la Ensenada, San Sebastian, Oct. 12, 1750, AGI, Caracas, 929. *"Tyranny, oppression, mistreatment":* José de Iturriaga, *Manifiesto, que con incontestables hechos prueba los grandes beneficios, que ha producido el establecimiento de la Real Compañía Guipuzcoana de Caracas . . .* ([Madrid?], 1749), 13f.

his country estate." When royal troops finally put down his rebellion for good in 1732, Andresote fled to Curaçao, presumably remaining there in exile for the rest of his life.[8]

Nine years later, another anti-Company protest broke out in San Felipe, a city near the site of Andresote's uprising. The uprising started in 1741 when San Felipe's inhabitants expelled Ignacio Basasábal, a Company-backed teniente known for his zealous prosecution of contrabandists. The protestors took control of the town and plotted various actions against the Caracas Company, including setting fire to a nearby Company factory. Like the Andresote rebels, San Felipe's insurgents received arms from the Dutch. After several months, royal soldiers put down the revolt, entered the city, and reinstalled Basasábal.[9]

Although both the Andresote and San Felipe uprisings expressed popular anger at the Caracas Company's commercial policing, several factors explain why neither rivaled León's Rebellion in size and scope. First, both revolts lacked a distinct, driving ideology. San Felipe protesters rallied around the idea of expelling their local official but never moved much beyond these personal politics. The Andresote Rebellion developed a split personality that vacillated between freedom for contrabandists and the empowerment of Afro-Venezuelans. The rebels frequently pursued no greater cause than the survival of their own insurgency.[10]

Both revolts also failed to encompass a broader base of support and, most important, the aid of elites. In San Felipe, this was because the rebellion never reached outside the confines of the city. Andresote's insurgency initially held

8. Linda M. Rupert has identified four eighteenth-century uprisings before the León Rebellion in which smuggling was a factor in colonial agitation (Rupert, *Creolization and Contraband: Curaçao in the Early Modern Atlantic World* [Athens, Ga., 2012], 203). To my knowledge, the largest concentration of primary source material on the Andresote Rebellion is Expediente sobre el zambo levantado llamado Andresote años de 1732 a 1733, AGI, SD, 782. The major secondary source on the rebellion is Carlos Felice Cardot, *La Rebelión de Andresote (Valles del Yaracuy, 1730–1733)* (Caracas, 1952). "Agreed to foment this uprising": Don Sebastian García de la Torre, governor of Venezuela, to the Council of the Indies, San Phelipe, Apr. 4, 1732, AGI, SD, 784. "Received with great applause and satisfaction": de la Torre to the king, Caracas, Oct. 22, 1732, AGI, SD, 782.

9. Tenientes were rural sheriffs who were the most important officials in Venezuelan communities before the arrival of the Caracas Company. Their role was one of both police officer and justice of the peace. See Ferry, *Colonial Elite,* 141. The largest group of documents on the San Felipe riot can be found in Expediente sobre el tumulto de la ciudad de San Felipe, Provincia de Caracas, 1741, AGI, SD, 788. The definitive study of the rebellion is León Trujillo, *Motín y sublevación en San Felipe* (Caracas, 1955). Trujillo views the León Rebellion as the direct ideological descendant of the San Felipe uprising.

10. Felice Cardot, *La Rebelión de Andresote,* 15, 49.

sway over local elites involved in the contraband trade; they saw the Afro-Venezuelan chief as their puppet. As the uprising progressed, however, white planters and traders became horrified by rebel rhetoric proclaiming that "the time has arrived when the whites will serve them or they [blacks] will kill them all." The veracity of these declarations is uncertain, given that royal officials included the racially charged language in their leading questions to witnesses of the uprising. Nevertheless, the tone of the documents demonstrates that elite opinion of the Afro-Venezuelan-led rebellion had soured.[11]

The San Felipe and Andresote uprisings never attained the critical mass of León's Rebellion because their partisans never reached Caracas. The short duration and small geographical scope of the San Felipe riot failed to attract significant attention in the capital. Andresote's two-year revolt owed its longevity more to the guerrilla tactics of its perpetrators and the rugged jungle terrain of its setting than to any provincewide participation or sympathy from the center. Ultimately, these two protests had little impact on the Caracas Company's control over Venezuela but indicate the consistent current of unrest that Juan Francisco de León would later channel into a substantial movement.[12]

Spain's competitors acutely recognized and sought to capitalize on local frustration with the Caracas Company. In addition to the Dutch interventions in the pre-León uprisings, English subjects also sympathized with anti-Company protests. One Boston newspaper cheerily recognized the bravery of "Andrew Scoso [Andresote] a Mulatto agitated by a generous Passion of relieving his distress'd Countrymen." Foreigners, particularly the English, made several overtures to Venezuelan coastal inhabitants encouraging them in rebellion against the Company and the Spanish crown. During the War of Jenkins' Ear, English admiral Charles Knowles sought to create a fifth column of Venezuelans disaffected by the Company to aid his invasions of La Guaira and Puerto Cabello in 1743. He sent leaflets in Spanish ahead of himself to both ports, explaining that the war between the English and Spanish had begun only out of need

> to reprimand the insolence of these pirates commonly called coast guards of which the Viscayans [Basques from the province of Biscay] are particularly noteworthy. They practice acts of cruelty and barbarism not just against the English, but against their own countrymen, the Spanish, treating them worse than Turks, jailing

11. "Whites will serve them": Declaración de Don Francisco Leal, asistente en los pardos de Guama, San Felipe, July 10, 1732, AGI, SD, 782.

12. Felice Cardot, *La Rebelión de Andresote,* 16, 21–22.

them, violating their ancient right to trade with other nations, and daily throwing them into the galleys.

Knowles proposed to establish a British colony at Puerto Cabello and promised protection from marauding Company forces. One British officer involved in the campaign recalled Knowles's orders to his subordinates: they were

> to let the Inhabitants of the Country know, that the *English* did not come there to take from them their Rights, Religion, or Liberties, but that they would from us enjoy them with greater Certainty, and more Happiness, than when under the Tyranny and Cruelty of the *Guiapesco* Company, which we were now come to rid them of.

Six years later, during Juan Francisco de León's rebellion, the rebel chief received a letter from British captain Ian Burr lamenting that the province's inhabitants found themselves "enslaved and impeded from trade and commerce" and offering the military aid of his convoy of three ships if León's forces would swear allegiance to the British sovereign.[13]

That none of these plots succeeded in swaying imperial loyalties confirmed the strength of Venezuelan fidelity to the Spanish crown. Public pronouncements and correspondence from subjects in the region continued to refer to the king and the imperial authority he represented with reverence. His sovereignty in law and government, along with the common bonds of language and Catholicism, affixed colonial allegiances that geographically close but culturally dissimilar empires could not pry loose. Unwillingness to join foreign invasion schemes also signified that the concerns that animated the colonial commercial frustrations and the larger León Rebellion were local in nature. Nonetheless, foreign entreaties to rebellion demonstrated that locals' frustration at the Caracas Company's control over the commercial, political,

13. "A Mulatto agitated by a generous Passion": "Barbados, March 3," *Boston Weekly News-Letter,* Apr. 20, 1732, 2. I wish to thank Charles Foy for providing me with this citation. "Reprimand the insolence of these pirates": Don Carlos Knowles Cavallero Comandante en Principal de una Escuadra de Fragatas de S. M. Bretanica de presente en la Costa de Caracas, a los Vecinos y Moradores de la provincia de Benevuela, n.d., AGI, Caracas, 927. "Tyranny and Cruelty of the *Guiapesco* Company": *Journal of the Expedition to La Guira and Porto Cavallos in the West-Indies, under the Command of Commodore Knowles* (London, 1744), 6–7. "Enslaved and impeded from trade": Captain Ian Burr to Juan Francisco de León, on board the ship "El Aspa," Puerto de Unare, Oct. 2, 1749, in Chitty, ed., *Juan Francisco de León: Diario,* 189. The authenticity of this letter was challenged by interim governor Julián de Arriaga, who believed it was a forgery. See Fray Don Julian de Arriaga y Rivera to Marques de la Ensenada, Caracas, Apr. 5, 1750, AGI, Caracas, 418.

and military resources of the province had intensified to the point where it was discernable across imperial boundaries.

## MARCHING ON CARACAS: THE REBELLION OF JUAN FRANCISCO DE LEÓN

Nowhere was creole frustration over the Basque monopolization of Venezuela more palpable than in Panaquire. The town was formed early in the eighteenth century from the boom in cacao production and became the bedrock of Juan Francisco de León's rebellion. Located in the fertile Tuy River valley just inland from the coast, Panaquire was an ideal location for Canary Islands immigrants to settle and grow cacao. Royal permissions and economic hardships back home brought Isleños to populate what had been a jungle at the turn of the eighteenth century. They found fellowship with Canary Islanders who lived in the Candelaria district of Caracas. Although the crown initially encouraged the efforts of these small cacao planters, the Caracas Company and governors beholden to it viewed these Isleños as a nuisance. Officials connected them to illicit trade and portrayed them as shifty, lazy, and rebellious. In 1750, the interim governor of Venezuela, Fray Julián de Arriaga y Rivera, conflated "*zambos, mulatoes, negroes, Ysleños,* deserters, and other elements of vagrants *(gente vaga)* that only obey the *alcalde* if they like and if not, they laugh at him and the priest. Most of them make a living combining the bounty of the haciendas and throwing themselves into [illegal] commerce on the coast."[14]

Such characterizations sprang from the weak royal presence in the Tuy River valley and the ease with which cacao could be shipped downriver and out to coastlines frequented by Dutch smugglers. The valley was a jungled backwater, but it also served as a back door into Caracas, whose principal river, the Guaire, was a tributary of the Tuy. The valley's inhabitants enjoyed autonomy

14. John Lynch, "Spanish America's Poor Whites: Canarian Immigrants in Venezuela, 1700–1830," in Lynch, *Latin America between Colony and Nation: Selected Essays* (New York, 2001), 58–61; James J. Parsons, "The Migration of Canary Islanders to the Americas: An Unbroken Current since Columbus," *Americas,* XXXIX (1983), 464–466; Gilbert C. Din, *The Canary Islanders of Louisiana* (Baton Rouge, La., 1988), 10; Castillo Lara, *La aventura fundacional de los Isleños,* 11; Francisco Morales Padrón, "La Real Compañía Guipuzcoana de Caracas y la sociedad venezolana," in Ronald Escobedo Mansilla, Ana María Rivera Medina, and Alvaro Chapa Imaz, eds., *Los vascos y América: Actas de las jornadas sobre el comercio vasco con América en el siglo XVIII y la Real Compañía Guipuzcoana de Caracas . . .* (Bilbao, 1989), 215. *"Zambos, mulatoes, negroes, Ysleños":* Fray Don Julian de Arriaga y Rivera a los factores en que les significó su juicio sobre el estado de la Provincia y Compania, Caracas, Mar. 29, 1750, AGI, Caracas, 929.

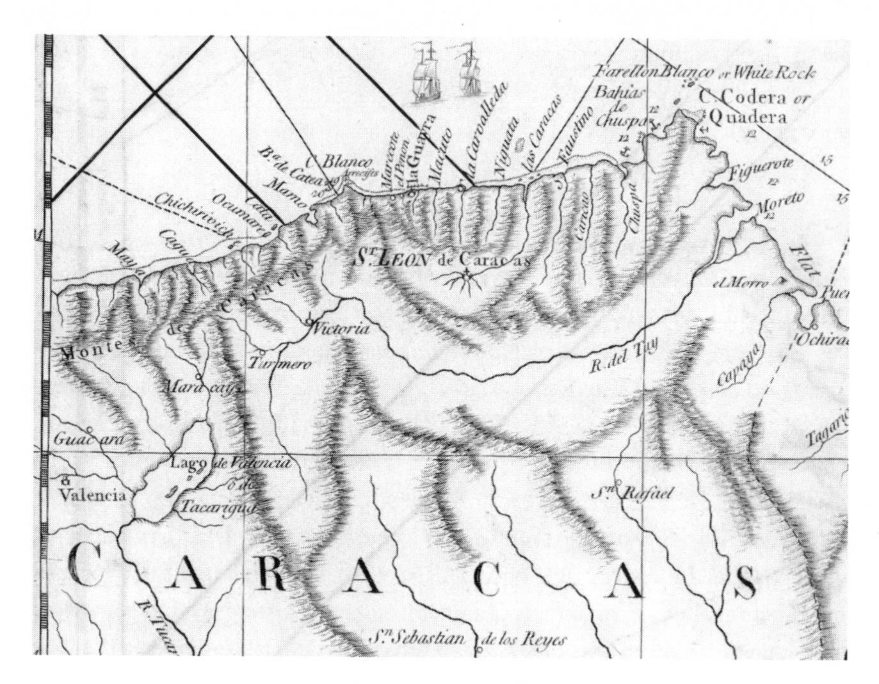


FIGURE 10. The Tuy River Valley. Detail of *The Coast of Caracas, Cumana, Parla, and the Mouths of Rio Orinoco, with the Islands of Trinidad, Margarita, Tobago, Granada, St. Vincent Etca.* By Thomas Jefferys. 1775. *The David Rumsey Map Collection, www.davidrumsey.com*

in a neglected area alongside convenient access to both Caracas and the coastline farther east. By the eighteenth century, riverine cacao plantations like those on the banks of the Tuy began to outnumber coastal ones.[15]

To combat the perceived lawlessness of the region, authorities restricted trade and movement with new rules. In 1735, Governor Martín de Lardizabal, a Basque, issued an order banning any non-Company commercial activity on the coasts of the province of Venezuela east of La Guaira. Instead, all cacao would have to be trucked overland across poorly maintained roads that became impassible in the rainy season, or brought by Company ships to La Guaira. The restrictions did not even allow commercial fishing on the coasts. They came on the heels of earlier decrees that mandated all cacao haciendas be planted at least fifteen leagues from the river and that boat building be prohibited.[16]

These orders designed to slow contraband commerce caused poverty

15. Ferry, *Colonial Elite,* 105–106.

16. Castillo Lara, *La aventura fundacional de los Isleños,* 166, 170–171; Ferry, *Colonial Elite,* 144.

and pushed subjects into the black market. Subjects elsewhere felt a similar squeeze on their commercial freedoms. A petition from the citizens of Caracas attributed their plight to living in a dysfunctional province where "there are many sellers and abundant produce, but few or only one buyer." Clergy complained that tithes and contributions from cacao-producing parishes were insufficient to support their churches. One priest summed up the unintended consequences of increased policing of trade by arguing that shuttered ports would "prohibit residents from exporting cacao by way of legal commerce and, as a consequence, open the danger of illicit trade because only criminals *(vasallos de mala ley)* and foreign ships would come to these less-traversed ports." By this line of thought, limiting access to the Tuy Valley actually encouraged contraband trade.[17]

Officials from Caracas wishing to limit independent commerce met stubborn resistance, especially in primarily Isleño areas. Teniente Juan Francisco de León, the titular leader of the coming revolution, presided over local government in the region. A cacao planter who had been instrumental in Panaquire's founding, León was pro-Isleño and reviled the Basques. Governor Lardizabal's successor, José Gabriel de Zuloaga, responded to continued illegal settlement and trade on the banks of the Tuy River by threatening to prohibit cacao cultivation in the area and to revoke Panaquire's charter in 1743. Official investigations hinted at plots to depose or assassinate both Lardizabal and Zuloaga. An uneasy standoff developed as the Basque governors' desire to rein in contraband suffered from Isleño disobedience and local governmental autonomy.[18]

By the end of the 1740s, Panaquire's simmering frustration boiled over into a provincewide rebellion owing to new Company attempts to assert governmental control over the Tuy River valley. On April 3, 1749, Martín de Echeverría arrived in Panaquire to assume the position of prize court judge of the

17. Here I am building on Ferry's extensive interpretation of conditions in the Tuy Valley; see his *Colonial Elite,* 106–139. "Few or only one buyer": Ciudad de Santiago de Leon de Caracas to the King, Caracas, Nov. 19, 1741, AGI, Caracas, 925. "Prohibit residents from exporting cacao": Memorial de Padre Pedro Díaz Cienfuegos, 1745, AGNV, Diversos, XXVII, fols. 2–16, quoted in Castillo Lara, *La aventura fundacional de los Isleños,* 174n. See also Las Religiosas Dominicas to the King, representan los graves perjuicios que se le siguen, por la restricción de buques a que se ha reducido el embarque de cacao en aquella Provincia, Caracas, Nov. 27, 1731, AGI, Caracas, 925.

18. Castillo Lara, *La aventura fundacional de los Isleños,* 167; Council of the Indies to the King, Madrid, May 25, 1745, AGI, Caracas, 418; Cuestionario de Juan Francisco de León, Caracas, Feb. 8, 1752, AGNV, León, II, fols. 266–272, in Mijares, ed., *Documentos relativos,* 181; Otto Pikaza, *Don Gabriel José de Zuloaga en la gobernación de Venezuela (1737–1747)* (Seville, 1963), 88; Morales Padrón, *Rebelión contra la Compañía de Caracas,* 42.

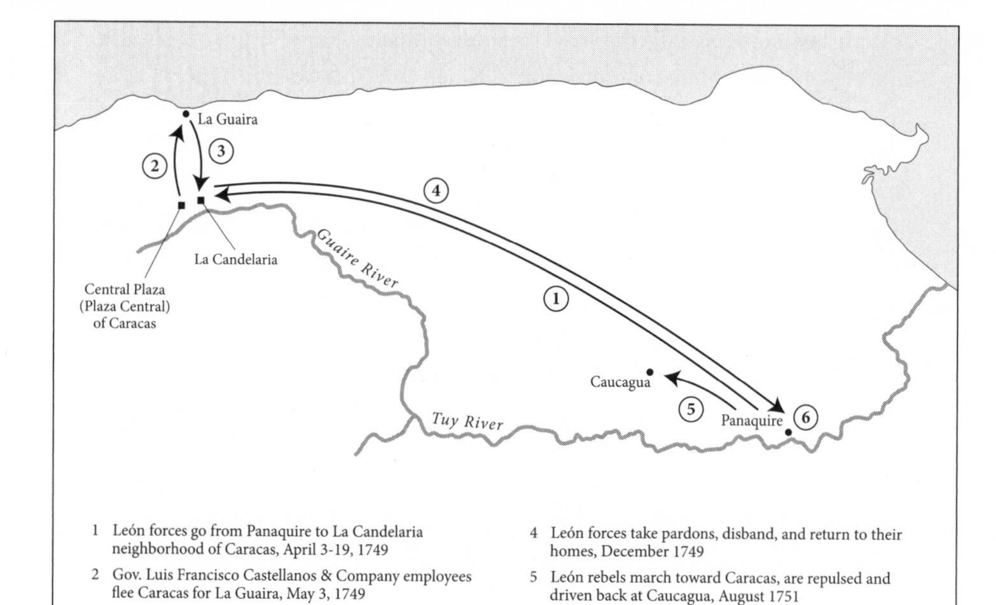


MAP 4. The Rebellion of Juan Francisco de León.
*Drawn by Christine Riggio*

town. Being that he was an outside official handpicked by the Caracas Company to judge captured contrabandists, Echeverría's appointment drove the townspeople to revolt. Believing erroneously that Echeverría intended to replace him as teniente, Juan Francisco de León met the official and informed him that the town would not accept Echeverría in any official capacity. When Echeverría pressed the issue, León's forces fired on him, and Echeverría withdrew. The rebellion of Juan Francisco de León had begun.[19]

The uprising, which lasted from 1749 to the beginning of 1752, comprised four phases. In the first phase, León marched on Caracas with an army of six to eight hundred armed men. Three-quarters of León's forces were Isleños or Spaniards by ancestry, whereas the rest were blacks, mulattos, zambos, and a few Indians. The protestors' social classes ran the gamut from wealthy planters to middling tradespeople to slaves. León's forces won this broad base by convincing Venezuelans not involved in cacao production that the expulsion of

19. Juan Francisco de León to Governor Castellanos, Chacao, Apr. 3, 1749, AGI, Caracas, 937; Confesión de León, Caracas, Feb. 9, 1752, AGNV, León, fols. 277–284, in Mijares, ed., *Documentos relativos*, 195; Ferry, *Colonial Elite*, 144.

FIGURE 11. Chronology of Events in the Rebellion of Juan Francisco de León

| | |
|---|---|
| April 3, 1749 | Expulsion of Martín de Echeverría from Panaquire (beginning of rebellion) |
| April 20, 1749 | Rebels enter the Central Plaza of Caracas |
| May 3, 1749 | Governor Luis Francisco Castellanos flees Caracas |
| November 1749 | Governor Julián de Arriaga succeeds Castellanos and arrives in Venezuela with reinforcements |
| December 1749 | Arriaga pardons the rebels |
| May 1751 | Governor Phelipe Ricardos succeeds Arriaga |
| August 1751 | Caracas Company reestablished. León rebels begin marching back to Caracas and a skirmish takes place |
| September 1751 | Manhunt for León and his remaining rebels ensues |
| January 1752 | Juan Francisco de León caught and tried for his crimes |

the Caracas Company would serve their interests, as well. One of León's subordinates told a group of "tailors, barbers, cobblers, and other tradesmen" that

> though they did not own a cacao hacienda or plant tobacco, by expelling the company they would enjoy benefits in the purchase of their goods and in the compensation for their work. The barber normally given a half *real* for each haircut would now receive two because there would be more money.

On the other end of the socioeconomic spectrum, León received anonymous letters of support from elite Caraqueños who later fed and sheltered his men when they got to Caracas.[20]

León sent letters of protest ahead of him, airing common grievances as he marched toward the capital. He accused the Caracas Company of impoverishing the province by lowering cacao prices to levels that forced producers to abandon their haciendas. He also charged individual Company officials with

20. On the composition of León's supporters, see Auto de Domingo de Aguirre, Apr. 20, 1749, in Chitty, ed., *Juan Francisco de León: Diario,* 8; Acta del Ayuntamiento de Caracas, Apr. 20, 1749, AGNV, León, II, fols. 228–239, in Mijares, ed., *Documentos relativos,* 25, 173. "By expelling the company they would enjoy benefits": Confesión de Matias de Ovalle, Caracas, Jan. 5, 1752, ibid., 174. For León's elite supporters, see Juan Francisco de León to Governor and Captain General Don Phelipe Ricardos, Dec. 16, 1751, AGI, Caracas, 421; Ferry, *Colonial Elite,* 148.

setting obscenely high prices on food and goods, smuggling for their own enrichment, and generally abusing Venezuelan subjects. Reports of bread shortages in the two years leading up to the rebellion buttressed his arguments. León demanded the immediate expulsion of the Compañía Guipuzcoana and all Basques from the province.[21]

Although the invaders conveyed the appearance of an armed revolt, the initial stages of the León uprising in Caracas were peaceful and orderly. By April 19, 1749, León's forces were on the outskirts of the city in the Isleño-dominated neighborhood of La Candelaria. Governor Luis Francisco Castellanos had no standing army, so they held him as a de facto hostage. Despite the rebels' control over the city, no looting or violence took place. All correspondence and public proclamations from León's men asserted their loyalty to the king and agreed that the uprising's only mission was the destruction of the Company. León and the governor declared an open town council meeting *(cabildo abierto)* to voice complaints over the Company. Ninety-seven attendees showed up for a meeting that normally produced no more than a dozen people. The cabildo's show of solidarity and Governor Castellanos's own captivity persuaded him to declare the expulsion of the Company and all Basques. On the night of May 3, after fifteen days of captivity, the governor disguised himself as a friar and fled to La Guaira. He joined Company employees, many of whom had already retreated from Caracas. Like ruling officials in the Comunero Revolt of 1780–1781 in New Granada, the governor of Venezuela declared all proclamations he had made in Caracas null and void and commenced to wait for reinforcements.[22]

21. For complaints of bread scarcities, see the following in AGI, Caracas: Declaración de Juan Camejo, vecino de Caracas, Caracas, Dec. 14, 1747, 891; Declaración de Francisco Domingo Bejaramo, Caracas, Dec. 15, 1747, 891; Petición de Juan Manuel de Goizueta, Factor de la Compañía Guipuzcoana, Jan. 9, 1748, 891. For León's writings on these subjects, see Carta de Juan Francisco de León to Governor Castellanos, Chacao, Apr. 19, 1749, 937; Extracto de carta del Gobernador de Caracas, n.d., 418; Juan Francisco de León to Domingo Aguirre, Caracas, Nov. 5, 1749, 418; Interrogatorio, n.d., 418; El Cabildo, Justicia, y Regimiento de la Ciudad de Caracas to the King, Caracas, Jan. 14, 1750, 419.

22. On León's entrance into La Candelaria and Caracas, see Petición del abogado José Pablo de Arenas, a nombre del Capt. Leon y demás vecinos y naturales de la provincia, n.d., in Mijares, ed., *Documentos relativos,* 29–30. On León's correspondence, see Ferry, *Colonial Elite,* 148; Morales Padrón, *Rebelión contra la Compañía de Caracas,* 71. In contrast to the standard closed cabildo, the cabildo abierto in Spanish tradition was an open meeting of prominent townspeople called in the event of an emergency. See Richard Graham, *Independence in Latin America: Contrasts and Comparisons,* 3d ed. (Austin, Tex., 2013), 175. On voiding proclamations from the Comunero Revolt, see David F. Marley, *Wars of the Ameri-*

Castellanos's flight changed the dynamics of the uprising. No longer could it simply be classified as a protest, for León's men had run a crown-appointed official out of the capital and into hiding. From this point onward, León and his men evinced a more anxious and defensive tone. They shifted blame onto the governor for running away and leaving the province vulnerable to slave revolts and other tumults. They also attempted to legitimize their protests and petitions with the help of notaries public and asked colonial officials to bring them legal counsel.[23]

Though they continued to petition for an end to the Company and its abuses, the insurgents sensed the strategic urgency of the moment. They blockaded the road to La Guaira to starve Company partisans of inland supplies and fought several skirmishes in late July 1749 with Company troops between the two cities. León's supporters now held Caracas with a force estimated to be between four and seven thousand men. The arrival of new interim governor Julián de Arriaga, 300,000 pesos of Mexican silver, and reinforcements in November 1749 altered negotiations. Arriaga was more conciliatory than Castellanos. He conceded to the rebels that the king would reevaluate the Caracas Company and fix the worst of its abuses. Shortly after assuming command, Arriaga marched to Caracas and met with León. By this juncture, the rebel leader's forces had become fearful of the consequences of being labeled traitors. In December 1749, they were more than willing to take the pardon extended to them by Arriaga, as long as the Company's demise seemed assured.[24]

---

*cas: A Chronology of Armed Conflict in the Western Hemisphere, 1492 to the Present,* II (Santa Barbara, Calif., 2008), 527.

23. León's relationship with slavery was a complicated one. He was a slave owner but also incorporated slaves and free people of color into his rebellion. Although he did not remark upon it, León most likely separated slave-led uprisings from revolts that contained slaves among their numbers. In the case above, he invoked slave revolt as a rhetorical specter meant to demonstrate to higher authorities the instability produced by the governor's irresponsible flight from the city. See Juan Francisco de León to Governor and Captain General Castellanos, Caracas, n.d., AGNV, León, I, fol. 4, in Mijares, ed., *Documentos relativos,* 39.

24. Auto de Gregorio del Portillo, Escribano Público, Caracas, Aug. 1, 1749, Auto del Teniente General Domingo de Aguirre y Castillo, Caracas, Aug. 2, 1749, in Chitty, ed., *Juan Francisco de León: Diario,* 115–116; Ferry, *Colonial Elite,* 152. There is little discussion in primary sources as to how the rebellion expanded from the original force in Panaquire to the figure of four to seven thousand supporters. It is difficult to say with certainty whether these accounts of crowds contained intentional hyperbole meant to dramatize the circumstances or were, in fact, accurate representations. On Arriaga's arrival and subsequent actions, see Alejandro Cardozo Uzcátegui, *Los mantuanos en la Corte española: Una relación cisatlántica (1783–1825)* (Bilbao, 2013), 150; Domingo de Aguirre y Castillo to Don Julian de

In the second phase of the rebellion, a year and five months of tense peace settled over Caracas. León's army disbanded and went home. Governor Arriaga still worried about their potential return. His term ended in May 1751 with the appointment of his successor, Phelipe Ricardos—the Company's choice to replace Arriaga. He took command and immediately began to execute orders to capture Juan Francisco de León and his accomplices and reestablish the Company. Despite more favorable trade provisions for colonists, the Company's return in any form was intolerable for León and his closest supporters.[25]

The third phase of the rebellion saw the destruction of the peace. León, incensed by the reestablishment of the Company, marched toward Caracas again in August 1751. The province was abuzz with rumors of thousands of León partisans rising up in various cacao-producing districts. This new revolt lacked the crucial support of the elite, however, who had come dangerously close to being branded traitors during the first phase of León's rebellion. With much more grave potential consequences for insurgents this time around and more for them to lose, many elites refused to back an uprising that did not seem assured to succeed. This fact, combined with the troops assembled by Ricardos, frustrated León's plans of a second trip to Caracas. León's men ran into forces sent by the governor to apprehend him and fought a skirmish in the small, outlying town of Caucagua. In the process, they wounded a royal officer. The incident represented the turning point in the uprising. The insurgents now had drawn blood and could no longer sustain their claims of a peaceful protest movement. During the skirmish, the governor's troops nearly surrounded León's party. After escaping, León's men, who feared the governor's substantial forces, began to desert in large numbers. León himself escaped capture by catching passage aboard a Dutch ship that transported him eastward down the Venezuelan coast.[26]

Retreat marked the fourth stage of the León Rebellion. The Leonistas began to resemble a group of hunted men more than an army. On September

---

Arriaga, Dec. 5, 1749, AGI, Caracas, 418; Fray Don Julian de Arriaga to Sr. Marques de la Ensenada, Caracas, Jan. 14, 1750, AGI, Caracas, 419; Nuñez, *Miranda / Juan Francisco de León,* 85; Hussey, *Caracas Company,* 133.

25. Cardozo Uzcátegui, *Los mantuanos,* 225; Testimonio de Bernardo Curbelo, vecino de Victoria, July 1, 1751, AGI, Caracas, 420.

26. For rumors of the rebel numbers, see Juan Rossel to Governor Phelipe Ricardos, June 27, 1751, and Antonio Baez to Governor Don Phelipe Ricardos, Maracay, June 29, 1751, AGNV, León, I, fols. 132, 135–136, in Mijares, ed., *Documentos relativos,* 80–81. For reports on the end of elite support for the rebellion, see Fray Don Julian de Arriaga y Olivera to Marques de la Ensenada, Dec. 7, 1751, AGI, Caracas, 421; Auto de Domingo de Aguirre, Caracas, Oct. 9, 1749, in Chitty, ed., *Juan Francisco de León: Diario,* 147–150.

13, 1751, the governor published a decree offering a reward for the capture of León and his men. The governor's forces pursued the fugitives for more than four months. Finally, in January 1752, León—hungry, beaten down, and tired of running—turned himself in along with his sons and several of his supporters. Authorities apprehended other rebels later. The weary leader wrote in a final letter to Governor Ricardos that the deck had been stacked against him by a government run by Basques who "declared me culpable and . . . pursued me. They have dishonored me and taken my livelihood as well as that of my sons, my wife, and the rest of the poor in this Valley of Panaquire."[27]

The aftermath of León's rebellion produced tremendous upheaval for both its participants and the province as a whole. Company ships carried León and his sons in chains to Spain. León died of disease in prison shortly after his arrival in Cádiz. His sons served lengthy terms in the presidios of Spanish North Africa. Spanish judges exiled twenty-eight other confidants of León and condemned them to forced labor. These ardent followers were sent to Spain, North Africa, Havana, Veracruz, and the Canary Islands, confirming the perceived need to separate and isolate the dangerous instigators of unrest. Authorities also executed more than ten Leonistas.[28]

In addition to dispensing justice, colonial officials sought to make an example of León through heavily symbolic gestures. During the last days of the rebellion, the governor's forces left the head of one executed rebel on the doorstep of León's Panaquire home and another on the royal road entering the city. Royal officials tore down León's city house in La Candelaria, salted the earth so that nothing would grow on the land, forbade the utterance of his name, and placed a plaque on the site declaring his infamy as a traitor to the king. The colonial government simultaneously attempted to emphasize León's villainy and to blot out his existence. The contradiction in this approach revealed profound anxieties concerning the influence of smuggling in peripheral unrest.[29]

27. Auto de Don Phelipe Ricardos, Caracas, Sept. 13, 1751, AGNV, León, I, fols. 387–388, in Mijares, ed., *Documentos relativos,* 116. "Declared me culpable": Juan Francisco de León to Governor Don Phelipe Ricardos, Dec. 16, 1751, AGI, Caracas, 421.

28. Noticia de las Personas que se deben embarcar en los navios, el Pablo Galera y la Concordia que están para hazer viaje a España; en el Don Juan Yturraldi, para Veracruz, Caracas, Nov. 14, 1751, AGI, Caracas, 421; Governor Don Phelipe Ricardos to Joseph Banfi, Caracas, Mar. 2, 1752, AGI, Caracas, 421; Nuñez, *Miranda / Juan Francisco de León,* 95–101.

29. Spanish colonial officials would perform a similar ritual of property and memory destruction on the house of Andean rebel Túpac Amaru in 1781. See Don Phelipe Ricardos to Marques de la Ensenada, Caracas, Sept. 11, 1751, AGI, Caracas, 421; Auto de Don Phelipe Ricardos, Caracas, Feb. 5, 1752, AGI, Caracas, 421; Stavig, *World of Túpac Amaru,* 248. The practice of salting the earth of a rebel or traitor's dwelling can be traced back to biblical

Alterations to the colony's defensive capabilities followed the punishment of rebel instigators. The instability produced by continued vitriol and open revolt directed at the Caracas Company convinced colonial bureaucrats of the need for an increased military presence in the province. The Bourbon push for standing armies in Spanish America might have had its origins in the events of 1749–1751 in Caracas rather than the siege of Havana a decade later. Once the dust settled after the uprising, Governor Phelipe Ricardos installed a permanent garrison of troops in Caracas at a cost of 100,000 pesos annually. Authorities paid for this contingent, as well as other projects, by more than doubling the alcabala tax from 2 percent on all goods to 5 percent. No doubt prompted by memories of the chaos of the uprising, successive governors continued to maintain this standing army. Even the audiencia of Caracas, founded in 1786, owed its existence in part to volatile protests against the Caracas Company. The military vulnerabilities of placing the province under the jurisdiction of the distant audiencia of Santo Domingo had proved devastating and justified the creation of a new audiencia in Venezuela.[30]

Furthermore, the León uprising spurred administrative and commercial reforms. There had been few debates in Spain about the León Rebellion while it raged. After its subdual, the king and the Council of the Indies became mindful of the explosive possibilities of provincial hatred for the Caracas Company. In a series of decrees between 1751 and 1753, they mandated that the Company submit to increased imperial oversight to curb abuses and prevent future rebellions. To make the Company's books and practices more transparent to authorities, the crown ordered its headquarters transferred from the Basque city of Pasajes to Madrid in 1751. The king also stipulated that a commission consisting of the governor, a Company factor, and a representative *(regidór)* from the Caracas cabildo set new annual price lists on European goods and cacao. As a result, the price paid to Venezuelan producers for their cacao increased. Other mandatory changes put Venezuelans on the Company's board of directors and allowed them to be stockholders. Finally, the crown quieted

---

times. See R. T. Ridley, "To Be Taken with a Pinch of Salt: The Destruction of Carthage," *Classical Philology,* LXXXI (1986), 140–146.

30. On consequences of the rebellion and higher taxes, see Ferry, *Colonial Elite,* 5–6, 247; Rosario Salazar Bravo, *El comercio diario en la Caracas del siglo XVIII: Una aproximación a la historia urbana* (Caracas, 2008), 198–199. On the maintenance of the standing army, see Sucre, *Gobernadores y capitanes generales de Venezuela,* 277–279. On the creation of the audiencia of Caracas, see Alí Enrique López Bohórquez, *Los ministros de la Audiencia de Caracas (1786–1810): Caracterización de una elite burocrática del poder español en Venezuela* (Caracas, 1984), 38, 63.

the fears of Venezuelan producers and merchants that the Company sought to monopolize Venezuelan cacao shipping to Mexico and cut Venezuelans out of a cost-effective means to transport chocolate to this crucial market. It abrogated the Company's rights to trade cacao with New Spain, ended the alternativa system that had given Company ships the right to load cargoes at Venezuelan docks before private traders, and reserved one-sixth of all Company ships bound for Spain to transport producers' cacao on their own accounts.[31]

Regardless of these new concessions, most Venezuelans continued to resent the Caracas Company. Some elite families dropped their opposition to the Company after they managed to marry into the families of Basque company men to expand their influence in Venezuela and in the Spanish court; Creole-Basque unions no doubt drained elite support from the León rebels during the uprising just as they cooled frustrations after it. Notwithstanding these relationships, other Venezuelans viewed the Company as an intruder that prosecuted colonists and their foreign trading partners for their role in the smuggling economy and still attempted to monopolize all trade. These sentiments remained decades after the León Rebellion. As late as 1778, a Spanish bureaucrat wrote to José de Gálvez, the minister of the Indies, informing him, "The residents of Caracas complain bitterly of the monopoly and extortions of the Company whose unsatisfactory prices would have discouraged the Caraqueños entirely were it not for the recourse of contraband trade, which they find absolutely necessary." Estimates are hard to calculate, but it appears that

31. In the decade that followed the royal decrees, Company factors continued to complain about crown-mandated cacao price lists, particularly for cacao being sold in Spain, and the removal of their headquarters from the Basque Country. These petitions were ineffectual. See D. Martin de Meinege a la Provincia de Guipuzcoana, Azcoytia, Apr. 10, 1757, AGI, Caracas, 930; Real Compañía Guipuzcoana de Caracas: En su Junta particular, Madrid, May 14, 1759, AGI, Caracas, 930. On changes to the Caracas Company, see Real Compañía Guipuzcoana de Caracas, *Real Cedula de Fundacion de la Real Compañia Guipuzcoana de Caracas, y reglas economicas de buen govierno, con que la estableciò la M.N. y M.L. Provincia de Guipuzcoa, en Junta General del año de 1728* (Madrid, 1765), 140–145; Raquel Rico Linage, *Las Reales Compañías de Comercio con América: Los organos de gobierno* (Seville, 1983), 27; Estornés Lasa, *La Real Compañía Guipuzcoana de Navegación,* 22; Hussey, *Caracas Company,* 152; Ramon Aizpurua, *Curazao y la costa de Caracas: Introduccion al estudio del contrabando en la provincia de Venezuela en tiempos de la Compañia Guipuzcoana, 1730–1780* (Caracas, 1993), 180; Morales Padrón, *Rebelión contra la Compañía de Caracas,* 138–139. On anxieties about shipping cacao to Mexico, see Eduardo Arcila Farías, *Economía colonial de Venezuela* (Mexico City, 1946), 190–205; Ferry, *Colonial Elite,* 165, 179–190. To compensate for the loss of its privileges in New Spain, the Caracas Company diversified its geographic reach in and around Venezuela, opening up new warehouses in Maracaibo in 1753 and in Guayana, Cumaná, Margarita, and Trinidad in 1776. See Cardozo Uzcátegui, *Los mantuanos,* 222.

despite the post-León legal trade opportunities presented to Venezuelans by the reformed Caracas Company, contraband trade occurred with greater frequency. With its authority to dictate the terms of trade and harry contraband commerce substantially restrained owing to oversight from Madrid and Caracas, the Compañía Guipuzcoana faced no further revolts. It continued to generate modest profits in Venezuela until its demise in 1784.[32]

It was not revolt but trade liberalization that broke the Company's back. The comercio libre decrees, begun in 1765 and greatly expanded in 1778, signified a monumental shift in imperial commercial thought. For the first time, a range of Spanish American ports and peninsular ports outside of Cádiz and Seville could trade legally with one another without needing to obtain special permission. As noted earlier, comercio libre did not extend to Venezuela; trade liberalization would not come to the province until 1789 owing to the lingering presence of the Caracas Company. In the years leading up to the opening of free trade in Venezuela, Bourbon reformers pilloried the Company as an institution holding Venezuela back from its lucrative agricultural and commercial potential. On the heels of the 1778 comercio libre decrees, the crown retracted the organization's monopoly over Venezuela's cacao trade in 1781. This was the death knell for the Compañía Guipuzcoana.[33]

### IDEOLOGIES OF THE INSURGENTS

The petitions and correspondence of the León rebels demonstrated cohesive moral, commercial, and communal belief structures. These ideologies, which in times of peace might have remained undocumented, found their way onto the page as a result of the chaos that enveloped the province and captured the attention of colonial functionaries. Moreover, León and some of his forces were literate and used the nearly three-year duration of the rebellion to express, in many cases through their own words, what their protest meant to

32. On Creole-Basque unions, see Cardozo Uzcátegui, *Los mantuanos,* 170. "Complain bitterly of the monopoly": Informe de Agustín Moreno Enríquez, remitido al Ministro de Indias, José de Gálvez, Amsterdam, Feb. 11, 1778, rpt. in Aizpurua, *Curazao y la costa de Caracas,* 391. On legal trade after the rebellion, see Joseph Luis de Cisneros, *Descripción exacta de la provincia de Venezuela* ([1764]; rpt. Caracas, 1981), 131–164; Arcila Farías, *Economía colonial de Venezuela,* 259; Gerardo Vivas Pineda, *La aventura naval de la Compañía Guipuzcoana de Caracas* (Caracas, 1998), 212. Luis González F. estimates that 20,000 fanegas of cacao left Venezuela illegally in 1761 (González F., *La Guayra conquista y colonia* [Caracas, 1982], 118).

33. Arcila Farias, *Economía colonial de Venezuela,* 349–350; Aizpurua, *Curazao y la costa de Caracas,* 172.

them. Their writings and actions showcased at least four political ideologies. These ideologies testify to the complexity of the revolt and further reveal the transformative impact that contraband trade had on Venezuela.[34]

First, the abundance of smuggling in Venezuela produced a distinctive brand of economic thought that was both reactionary and forward thinking. Subjects' petitions both before and during the rebellion called for a return to the days of limited metropolitan commercial involvement in the region, before the "despotism and absolute dominance" of the Company took hold. Despite an appalling lack of legal trade in the late seventeenth and early eighteenth centuries, few subjects complained of the way things had been before the rise of the Basque venture. Rather, a 1750 Caracas cabildo petition called for the return of register ships as the only trade from Spain. It was the unstated assumption of the cabildo's request that the reappearance of this system, without a dramatic increase in the quantity of register ships, would lead to an economy dependent on smuggling.[35]

At the same time that illicit trade's hold on the province produced intransigence toward change, it also, paradoxically, prefigured the liberalization of trade to come in most of the Caribbean. Juan Francisco de León's own designs for an ideal trade system harbored many of the principles of free trade. He believed that Venezuelan-produced cacao should find its way to market by the most expedient means. In return, goods should come to Venezuela from many separate places but with no obligation for Venezuelans to buy any of them. Other colonists spoke of the benefits of a plurality of merchants in commercial matters. These tendencies toward unrestricted commerce were not lost on the governor of Venezuela, who noted that "untold numbers of Canary Islanders are vendors and petty merchants. They are, in my eyes, the contrabandists of the coast and it is liberty that they love. As the majority of them are not married, nor in possession of haciendas, they foment revolt with little risk." From the standpoint of provincial authorities seeking to contain Venezuela within a preordained company system, all overtures toward commercial flexibility smacked of a pro-smuggling agenda.[36]

34. See William B. Taylor's work on peasant unrest in colonial Mexican villages (Taylor, *Drinking, Homicide, and Rebellion in Colonial Mexican Villages* [Stanford, Calif., 1979], 9).

35. "Despotism and absolute dominance": El Cabildo, Justicia, y Regimiento de la Ciudad de Caracas al Rey, Caracas, Jan. 14, 1750, AGI, Caracas, 419. On the return of register ships, see also Extrato de las quejas que ha havido de Caracas de el establecimiento de la Comp. Guipuzcoana sobre perjuicios que esta causa a aquellos naturales y vecinos de las resoluziones tomadas por el Rey, Madrid, Sept. 2, 1749, AGI, Caracas, 419.

36. Representación de León, n.d., AGNV, León, I, fols. 119–126, in Mijares, ed., *Documen-*

It is worth noting that, although Venezuelans' commercial modus operandi involved trade with foreigners, they maintained fidelity to the monarchy and the conventions of the Spanish legal system. The rebels did not see their protest as treasonous. Like the Quito, Túpac Amaru, and Comunero rebels to come, the León insurgents appealed to an earlier governing pact that legitimized limited self-government and the right to rise up when entities (except the monarch) challenged community rights. For Spanish Americans, Bourbon policies threatened the transformation of overseas possessions from equal kingdoms in a monarchy into the more pejorative status of colonies in an empire. The Caracas Company's burdensome presence in the province was all the more onerous because the organization existed outside the legitimacy of the monarchical pact. Cutting out this cancer would reaffirm Venezuelans' proper role in the Hispanic world to which they felt affinity. Hence rebels, in the very act of surrounding the governor's palace, pledged that for the king "we sacrifice and will continue to sacrifice our throats."[37]

The insurgents obsessed over the notarization and legal representation of their nearly bloodless uprising. They called together juntas of Caracas's most elite subjects to confirm the legitimacy of their protests. Juan Francisco de León even sent one of his lieutenants, Miguel de Fuentes y Abreu, on a voyage to Spain to deliver petitions directly to the king. Unfortunately, the governor of Cuba seized Fuentes y Abreu's papers, which proclaimed the loyalty of the supposed insurrectionists to the crown, and prevented them from reaching Madrid. Though they shouldered weapons, the insurgents clearly believed that their actions differed little from sending a complaint letter to the king. Juridical maneuvers and popular uprisings were not mutually exclusive.[38]

---

*tos relativos,* 72–74; Extrato de las quejas que ha havido de Caracas de el establecimiento de la Comp. Guipuzcoana, AGI, Caracas, 419. "Foment revolt with little risk": Arriaga to Sr. Don Joseph Banffi, Caracas, Feb. 25, 1750, AGI, Caracas, 418.

37. For popular appeals of this nature in other eighteenth-century South American rebellions, see Thomson, *We Alone Will Rule,* 12; Phelan, *People and the King,* xviii; McFarlane, "Rebellions in Late Colonial Spanish America," *BLAR,* XIV (1995), 319, 323, 330. Elliott refers to this pact between ruler and subjects in a monarchy and the recourse of rebellion when it was not respected as "contractualism." He identifies contractualism as a defining characteristic in both Spanish and British American uprisings in the eighteenth and nineteenth centuries (*Empires of the Atlantic World,* 349–350). "Sacrifice . . . our throats": Copias de Cartas de Juan Francisco de León al Sr. Gefe de Esquadra, Sr. Fray Julian de Arriaga, Nov. 29, 1749, AGI, Caracas, 418.

38. Junta, Caracas, Apr. 22, 1749, AGI, Caracas, 937; Francisco Caxigal de la Vega, Governor of Cuba, to Sr. Marques de la Ensenada, Havana, July 23, 1749, AGI, Caracas, 423, 937. This act of petitioning the king or royal officials in the wake of uprisings was also a part of the

Second, the León rebels rationalized the decision to take up arms by claiming that they were bound by conscience to protect the province's moral economy. E. P. Thompson notes, "It is possible to detect in almost every eighteenth-century crowd action some legitimizing notion." What made justifying the León Rebellion so difficult was that the basis of its justification was a customary yet illegitimate practice. Petitions to royal officials or the king could not directly advocate unrestricted commerce with foreigners, which would brand the petitioners as lawbreakers. Yet León's insurgents, both before and during the rebellion, spoke of smuggling as a necessary means of sustenance for the impoverished. Descriptions of the province emphasized its residents as desperate. The Caracas cabildo pleaded for the delivery of "the most moderate and limited clothing and necessary and indispensable foodstuffs like bread, wine, and olive oil." Before the uprising, León noted that prices for cacao had dropped so low that some Isleños were selling off their devalued haciendas to the Company at fire sale prices. Such accounts displayed a powerful sentiment that the Company's stranglehold on licit and illicit trade had transgressed commonly agreed-upon thresholds of economic justice. Though he viewed the uprising with horror, interim governor Julián de Arriaga seconded León's views on the detrimental consequences of low cacao prices. The magistrate asked Company merchants whether ruined hacendados could now afford even "a hat for themselves or a shirt for their sons." One parish priest explained the rebellion through scripture: the Israelites asked for relief from oppressive taxes imposed by Solomon's son Rehoboam and rebelled when their demands were not met. "The people ask for justice," wrote the priest. "Allowing oppression to breathe will incline them to rebellion." Abrogation of a commercial sense of fairness justified smuggling and popular protest and challenged the perceived immorality of both offenses.[39]

---

San Felipe uprising, whose participants attempted to send appeals to the viceroy in Bogotá in 1741. See Trujillo, *Motín y sublevación,* 84. On South American rebellions and juridical strategies more broadly, see Stavig, *World of Túpac Amaru,* xxvi; Serulnikov, *Subverting Colonial Authority,* 138.

39. "Some legitimizing notion": Thompson, "Moral Economy of the English Crowd," *Past and Present,* L (1971), 78. In the eighteenth-century Atlantic world, it was not uncommon for subjects to rebel against governments to support smuggling while never explicitly stating as much. Shannon Lee Dawdy argues that the 1768 revolt of French and German settlers against the recently installed Spanish government in New Orleans had more to do with protecting illicit interimperial trade against Spanish mercantilist policies than the stated complaints of the rebels that Spanish rule would bring economic ruin (Dawdy, *Building the Devil's Empire: French Colonial New Orleans* [Chicago, 2008], 130). For León's views, see Interrogatorio de Juan Francisco de León, n.d., AGI, Caracas, 418. "Necessary

The study of smuggling points to a more capacious definition of the moral economy. In the case of eighteenth-century coastal Venezuela, rather than seeking governmental support to regulate the market, protestors promoted the return of the deregulated exchange they had long used to maintain themselves. Certainly they wished to end the mutually profitable relationship between the Spanish crown and the Caracas Company, founded on the latter's exclusivist privileges. But they also wanted to preserve a status quo of imperial neglect that would allow them access to efficient commercial relationships with a range of foreigners. The León partisans were not hidebound to local exchange. Rather, they resorted to the moral economy in order to justify trans-imperial trade.[40]

Evidence of rebel dependence on Dutch trade demonstrates a third ideological strain: that of commercial autonomy. Anxieties about the participation of Dutch forces from Curaçao peppered royal correspondence on the León Rebellion. Dutch ships ferried arms, supplies, and food to the rebels via the Tuy River in exchange for cacao. They assaulted Caracas Company ships and broke up blockades at the mouth of the river. In 1751, during the height of the manhunt for Juan Francisco de León, Dutch and English smugglers routed and captured several Spanish coast guard patrols closing in on León. Like the rebel chief Andresote before him, León escaped to safety aboard a Dutch vessel. Venezuelan governors and Company officials alike blamed the Dutch

---

and indispensable foodstuffs": Acta de la Asamblea que celebraron los Notables de Caracas en la Sala del Ayuntamiento, Apr. 22, 1749, AGNV, León, I, fols. 19–29, in Mijares, ed., *Documentos relativos,* 32–33. "A hat for themselves": Don Julian de Arriaga y Rivera to Don Juan Manuel de Goyzueta and Don Mathiais Urroz, factors of the Compañía Guipuzcoana, Caracas, Mar. 29, 1750, AGI, Caracas, 418. "The people ask for justice": Doctor Don Manuel de Sossa y Betancurt to Governor Castellanos, Caracas, July 25, 1749, in Chitty, ed., *Juan Francisco de León: Diario, 1749,* 96–97. This sense of smuggling as a means of achieving economic justice and basic needs was not unique to Venezuela. Sherry Johnson contends that mid-eighteenth-century Cubans participated in illicit commerce during periods of domestic tranquillity, but especially after catastrophic events such as hurricanes. See Johnson, *Climate and Catastrophe in Cuba and the Atlantic World in the Age of Revolution* (Chapel Hill, N.C., 2011), 195.

40. Adrian Randall and Andrew Charlesworth describe the need for a wider understanding of the moral economy. To do this, "Edward Thompson's methodology of placing accounts of protest in a context of 'thick description' needs to be taken forwards towards attempting a 'total history' of riotous, and non-riotous, communities, a history which will take account of the changing social, economic and political context from which protest emanated and of the rich variety of forms which protest took" (Randall and Charlesworth, "The Moral Economy: Riot, Markets, and Social Conflict," in Randall and Charlesworth, eds., *Moral Economy and Popular Protest: Crowds, Conflict, and Authority* (New York, 2000), 12–13.

for agitating the rebellion and sent spies to Bonaire and Curaçao to gather intelligence. Their worries were not misplaced. Imperial regulators realized the implication of Venezuelan smugglers-cum-rebels contracting with the Dutch for trade in peacetime and for firepower in wartime. The insurgents' reliance on their non-Spanish Caribbean neighbors in moments of upheaval as arms dealers and naval muscle demonstrates the close, symbiotic relationship that Venezuelan coastal inhabitants shared with foreign traders and their independence from legally sanctioned modes of trade. By the time of the León Rebellion, Dutch trade had supplanted Spanish mercantile networks for many Venezuelan traders and producers. Spanish attempts to rein in this commercial self-rule risked betraying coastal subjects' faith in Spanish political legitimacy, which rested on benign neglect of unlicensed trade to compensate for a scarcity of legal trade goods.[41]

Fourth, the León Rebellion highlights smuggling's importance in the gradual evolution of a place-bound creole identity. As Venezuelan subjects began openly to protest the Caracas Company's involvement, the accompanying unrest forced them to define more clearly who they were and what they stood for. They identified the Company and Basques as outsiders to their community. Isleños countered characterizations of themselves as petty criminals by demonizing the Basques. Public pronouncements and correspondence of the León rebels spoke of the Basques as a generally immoral, arrogant, and violent lot. It should be noted that the protestors did not use Basques as generic stand-ins for peninsular Spaniards in León's time. Nor did they detail some deeper history of Basque-Isleño rivalry transplanted from Europe. Instead, the testimonies of León's followers were quite specific to the time and place of their grievances against Caracas Company employees and their associates. Accounts outlined crimes committed by Basques and their dependents against Venezuelans, including the rape of women, the poisoning of Venezuelan sailors working aboard Company ships with rotten food, and the torture of prisoners. León went so far as to place blame for the 1730 rebellion of Andresote squarely on the shoulders of the Basques. According to him, the uprising was in part revenge for an incident in which a group of Vizcayans broke into Andresote's house, beat him, tied him up, and then raped his wife and daughter. "Long live

41. On Dutch interference, see Governor Don Phelipe Ricardos to the Marques de la Ensenada, Caracas, Sept. 11, 1751, AGI, Caracas, 421; Declaracion de Don Liendo Manuel de Agreda, Caracas, Sept. 3, 1751, AGI, Caracas, 420; Testimonio de Phelipe Niman, residente de Capaya, Aug. 24, 1751, AGNV, León, I, fol. 368–369, in Mijares, ed., *Documentos relativos,* 107; Iturriaga, *Manifiesto,* 2 f. On León's escape, see Morales Padrón, *Rebelión contra la Compañía de Caracas,* 114.

the king and death to the *Viscainos*" became a frequent refrain of the León insurgents. What started as Isleño rhetoric morphed into a provincewide critique of imperial economic imposition.[42]

The interethnic pejoratives of Isleño protests were a part of defining belonging in Venezuela. They exposed the fault lines in white ethnogenesis in the province. European ethnogenesis in the Americas evolved from the exclusion of Africans and indigenous peoples, but also from durable ethnic associations from the Old World that complicated the formation of creolized whiteness. Basque-Isleño rivalry in coastal Venezuela challenged the coherence of a white, pan-Spanish consciousness. Both Basques and Canary Islanders engaged in stereotyping and ethnocentrism designed to define their rivals as morally deficient, unworthy subjects. According to the discourse of contemporary documents, Basques were duplicitous and self-serving mercantile enforcers, whereas Canary Islanders were disloyal smugglers. Ethnicity in this context evolved from a shorthand for geographic origins into a descriptor of occupational identity, lawfulness, and legitimacy. The León rebels, whose core constituency was Isleños, used all of these categories to demarcate the Company and its Basque retinue as interlopers. The insurgents blamed their commercial improprieties on the poverty produced by Basque impositions. In doing so, they simultaneously reiterated their connection to Venezuelan soil and to rightful subjecthood.[43]

By attempting to expel the outsiders and reaffirming Isleño identity, the revolt's participants gained a clearer sense of communal self. As in the Andean rebellions of Túpac Amaru, Túpac Katari, and Tomás Katari, what began as a revolt over local and ethnic grievances struck a chord with the greater province

42. On blame for the Andresote Rebellion, see Interrogatorio, n.d., AGI, Caracas, 418; Juan Francisco de León to the Governor and Captain General Don Phelipe Ricardos, Dec. 16, 1751, AGI, Caracas, 421. "Long live king and death to the *Viscainos*": Certificacion de Manuel de Salas, Thesorero y Lorenzo Rosel de Lugo, Contador de la Real Hacienda, Caracas, Apr. 22, 1749, AGI, Caracas, 937. This rallying cry trod on the well-worn turf of "Long live the king and death to bad government" slogans of the past.

43. James Sidbury and Jorge Cañizares-Esguerra advocate for contextual readings of identity formation and caution against rigid theorizations of creolization that depend on imperial designations. In Spanish America, they note a "precocious pan-Spanish ethnicity" that "surfaced much earlier in Spanish America than in Spain." Basque-Isleño tension in the context of the León Rebellion indicates an awareness of Spanish-ness rooted in proper subjecthood, but also the desire to exclude other Europeans from that subjecthood (Sidbury and Cañizares-Esguerra, "Mapping Ethnogenesis in the Early Modern Atlantic," *WMQ*, 3d Ser., LXVIII [2011], 203; see also 199–203).

and grew into a broad insurgency.[44] Nicolás León, Juan Francisco's son, wrote, "We are obliged to defend our homeland *(nuestra patria)* because if we do not, we will be made the slaves of all others." Rhetorically, the rebels freely employed the term "patria" to denote shared rights and privileges (among them commercial liberties) that had to be defended. We must resist the teleological urge to completely equate their use of this word with the protonationalism that it would come to represent during the independence period. Many separate developments over the next sixty years would influence Venezuelan identity irrespective of smuggling or the León Rebellion. Imperial loyalty was not a totalizing consciousness. It could be a buffet from which some elements of an imperial platform were chosen and others rejected. León's rebellion, the largest popular protest in Venezuela before the independence period, nurtured a creole identity that upheld commercial liberty from the metropole even as it held fast to loose Spanish imperial loyalties.[45]

## CONCLUSION

The uprising of Juan Francisco de León, though short in duration and largely nonviolent, cast a long shadow over Venezuelan commercial and political affairs. Although labeling the event itself a failed independence movement or even a precursor to the independence struggle overstates its place in Vene-

44. William Taylor has demonstrated the importance of outsiders as enemies within tight-knit communities. Resisting the outside world provided rural villages with a common sense of identity from which rebellion sprung (Taylor, *Drinking, Homicide, and Rebellion,* 153). I extend Taylor's argument to encompass not just individual villages but entire coastal regions of the province of Venezuela. Joseph Pérez's work compares the León rebels to the Comuneros of Paraguay and finds that both chose to represent themselves as place-bound corporate entities as a result of their opposition to those who would constrict their economic opportunities (Pérez, *Los movimientos precursores,* 41–44). For comparisons to the Amaru and Katari rebellions, see Charles F. Walker, *The Tupac Amaru Rebellion* (Cambridge, Mass., 2014), 38–39, 61–64; Stavig, *World of Túpac Amaru,* xxvi; Serulnikov, *Subverting Colonial Authority,* 3–4.

45. "Obliged to defend our homeland": Nicolás León to Sr. Capitan Don Santiago, Caucagua, Aug. 17, 1751, AGNV, León, I, fol. 188, in Mijares, ed., *Documentos relativos,* 88; Nuñez, *Miranda / Juan Francisco de León,* 62. Commenting on Nicolás León's statement, John Lynch asserts that "*Patria,* of course, did not mean nation, but it may have indicated a sense of regional identity, an awareness of Venezuelan interests and a belief that local communities had a right of protest against abuse of power by the Spanish authorities and their colonial officials" (Lynch, "Spanish America's Poor Whites," in Lynch, *Latin America between Colony and Nation,* 64).

zuelan history, the rebellion did represent the distillation of major tensions in the province. Smuggling informed creole constructions of moral economy, independent trade, and autonomous local identity that inspired Venezuelan subjects to rise up against the Compañía Guipuzcoana and the royal government. These salient issues continued to loom on the political horizon as Spanish America came closer to independence.

The Caracas Company faced no more challenges to its rule from armed masses after the revolt ended in 1752, but continued grievances over the monopoly lurked just beneath the surface. In 1780, José de Ábalos, the first intendant of Venezuela, summarized the anxiety produced by the Company's continued disturbance of creole economic aims and subsistence practices.

> The name of the King, of his ministers and of all Spaniards is heard by the leaders of this country with the greatest disgust, aversion and dislike simply on account of the Company, which seems to them to be the original sin which gives rise to their wrongs. And truly this error seems at times excusable; in a sense it is true that they suffer a kind of slavery, enjoying no benefit from the operations of the Company, and oppressed by the necessity to put through its miserly hands those few products which they are able to cultivate, after seeing lifeless and buried the multitude of other products which ought to flourish in the province to the great gain of the Royal Treasury, the outstanding good of the State and the immense profit of both continents. The woeful and rancorous tone of their laments increases daily, and unless His Majesty grants them the open trade for which they sigh he can no longer count on the fidelity of these vassals, since they will lend their ears and hearts to any hint and help offered them by the Crown's enemies, and it will be impossible or very difficult to cure this ill. This is not an empty prophecy, but the forecast of one who knows the country well.

Ábalos argued for the destruction of the Company until its demise in 1784. The intendant understood that unrestricted trade and autonomous commercial connections had become central to the moral economy of coastal dwellers. Attempts to restrict these features of community life in the province served more to irritate the populace than to correct its behavior.[46]

One final anecdote about the León Rebellion underscores the intercon-

46. "The name of the King": José de Ábalos to José de Gálvez, Sept. 27, 1780, AGNV, Intendencia, IX, fols. 109–119, quoted in Guillermo Morón, *A History of Venezuela,* trans. John Street (New York, 1963), 85.

nectedness of Venezuelan society, smuggling, and political protest in the Bourbon period of Spanish rule. As mentioned earlier, one of the punitive rituals of crushing León's uprising involved tearing down his house and erecting a plaque on the site to mark his treachery. Almost sixty years later, on September 20, 1811, two articles ran in the *Gaceta de Caracas* detailing a request from the director of public works for the province to remove the plaque. One of these articles, written only two months after Venezuela's congress had declared independence from Spain, noted that the plaque had been erected many years before

> to unjustly stain the memory of Juan Francisco de León. He led those valiant men that tried to throw off the heavy mercantile yoke from which the avarice and despotism of the Spanish kings monopolized the commerce of these provinces. This they did by way of the unscrupulous Compañía Guipuzcoana, under whose exclusive privileges Venezuelans groaned for more than forty years.

Despite the passing of more than a half century, León's rebellion and its significance remained fresh in Venezuelan popular memory.[47]

47. "Unjustly stain the memory of Juan Francisco de León": "Decreto," "Demonstración Patriotica," Sept. 20, Oct. 15, 1811, in *Gaceta de Caracas,* III (Caracas, 1983).

# CONCLUSION

## *Altered States*

Do the foreigners introduce their goods into all these seaports and entrances to the kingdom? It is true and well known that they do this along the whole coast and kingdom, not only among private subjects of all types, but also among those entrusted with royal positions and honors. Why is such disorder not restrained? Why does no one try to impede such pernicious importation and commerce? They try. All the viceroys and governors arrive with strictest orders from the court to be vigilant against illicit commerce and to put an end to it. But even those who govern with true zeal, and without an eye to their own interests or what they can take with their hands, find neither good wishes nor happy results from the measures they take.

ANTONIO JULIÁN, *La perla de la America, provincia de Santa Marta, reconocida, observada y expuesta en discursos historicos* (1787)

The words of Jesuit priest Antonio Julián reveal just how interconnected (illicit) trade, government, and the behavior of subjects were in the eighteenth-century Caribbean. The most telling part of Julián's passage, aside from its acknowledgment of the ubiquity of contraband commerce, is its rhetorical pessimism in assessing what could be done about this "pernicious" problem. Julián implies that a governmental official intent on defending the crown's commercial prerogatives would meet a chilly response from subjects in the Americas. That "neither good wishes nor happy results" would accompany a well-meaning administrator's attempts to enforce the law pointed darkly to how disentangled Spanish America's populace had become from the bedrock commercial policies of the empire. The prevalence of an alternate economic and social world of illicit trade, though not a new development, troubled eighteenth-century Spanish imperial reformers who sought to rebuild a sense of political sovereignty and financial control over Spain's overseas territories.

Nonconforming patterns of economic activity in the early modern Atlantic, such as smuggling, force us to reevaluate our perceptions regarding the practices, societal ties, and belief structures of traders and their associates. The influence of commercial actors on the communities where they operated stretched well beyond the realm of the market. The manner in which merchants conducted business, along with how governments regulated their actions, determined commercial and material conditions for everyday subjects. Merchants' and consumers' interactions with the international black market also had the power to alter legal standings, consumption practices, social networks, and political agreements. Smuggling is not unique among early modern economic activities in its ability to evoke the broader societal impacts of human labor and exchange. Rather, its criminality produced a revealing yet ambiguous corpus of records that speak to the paradox of commonplace actions in legally punitive contexts.[1]

Foreign and domestic smugglers circulating around Venezuela used Atlantic and, more specifically, circum-Caribbean markets to satisfy tangible and immediate needs that their empires of origin failed to fulfill. Trade-starved Venezuelans yearned for the sustenance and comfort that European-manufactured food and clothes provided. Merchants from many nations hoped to make a profit by discreetly siphoning lucrative cacao from the Venezuelan coast. Rootless maritime workers (and sometimes the enslaved) conceived of smuggling as a preferable occupation to working on plantations and in the navies of the Caribbean.

Additionally, participants in contraband trade utilized Atlantic sites of exchange to accomplish more complex economic and political objectives. In the seemingly trivial details of covert trading, we see more than just how transactions occurred. Rituals of evasion and the legal proceedings against contra-

1. As an example of this thinking, Bernard Bailyn explains, "Of [the Atlantic] economy much is known, in terms of the magnitudes and chronology of the flow of goods, the size of markets and productive capacities. But one wants to know more, not so much of statistical aggregates as of the shaping circumstances, inner processes, and patterns of entrepreneurship that developed in response to the opportunities that appeared" (Bailyn, "Introduction: Reflections on Some Major Themes," in Bailyn and Patricia L. Denault, eds., *Soundings in Atlantic History: Latent Structures and Intellectual Currents, 1500–1830* [Cambridge, Mass., 2009], 10).

bandists elucidate what subjects hoped to gain through criminality. Both Spanish and non-Spanish subjects gained some measure of commercial self-determination apart from their empires. Particularly for Venezuelans marginalized by the Caracas Company, smuggling eased the burdens of economic subordination, and the foreign contact it provided helped sustain defiance of Company rule. On the other side of the equation, Spanish imperial administrators and political economists struggled to quell the most corrosive effects of illicit commerce on Spanish finances and sovereignty while brainstorming palatable incentives to legal trade. Stuck in the middle of these concerns, officials on the ground in Spanish America relied on smuggling to pacify subjects, to sustain valuable merchant communities, and to line their own pockets through willful disregard of commercial law.[2]

Records of smuggling allow historians to see how people from all walks of life concretely connected to the Atlantic world. When used without care, "Atlantic world" can be a nebulous term that disregards specific historical contexts and circumstances in pursuit of transnational and transcultural commonalities. The history of contraband trade goes against narratives of effortless connection, for there was struggle and violence in projects of commercial integration. Borders and deception figured into interimperial relations just as much as cultural exchange and trust did. In smuggling, we see how subjects of different empires interacted, how Atlantic connections worked, and how empires sought to break up or co-opt these linkages.[3]

The paths of smugglers provide an appraisal of how little imperial understandings of entangled spaces influenced the interactions of mobile subjects outside the courtroom. One measure of foreign penetration into Venezuelan commerce was the familiarity between outsiders and Spanish subjects. Dutch smugglers knew the contours of the Venezuelan coast as if it were their own dominion and counted Venezuelan coastal inhabitants among their most habitual business associates. Both groups desired freedom of movement, association, and safe passage.[4]

2. Writing about the trade policy of the British and Spanish Empires, J. H. Elliott observes that both powers held "the same set of assumptions about the proper relationship of overseas settlements to the mother country. This was to be a relationship in which the interests of the settlements were ruthlessly subordinated to those of an imperial metropolis bent on identifying and developing in its transatlantic possessions those economic assets that most nearly complemented its needs" (Elliott, *Empires of the Atlantic World: Britain and Spain in America, 1492–1830* [New Haven, Conn., 2006], 114).

3. Pierre Gervais, "Neither Imperial, nor Atlantic: A Merchant Perspective on International Trade in the Eighteenth Century," *HEI*, XXXIV (2008), 468–469.

4. Eliga H. Gould has argued that, at least as far as British and Spanish imperial inter-

The battle between Spanish commercial enforcement officials and smugglers over the traversing of artificial borders highlights the plebeian cosmopolitanism produced by black market trade. Despite obstructions, it is remarkable that participants in covert commerce were so successful as transimperial brokers and sociocommercial integrators for the neglected communities in which they traded. They crossed legal jurisdictions and entered into risky business relationships at times of dangerous warfare and chaos in the Caribbean. Subjects of multiple empires ended up in places they should not have been, according to the logic of political maps. Through commerce, Sephardic Jews renewed family connections across separate linguistic and cultural zones. Enslaved and free people of color passed through multiple slave societies as illicit traders or as contraband cargo themselves. The Spanish penal system shipped condemned foreign smugglers all over the empire to work as laborers or soldiers. By contrast to gentlemen adventurers and intellectuals associated with early modern cosmopolitanism, smugglers in the seas around Venezuela came from much less elite backgrounds and sometimes crossed imperial boundaries against their will.[5]

Spanish imperial administrators and even Spanish American judges had

---

action was concerned, many of the coastal spaces of the Caribbean basin and North America can be viewed as "entangled worlds" owing to the mutually influencing presence of both empires (Gould, "Entangled Histories, Entangled Worlds: The English-Speaking Atlantic as a Spanish Periphery," *AHR,* CXII [2007], 764–786). Gould's concept is particularly enlightening for places where smuggling and other forms of unsanctioned interimperial exchange occurred. Unlike borderlands studies, it does not mandate overlapping imperial claims to a territory as a precondition. Following this definition, the majority of settlements in the coastal Americas and certainly in the circum-Caribbean were entangled spaces. A survey of Atlantic research by Jorge Cañizares-Esguerra and Benjamin Breen argues that all Atlantic spaces were entangled in this manner and that hybridized individuals such as smugglers and slaves linked together these multi-imperial bodies (Cañizares-Esguerra and Breen, "Hybrid Atlantics: Future Directions for the History of the Atlantic World," *History Compass,* XI [2013], 600).

5. I am patterning the term "transimperial brokers" on Alison Games's description of "cultural brokers" as "those people in the Americas, indigenous, European, or of mixed race, who moved freely between cultures and who played important roles in mediating the moments when mutually incomprehensible societies conflicted or engaged in any number of ways" (Games, "Atlantic History: Definitions, Challenges, and Opportunities," *AHR,* CXI [2006], 752). See also Games, *The Web of Empire: English Cosmopolitans in an Age of Expansion, 1560–1660* (New York, 2008). As Lauren Benton points out, maritime actors not only transgressed imperial statutes but also "extended the reach of the law, helped to form new political communities, promoted challenges to imperial designs, and created variations of familiar legal practices" (Benton, *A Search for Sovereignty: Law and Geography in European Empires, 1400–1900* [New York, 2010], 3).

difficulty fitting the irrepressible presence of Atlantic smuggling into the closed system they were tasked with upholding. The reader of prize court records notes a certain awkwardness in watching multiple empires come into contact. Scribes fumbled with and egregiously misspelled foreign names. In many cases, investigators of illicit trade assumed that foreign merchants were spies or the vanguard of an invading force, marching in lockstep with their empire's intentions. They viewed itinerancy with suspicion. Ideas of what constituted contraband also varied tremendously between the accuser and the accused. These misunderstandings often sprang from the legal pluralism of the multi-imperial Caribbean. "Illegal trade" was illegal, but not by everyone's laws.[6]

Yet the broad mental geographies of contrabandists should not decouple them from narratives of colonialism. In fact, smugglers' interpersonal and legal relationships bear out many of the patterns of colonial historiography. The power of kinship, the importance of material culture, the rights and definitions of subjecthood, and the multiple interpretations of political corruption are all historical problems of early modern society *and* illicit commerce. Additionally, the political conflicts of smuggling reflect wider Bourbon-era popular protests and rebellions in the colonies deriving from tensions between increased royal authority and entrenched local power structures. All of these themes, like contraband trade, shaped Spanish imperialism on the periphery.

Navigating subverted, but still powerful, commercial codes became a preoccupation for Spanish American subjects and foreigners involved in illicit trade. They looked for advantageous positions in a flawed system by utilizing their social connections, bureaucratic positions, and wealth. Smugglers lacking these points of leverage were likely to be prosecuted and punished. Still, unrespected regulations and their human consequences could be long lasting. As prize court sentences demonstrate, Spanish commercial codes maintained their power to discipline offenders when not disarmed by social influence or bribes. Convicted foreign contrabandists faced dislocation, long periods of forced labor or military service, and occasionally capital punishment, even though their trade with Venezuelan subjects was commonplace. Clashes between foreigners and royal or Caracas Company coast guards put coastal inhabitants in the crossfire of an undeclared conflict zone. Though interimperial

6. As political scientist Moisés Naím observes regarding contemporary global smuggling, "Illicit trade is a type of crime. After all, illicit trade by definition takes place outside the rules. But herein lies a complicating problem: *whose rules?*" (Naím, *Illicit: How Smugglers, Traffickers, and Copycats Are Hijacking the Global Economy* [New York, 2005], 184).

trade was a victimless and casual practice, enforcement of its prohibition spurred extensive violence and retribution.

Littoral people of multiple empires mitigated conflict and criminalization in Venezuela by creating alternate social norms and moralities. Venezuelan communities involved in smuggling developed acceptable thresholds of criminality and bureaucratic corruption. They punished smugglers and authorities alike who transgressed these limits. Colonists also resisted monopolization of their markets by individuals, factions, the Spanish state, or the Caracas Company. Throughout the eighteenth century, they defended a moral economy of smuggling, at times with arms.

Faced with legal condemnation on one hand and the dearth of legal trading options on the other, Venezuelans, like many subjects in the peripheral Americas, forged their own individual relationships with commercial crime and colonial rule. They used contraband trade and other practices technically outlawed by the state to ensure their local autonomy and flexibility, even as they upheld their loyalty to the Spanish crown. Some maritime workers became full-time professional smugglers committed to the business. Other people, like petty producers, availed themselves of the black market only occasionally to pick up supplies for personal consumption.[7]

Ultimately, smuggling in eighteenth-century Venezuela illustrates the tension most characteristic of colonialism: that replicated societies eventually become self-sufficient and self-aware. The fight for how coastal inhabitants would provision themselves represented a negotiation over imperial support for colonies and colonial obligations toward empires. When left to tacit levels of acceptability, smuggling acted as a safety valve to relieve the pressures of imperial relationships. Those who tampered with contraband trade risked the explosion or subversion of these compacts.

Then as now, broken or disregarded laws that still have the force and authority of the state behind them can produce a strange and elaborate kabuki theater. Citizens devise complicated and evasive measures to transgress legal

7. Shannon Lee Dawdy writes, "The Americas, in particular, were dotted with countercolonial fiefdoms and syndicates just as likely to be operated by disloyal Europeans as by indigenous natives, creoles, pirates, or maroons. . . . These pockets were connected by intricate, intercoastal networks that in many ways disregarded the mainstream of the Atlantic world. Thus, my more global argument is that colonialism frequently creates conditions that foster not only cultures of resistance, but also circuits of seditious power and contraband flow—what one might, without irony, call *rogue colonialism*" (Dawdy, *Building the Devil's Empire: French Colonial New Orleans* [Chicago, 2008], 4).

statutes while still avoiding prosecution. In time, ordinary people become adept at eluding the law and come to think of their subversion as a normal, natural course of events. Indeed, they see fines and other punishments as just the costs of doing business. Many citizens find those officials who enforce the law to be more immoral than themselves. Perhaps authorities or even whole states decide that they can extract profit from this competing structure. Modern populations negotiate archaic systems that have lost their meaning just as adroitly as early modern subjects once did.[8]

8. Peter Andreas finds centuries-old continuity in how naturally citizens learned the language and practices of deception that constituted contraband trade in many separate periods of American history. He goes on to scoff at the notion that crime has gone global only in the twenty-first century: "Illicit globalization is not entirely new. Indeed, rather than a new threat to America, it is the continuation of an old American tradition" (Andreas, *Smuggler Nation: How Illicit Trade Made America* [New York, 2013], 331). In his journalistic investigation of lawlessness on the early-twenty-first-century oceans, William Langewiesche offers a similar picture of oceanic regulators, shipping companies, and miserly ship owners going through the motions to create the appearance of a regulated sea. In reality, nearly anarchic conditions over the world's oceans make for incredibly cheap and efficient shipping but also produce global social ills. These include "the playing of the poor against the poor and the persistence of huge fleets of dangerous ships, the pollution they cause, the implicit disposability of their crews, and the parallel growth of two particularly resilient pathogens that exist now on the ocean—the first being a modern strain of piracy, and the second its politicized cousin, the maritime form of the new, stateless terrorism" (Langewiesche, *The Outlaw Sea: A World of Freedom, Chaos, and Crime* [New York, 2004], 7).

# index

*Page numbers in italics refer to illustrations.*

MIX
Paper from
responsible sources
FSC® C013483
FSC
www.fsc.org